How We Learn

Monisha Pasupathi, Ph.D.

THE
GREAT
COURSES

PUBLISHED BY:

THE GREAT COURSES
Corporate Headquarters
4840 Westfields Boulevard, Suite 500
Chantilly, Virginia 20151-2299
Phone: 1-800-832-2412
Fax: 703-378-3819
www.thegreatcourses.com

Monisha Pasupathi

Associate Professor,
Department of Psychology
University of Utah

Professor Monisha Pasupathi is an Associate Professor in the Department of Psychology at the University of Utah, where she has served on the faculty since 1999. She completed B.A. degrees in Psychology and English Literature in 1991 at Case Western Reserve University and, having found that academia was her natural habitat, immediately went on to complete her Ph.D. in Psychology at Stanford University in 1997. She subsequently completed a postdoctoral fellowship at the Max Planck Institute for Human Development's Center for Lifespan Psychology between 1997 and 1999.

Professor Pasupathi's research examines how people of all ages learn from their experiences, with a particular focus on learning about the self via telling stories. People tell stories about their everyday lives, and as they do so, they draw conclusions about what they are like, what others are like, and how the world works. The audiences for these stories contribute by supporting the stories, but also by challenging them.

Professor Pasupathi teaches courses in research methods, adult development and aging, and social and personality psychology, along with an occasional specialty class in memory and self, to approximately 100–150 students per year. She is especially proud of her research methods courses, which she views as providing critical skills in the evaluation of research to any member of society; this aspect of her teaching has given her a strong side interest in scientific reasoning and literacy.

During her time at the University of Utah, Professor Pasupathi has received recognition for her teaching on 3 separate occasions. She was named Best Psychology Professor by Utah's chapter of Psi Chi, The International Honor

Society in Psychology. Psi Chi also awarded her the Outstanding Educator Award and Favorite Professor Award.

Professor Pasupathi coedited the book *Narrative Development in Adolescence: Creating the Storied Self*. She has also authored and coauthored chapters for more than 10 books, including *The Handbook of Aging and Cognition*, *Identity and Story: Creating Self in Narrative*, and the *Encyclopedia of Human Relationships*. Her research has also been published in scholarly journals, including *Psychology and Aging*, *Journal of Personality and Social Psychology*, and *Developmental Psychology*.

Since her graduate years, Professor Pasupathi has been delivering community lectures in an effort to make psychology relevant and interesting to the public. Her first talk, given to the Kiwanis Clubs of Menlo Park, focused on marriage and aging. Most recently, she worked in collaboration with neuroscientist Christopher German and The Leonardo interactive museum to craft a public presentation on the relationship between self, memory, and the brain. She also works with the Utah Symposium in Science and Literature, an organization that brings innovative, integrative presentations connecting science and the arts to a general public audience in Salt Lake City.

In her nonwork life, Professor Pasupathi enjoys the mountains, reading, cooking, and the many stories that her children, husband, and extended family provide. You can learn more about her and her research at http://www.psych.utah.edu/monishapasupathi. ∎

Table of Contents

Table of Contents

Table of Contents

How We Learn

Scope:

Learning—the acquisition of new knowledge or skills from experience—is a complex process. Without learning, you couldn't walk, speak, operate a computer, drive a car, or tell a great story. This course explores the newest research on how we acquire new knowledge and skills—from birth through late life. We now know that learning depends on what is learned, how and why it is learned, and by whom, and each of these issues will be examined throughout the course.

In the first segment of the course, you will encounter the early efforts to explain learning in terms of associations, rewards, and punishments—and where those early efforts fell short. The history of research on learning presents an interesting story because for a while, researchers believed that learning was a single simple process that could be applied across various species, including pigeons, rats, dogs, and people.

In the second segment, you'll learn that learning is not passive: It doesn't involve a pouring of information into an empty brain, and there's no tabula rasa, or blank slate. You will discover how learning depends on what we already know—for adults and for newborns—and you will determine what newborns must know at birth in order for them to learn so much so quickly.

The third segment of the course examines how we learn different things—a second language, a dance, a new city, a problem-solving strategy, a body of scientific knowledge, and how to tell stories. Learning can involve skills or knowledge and visual or verbal information, just to name a few distinctions. Not everything is learned in quite the same way, and not everything is equally easy for us to learn. We learn motor skills and language in ways that have both overlaps and differences. We learn how to get around a city in ways that are comparable to learning how to tell a story—but that are also distinct. The broad view of this section will allow you to draw some conclusions about what is true for learning across different areas and what is specific to particular types of learning.

The fourth segment of the course explores the idea of metacognition, or knowledge about learning. You will discover some of the basic cognitive abilities that allow learning, and you will examine the way in which we learn both information and context—but not equally well. You'll discover when and how paying attention improves learning, and perhaps most importantly, you'll analyze people's ability to judge their own learning and to make strong strategy choices about how to learn better. You'll also consider the role of emotion, motivation, and goals in learning: Is it better to learn when you are in a good mood? Do you have to be interested in things to learn them?

Finally, in the last segment of the course, you will consider how learning is different for different people. Recall a learning situation in which you have envied the people around you, who seemed to learn so effortlessly and so quickly. What is the difference between you and those other individuals? Is it that they are smarter? Are they more motivated by the material they're learning? Do they have different learning styles that fit better with the instructor? Is it because they're older and more experienced or younger and more energetic?

By the time you complete this course, you will appreciate the incredible breadth of what we learn in our lifetimes, understand the commonality and diversity across that learning, and perhaps understand how you can maximize both how much you learn and how much you enjoy learning. ■

Myths about Learning

Lecture 1

Although our intuitions about how we learn may have grains of truth, they're often—to a larger extent than we realize—misconceptions, and they're based on an imperfect understanding of people and animals as learners. In much of this course, we will consider the ways in which we are right and wrong about how we learn. In this lecture, we'll define what it means to learn, and we'll discuss some concepts that are relevant for learning—that are maybe close to the idea of learning but are not quite the same—such as development and memory.

Myth 1: Learning is aware and purposeful.

- We don't always have awareness of the learning process or its outcomes. In addition, we learn all the time and we often do so without awareness that we're learning—without actually meaning to learn anything at all.

- For example, if you suddenly start wearing a different pair of glasses to the grocery store than you normally wear, your favorite cashier might not recognize you because, without realizing it, what she had learned about the way your face looks was connected to a specific pair of glasses. Many people experience this from both sides—being recognized or not, or failing to recognize someone—when one minor thing has changed.

Myth 2: People, especially intelligent people, basically already know how to maximize learning.

- This myth is related to the idea that learning is largely something we're aware of and, therefore, something we know how to optimize. In fact, there's evidence that people choose less-than-ideal strategies for learning.

- Furthermore, our judgments of what we've learned well, what we don't yet know, what we do and do not need to practice are not as accurate as they could be.

- For example, our experience of learning as effortful may mislead our judgments of whether we learn something, and consequently, our ideas about what we need to practice and what we can stop practicing are also wrong.

Myth 3: When learning is going well—when we're really learning—we feel confident, successful, and clear.
- In fact, the learning process is not quite that straightforward. Moments of confusion, frustration, uncertainty, and lack of confidence are part of the process of acquiring new skills and new knowledge.

- However, learning is going on all the time—even in those less confident moments—and sometimes those moments are necessary before we achieve a new level of understanding.

Myth 4: Emotion is a problem for rationality, and therefore, getting emotional messes up learning.
- The idea that getting emotional messes up learning or makes it difficult to learn may have a grain of truth, but it is probably more accurate to view emotion as changing the orientation we have toward learning, narrowing our focus when we're learning, or broadening that focus.

- When we are feeling angry or anxious, that may help us focus our attention very narrowly. When we're feeling good, we're likely to broaden and make new connections more easily—and maybe even make more creative connections. Different types of learning and different learning situations may call for one or the other kind of focus. Additionally, emotion can help or hinder learning, depending on what emotions we're talking about and what is being learned.

Myth 5: If someone doesn't find something interesting, he or she won't or cannot learn it.

- We often think that interest helps learning. Of course, it's true that being interested in learning something can help us learn it, and people have things they can do to cultivate interest and engagement. There are ways to increase your motivation to learn.

- It turns out that foundational learning can actually foster the development of interest. In other words, we usually think interest helps learning, but learning can also help us develop an interest—another reason to stick it out through early frustration.

Myth 6: People learn from getting rewarded and punished.

- Many of us think that we learn from consequences, and we sometimes treat our pets and our children in precisely this way. However, people and animals explore their worlds for the sake of learning.

- In addition, learning seems to be an innately motivated action. For example, infants who are learning to walk experience a lot of painful consequences, but this doesn't deter them from carrying on with the project of learning to walk.

- For a dog who learns to sit when you say "sit," perhaps after many treats, the reward is not necessarily what drives learning. The dog actually might figure out what you want relatively quickly. Instead, what the reward does is encourage the dog to demonstrate what it has learned.

Myth 7: Intelligent people learn more easily and better than less intelligent people.

- This myth seems so logical, that there are some of us who are smarter than others—those people who do very well on IQ tests—and that having a higher IQ means you have an easier time learning new things.

- However, being smarter by scoring higher on IQ tests might actually mean you've already learned more—not necessarily that learning was easier for you in the first place.

Myth 8: Learning is like opening up your brain and having stuff dumped into it.

- Learning is not passive, and it doesn't happen on an empty brain. We are transforming information in our environments all the time in order to learn; some of those transformations are completely without our awareness.

- In addition to that transformation that is occurring, learning actually depends on prior knowledge and assumptions because the transformations we make allow us to connect new experiences and new information to what we already know.

Myth 9: People of all ages learn basically the same way; learning is learning.

- There is an enormous amount of evidence that people of different ages learn somewhat differently. First, if learning depends on prior knowledge, then children and adults have different prior knowledge of the world.

© Stockbyte/Thinkstock.

Children learn from their experiences to wait patiently for their turn to speak in class.

- In addition, the ability to reflect on what we are learning—to think critically as we're in the process of learning—develops. The brain matures from birth to adulthood in ways that allow us to engage in critical thinking about evidence and sources of information as we learn. In childhood, the brain has more of a limited capacity for that kind of critical reflection, which in turn affects how children learn

- Also, the learning limitations go in both directions. There are things that babies are good at learning and adults are not so good at learning—such as language—and there are things adults are capable of learning and young children are not so competent at learning—such as evidence-based reasoning—even with a lot of help.

Myth 10: You can't teach an old dog new tricks.

- This myth implies the idea that learning new things is only something children do well. However, given good health, even people who are very old are able to learn new things.

- Learning does change as we age. There are changes in how quickly we learn, and there are changes in what we care about and are interested in learning. Therefore, it's not that learning is the same in old age as when we are young; instead, learning is possible for people across the lifespan. Old dogs are always learning new tricks, provided they want to do so and provided they take the time to do so.

What Is Learning?

- Dictionary definitions of learning define it as a change in a person's understanding, knowledge, or abilities that arises from the person's experience.

- This definition encompasses things we learn consciously and know that we've learned—such as changes in understanding and knowledge—and things we might acquire in a less conscious way—such as learning how someone's face looks. It focuses on change, which gives us a way of thinking about how to tap into learning, and it emphasizes that learning comes from experience.

- At the end of the course, we'll revisit the definition and we'll think again about whether it encompasses the points that we've raised along the way.

Learning versus Development and Memory

- Development can be defined in ways that actually include learning as one of the ways development happens—and in ways that exclude learning from the idea of development.

- In this course, we will view development as referring primarily to brain-based maturation, changes in abilities that are going to happen regardless of the specific experiences that a child has.

- Most changes from childhood through old age combine developmental processes, such as the maturation of our brains with specific experiences that we learn from. Therefore, most of what changes about our lives involves some combination of maturation and learning.

- Memory is also not the same as learning. Memory is our ability to store and recall past experiences in various ways, and learning is the acquisition of new information and abilities.

- Without memory, we can't keep what we learn. In fact, without memory, there would not be learning. In many cases, we know we've learned because we can recall information. Therefore, in many cases, memory is how we know people have learned.

- Learning is your acquisition of new knowledge, but to say that knowledge has been acquired, we also mean that you can store and recall it using memory systems.

- Learning both changes the brain and depends very intimately on the changes that have already occurred in the brain—our store of knowledge. Learning is a way of changing the brain, and the brain allows us enormous sophistication and flexibility in the learning process.

- The main point of this course is that learning is a complicated process that depends in part on what is being learned, how and why, and by whom.

Suggested Reading

Doidge, *The Brain That Changes Itself.*

Question to Consider

1. Consider learning experiences you would term successful as well as those you would term failures. Consider the sense of effort versus ease you had and the emotional qualities of the experiences. Consider whether you had an easy time motivating yourself or struggled to stay with it. What are the characteristics of good and bad learning experiences?

Myths about Learning
Lecture 1—Transcript

Imagine this: You were born and raised in sub-Saharan Africa, and you're making a living as a subsistence farmer. You're living with none of the modern conveniences of a typical Western life. When war comes you and your family are displaced, and after some time in a refugee camp you're resettled in the United States.

You will need to learn virtually everything—how to use a toilet, how to turn on a light, how to cross a street, how to speak a new language—and you need to learn new skills that will help you make a living in a completely alien world.

Or let's move a bit closer to home. Imagine you're traveling in Berlin, Germany for the first time in many, many years. You thought you knew how to get from Alexanderplatz in the former East to the zoogarten in the former West, but all that new construction means you're now thoroughly lost. You need to dredge up your high school German and use it to learn a new spatial map of the city.

Or consider this: Through an unfortunate incident, you managed to break both your arms. With the casts on, you become aware of just how often your ways of moving around depend on your arms. You realize you've been using those arms to get in and out of cars, to go up and down staircases, to help you balance on trails, and now you're going to have to relearn how to do those things using different muscles and different movements.

I'm Monisha Pasupathi and this course is about how we learn.

Let's begin by considering some of the ways you might think about learning. Although our *a priori* intuitions about how we learn may have grains of truth, they're often to a larger extent than we realize, misconceptions, and they're based on an imperfect understanding of people and animals as learners. In much of this course, we will consider the ways in which we are right and wrong about how we learn.

In this lecture we'll define what it means to learn and we'll discuss some concepts that are relevant for learning, maybe even close to the idea of learning, but which are not quite the same thing—concepts like development and memory.

I'll close by giving you a brief overview of the main point of the entire course, which is that learning is a complicated process that depends in part on what is being learned, how and why, and by whom.

So first some myths, an abbreviated myth-busting about learning, and a sampling of some of the things we will discuss in greater depth in later lectures.

Myth 1: Learning is aware and purposeful.

This is a myth in a couple ways. We don't always have awareness of the learning process or its outcomes. Sometimes you think you've learned how to do something, only to find when push comes to shove, you haven't. Also, you learn all the time and you often do so without awareness that you're learning, and you often do so without actually meaning to learn anything at all. The arm example above highlights this. You've learned to move using your arms, without realizing that, until something happens and you have to learn to move without them.

Here's another example. Imagine that you have several different pairs of glasses. Sometimes you get in the habit of wearing one pair consistently for a period of time, and then suddenly you remember, "Oh yeah, let me wear the purple glasses today." When you walk into the grocery store where you're a regular, recognized customer, your favorite clerk doesn't seem to recognize you. What's going on? Well, given her job, she was probably generally paying attention to your purchases and your overall appearance, but on some level, she learned how your face looks. Though she wasn't aware of it, and she didn't do it on purpose, what she learned about how your face looks was connected to a specific pair of glasses.

When you changed glasses, you changed something about your face, and the clerk had difficulty recognizing you. She had learned one version of you with a particular pair of glasses, not the version with the purple glasses.

Many people experience this from both sides—being recognized or not, or failing to recognize someone—when one minor thing has changed. We've learned something without awareness and without meaning to learn it.

Myth 2: People, especially college educated, smart people, basically already know how to maximize learning.

This myth is related to the idea that learning is largely something we're aware of, and therefore something we know how to optimize. In fact, there's good evidence that people choose less than ideal strategies for learning. My undergraduate students are no exception. Also, our judgments of what we've learned well, what we don't yet know, what we do and do not need to practice, are not as accurate as they could be.

For example, our experience of learning as effortful may mislead our judgments of whether we learn something, and consequently, our ideas about what we need to practice and what we can stop practicing are also wrong. This idea of not being completely good at judging our own learning is also linked to a third myth.

Myth 3: When learning is going well, when we're really learning, we feel confident, successful, and clear.

In fact, the learning process is not quite that straightforward. Moments of confusion, frustration, uncertainty, and lack of confidence are part of the process of acquiring new skills and new knowledge.

Often, moments of confusion and uncertainty are moments where you think, "Geez, is it really worth the effort to do this? Am I ever going to master this new thing?" It feels like your brain and your mind are going in circles and like nothing is getting in. But, learning is going on all the time, even in those less confident and clear and successful moments, and sometimes those moments are necessary before we achieve a new level of understanding. And in fact, this is related to another myth people often have.

Myth 4: Emotion is a problem for rationality and therefore getting emotional messes up learning.

The idea that getting emotional messes up learning or makes it hard to learn may have a grain of truth as well, but it is probably more accurate, as we'll see, to see emotion as changing the orientation we have towards learning, narrowing our focus when we're learning, or broadening that focus out.

When we are feeling angry or anxious, that may help us focus our attention very narrowly. When we're feeling good, we're likely to broaden out and make new connections more easily, maybe make more creative connections. So, different types of learning and different learning situations may call for one or the other kind of focus. And the upshot is that emotion can help or hinder learning, depending on what emotions we're talking about and what's being learned. Again, this is something we'll focus on in more detail later in this course.

Myth 5: If someone doesn't find something interesting, he or she won't or cannot learn it.

We often think that interest helps learning, and in discussions of teaching we often ask ourselves, "How can we better engage students with this material? How can we make them want to learn it?" Of course it's true that being interested in learning something can help us learn it. And, as we'll discuss in this class, people have things they can do to cultivate interest and engagement. There are ways to increase your motivation to learn.

But here's a surprise. It turns out also that a little foundational learning can actually foster the development of interest. That is, we usually think interest helps learning, but it turns out, learning can help us develop an interest, and that's another reason to stick it out through early frustration.

Myth 6: People learn from getting rewarded and punished.

Many of us think that we learn from consequences, and we sometimes treat our pets and our children in precisely this way. There are many aspects of this myth that need more careful thought, as we will see in this course.

First of all, people and animals explore their worlds for the sake of learning. Learning seems to be an innately motivated action. To name just one example, infants who are learning to walk experience a lot of painful consequences. They fall, they scrape themselves, and they cry about it, but this doesn't actually deter them from carrying on with the project of learning to walk. People will even try out actions they've seen other people do, and they'll do that if there isn't any obvious reason to do so. They'll do it just to find out what information they can get from doing that action.

Try staring at the sky on a crowded sidewalk some time. Passersby will stop and look because they want to know what's out there. They think something might be learned and they don't want to miss out.

Even for your dog, who learns to sit when you say, "Sit"—maybe after a lot of treats—the reward is not necessarily what's driving learning. The dog actually might figure out what you want with "sit" relatively quickly. Instead what the reward does is to encourage the dog to demonstrate what he has learned. You can't get in your dog's head to figure this out, but we will consider some experiments that make this idea of rewards causing learning seem less likely and make the idea of rewards motivating the demonstration of learning more reasonable and more likely.

Myth 7: Smart people learn more easily and better than less smart people.

This is a myth to which, honestly, I partly subscribed prior to developing the course. It seems so logical, that there are some of us who are smarter than others—those people who do very well on IQ tests—and that in fact being higher in IQ means you have an easier time learning new things.

Later in this class you will learn, as I did, that being smarter by scoring higher on IQ tests might actually mean you've already learned more, not necessarily that learning was easier for you in the first place.

Myth 8: Learning is like opening up your brain and having stuff dumped into it.

Learning is not passive and it doesn't happen on an empty brain. We are transforming information in our environments all the time in order to learn. Some of those transformations are completely without our awareness. For example, patterns of light waves get transformed into your perception of edges, objects, and drop-offs without any awareness on your part, but your eye and brain are transforming sensory information in order for you to see the world. Then these pieces of information get further transformed into a mental map of your office or your building or your city, and at that point you may be more aware of that transformation process.

Further, in addition to all that transformation, learning actually depends a lot on prior knowledge and assumptions because the transformations we make allow us to connect new experiences and new information to what we already know.

Now there's one really delightful example of this and it comes from a study of golfers and non-golfers. The people in this study were asked to learn and to remember different actions like, "turn on the lamp" or "putt to the target." And as you can see, some items were golf-related and others weren't. The items were given to the participants in one of three ways—as a sentence on a card, in a video on a computer, or the person was actually asked to do the task physically. Then participants were asked which items they remembered as a test of learning, and as it turns out, golfers were superior at remembering golf actions. This was really true when they had actually learned the actions by doing them.

Now, for a present consideration of this myth, what's important is why golfers might have an easier time learning golf-relevant actions. They were not superior at learning other actions. They were just like non-golfers. They weren't smarter in general and they weren't more interested in general. But here's the thing, for the golfers, putting to a specific target in a room has many more connections to their own experience and their expertise. To golfers the golf clubs are more distinctive. They can make comparisons of the putt to known golf courses, and all of that draws on their prior learning of golf. Moreover, all of that makes each enacted golf action distinctive and easily learned and recalled—but only for golfers.

Myth 9: People of all ages learn basically the same way; learning is learning.

So, I can teach my preschooler grandchild about science the same way I would teach my adult child with simpler concepts. Right? No. This is another myth. There is enormous evidence that people of different ages learn somewhat differently, for several reasons.

First, if we just learned today, learning depends on prior knowledge, then kids and adults have different prior knowledge of the world. Second, the ability to reflect on what we are learning—to think critically as we're in the process of learning—develops. It's not something younger kids can do easily, and it may not be something that young kids can be taught to do. Rather, the brain matures from birth to adulthood in ways that allow us to engage in critical thinking about evidence and sources of information as we learn. In childhood, the brain has more limited capacity for that kind of critical reflection, and that in turn affects how kids learn.

Also, as we'll see, the learning limitations go in both directions. There are things babies are good at learning and adults are not so good, like language. And there are things adults are capable of learning to do, like evidence-based reasoning, and young kids are not so competent at learning, even with a lot of help.

Myth 10: You can't teach an old dog new tricks.

Well, that last myth was the idea that age doesn't matter for learning, but there are also myths about age making all the difference, and these myths usually point to the idea that learning new things is something only children do well.

My guess is that by being in the audience you don't endorse this myth. But, let me underscore that this is a myth. Given good health, even people who are very old are able to learn new things. Consider this example. Weight training and balance training interventions are being employed with frail, nursing home–dwelling elderly populations. Now, these interventions are aimed at improving strength and balance, preventing falls and reducing the likelihood of broken bones. But here's the catch: They require that people learn new things. They require that people acquire new a movement skill, learn exercise sequences, and acquire new muscle capabilities, and that's also learning. And, even this most vulnerable population can do so successfully.

Now, I can give you another example, and this one is closer to how we typically think of learning. Two of the recent Ph.D. graduates in the program where I teach were 50 or older at the time they received their degree. Now, to get that degree, they had to master statistical techniques that were not even developed when they were 20. They had to acquire knowledge related to their interests—one in cardiovascular health and stress, a high-tech, biologically oriented area of our field—and they had to master that knowledge so well that they're now deemed ready to expand what we know with their own independent research.

In talking with one of these women recently, I came to discover that in her lifetime, she had worked as a bank teller, raised five children, run her own business, provided full-time care for an aging parent, and returned to college, in roughly that order.

Now, when I put it this way she sounds utterly extraordinary, doesn't she? But the fact is that in each of those successive lives, she simply was open to the idea of learning something new and willing to invest energy and time in doing so. And in my most recent undergraduate class, I had a student in his 70s. His scores on the exams were so high relative to his much younger peers, and one explanation was that he was simply brilliant. But, it turned out, when I spoke with him about how he was getting this incredible level of performance on the exams, he just had very strong study skills—so much so that I asked him to explain to others what he did to prepare for tests, so they could do likewise. He was studying the material a little at a time, every day, and connecting it to other things he knew.

Now, as we'll discuss in this class, learning does change as we age. There are changes in how quickly we learn. Something my 70-year-old undergraduate student noted about his own studying was that it took him more time than it would have when he was young man. And also, there are changes in what we care about and are interested in learning. So, it's not that learning is the same in old age as when we are 20, but the important message here is that learning is possible for people across the lifespan. So, old dogs are always learning new tricks, provided they want to do so and provided they take the time.

While I could go on with myths of learning, in this first lecture on how we learn, I would also like to lay out some important concepts that I'd like you to keep in mind throughout the course.

Now, first of all, what is learning? We just swept through things like recognizing faces, learning lists of actions, and remembering them, issues of interest, of golf knowledge, of language learning, and even the idea that lifting weights involves acquiring muscle skills.

Dictionary definitions of learning define it as a change in a person's understanding, knowledge, or abilities that arises from the person's experience, and that's a good definition to start with. Here's why. It encompasses things we learn consciously and know that we've learned, like changes in understanding and knowledge, and things we might acquire in a less conscious way, like learning how someone's face looks. It focuses on change, which gives us a way of thinking about how to tap into learning, and it emphasizes that learning comes from experience.

At the end of the course, we'll revisit the definition and we'll think again about whether it encompasses the points that we've raised along the way.

Next, learning is easy to confuse with some other things, and in particular here, I'm concerned with confusing learning with development and confusing learning with memory.

What is the difference between learning and development? Development can be defined in ways that actually include learning as one of the ways development happens, and in ways that exclude learning from the idea of development, and that's why this difference is somewhat tricky.

In this course, we'll think about the difference between development and learning in this way: We will view development as referring primarily to brain-based maturation—changes in abilities that are going to happen regardless of the specific experiences that a child has. And what we shall see is that most changes from childhood through old age combine developmental processes, like the maturation of our brains, with specific experiences that we learn from. So, most of what changes about our lives involves some combination of maturation and learning.

For example, kids all need to learn to wait patiently for their turn at say, a drinking fountain. Now, they learn this from experiences—experiences where adults tell them to wait and help them to wait patiently, without shoving, and they also learn it from experiences of being pushed and shoved, which they usually don't find very nice. But, children can't quite master patiently waiting their turn until their brain has developed an ability to inhibit, or suppress, a behavior that you want to do. So you have to both learn what is appropriate behavior through your experiences, and have the brain maturity that lets you do what's appropriate, and not what may be more desired, like shoving ahead to get the first turn.

Another way to think about this is that development is not the same as learning, but learning is one major contributor to development. Learning is also not memory. Memory is our ability to store and recall past experiences in various ways. And learning is the acquisition of new information and abilities.

However, you can see that these two concepts have what Patricia Bauer, a noted researcher of children's memory development, calls a "horse and carriage" relationship. Without memory, we can't keep what we learn. And in fact, without memory, there would not be learning. And in many, many, many cases, we know we've learned because we can recall information. In this course, we won't cover memory research in detail, and we will especially not spend much time addressing how memory works. But, we will often draw on findings from memory work to illustrate aspects of learning, because in many cases memory is how we know people have learned.

For example, suppose you want to learn about the role of nutrition in the rising rates of obesity in the Western, industrialized society. Now, you might go about learning this by reading articles in the newspaper or in journals. You might discuss those articles. You might talk to experts or your family physician. You might consult Professor Google, and so on—lots of ways that you could go about acquiring this knowledge.

Now, if I wanted to know what you've learned, I need to give you some type of test—an essay exam, a multiple choice test. And if this is sounding a little bit like a college class example, I'm sticking to what I know here. I'm going to take exam performance as an indicator of what you have learned.

But, you also have to draw on the capacity to remember—to store and recall experiences of reading and learning about obesity—in order to perform well on that exam. So, learning is your acquisition of that new knowledge, but to say that knowledge has been acquired, we also mean that you can store and recall it using memory systems.

Before I move on to some notes about how this course is organized, I wanted to make one last important note for you, and this one about learning and the brain. Learning both changes the brain and depends very intimately on the changes that have already occurred in the brain—our store of knowledge. And we're not going to spend a lot of time discussing brain-based work in this course because there's so much more to say about how we learn just in terms of our behaviors. But, learning is a way of changing the brain, and the brain allows us enormous sophistication and flexibility in the learning process.

So now, to the course. Learning—the acquisition of new knowledge or skills from experience—is a complex process. Otherwise, we could cover it in a single lecture. The way we are going to approach that complexity is this way: We're going to say that learning depends on what is learned, how and why, and by whom.

In the opening part of the course, we will spend a little time on the history of research on learning because for a while, researchers tried to pretend learning was one simple process, and we could apply it to pigeons, rats, people, and some slobbering dogs; and this didn't work. Then, we'll talk a little bit about how learning is neither passive (it's not pouring information into an empty brain) and there's no tabula rasa (no blank slate) in learning.

After that, we'll move on to consider what is learned. Learning can involve skills or knowledge, visual or verbal information, just to name just a few distinctions. Not everything is learned in quite the same way, and not everything is equally easy for us to learn. We learn motor skills and language in ways that have both overlaps and differences. We learn how to get around our city in ways that are comparable to learning how to tell a story, but also distinct.

Of course, what we're learning, in part, determines how and why it's learned. And this is something we'll address in the fourth section of the course. We'll consider some of the basic cognitive abilities that allow learning along with the way we learn both information (what), and context, (where, how, from whom, but not equally well). And we'll also look at the role of emotion and motivations and goals in learning.

Perhaps most importantly, in this section of the course, we will look at people's ability to judge their own learning, and to make strong strategy choices about how to learn better.

The final section of the course will deal with individual differences—who's learning? We've all been in a learning situation and envied the person next to us, who seemed to do things so effortlessly and well, right away. What is the difference between us and that individual? Is it that the person is smarter? Are they more motivated by the material they're learning? Do they have a different learning style, one that fits better with the instructor? Is it because they're older and more experienced, or younger and more energetic?

Along the way, we'll extract information that helps each of us to learn more effectively and more deliberately, as well as to just deeply appreciate how amazingly capable we are of learning.

In the next lecture, we'll take a brief historical tour of early work on learning. We will see that the research findings in this area taught us a great deal about learning, even if the way we interpret those findings has changed over time.

Why No Single Learning Theory Works
Lecture 2

C
an we have a theory of learning that applies to everyone learning and everything to be learned? This was arguably the ambition of early learning theories. Researchers developed and actively tested these theories through the 1960s, and the work they did continues to inform our understanding of learning processes even today. In this lecture, we will get a sense of just how much we learned about learning using these early approaches, but we will also discuss how these approaches fell short of explaining the vast array of learning that people and animals do.

Classical Conditioning

- The kernel of learning theories is that learning in everyday life involves associating two things with one another. For example, an infant learns that the parent's appearance signals comfort and food. How we acquire these associations between two different stimuli is important, and it's a foundational question in the science of learning.

- Early studies of this type of learning called it classical conditioning, which looks at learning of the association between two stimuli, or things that stimulate a response, by capitalizing on instinctive or reflexive responses. These are behaviors that aren't voluntary—such as blinking or salivating—and they seem to be built into an organism.

- In the most famous work on classical conditioning, Ivan Pavlov looked at salivation, which is a reflexive response to having food placed in your mouth—an effect that occurs in both dogs and humans. Pavlov paired two events to see if the dogs could acquire the association.

- For Pavlov, the first event was food. It was a meat powder that he gave his dogs, and he called this the unconditioned stimulus. When the dogs were given the meat powder, they produced saliva, and Pavlov called this the unconditioned response. However, prior to giving the dogs the meat powder, Pavlov also rang a bell. The bell tone was the conditioned stimulus. Salivating to the bell, rather than the food, is what Pavlov called a conditioned response. This indicates that the dog has acquired an association between the bell tone and the arrival of the meat powder.

- At first, even though the bell is occurring right before the arrival of food, dogs don't salivate to the sound of the bell, but after a number of exposures to the bell, followed by the meat powder, they start to do so. The salivation to the bell is a conditioned response, and it shows the dogs have come to associate that bell tone with being given the meat powder.

- What it takes for a dog or any animal or human to acquire associations like this are three things: repetition, temporal contiguity, and differential contingency.

- Repetition is being exposed—often multiple times—to the pairing of two stimuli. Temporal contiguity means that the two stimuli have to happen close enough together in time. Differential contingency means that when the conditioned stimulus occurs, the unconditioned stimulus will come.

- Once an association is learned, the animal or human may generalize that association—that is, apply that learning to similar situations. If the associations are too specific, the kind of learning they support won't be very useful. Associations need to accommodate some variability to be truly useful.

A Few Questions
- Are there factors that make the learning of associations stronger? What is meant by the term "stronger" is that the conditioned response is either more intense or it's more consistently produced.

- If a conditioned stimulus is uniquely predictive of an unconditioned stimulus, then conditioning is stronger than when that's not the case. If only one sound signals one event, the arrival of the meat powder, the conditioning is stronger than if food arrives after the dog hears many different sounds.

- In fact, if you try to add a second conditioned stimulus when the animal has already learned the first one, they don't actually learn the second one. For example, if Pavlov's dogs are given both a light and the bell, they don't learn to salivate to the light because it's redundant. In other words, learning is efficient.

- Are there factors that make the learning of associations weaker? If you repeatedly present the conditioned stimulus without the unconditioned stimulus, you'll get a decline in the likelihood that the animal is going to give you the conditioned response. If you keep ringing the bell and there is no meat powder, the dog will stop salivating.

The Little Albert Experiment
- Associations don't always involve responses we view as neutral, such as salivation. One of the most famous examples of classical conditioning involved John B. Watson and Rosalie Rayner's conditioning of fear in a young infant that they called Albert.

- The goal of the study was to get Little Albert to respond to rats with fear by being presented with rats in conjunction with a loud, unpleasant noise. Eventually, Little Albert acquired a fear reaction to rats, and he generalized that fear reaction to white, furry animals of all kinds.

- The point of the Little Albert experiment was to demonstrate that phobias were learned behaviors—not inborn as had been previously thought. The experiment also suggested that you could treat phobias the way you would extinguish any conditioned response—by extinction.

Problems with Classical Conditioning

- With classical conditioning, there's very little attention to the awareness of learning or the idea that people may actively try to learn something, which we know they do, and there's no attention to the idea of feedback.

- A comprehensive treatment of learning has to account for the many cases in which we aren't passive recipients of environmental events, but actively altering the environment to achieve particular goals.

- The idea that there are consequences of our behavior—that rewards and punishments are important aspects of how we learn—is a very entrenched idea that is used in many different situations. This idea matches intuitions we have about the pursuit of pleasure, and it also seems to take into account the fact that we do consider consequences when we are engaging in our behavior.

Operant Conditioning

- Around the turn of the 20th century, Edward Thorndike observed cats figuring out how to open a latch and escape from their cage into an adjacent enclosure that had a large dish of salmon. At first, the cats had to engage in trial and error to accomplish the task, but once they figured out how to open the latch, latch-opening behavior increased.

- Thorndike articulated what he called the law of effect as a rule about how behavior might be governed by its consequences. The law of effect implies two things: An important class of associations that we learn are the ones between what we do and the consequences of that behavior, and we change our behaviors when we've learned those contingencies.

- Thorndike also noted that we can have positive or negative consequences, and they can either occur or cease, and behavior should vary accordingly, provided we learn the behavior and consequence associations accurately.

© iStockphoto/Thinkstock.

Good students learn to associate dedicated study habits with the reward of high grades.

- Following this reasoning, researchers began to conduct experiments to see how they could alter behavior by changing or controlling the consequences that were attached to behavior. This research area was termed operant conditioning, and it differed from classical conditioning because it emphasized associations between behaviors and consequences—rather than associations between two stimuli.

- The assumption of operant conditioning is that when an animal is rewarded for a behavior, increases in the behavior show that the animal has learned to associate the behavior and reward.

- As with classical conditioning, it's important that the reward be contingent on the response for the person or the animal to learn the association. The reinforcer has to follow the behavior when it occurs. However, you can alter the rewarding to maximally shape behavior—to form the strongest association.

- On a fixed ratio schedule, every time the animal presses the lever 10 times, it gets a food pellet. On a variable schedule, the animal gets a food pellet, on average, when it presses the lever 10 times—but the actual number of lever presses varies over time. This creates a bit of uncertainty; you never know quite when you're going to get a reward.

- If you want to have someone engage in a behavior maximally, a variable ratio schedule is a very good one to use. In animal research, the animal will respond at a high rate all the time because it can never tell exactly when the reward is going to come again. Gambling with slot machines is an example.

Problems with Punishment

- With punishment, because the behavior you're going to punish is already happening, it must already be rewarded in some way—according to operant conditioning researchers. Unfortunately, it is not always very easy to know what that reward is, but you need to figure it out before your punishment will work.

- Punishments slow down people's responding, even when they are given in the presence of rewards, and they also will lead people to find an alternative way to get that reward.

- Punishment works, but it works best when it is maximal, immediate, and not introduced in mild form. When we punish children, we often violate these principles. We sometimes delay punishment, or we start with milder punishments and we work toward more severe consequences. What the research says is we have to jump on bad behavior with as severe a response as we think appropriate.

Complications with Punishment and Classical Conditioning

- The theories of punishment and classical conditioning cannot explain what is rewarding or reinforcing outside the narrow range of innate drives, such as hunger and thirst. For example, some animals will press a lever just to make a light turn on.

- Another complication in what counts as a reward comes from research that suggests that behaviors that are more often chosen in a free-choice situation are reinforcers for less frequently chosen activities. For example, given a choice between running several miles and eating a piece of cake, all else being equal, most people would take the cake. The cake can then be a reinforcer for the running, but not vice versa.

- Some stimuli become reinforcers because they're associated with desirable items. The clearest examples of this are token economies. Money is the most famous token economy, in which we have these papers that we can exchange for things we actually want.

- Simply having control over events is reinforcing. In addition, there's evidence that people learn without any rewards. For example, child development researchers have shown that children will even imitate someone who's clearly failing at their intended goal.

- One of the most difficult parts of learning theory initially was that researchers wanted to avoid considering anything that wasn't directly observable. However, a person's own ideas about the world play a role in whether a reward is really a reward.

- Considered this way, it makes more sense that control over the environment is itself rewarding and that animals and people exhibit latent learning—learning that's already occurred but they haven't yet demonstrated in their behavior. It also makes more sense for explaining how we learn complicated things—such as token economies—and for understanding the paradoxical features of punishment.

Suggested Reading

Beck, Levinson, and Irons, "Finding Little Albert."

Powell, Symbaluk, and MacDonald, *Introduction to Learning and Behavior.*

Rankin, et al., "Habituation Revisited."

1. Studies of classical and operant conditioning suggest some useful ways of training a pet to do a trick or of training ourselves to do something new. Consider how you might apply principles of reinforcement to change a habit you'd like to alter.

2. Can you explain how people understand that "the dog bit the man" and "the man bit the dog" mean different things using only the idea of learned associations between stimuli or between stimuli and responses? Why or why not?

Why No Single Learning Theory Works
Lecture 2—Transcript

Can we have a theory of learning that applies to everyone learning and everything to be learned? This was arguably the ambition of early learning theories. Researchers developed and actively tested these theories through the 1960s, and the work they did continues to inform our understanding of learning processes even today.

In this lecture, I want to give you a sense for how much we learned about learning using these early approaches. I also want to begin to talk about how this fell short of explaining the vast array of learning that people and animals do. In particular, these theories ignored the role played by who the learner is, why the learner is learning, and they failed to offer a very good explanation for why some things seem harder to learn than others.

The kernel of learning theories is that learning in everyday life involves associating two things with one another. An infant learns that the parent's appearance signals comfort and food. A student that the ending of the music indicates the class is about to begin. A student might also learn that good study habits yield the reward of high grades, or a stockbroker that extensive overtime yields a larger bonus.

My personal favorite is one that happens every evening at my house. One of the grownups says the words, "Did anybody feed the dog?" and the dog goes immediately to his bowl and stands there, waiting. I actually bet he starts to salivate, too. So my dog has an association between the phrase, "Did anybody feed the dog?" and the appearance of food in his bowl. When he hears the phrase, he demonstrates he's learned this association by behaving as though he's getting ready to eat.

Now an important thing about the study of these associations is that I don't speculate at all about what is in my dog's head; rather, I'm just noting that he's demonstrating an association or a link between one event (the words, "Did anybody feed the dog?") and a second event (the arrival of food in his bowl).

How we acquire these associations between two different stimuli is an important and it's a foundational question in the science of learning. Early studies of this type of learning called it classical conditioning. Classical conditioning looks at learning of the association between two stimuli, two things that stimulate a response, by capitalizing on instinctive or reflexive responses. These are behaviors that aren't voluntary, and they kind of seem to come built into an organism. So you might think of sweating or blinking or salivating.

In the most famous work on classical conditioning, Pavlov looked at salivation, which is a reflexive response to having food placed in your mouth. That's true for dogs and for humans. You can actually try this at home today. If you think about your favorite food and vividly imagine how that food tastes and feels in your mouth, you will actually experience an increase in saliva production right now.

Before I go on to tell you a little more about classical conditioning research I need to introduce some terminology, and I'm going to do it with the salivation example. Pavlov set up a kind of weird little apparatus for investigating conditioning. He had dogs in a cage and, in a slightly gruesome twist, he surgically placed their salivary glands outside their jaw, and this actually allowed him to measure saliva production more easily. Then Pavlov paired two events to see if the dogs could acquire the association.

For Pavlov, the first event was food. It was a meat powder that he gave his dogs, and he called this the unconditioned stimulus. Now, when the dogs were given the meat powder they produced saliva, and Pavlov called this the unconditioned response. But, prior to giving the dogs the meat powder, Pavlov also rang a bell. The bell tone was the conditioned stimulus. Salivating to the bell, rather than the food, is what Pavlov called a conditioned response. This indicates that the dog has acquired an association between the bell tone and the arrival of the meat powder.

At first, even though the bell is occurring right before the arrival of food, dogs don't salivate to the sound of the bell, but after a number of exposures to the bell, followed by the meat powder, they start to do so. The salivation to the bell is a conditioned response, and it shows the dogs have come to associate that bell tone with being given the meat powder.

The example of my own dog can actually be interpreted very similarly. He's come to recognize a certain sequence of sounds—the "feed," the "dog" with a question intonation—as signaling the arrival of food in his dish. Now, what it takes for a dog or any animal or human to acquire associations like this are three things: repetition, temporal contiguity, and differential contingency. Let me explain what those three words really mean.

Repetition is being exposed multiple times to the pairing of those two stimuli. It's very rare to learn that two stimuli are associated with only one exposure, although it can happen. Mostly, however, we need to see those stimuli happen together repeatedly. We need to hear the bell and get the meat powder over and over.

Now, temporal contiguity means that the two stimuli have to happen close enough together in time. It's pretty hard to acquire associations between events that are widely spaced in time. This fact actually is probably connected to some of the difficulties we humans have with being responsive to the long-term outcomes of our immediate behavior. So for example, there are many outcomes regarding health in later life that have to do with behaviors we've engaged in years earlier. It's hard for us to learn those associations.

Finally, differential contingency of the conditioned stimulus, unconditioned stimulus pairing is a super technical way of saying that the conditioned stimulus (in Pavlov's case this is the bell) has to be informative about the occurrence of the unconditioned stimulus (the arrival of the meat powder). What this means is when the conditioned stimulus occurs the unconditioned stimulus will come. If we said, "Did anybody feed the dog?" all of the time before and after our dog has been fed and at random intervals throughout the day after which we didn't feed him he probably wouldn't acquire that association between that question and the arrival of food.

Once an association is learned, you can see that the animal or human may generalize that association—that is, apply that learning to similar situations. For example, let's consider a study in which birds are conditioned to respond with pecking to an 800 Hz tone. Now, if you then go on and you play a variety of tones for the birds, you're going to see that some conditioned responding, some pecking, happens around 800 Hz as well. So, the 800 Hz tone might get you the maximal pecking, but there's going to be pecking to tones that are sort of close to that 800 Hz tone.

This is actually a very important feature of conditioned associations, specifically in learning in general. If they were too specific—those associations—you can see that the kind of learning they supported wouldn't be very useful. Associations need to accommodate some variability to be truly useful. For example, words can be uttered with variations in pronunciation even if the same person is saying the word. Those variations happen because of the other words in the sentence, the surrounding environment, and so on. Different people definitely pronounce the same word in different ways— tomato/tomahto, potato/potahto. We can still recognize the word that's being said.

An associative learning mechanism that required us to pronounce words in a single way would be problematic for understanding language. But in fact, you probably don't even notice these variations, except in unusual circumstances—when the variations actually make it problematic to understand. So for example, you might think of someone with a particularly strong accent.

As people interested in learning, one important question is whether there are factors that make those associations, the learning of those associations, stronger. And what we mean by that is that the conditioned response is either more intense or it's more consistently produced. Now, to think about these factors, we can go back to differential contingency, and that has to do with the unique informative value of the condition stimulus for the conditioned response to occur.

If a conditioned stimulus is uniquely predictive of an unconditioned stimulus, than conditioning is stronger than when that's not the case. If only one phrase or one sound signals that one event, the arrival of the meat powder, the conditioning is stronger than if food arrives after the dog hears a lot of different kinds of words, like, "The dog is hungry. The dog needs to be fed. The dog wants food." And so on.

In fact, it actually turns out that if you try to use two condition stimuli (you add a second when the animal has already learned a first one), they don't actually learn that second one. So Pavlov's dogs, for example, if they're now given both a light and the bell, they don't learn to salivate to the light. It's redundant so they just don't learn it. And one way to think about this is to think that learning is efficient.

Now, a second important question actually relates to the matching between the conditioned stimulus and the unconditioned stimulus. It turns out rats very easily learn to associate a taste with nausea in experiments that link some tastes with poisons and others not. And rats learn very easily to connect lights or noise with shock, and to respond to a light or a noise by running away from the area where they're shocked. But if you try to cross those stimuli things don't work so well. It's hard to associate light with nausea, and it's hard to associate tastes with shock.

You can also ask how to weaken associations. Now, the simplest route to extinction of an association is to present that conditioned stimulus, like the bell, without the unconditioned stimulus. And if you repeatedly present the conditioned stimulus without the unconditioned stimulus, you'll get a decline in the likelihood that the animal is going to give you that conditioned response. If I keep ringing the bell and there is no meat powder, the dog will stop salivating.

And one way to think about this is that if you do this, if you present the conditioned stimulus without the unconditioned stimulus, you're undermining that differential contingency. You're actually making the conditioned stimulus less informative about whether the unconditioned stimulus is coming.

Associations don't always involve responses we view as neutral, like salivation. One of the most famous examples of classical conditioning involved Watson and Raynor's conditioning of fear in a young infant that they called Albert.

Now, the goal of the study was to get Albert to respond to rats with fear, and the way they accomplished this was that they would present the rats to the infant in conjunction with a loud, unpleasant noise. And eventually, Little Albert acquired a fear reaction to rats, and he generalized that fear reaction to white, furry animals of all sorts. In fact, the point of the Little Albert experiment was to demonstrate that phobias were learned behaviors, not inborn as had been previously thought.

The Little Albert experiment may seem cruel, and it's probably not repeatable in today's world because protections for children in research have strengthened, but it suggests that you can treat phobias the way you would extinguish any conditioned response, by extinction.

In fact, there are two versions of this type of therapy for phobias that are actually in use today. Both incorporate a basic extinction type of thinking. One is called flooding and response prevention and the other is called systematic desensitization or counter conditioning. In both cases, you expose people to the scary stimulus, and you do something to prevent them from having a full blown fear reaction, such as relaxing breathing or other kinds of techniques. And the result, after some time, is that that fear response is extinguished. No more phobia.

So, classical conditioning seemed to get us very far, but there are some holes here. First of all, there's very little attention to the awareness of learning or the idea that people may actively try to learn something—which we know they do—and there's no attention to the idea of feedback in this approach to learning.

Consider a cartoon by Mark Stivers, which depicts the same Pavlovian dog scenario we discussed earlier. But this time, one of the dogs turns to the other dog and says, "Watch what I can make Pavlov do. As soon as I drool, he'll smile and write in his little book."

The cartoon is funny but the deeper message is about features of learning that can't be explained by learning to associate two stimuli in such a way that you can evoke a conditioned response.

A comprehensive treatment of learning has to account for the many cases in which we aren't passive recipients of environmental events, but actively altering the environment to achieve particular goals.

The idea that consequences of our behaviors—rewards and punishments are important aspects of how we learn—is a very entrenched idea, and you can find this idea operating in many different situations. The idea has a lot of appeal. It matches intuitions we have about the pursuit of pleasure, like if it feels good, we're going to do it. And it also seems to at least start to take into account the fact that we do consider consequences when we are engaging in our behavior.

Around the turn of the century, Thorndike was observing cats figuring out how to open a latch and escape from their cage into an adjacent enclosure that had a large, smelly dish of salmon.

At first cats had to do a lot of trial and error to accomplish the task, but once they figured out how to open the latch, not surprisingly, latch-opening behavior increased. Thorndike observed this and he articulated what he called the law of effect as a rule about how behavior might be governed by its consequences.

Thorndike's law of effect implies two things. First, an important class of associations that we learn are the ones between what we do and the consequences of that behavior. Second, the law of effect implies that we change our behaviors when we've learned those contingencies.

Now, Thorndike also notes that we can have positive or negative consequences, and they can either occur or cease, and behavior should vary accordingly, provided we learn the behavior and consequence associations accurately. So after this, researchers began to conduct experiments to see how they could alter behavior by changing or controlling the consequences that were attached to behavior.

These experiments varied widely and they ranging from conditioning rats to press levers or getting pigeons to peck lights in exchange for food rewards, to giving monetary rewards to human participants who were engaged in different kinds of problem solving. This research area was termed operant conditioning research, and it differed from classical conditioning because it emphasized associations between behaviors and consequences, rather than associations between two stimuli.

The assumption is that when an animal is rewarded for a behavior, increases in the behavior show that the animal has learned to associate the behavior and the reward.

Now, all this makes a ton of sense to our intuitive ideas about how people and animals learn to behave. If I want my dog to sit, I get him to do it, and then give him a liver snack. He will sit for me every chance he gets after that—though it might take a couple liver treats.

If I want my child to perform well in school, I pay him a dollar for every A he receives on an assignment, and since he's quite the mercenary child that works pretty well. But then, not surprisingly, if I stop the rewards, the behavior might eventually stop, too.

As with classical conditioning, it's important that the reward be contingent on the response for the person or the animal to learn the association. The reinforcer has to follow the behavior when it occurs. However, you can ask just how much rewarding should happen in order to maximally shape behavior, to form the strongest association, and it turns out there are actually some options.

A fixed ratio schedule is one option. And what that means is every time you press the lever 10 times you get a food pellet. Every time you get three 100% spelling tests in a row you get a dollar. And this is a lot like peace work in factories.

Another alternative is called a variable ratio reinforcement schedule. This is a little different. In a variable schedule, on average you get a food pellet every time you press the lever 10 times. But the actual number of lever presses varies over time. Sometimes you have to press 12, other times you only have to press eight. And what this does is it creates a little bit of uncertainty. You never know quite when you're going to get a reward.

So, how do these different approaches to rewarding people work for maintaining a behavior? If you want to have someone engage in the behavior maximally, a variable ratio schedule is a very good one. In animal research, the animal will respond at a high rate all the time because it can never tell exactly when the reward is going to come again.

Now, for human beings, gambling with slot machines is exactly the same scenario. It exposes you to variable ratio reinforcement. The machines are actually programmed to pay off at variable ratio schedules. And if you visit a casino you see something that looks a lot like pigeons and levers. You see sort of a mechanical rate of shoving coins into slots and pulling levers.

Another everyday example for many of us actually involves whining children. If you consider that when you shop with children, they whine for toys and candy and so on. Now, most parents say "no" to this whining most of the time, but virtually every parent occasionally gives in. And this creates a variable ratio reinforcement schedule. That's the reinforcement schedule that's guaranteed to create strong, escalating responding. In other words, we're doing exactly what we need to do to increase whining.

Well, what are we supposed to do? Actually, one thing to do with the child case is actually advice that you'll see in many parenting books. So, the idea is that first the child has to ask in a normal, not whining voice for the desired object. And then, the parent has to make an immediate, firm, and fast decision about saying "yes" or "no" and stick to the decision. And if the whining voice is there from the start the answer is always no. It's really good advice but it's really hard to follow.

Well, these two examples actually bring me to the issue of punishment. Whining is an aversive behavior—nobody likes to hear it. And gambling is a risky behavior, and in many cases, we respond to risky or aversive behaviors not with rewards, but with punishments.

So, do punishments act so of like anti-rewards? Not precisely. Does punishment work? It can, but there are some kinds of tricky things about punishment.

One is that the behavior you're going to punish is already happening, and so it must already be rewarded in some way, according to operant conditioning researchers. So punishment is happening in conjunction with some reward, and knowing what that reward is is not always very easy. What reward are you giving your whiney child? You're going to have to figure that out before your punishment is really going to work.

Now, one study of this looked at people pressing a button for a reinforcement, for a reward, and they had to press the button 500 times to get the reinforcer. Now, if the button also makes a bad noise, it takes them 18 minutes, as opposed to three minutes to get to 500 presses. If you give them the option of another button that doesn't make the noise, they completely stop with the button that makes a noise.

So what that tells us is punishments slow down people's responding, even when they are given in the presence of rewards, and they also will lead people to find an alternative an alternative way to get that reward.

But, we can also think about another study of rats that were trained to press levers for food. Now, in this particular study, food was given in response to lever pressing. So there was a reward in place. Now, all of the sudden the researchers changed the rules of the game and the rats are going to get punished when they pressed. Now, this is cruel, but it's important for understanding punishments. One group of rats got punished immediately, right when they pressed the lever. Another group of rats got punishment sort of a little bit delayed, and a final group of rats got punished in a noncontingent way. And in fact, what happened was they got shocked while they were lever pressing, but the shocks were not connected to their lever pressing. They don't have any way to stop it and they don't have any way to predict it.

This last group, the noncontingent group is kind of a critical group because just getting shocked could suppress the rat's lever pressing for reasons that have nothing to do with punishment. In fact, rats actually tend to freeze when they're fearful, and that's going to inhibit their ability to lever press.

In this study, the punishment group, almost completely stopped responding by the second shock. That immediate punishment seemed to work really well. Now, for the delayed punishment and the noncontingent shock groups, they're a little bit suppressed in their responding, which suggests there's a little bit of fear going on there, but they didn't unlearn the behavior—that is, they didn't stop lever pressing.

What all this tells us is that punishment works, but punishment works best when it is maximal, immediate, and not introduced in mild form. When we punish children, we often violate these principles. We sometimes delay punishment, "Just wait 'til your dad gets home." We start with milder punishments and we work towards more severe consequences. And, those are approaches to punishment that don't work. What the research says is we have to jump on bad behavior with as severe a response as we think appropriate.

Now, between this and classical conditioning, it may seem like we've accounted for everything. We have an account of how people learn associations between different events in the environment, and how they learn associations between their behavior and its consequences, but there are some complications, and when we think them through, it's hard to feel like our initial theories of learning are adequate.

Let's consider some of the evidence that these theories don't explain very well. First, these theories cannot explain what is rewarding or reinforcing outside the narrow range of innate drives, like hunger, thirst, and maybe for people and social animals a need for praise from others. But monkeys and rats and other animals will press a lever just to make a light go on. There's no need satisfied by turning on lights that we know about, but animals clearly experience that as a reward.

Another complication in what counts as a reward comes from work by Premack in the late '50s and early '60s. And this work suggested that behaviors that are more often chosen in a free-choice situation are reinforcers for less frequently chosen activities. That's kind of abstract, so let me give a concrete example. Given a choice between running several miles and eating a giant piece of chocolate cake, all else equal, I'd take the cake. Now, the cake can then be a reinforcer for the running, but not vice versa.

But, as Premack kept working, the relativity of reinforcers became clearer—like water is reinforcing when you're thirsty but not when you've just had a giant glass. Now, in learning theory, as we've talked about it, there's no way to explain how a reward is sometimes less rewarding than at other times.

Some stimuli become reinforcers because they're associated with desirable items. The clearest examples of this are token economies. Money is the most famous token economy around, where we have these papers and we can exchange them for things we actually want, but even my son's third grade classroom has a very serious token economy going where kids get little tokens for good behavior and they can exchange them for candy or toys.

But, consider the complexity of associations that have to be learned. You get tokens as a result of behaviors—that's operant conditioning. Tokens go with candy or toys—that's classical conditioning. But the kids' behaviors, the rewards that connect to tokens are widely varying, and this is just outside the bounds of generalization that we've talked about with respect to classical or operant conditioning.

Finally, some evidence from infants responses to a mobile they can control, and from research on learned helplessness, really point to the idea that having control over events is reinforcing, in and of itself. Infants smile and coo at a mobile that they control by kicking, but not at one they don't control, even if they're getting the same visual and auditory experience. And, when animals are exposed to shocks they can't control, they get withdrawn and apathetic. They stop behaving at all, and this is called learned helplessness.

Control over events is a very strong reinforcer, and we can see that when we look at the paradoxical rewards of punishments. So how can punishment be a reward? Take an example familiar for many of us: A married couple attempt to have a serious, interesting conversation about political events at the dinner table. The five and eight-year-old don't find this very interesting or rewarding, but their attempts to hijack the conversation get ignored, and in short order, the five-year-old begins to spit her food at her brother. This results in a quick and very abrupt shift of parental attention to the children, combined with punishment, scolding and reprimands. Now, from the adult perspective, what's just been delivered is punishment.

But, if you think about how reinforcing control is, what the five-year-old has just pulled off is to control the response she received and to get the attention she desired.

Finally, there's evidence that people learn without any rewards from many studies. One example consists of what's called latent learning. Remember the myth from the first lecture that we always know when we're learning? We don't. Consider a famous study by Tolman and Honzik, and in this study rats were turned out into a maze. Some of the rats were just allowed to explore without any rewards or punishments. Other animals were given a rewarded for going a certain route within the maze. Now, a third group of rats weren't given any rewards initially, but 10 days into the study, they were given a reward for going a particular route. At this point, the newly rewarded rats demonstrate that they've, in fact, learned the correct route because they are much faster to being going that route than the rats that were rewarded from the beginning—that is, it takes them less time to start demonstrating the desired route.

And this can only be the case if they actually learned the maze, and what the reward is doing is just incentivizing, or giving them the incentive, to make sure of their learning in a particular way.

In related studies, child development researchers have shown that children will even imitate someone who's clearly failing at their intended goal. Now, why would a child imitate someone who isn't getting what they want?

One of the most difficult parts of learning theory initially was actually that researchers wanted to avoid considering anything that wasn't directly observable. So, you can see the meat powder and you can hear the bell and you can measure the saliva, but you can't talk about the dog having an expectation because that isn't measurable in the same way as those other things.

But, the complexities of rewards and associations that we've been talking about make more sense if we think people aren't merely learning associations between two stimuli that are reflected in observable behavior, but rather that they're processing their experiences in the service of building a representation of the world in which they live, and that representation is housed in the black box of their mind. In other words, a person's own ideas about the world play a role in whether or not a reward is really a reward.

Considered this way, it makes more sense that control over the environment is rewarding, in and of itself, and that animals and people exhibit latent learning—learning that's already occurred but they haven't yet demonstrated in their behavior. And it also makes more sense for explaining how we learn complicated things, like a token economy, and for understanding those paradoxical features of punishment.

At the heart of this move from thinking about learning solely in terms of classical or operant conditioning to a theory that factored in the subject's representational view, the person's understanding of their world was what is called the information processing revolution, and we're going to consider it in more detail in our next lecture.

Learning as Information Processing
Lecture 3

I n the last lecture, we learned that in attempting to create a theory of learning that avoided representations, expectations, and other immeasurable concepts, researchers in the field of learning actually became increasingly incapable of explaining even some pretty straightforward concepts—such as learning without rewards or the fact that rewards are relative. In addition to the issues that were raised in the last lecture, the restriction on talking about mental states and processes meant that learning theories were unable to explain some very important phenomena in the area of language processing.

Information Processing

- Consider the following three sentences: We have to be at school by 6 pm. The performance begins at 6 pm. At 6 pm, the play will start. They all mean more or less the same thing, but they are three different stimuli from a behaviorist and conditioning approach. It is difficult to explain how these three different sentences are understood in the same way by the person hearing them.

- If we only have behaviorist and conditioning approaches to work with, then we have to resort to the very cumbersome idea that over time all three sentences have become associated with the same response—showing up at school by 6 pm. That's problematic because once you have one stimulus associated with a response, it's not easy to learn a new association to that response.

- Once we allow ourselves to talk about meaning and representations, however, it's very easy. While the surface form of the three sentences is different, the underlying meaning for the person—the information they contain—is the same, and they're going to result in the same behavior.

- Many other aspects of language use were difficult to explain with behaviorism, such as the way people can generate many different sentences that are all grammatically correct. Early learning theories require that we were exposed to those sentences before we could generate them, but this isn't the case.

- People make sentences that nobody has ever heard before, and a person's ability to create a new sentence only works if we have the idea of rules, which aren't observable parts of the environment. The idea of rules means we have to imagine what's going on inside people's heads, and that's completely unacceptable in a classic behaviorist approach to learning.

- As conditioning paradigms were running into trouble, there were some exciting developments going on in computing, including the development of the first computers, which gave rise to a corresponding development that's referred to as information theory.

- The language and concepts in the computing world turned out to be helpful in thinking about the way the human brain might learn. Information theory emphasizes how information is coded and recoded and how it can be decoded or understood as it gets transferred across various media.

- From this perspective, we can think about learning as the acquisition of new information and the ability to use that information in some way—to repeat it, for example. In this way, learning occurs as people take in, store, and then use information.

- An information-processing approach to learning means that learning happens as people encounter information, connect it to what they already know, and as a result, experience changes in their knowledge or their ability to do certain tasks.

- The kind of information we encounter can actually be quite varied, and both learning and the demonstration of learning can be thought of as translations of information from one medium into another.

- An information-processing approach identifies different stages of the learning process. Initially, new information must be encoded—that is, translated from perceptual experiences into a representation in the mind. Once it's in the mind, we may or may not further work with the representation; this can be compared to the process of a rehearsal.

Verbal Learning

- These two stages, encoding and rehearsal, represent aspects of learning that can vary. There are many ways we encode information, and there are different ways we rehearse it once we have it encoded. On some later occasion, we may have to retrieve that representation in order to demonstrate our new learning. The basic approach to studying learning from this perspective is often verbal learning—that is, learning lists of words.

- When we ask people in verbal learning paradigms to learn lists of words or word pairs to demonstrate their learning in tests of memory, we divide the learning process into three information-processing stages: encoding, storage, and retrieval.

- During encoding, people are taking in new information and are making sense of it. For example, you're both hearing what someone else is saying and drawing on your past experiences to transform the sounds the other person is making into something meaningful and understandable.

- In fact, encoding operates through a variety of short-term information stores, and within each of those stores, information is being transformed. Researchers call that storage space working memory. Within working memory, we think about the meanings of words and link them to memories we already have.

- Processes of rehearsal also draw on our established knowledge, which you can think of as long-term memory. Encoding is central to our understanding of learning today, and differences in encoding matter for how well we learn.

- Storage, in an information-processing account, refers to keeping information we have learned over time. The storage part of the process of learning is actually the most difficult to test, measure, or observe.

- During retrieval, people make use of the information they previously learned. For example, you might be asked to recall information, to recognize something previously learned, or to demonstrate use of prior learning without even thinking about it.

- Retrieval is not the same as learning, and we might think of retrieval roughly as memory. Retrieval is often one of the only ways we have of knowing that something has been learned.

- Retrieval is not only a demonstration of past learning; it's also a re-encoding. That is, every time you recall information, you re-encode it. You retrieve it and use it, and the information is actually changed because you've retrieved it and used it. In this way, although retrieval often gets thought of as a way of demonstrating previous learning, it turns out retrieval is also an important way to improve learning over time.

Information Processing versus Conditioning
- Conditioning couldn't explain why water is rewarding sometimes and not other times. Information processing says that encoding is a function both of the stimulus—the water—and the prior experience of the perceiver, and experience varies over time. When recent experiences have left a person or animal hungry, food rewards are enticing. When this is not the case, food rewards are less appealing.

- In addition, what rewards us and reinforces our behaviors varies from one person or animal to the next. Because of this, one major factor in learning involves the way that our previous experience changes how we encode information.

- Conditioning paradigms have a difficult time explaining why people would learn without rewards or incentives, although people do. Information-processing theories, by contrast, suggest that we're fundamentally oriented toward making sense of our worlds and that information is its own kind of reward.

- In conditioning work, variability in how people or animals learn was limited to variations in the way stimuli were presented or that responses were rewarded or punished. By contrast, in an information-processing paradigm, we can actually look at variability in how people engage with the material to be learned. We can ask, in limited ways, what's in the subject's head. When studying humans, we often do this with verbal materials.

- Consider that some things don't help us learn. Numerous studies show that simply repeating information over and over doesn't actually help us learn it very effectively. Unfortunately, it turns out that merely intending to learn a list of words also doesn't help us learn them.

- While intentions to learn material and simple repetition don't seem to help us, something called elaborative encoding does. Study after study reinforces this finding, and it has direct applicability to a lot of the learning we do.

- In practice, this means that going over notes is less effective than reading and thinking about how material can be connected to other things we already know; thinking about clever mnemonic devices that would help us recall material; or otherwise engaging in deeper, more elaborated thinking about the material we're trying to learn.

- Elaborative encoding works better for learning because, in most cases, it approximates how we're going to use the information we're trying to learn. A phenomenon called transfer-appropriate encoding shows that the more your learning method approximates the way you're going to need to use the information you're learning, the better your learning will be. In fact, if you're learning specifically to be able to do well on a test, testing yourself over and over again represents a way to learn material that's very effective.

- Every time we recall things we've learned, that occasion of recall functions as a new learning episode. In other words, when you engage in

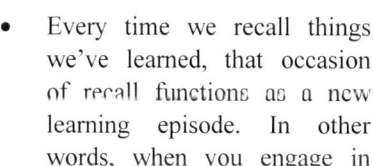

Retention testing is a way of using the material we've learned; for many of us, we retention test ourselves on reading every day.

retrieving learning, you give yourself another chance to encode. There is a phenomenon called hypermnesia that shows just how effective repeated retrieving can be for learning.

- Hypermnesia means that when you test retention—when you engage in testing over and over again—you actually end up increasing what you remember over time. This is a very powerful and important idea for those of us who want to continue to learn things or to remember what we've already learned.

- Research in this area suggests that different types of information may be differentially easy or difficult to learn. In addition, studies suggest that pictures may be easier to learn than words, which is why so many memory techniques make use of visual imagery to help people remember things.

Learning and Forgetting

- Material we learn is forgotten when it's not used, and retention testing is also a way of using the material we've learned. In some cases, as it is with reading, we retention test ourselves every day. In other areas, such as with foreign language learning, we may not very frequently make use of that past learning, so it's not surprising that we end up forgetting or losing much of what we initially learned.

- Information-processing approaches to learning give us much more flexibility than classical or operant conditioning theories about learning. Information processing allows us to think about how learning changes depending on who's doing it and how they're going about doing it.

- The idea of transfer-appropriate encoding also reminds us that why we're learning is important, and matching how we are learning for the purposes we have in mind is going to be important for enhancing the effectiveness of our learning.

- Perhaps the most important part of the information-processing approach, however, is that information-processing approaches demand that we consider not just the material to be learned, but also the past experiences and expectations that we bring to that learning experience. In other words, there is no tabula rasa; there's no blank slate.

Suggested Reading

Baars, *The Cognitive Revolution in Psychology.*

Question to Consider

1. How might information-processing ideas about learning be applied to learning a new dance or hoping to improve one's golf swing?

Learning as Information Processing
Lecture 3—Transcript

Recall that last time we talked about how behaviorist theories. In attempting to create a theory of learning that avoided representations, expectations, and other immeasurable concepts, researchers in the field of learning actually became increasingly incapable of explaining even something pretty straightforward—like learning without rewards, or the fact that rewards are relative.

In addition to the issues that we raised in the last lecture, the restriction on talking about mental states and processes meant that learning theories were unable to explain some very important phenomena in the area of language processing.

Consider the following three sentences: We have to be at school by 6 pm. The performance begins at 6 pm. At 6 pm, the play will start. They all mean more or less the same thing, right?

But these are three quite different stimuli from a behaviorist and conditioning approach, and so it then is difficult to explain how these three different sentences are understood in the same way by the person hearing them. If we only have behaviorist and conditioning approaches to work with, then we have to resort to the very cumbersome idea that over time all three sentences have become associated with the same response—showing up at school by 6 pm. And that's problematic because, as we noted last time, once you have one stimulus associated with a response, it's not so easy to learn a new association to that response. Remember the example: when bell ringing was associated with the arrival of meat powder and therefore salivation, and then you add a light to the bell, the light just didn't work as well. And in fact, sometimes animals didn't learn to salivate to the light at all.

Once we allow ourselves to talk about meaning and representations, however, it's very easy. While the surface form of the three sentences is different, the underlying meaning for the person, the information they contain, is the same. In other words, they're three different ways of conveying the same information, and they're going to result in the same behavior.

Many other aspects of language use were difficult to explain with behaviorism, like the way people can generate many different sentences that are all grammatically correct. Early learning theories require that we were exposed to those sentences before we could generate them, but this isn't the case. People make sentences that they've never heard before. People make sentences that no one has ever heard before. And a person's ability to create a new sentence that they've never heard before only works if we have the idea of rules. This is the idea that there are rules about how words can be combined, and a person knows the rules and can then use them to make lots of different sentences.

But rules aren't observable parts of the environment, and they're not an observable behavior. The idea of rules, again, means we have to imagine stuff inside people's heads, and that's completely unacceptable in a classic behaviorist approach to learning. That classic approach only recognizes stimuli we can see and behaviors we can measure.

As conditioning paradigms were running into trouble, there were actually some exciting developments going on in computing, including the development of the first computers. And this gave rise to a corresponding development that's referred to as information theory.

The language and concepts in the computing world turned out to be helpful in thinking about the way the human brain might learn. Information theory emphasizes how information is coded and recoded, and how it can be decoded or understood as it gets transferred across various media.

So a piece of information I'd like to give my husband about when we need to arrive at a school performance moves from a thought or piece of knowledge I possess, to a series of sounds, words, which he can then recode into information, and use to respond appropriately.

From this perspective, we can think about learning as the acquisition of new information, and the ability to use that information in some way—to repeat it, as is the case often in more academic kinds of learning—or to make use of that information. For example, when we learn how to apply for a driver's license by reading a website, and then we make use of that learning by actually going through the process of applying for the driver's license. So in this way, learning occurs as people take in, store, and then use information.

Today, we'll focus on three issues. First, what is this information processing approach anyway? Second, how do we know this approach is useful or needed? And third and finally, does this approach actually better let us make sense of the way that who, what, when, where, why, and how we learn, matter?

What does an information processing approach to learning mean? Well, for learning, an information processing approach means that learning happens as people encounter information, connect it to what they already know, and as a result, experience changes in their knowledge or their ability to do certain tasks.

The kind of information we encounter can actually be quite varied. So, we can think of classroom learning as offering certain kinds of information, but also if you learn a new dance, you can think of the process of watching the new steps and sequence, recoding that visual information into a mental representation, and then translating that representation into a motor movement sequence as you repeat the steps you watched. So both learning and the demonstration of learning can be thought of as translations of information from one medium into another.

An information processing approach identifies different stages of the learning process. Initially, new information must be encoded—that is, translated from perceptual experiences into a kind of representation in the mind. Now, once it's there in our head, we may or may not further work with the representation. Something we often kind of think about that working with as a rehearsal.

These two stages, encoding and rehearsal, represent aspects of learning that can vary. These are the how of learning in the information processing approach. There are many ways we encode information, and there are different ways we rehearse it once we have it encoded. On some later occasion, we may have to retrieve that representation in order to demonstrate our new learning. And, the basic approach to studying learning from this perspective is often verbal learning—that is, learning of lists of words.

We ask people in verbal learning paradigms to learn lists of words, lists of word pairs, to demonstrate their learning in tests of memory for those words or word pairs, and although a lot of the research I'll talk about has been done with lists of words, you can use a similar approach with pictures or sounds or spoken languages, numbers, other kinds of stimuli. There are many options. But, when we take this approach, we divide the learning process into three information processing stages.

Let me first describe these stages, and then we'll need to briefly consider why this stage-like understanding is a little bit oversimplified. Encoding. During encoding, people are taking in new information and they're making sense of it. For example, as I'm talking, you're decoding the meaning of the words and the sentences, and you're understanding what I'm saying. As you do so, and this is important, you're not just focusing on what I'm saying, you're transforming it in light of what you already know, including the meanings of the words and how they're connected in sentences I'm using, but you're also using what you know in terms of what you know about the concept of coding and what you understand stages to mean, and so on. You may not be specifically or deliberately aware of all the past knowledge you're using to do this encoding. The important point is that you're both hearing what I am saying, and you're drawing on your past experiences to transform the sounds I'm making into something meaningful and understandable.

In fact, encoding operates through a variety of short-term information stores, and within each of those stores, information is being transformed. For example, if I present you with a list of words, it's represented as sensory information visually, if I'm showing you the words on a page, and then it moves to a short-term storage kind of space in the mind, within which you can work with or rehearse those presented words. That storage space is called, by researchers, working memory.

Within working memory, we engage in processes that we refer to as rehearsing the words. We think about their meanings. We link them to memories we already have, and so on. Those processes of rehearsal also draw on our established knowledge, which you can think of as long-term memory.

Encoding is central to our understandings of learning today. We're going to have a lot to say about how differences in encoding matter for how well we learn. The other two parts of an information processing approach apply, in a way, to issues of how well learning sticks once we've done it, and how we can demonstrate learning. These are called storage and retrieval.

Storage, in an information processing account, refers to keeping information we have learned over time. Ultimately, the way things are stored depends on long-term or lasting changes, in the way our neurons connect with one another. This is something referred to as long-term potentiation. The storage part of the process of learning is actually the most difficult to test, measure, or observe, and we won't say much about storage, except for the last piece of information processing, which is retrieval.

During retrieval, people make use of the information they previously learned. This can take a variety of forms. For example, you might be asked to recall information. You might have to remember how to get to your new office or to recite the multiplication tables. You might need to recognize something previously learned. For example, can you recognize the face of the person waving at you? Or, can you correctly recognize which coat is yours from all the coats in the closet?

Or, you might demonstrate use of prior learning without even thinking about it. Every time you shift gears in a manual transmission car, you're retrieving a previously learned motor skill, but you're not aware of that process at all. Your conscious experience is that you want to shift, and you do so.

Now, retrieval is not the same as learning, and we might think of retrieval roughly as memory. It is important because retrieval is often one of the only ways we have of knowing that something has been learned. So retrieval is not the same as learning, but it's often going to be how we demonstrate that we or someone else has learned something.

For example, you know your child has learned something in school when she can tell you about it, and in telling you, she has to retrieve the information she has acquired. Or, recall the idea of shifting your car. Even though you're not conscious of the act of calling up, or retrieving that motor skill, the fact that you shift requires you to retrieve a specific motor pattern.

What I want to point out today is that retrieval is not only a demonstration of past learning. It's also a re-encoding. That is, every time you recall information, you re-encode it. You don't pull it up then put it back just the way it was. You retrieve it, you use it, and the information is actually changed because you've retrieved it and used it. In this way, although retrieval often gets thought of as a way of demonstrating previous learning, it turns out retrieval is also an important way to improve learning over time. We'll talk more about this in a later lecture.

Information processing approaches to learning, then, they often divide things into phases of learning and the demonstration that learning has been successful and of course, retained. But you may be thinking, "How is this better than the stimulus-response and stimulus association approaches of conditioning research?" Well, let's consider some of the issues that conditioning work did not address very well.

Let's start with variation and rewards. Remember that conditioning couldn't explain why sometimes water is rewarding and other times it's not. Information processing says that encoding is a function both of the stimulus, the water, and the prior experience of the perceiver, and experience varies over time. So, when an animal or a person's recent experiences have left them hungry, food rewards are enticing. When this is not the case, food rewards are less appealing. And in fact, in our broader who, what, when, where, and why framework, our experiences make each of us a very unique who. And as unique who's, what's going to reward us and reinforce behaviors for us is going to vary from one person or animal to the next.

Because of this, one major factor in learning involves the way that our previous experience changes how we encode information. We'll focus more on this issue in the next set of lectures and we'll return to it later in the course, when we think about how different people do or do not learn differently.

Now, a second issue that was poorly explained by conditioning was the idea of latent learning and observational imitation without any rewards.

Conditioning paradigms have a hard time explaining why people would learn without rewards or incentives, although they do. Information processing theories, by contrast, suggest that we're fundamentally oriented towards making sense of our worlds. We want to turn what's going on around us into meaningful information. Information processing paradigms actually imply that information is its own kind of reward. So, like the Alpine climbers who say they have to climb the mountain, because it's there, we seem to learn stuff because it's there to be learned.

Information processing accounts are particularly useful for thinking about what we learn, and how we learn it. In conditioning work, variability in how people or animals learn was limited to variations in the way stimuli were presented, or that responses were rewarded or punished. And what happened inside the minds' of those people and animals was off-limits or unscientific. So there wasn't any way to ask, what sense did the rat make of the lever and the food reward?

By contrast, in an information processing paradigm, we can actually look at variability in how people engage with the material to be learned. We can ask, in limited ways, what's in the rat's head, and in less limited ways, what's in the person's head. So, when studying humans we often do this with verbal materials, and the results can be really interesting.

First, consider that some things don't help us to learn. For example, when I was young, and I needed to phone someone with an unfamiliar telephone number, I looked up their number in the phonebook, and then I walked to the telephone on our wall, muttering the number over and over and over again under my breath until I could punch it into the touch pad. But, after doing this, I didn't retain that phone number later on. It wasn't a good way to learn a telephone number. And in fact, numerous studies show that simply repeating information over and over doesn't actually help us to learn it very effectively.

Well, one could say, the problem with that is that I might never have intended to learn the number. Suppose I was merely telephoning a person that I never will need to telephone again—a store, and I wanted to inquire about an item's availability; not a call I'd need to repeat. And perhaps it would work better if I had intended to learn that number.

Unfortunately, it turns out that merely intending to learn a list of words also doesn't help us to learn them. In one classic study, Hyde and Jenkins asked participants to look at a list of 24 words. They saw each word for three seconds. And as participants looked at each word, they were asked to do one of two things. They were either asked to determine whether the word contained the letters a or q, or they were asked to rate how pleasant the word was.

Now, notice that the second task requires people to think about the word meaning, and we'll come back to that later. Now, in this experiment, half of the participants were told they would later be tested on the words, and half were not told. And, the assumption here is that if you were warned about the test you would have the intention to learn the test words. Then, as is often the case in these studies, everyone was given a recall test.

If you looked at the results, you would notice two things. First, the participants who were told about the recall test, and those who were not told, had exactly the same performance. The promise, or the threat of a test, didn't help anyone learn the words better. So, presumably the intention to learn the words didn't really help. Second, the participants who thought about whether the words were pleasant or unpleasant recalled more words—just under 70 percent—than did the people who determined whether the words were spelled using a or q.

Why would this be? While intentions to learn material and simple repetition don't seem to help us, something called elaborative or deep encoding does. And this is one of the most robust findings in the literature on learning and memory. Study after study reinforces this finding, and it has direct applicability to a lot of the learning we do. Here's what it means in real terms: Going over notes is less effective than reading and thinking about how material can be connected to other things we already know, or thinking about clever mnemonic devices that would help us recall material, or otherwise engaging in deeper, more elaborated thinking about the material we're trying to learn.

There is a twist in all of this, however, which is that elaborative encoding works better for learning because, in most cases, it approximates how we're going to use the information we're trying to learn. In the laboratory, you can actually create circumstances where this is not the case.

For example, imagine that I give you a task where sometimes you have to come up with a rhyming word. Thinking about a rhyming word, is usually a type of shallow processing or shallow encoding. Now, on a different task, you might have to think about whether a word fits a sentence in terms of meaning. This is usually viewed as a deep or elaborative processing task. Then, I might give you two different kinds of retention tests to see what you've learned. In one test, you have to look at words and tell whether you've heard those words before or not.

The usual advantage for elaborative or deep encoding is observed here. People who thought about whether a word's meaning fit the sentence did better and people who identified rhyming words did poorly. Now, in the other test, you're given a list of cue words that rhyme with the original list of words, and you have to use the cue words to recall the list words. In this case, the rhyming participants actually outperform the deeper processing people.

What's going on? This is a phenomenon called transfer-appropriate-encoding. And what it means is that the more your learning method, the more your how, approximates the way you're going to need to use the information you're learning, the better your learning will be. In fact, if you're learning specifically to be able to do well on a test, testing yourself over and over again represents a way to learn material that's very effective. Studying the booklet for the driving test can help you pass the test, but studying for that test won't necessary improve your driving.

Now, I mentioned earlier that every time we recall things we've learned, that occasion of recall functions like a new learning episode. Another way of saying this is to consider that when you engage in retrieving learning, you give yourself another shot at encoding. And there is a phenomenon called hypermnesia that shows just how effective repeated retrieving can be for learning. Now, what is hypermnesia? In order to explain this concept I'm going to have to tell you about another experiment.

Erdelyi and Kleinbard showed participants 60 slides. Now, some participants in their study saw slides of simple picture sketches of objects, like a telephone. Others participants saw instead the word "telephone" on the slide. Participants looked at each slide for about five seconds. And at the end of the presentation, participants were given seven minutes to remember as many of the items they had been asked to learn as possible. On subsequent days, participants in this study were asked to complete recall sheets at least three times a day over the course of the next week, and each time, they were to take only seven minutes to recall.

If you plotted their results on a graph, with the y-axis indicating the number of items people remembered, and the x-axis showing the time since they initially learned, you would see distinct patterns for the two kinds of items over time. For the first several hours, you see a sharp rise in the number of items recalled for both pictures and words. Then the number of words recalled stays stable at about 50 percent recall, and the number of pictures actually increases to about 66 percent.

So, there are two things I want to draw your attention to here. First, both words and pictures show increases in retention over repeated testing. What is this about, and how does it relate to learning? This is the phenomenon of hypermnesia. What it means is that when you test retention, when you engage in testing over and over again, you actually end up increasing what you remember over time. And, this is a very powerful and important idea for those of us who want to continue to learn things or to remember what we've already learned. Testing or trying to recall things increases your chances of learning and retaining what you've learned.

Now, the second thing I want you to think about with respect to these results is that the data actually suggest different types of information, maybe differentially easy or difficult to learn. And, the study actually suggests that pictures may be easier to learn than words. And this is why so many memory techniques—a topic for a different course—make use of visual imagery to help people remember things.

But let me get back to learning and forgetting. Material we learn is forgotten when it's not used, and retention testing is also a way of using the material we've learned. Now, in some cases, as with reading for many of us, we retention test ourselves on reading every single day. But in other areas, for example, with foreign language learning or solving math problems, we may actually not very frequently make use of that past learning. And it's not surprising that we then end up forgetting or losing much of what we initially learned.

So, it happens that there's actually a substantial body of research looking at forgetting of material that was learned over time. And some of this work is actually quite old. For example, Ebbinghaus, around the turn of the century, asked people to learn lists of nonsense syllables, and showed that after people learned the syllables perfectly (that is, they could recall 100 percent of what he had taught them), their performance on a retention test tended to decay over time (that is, over time when they didn't use these nonsense syllables they lost them). They no longer had access to that learning or they unlearned.

So, classical conditioning helped us look at associations, but it didn't let us think about consequences. Operant conditioning let us think about rewards and consequences, but not why some things were rewarding and some things weren't, or things were sometimes rewarding and sometimes not, or why people actually learn without rewards. Both of these approaches assumed that what the person or the animal knew or previously learned didn't quite matter for how they were going to learn something new.

What we've talked about today is how essential it is to think about learning in terms of information, representations, expectations, and rules, and to understand that learning happens as a process of encoding, retrieval, and re-encoding. What kind of information matters; pictures are easier information than works. Why we are learning matters; if we learn in ways that don't actually correspond to what we need to do with our learning, it's actually going to be less effective for us. How we deal with information also matters; thinking about material, connecting it to what we already know, elaborative or deep encoding usually works best for learning.

Elaborative encoding brings me to what is perhaps the most important part of the information processing approach. Information processing approaches demand that we consider not just the material that's going to be learned, but also the past experiences and the expectations that we bring to that learning experience. In other words, there is, as we'll discuss in more detail next time, no tabula rasa. There's no blank slate in learning. Instead, we bring to every learning experience our intentions and expectations based on our broader goals, our perspective on what we are learning, and our shared and unique cultural history.

Creating Representations
Lecture 4

We seldom, if ever, learn passively by letting things wash over us. Learning does happen without our awareness, but even in that case, learning happens as we're engaged in purposeful action: We're pursuing other goals, and the learning that happens in those circumstances is affected by the goals we're pursuing. Furthermore, we learn in addition to everything else we already know, and what we already know changes our experiences as we learn. In this lecture, we'll discuss goals, or purposes, and how they affect learning. Then, we'll consider how past experience shapes current and future learning.

Learning and Motivation

- If we think about learning in terms of information processing, we can draw an imaginary line from a stimulus in the environment—a piece of information, an image, or a sound—through a series of transformations and repetitions based on previous knowledge and experience. That line ultimately ends up in learning.

- The stimulus can be anything defined in terms of energy—such as sound waves or light waves—and that energy is transformed into a sensory experience by our sensory systems. It is then transformed further into a perception, and we may combine perceptions into even more complex representations of our surroundings or into complex actions and reactions. This is the process of encoding.

- Representations and actions that we store and can then generate on our own—independently of the environment and independently of a stimulus—are considered learned. This is the process of retrieval.

- Goals shape what we learn as we go through experiences, and they affect our imaginary line at each stage in the process. Sometimes the goal is simply to learn about our environment and what the available options are. At other times, the goal is more narrowly focused, and the learning that occurs happens more incidentally with possibly more limited usefulness. Learning is also shaped by the goals we pursue as we engage with our environment.

- We learn what we need to learn to engage in our everyday actions. When we don't need to learn, we may actually not learn anymore. For example, when the goal of being able to stay in touch with friends can be met without memorizing phone numbers, we no longer invest effort, time, or energy in learning the numbers, and we actually don't learn them.

- Psychological research has shown that purposeful behavior shapes our learning, even when learning isn't our central purpose. However, human beings and other animals engage in a lot of spontaneous exploration. In fact, the exploration of our environments is a major motivating force. In other words, we often do have a chronic goal of learning.

Exploration as a Motivator
- In the 1950s, psychologist Kay Montgomery proposed that animals have two conflicting motivations: a drive to explore, or curiosity, and a fear of the unknown. He posited that the curiosity drive is innate and that it's aroused by novelty.

- In one study, Montgomery and his colleagues showed that rats would learn a simple maze much more quickly if they were rewarded with the opportunity to explore a more complicated maze. Therefore, getting to learn something more interesting actually serves as a reward.

- Montgomery also showed that rats who had a more complicated and rich environment when they were young actually become interested and curious in complicated environments—but not in simple, new environments. To some extent, what's novel and what stimulates curiosity depends a little bit on what you've experienced up until that point in your life.

- Human infants begin exploring almost from the beginning of life, even when their ability to move, see, hear, smell, and taste are very limited. This exploration has many functions, but it seems that it's rewarding for babies to simply understand their environment and what it offers.

- One of the biggest changes in a baby's behavior happens at the point where the baby is able to grasp an object. Grasping lets babies link how an object feels in the hand with how it looks to the eyes. Once babies move from grasping to crawling or walking, there is no stopping their exploration.

- You may think that exploration is the province of the young, but the act of exploration—the act of learning something new about your environment—is a motivator for most of us in our daily lives, at least in some areas. Exploration is a lifelong possibility.

Learning and Prior Knowledge
- The purposes we have as we go through our day and the purpose of exploration itself are not the only things people bring with them to a learning situation. Learning is not only purposeful; it's also driven, to some extent, by what we already know.

- There is no tabula rasa in learning. In other words, what we learn doesn't just come in and imprint some as-yet-unused piece of the brain; instead, what we learn is a result of what we've already learned.

- Just as with goals, along our imaginary line representing information processing, there are numerous points where we might see the importance of past experience in shaping present perception and representation—and by extension, learning.

- One point along that continuum is in the transformation of stimulus energy into sensation and perception. Some of the most compelling experiments in this area look at the connection between early deprivation and the ability to sense or perceive parts of the visual environment.

- In these studies, researchers vary whether a particular experience happens or doesn't happen, and then they look at whether that experience matters for a later ability to perceive or sense the environment. For example, it turns out that experience matters quite a bit for later visual perception.

- An example from visual perception concerns the ability to recognize faces. Interestingly, when people grow up in ethnically and racially homogenous environments, they're actually less capable of recognizing individual faces of people who come from a different racial or ethnic group—and possibly of associating names with those faces. This phenomenon is called the same-race bias.

- This bias can be overcome with exposure: As we see many diverse faces, we become better at discriminating between individual faces from people in an ethnic group that is different than our own. In fact, this kind of perceptual learning—the ability to tell the difference between different stimuli with exposure—happens in many contexts.

- Perception—the basic, initial phase of information processing in learning—is affected by our past experiences with stimuli. There is no tabula rasa, not even at the very beginning of information gathering for learning.

- Let's move a bit further along that processing path to the point where people need to take perceptions and combine them to create some meaningful representation. We learn some very interesting things about meaningful representation in early learning experiments that involve memory for words—and for illustrations.

- People have to make use of their own prior knowledge in order to use categories to help them learn and remember lists of words. Once they do so, they are prone to some distinctive and interesting errors. For example, suppose you are presented with the following list of words and are asked to learn them: bed, nightlight, reading lamp, pillow, blanket, dream.

- Later, when you are asked to recall the words you just learned, you're very likely to recall the word "sleep," even though it was not on the list. This is a very robust finding, which means that it is a very easy finding to repeat with different participants and different studies.

- Remembering that you learned the word "sleep" in this list is what researchers call a false memory. You spontaneously used a category you have—things related to bedtime and sleeping—to organize the words you were given as you learned them. Later, this organization actually makes you better at remembering the items that were on the list. It also makes you vulnerable to the error of remembering that "sleep" was on the list.

Categories and Scripts

- Just as our knowledge about categories helps us organize otherwise chaotic information, our knowledge about complex events and objects in the world, known as our schemata, help us learn from experiences.

- Schemata are defined as abstract knowledge structures, and they include things like plans and event sequences, which are also called scripts. Just as in a play, a script tells you what happens, in what order, for some type of event.

- These knowledge structures were originally conceived of in computer science—as people tried to figure out how to get computers to process information—and then they were applied to research on how human beings process information.

Just as in a play, a script tells you what happens, in what order, for some type of event.

- Roger Schank and Robert Abelson are two pioneers in this field, and some of their early work involved trying to make computers that could read and understand prose based on prior programming with a script. Reading and understanding are not quite the same as learning, but they are important steps in encoding.

- There are a variety of ways of testing the idea that there are scripts in people's heads—just as with testing whether there are categories in people's heads. In a sense, scripts are like categories, but scripts also have information about serial order, or the expected order in which events occur.

- One way of testing the idea of scripts involves asking people to learn and recall events and looking for false intrusions of script-relevant events that people were never told about.

- Furthermore, when people are asked to generate a script, or to draw inferences about what happens next in a story, they're more likely to choose something that's pretty central to the script rather than something that's more peripheral or could be left out.

- If you were asked to generate a script for eating out in a restaurant, you would include items like being seated, reading the menu, choosing something, waiting for the food, and asking for the bill. However, you probably wouldn't list things like visiting the bathroom or assessing the quality of the chairs because these are peripheral to the main idea of having dinner out. Leaving these items off your list suggests that scripts aren't just a memory for eating out, but they're actually a list of rules and events that are central to the event of eating out.

- We approach any learning situation with prior knowledge and with beliefs about categories and scripts, and these influence what we perceive, understand, learn, and later remember from material we're trying to learn. Two of the prominent features of prior knowledge are categories and scripts, but there are other kinds of prior knowledge—prior knowledge about body movements and scripts for muscle movements, for example—that also qualify as kinds of schemata and that also affect learning.

Suggested Reading

Bartlett, *Remembering.*

Questions to Consider

1. Categories and scripts are both friend and foe to learning in that they serve as aids to learning new material, but they can also produce errors in our learning and memory. Considering your everyday life, how important are the errors that are produced by category- or script-based distortions in learning?

2. Can you recall a time when you had to learn a new event script? What was that time? How did the experience unfold?

Creating Representations
Lecture 4—Transcript

In today's lecture, I want to make two general points about how we learn. First, we seldom, if ever, learn passively by letting things wash over us. Learning does happen without our awareness, but even in that case, learning happens as we're engaged in purposeful action. We're pursuing other goals. And, the learning that happens in those circumstances is affected by the goals we're pursuing. Second, we learn in addition to everything else we already know, and what we already know changes our experiences as we learn.

Now, as we've discussed already, these two aspects of learning posed a profound challenge to early theories because goals and prior experience are hard to observe. They're also foundational to much of what we will discuss through the remainder of the class. I'm going to begin with goals or purposes, and how they affect learning. Then, I'll consider some illustrations of how past experience shapes current and future learning.

Remember, that if we think about learning in information processing terms, we might draw a kind of line from a stimulus in the environment—a piece of information, an image, or a sound—through a series of transformations and repetition based on previous knowledge and experience. And, in the end that line ultimately ends up in learning.

Now, the stimulus can be anything defined in terms of energy, like sound waves or light waves, and that energy is transformed into a sensory experience by our sensory systems, and then further into what we call a perception. We may combine perceptions into then more complex representations of our surroundings or into complex actions and reactions. This process is what we've been calling encoding.

Representations and actions that we store, and can then generate on our own independently of the environment, independently of a stimulus, are considered learned. And that's what we've called retrieval—that process of generating the representation independently of needing a stimulus.

Now, goals shape what we learn as we go through experiences, and as you can imagine, goals are going to affect everything at each stage in this sort of processing line that I'm trying to draw out for you. Now, sometimes the goal really is simply to learn about our environment and what the available options are. But, at other times, the goal is going to be more narrowly focused and the learning that occurs happens more incidentally, with maybe more limited usefulness. But that learning is also shaped by the goals we are pursuing as we engage with our environment.

You may remember the example of the grocery clerk from earlier in the course. Her purpose was everyday recognition of you as a customer. She wasn't learning your face to be able to pick you out in the crowd or as you were wearing multiple disguises. She wasn't a private investigator.

One generality about learning is that we learn what we need to learn to engage in our everyday actions. When we don't need to learn, we may actually not learn anymore. For example, we're no longer as likely to memorize people's phone numbers as a child, or actually a teenager, I learned my friend's phone numbers by rote memorization. Because at that time, if you didn't learn the numbers, you had to look them up every time in the phonebook, and if you didn't have the phonebook handy or your friend's number was unlisted, you weren't going to be able to call your friends.

Now, we no longer do this because we need only type a phone number one time into our cell phones, and then we can call that person anytime we want to. In many cases, we don't even need to dial that number at all. So, one way to think about this is that when the goal of being able to stay in touch with friends can be met without memorizing phone numbers we no longer invest effort, time, or energy in learning the numbers, and we actually don't learn them.

Or, consider this: A student once asked me how to get to the Biology Department on my campus. I knew and had learned many landmarks on my campus at that point, but here's how I learned them: They were either relevant to my work (the location of my building, the classroom building where I taught, the Dean's office for my college, the best cafeteria for lunch, and the library) or the places I knew would be relevant to my non-work life as a runner (the best road to reach a nearby park, and so on). Now, I had no goals or needs involving the biology building, so as it turns out, I didn't know where it was located or what it looked like. And this was true despite the fact that I'd been walking by it every day for six years.

Now, some of the more fun illustrations of this aspect of learning in respect to goals come from work on learning about a series of events when we vary the goals people have for learning about them.

One of my favorite example studies is this: You might show people a set of relationship events that occur between a man and woman. And let's just say for the sake of thinking about this problem, first meeting, a first kiss, an argument about commitment, infidelity on the part of the man, hostile and angry treatment on the part of the woman, infidelity on the part of the woman, additional infidelity on the part of the man, culminating in conflict and a decision to divorce. Now, this is not a very happy story—I know—but it has a lot of drama and that's kind of nice for an experiment where you ask people to learn things.

Now, imagine that for some of the people, I ask them to learn about this list of events, to learn this relationship history while serving as the divorce lawyer for the woman. Now, for others I might ask them to do the same thing. Learn this relationship history, but serving as the lawyer for the man. Now, as you might imagine, when I later ask people to tell me what happened in the relationship to test what they've learned, people's learning of the events turns out to be partisan. The divorce lawyer for the woman under-learns and actually underestimates the negative actions of his client relative to the other party.

So, one point that can be made over and over and over again from research findings in psychology is that purposeful behavior shapes our learning, even when learning isn't our central purpose. Now, we'll revisit this issue in future lectures as we consider some findings on second-language vocabulary acquisition and the role of attention in learning more generally.

But I would leave you with an erroneous conclusion if we stop considering purposes at this point because one of the interesting things about most species that have been studied is this: Human beings and other animals engage in a lot of spontaneous exploration. And in fact, the exploration of our environments—and in our case that means both our physical and our social environment—is a major motivating force for us. In other words, we often do have a chronic goal of learning.

How do we know this? In the 1950s, a young psychologist named Kay Montgomery proposed that animals have two conflicting motivations: a drive to explore, which we might call curiosity, and another motive, which you might think of as a fear of the unknown.

If you have ever paused for a moment outside the door to the building where you're about to start a new job or a new school, you've probably experienced a moment where both of these motives were very strong, very salient for you.

Now, Montgomery posited that the curiosity drive was innate and that it's aroused by novelty. That is, whenever you encounter something new you experience curiosity or an interest in learning. In one study, he and some colleagues showed that rats would learn a t-shaped maze much more quickly if they were rewarded with the opportunity to explore a more complicated maze. So, getting to learn something more interesting actually serves as a reward. Montgomery also did something quite interesting. He varied rats' experiences in early life, and he showed that rats who had a more complicated and rich environment when they were young actually get interested and curious in complicated environments, but not in simple, new environments. So to some extent, what's novel and what stimulates curiosity depends a little bit on what you've experienced up until that point in your life.

Human infants begin exploring almost from the beginning of life, even when their ability to move and their ability to see and hear and smell and taste are very limited. And this exploration has many functions, but it looks like it's rewarding in and of itself for babies to understand their environment and what it offers.

So, if you think about young infants, in the newborn to six month phase, their ability to sit up or move or in some cases even hold their head up is fairly limited. One of the biggest changes in a young baby's behavior happens at the point where the baby is able to grasp an object. Now, prior to this point, babies spend a lot of time looking at things, and mouthing things that they're offered, because that's what they're able to do.

Once they can grasp an object, babies spend a lot of time doing so. And, any of us who have ever played with a baby know that they like to grab your fingers or your keys, your glasses, or anything that they can reach. And this grasping actually lets babies link how an object feels in the hand with how it looks to the eyes. And any parent is going to tell you that once babies move from grasping to crawling or walking there is no stopping their exploration.

Based on what I've said so far, you may think that exploration is the province of the young, but recently my mother phoned me to enthuse about a recently opened grocery store in our city. Now, there are three large grocery stores within about two miles of her house, and together with a some ethnic food stores, she's already able to buy any food items she might need. But, the opening of a new store was a cause for exploration. It's a novel stimulus and it provoked curiosity, followed by the need to share what she'd learned with others. What prices and items were available? Did the produce look better than at other places? Was there more variety? Were the employees nice? Now, all of these pieces of information are completely unnecessary, but the act of exploration alone, the act of learning something new about her environment, was a motivator for my mother, and this is true for most of us in our daily lives, at least in some areas.

So, exploration is at least a lifelong possibility, although we are going to return later in this class, to the question of whether exploration is uniquely salient in infancy and childhood as compared to later adulthood. Now, we touched on this in the first lecture when we promised to talk about the myth that you can't teach old dog new tricks.

The purposes we have as we go through our day, and the purpose of exploration itself, are not the only things people bring with them to a learning situation. Learning is not only purposeful; it's also driven, to some extent, by what we already know.

The second major point of this lecture is that there is no tabula rasa in learning. So, what we learn doesn't just come in and imprint some as-yet-unused piece of the brain; what we learn instead is a result of what we've already learned. Consider those rats who had complicated environments in rat puphood: They didn't find a simple maze very rewarding as adults. It wasn't novel. It didn't offer them much to learn. So what we've learned is a result of what we'd already learned, and it also determines what we're going to go on to learn next.

Now, to see how this works, let's revisit that line representing information processing—that line from a stimulus in the environment, a piece of information, an image, a sound—through a series of transformations and repetitions that ultimately results in learning.

As you can see, just as with goals, there are numerous points along that continuum where we might see the importance of past experience in shaping present perception and representation, and by extension, learning.

One is in the transformation of stimulus energy into sensation and perception. Some of the most compelling experiments here look at the connection between early deprivation and the ability to sense or perceive parts of the visual environment. The logic of these studies is straightforward. Researchers vary whether a particular experience happens or doesn't happen, and then they look at whether that experience matters for a later ability to perceive or sense the environment. For example, in later visual perception, and it turns out, experience matters quite a bit for later visual perception.

Some early studies deprived kittens of a certain type of visual stimulation at a point in early kittenhood where visual perception is developing. For example, researchers might make sure that a kitten never sees horizontal lines. (At this point, you can see why much of this work has been done with animals because it's difficult to control a human being's environment that thoroughly.) Now, if you do this to a kitten—if you raise a kitten in the absence of horizontal lines—what you get is a kitten who actually can't perceive horizontal lines in the future.

Now, if you're a visual perception researcher, this is the end of the story. But if you're interested in learning, we have to go one step further. Any kind of learning that requires the kitten to see horizontal lines is not going to be possible for this kitten. But for another kitten, whose early perceptional experience was normal and included horizontal lines, learning that requires horizontal lines is perfectly doable, perfectly straightforward.

Another example from visual perception concerns our ability to recognize faces. Interestingly, when people grow up in ethnically and racially homogenous environments, they're actually less capable of recognizing individual faces of people who come from a different racial or ethnic group. And this phenomenon is called the same-race bias.

What it means is that it is more difficult to learn people's faces, and possibly to associate names with those faces, if they're from a different group. This bias can be overcome with exposure. So as we see many diverse faces, we get better and better at discriminating between individual faces from people in an ethnic group that is different than our own. And in fact, this kind of perceptual learning—the ability to tell the difference between different stimuli with exposure—happens in many contexts. And we'll actually talk a little more about this kind of learning in the next lecture.

So, perception—that basic, initial phase of information processing in learning—is affected by our past experiences with stimuli. There is no tabula rasa, not even at the very beginning of information gathering for learning.

Let's move a bit further along that processing path to the point where people need to take perceptions and combine them to create some meaningful representation. We learn some very interesting things about meaningful representation in early learning experiments that involve memory for words.

So, in one early study by someone named Bousfeld, participants were given mixed up lists of words from a variety of categories. For example, consider the following list: daisy, saucepan, cat, rose, frying pan, geranium, dog, hamster. Now, at this point in the experiment I might ask you to tell me the words that I just told you—that is, to see which of the words you've learned.

Now, people do something quite interesting when you ask them to say these words. Rather than repeat the words back in order, they often do so organizing the words by category. In other words, people presented with this task say, "rose, geranium, daisy, saucepan, frying pan, cat, dog, hamster." So, they've spontaneously organized the list of kind of unrelated words into three categories. And this kind of finding tells us people are making use of what they already know to organize their learning—that is, they know that some of these words belong together because they're flowers, and they know that some of these words belong together because they're equipment used in cooking, and other words belong together because they're all animals. And so, they're using their category knowledge to organize their learning. And this is quite adaptive because it turns out that if you use categories when you're trying to learn a list of words you'll actually improve your learning.

Now, a different researcher named Barsalou did a different experiment, and he asked people in this case to generate categories from arbitrary lists of words. For example, I'm going to give you a list of four words: children, dog, stereo, blanket. What category might encompass these four items? Think for just a minute.

People given this task came up with a variety of things. For example, some people said, "These are things to take from your house in case of a fire." Others said, "These are the things you take to the park." You can get very creative with this task, and I think it's actually kind of a good party game. But, what you can see is that people actually can make enormously inventive use of what they already know, of their own past experience, to create a meaningful way of connecting a list of items that on the surface are just unrelated.

Another example from memory research involves making up funny sentences to help remember an arbitrary list, like, "The dog and cat put the hamster in the frying pan after boiling him in the saucepan and hey served him up with rose, geranium, and daisy petals." This strategy for learning makes use of your knowledge about sentences and about language, and it also makes use of surprising visual imagery in ways that you actually know are ridiculous, and even the ridiculousness relies on what you know about what is normal.

So, people have to make use of their own prior knowledge in order to use categories to help them learn and remember lists of words. Now, once they do so, they are prone to some distinctive and interesting errors. For example,

I might present the following list of words to you and ask you to learn them: bed, nightlight, reading lamp, pillow, blanket, dream.

Later, when I you what words you were asked to learn, you're very likely to recall that I asked you to learn the word sleep. This is a very robust finding, by which we mean this is a very easy finding to repeat with different participants and different studies. Remembering that you learned the word sleep in this list is what researchers call a false memory. In fact, the word sleep is not on the list. What happened? You spontaneously used a category you have—things related to bedtime and sleeping—to organize the words you were given as you learned them. And later, this organization actually makes you better at remembering the items that I gave you to learn. It also makes you vulnerable to the error of remembering that sleep was on the list.

So far, we've talked about how what we already know can help us make sense of, organize, and learn lists of words in a more effective way, and you can imagine similar approaches with pictures or other lists of concepts. Now, a more pointed illustration of this comes from the work of Sir Fredrick Bartlett, in the early 1900s, on people's ability to learn a folktale from a culture quite different than their own. To do this, Bartlett presented British adults with a series of folktales drawn from native cultures in other parts of the world, including Native American cultures, and he asked the British adults to learn and then retell the tales. And he used those retellings to look at their learning and their ability to retain what they had learned.

One of the stories was called the "War of the Ghosts." This is a North American, indigenous folktale, and Bartlett knew his participants had never heard it and wouldn't be familiar with it. So they couldn't draw on their specific prior knowledge of the story to help them learn and remember the details. Now, the second key thing about the "War of the Ghosts" is that it's difficult to understand in some places because the story actually requires you to understand a little bit about that originating cultures mythology and worldview. And in particular, it requires you to understand some assumptions like the following: Ghosts can come and talk to the living as though the ghosts are still alive and animate, and the living can be fooled about whether the ghosts are alive or dead. So, the gist of the story is that the two young men are seal fishing, and they're approached by a party of warriors.

Unbeknownst to these men, the warriors are ghosts. The warriors invite the two men to make war with them on a down-river group. One of the men refuses but the other one actually goes along to war. In the ensuing fight, the young man is killed, but he doesn't seem to realize this, and he returns with the ghosts to his home village. He tells his story, and then he falls down, and a black thing flies from his mouth, and he is then at that moment recognized by his home tribe as being dead.

Bartlett's participants read the story twice through. And then, 15 minutes later, he tested their retelling of the story to see what they had learned. So, how did prior knowledge, or in this case the absence of the right prior knowledge, affect learning? Well, as I said, for western Brits of the time there were some things in the story that don't quite make sense.

For example, Bartlett's British participants, they don't have this worldview in which ghosts walk around and get living people into trouble, and they also don't have the idea that people might not immediately recognize when someone is dead. So, participant's retellings of the story actually distorted the meaning of the word ghost in the story in ways that were more consistent with what British participants believed about the world in general. For example, one participant reported that the warriors were accused of being ghosts. Another participant reported that the clan's name was ghosts.

Now, these are errors in what's been learned about the "War of the Ghosts" but they're also errors that reflect the way that prior knowledge shapes what we understand about our situation and what we are able to learn.

In fact, just as our knowledge about categories helps us to organize otherwise chaotic information, our knowledge about complex events and objects in the world, known as our schemata, help us to learn from experiences.

Now, schemata are defined as abstract knowledge structures, and they include things like plans and event sequences, which are also called scripts. Just like in a play, a script tells you what happens, in what order, for some type of event like going to a restaurant, or hosting a birthday party. For Bartlett's participants, their scripts for young men going off to war were probably something like your own, and the idea of ghosts making mischief and dead people walking are not part of those scripts. Rather, the script for young men going to war involves some sort of provocation, at a minimum an insult which was one common distortion of the story. So, what you already know shapes future learning. Prior knowledge affects how you learn new things. As I've said before, no tabula rasa.

These knowledge structures were originally conceived of in computer science, as people tried to figure out how to get computers to process information, and then they were applied to research on how human beings process information.

Consider the following few sentences: John was feeling very hungry as he entered the restaurant. He settled himself at a table and noticed that the waiter was nearby. Suddenly, however, he realized that he'd forgotten his reading glasses.

We know right away that this problem is relevant because the next step is for John to read a menu. Yet this hasn't been mentioned, We know it and we understand these sentences because we have a script in our minds. We have a representation of what's involved in going to a restaurant.

Now, some of Schank and Abelson, two pioneers in this field, some of their early work involved trying to make computers that could read and understand prose based on prior programming with a script. Now, reading and understanding is not quite the same as learning, but as with all information processing ways of thinking about learning, reading and understanding is one of the important steps in encoding.

How do we know something like a script or a set of expectations about what will happen and in what order, how do we know this exists in people's heads? There's a variety of ways of testing this idea, just as with testing whether there's something like a category in people's heads. For example, just like with the false memory for the word "sleep" earlier, and just like with Bartlett's example of misremembering the "War of the Ghosts," we can ask people to learn and recall events, and we can look for false intrusions of script-relevant events that people were never told about.

One example would be a false memory for a statement about menu reading in the event description above. In this sense, scripts are like categories. But scripts also have other information. That includes information about serial order or the expected order in which events occur.

So, in other studies of scripts, participants are given a series of event descriptions to learn, and researchers can present items in or out of sequence with that script. We develop a standard script by asking a whole bunch of people what happens when you go to a restaurant and aggregating their answers so that we know what steps are endorsed by most people and what order is endorsed by most people. And then, if we present events in or out of order, people actually tend to distort the order of events so that it fits that kind of group script.

So, imagine for example, that you were accepted to two graduate programs and you interviewed on each campus after being accepted. Now, in retelling this to someone else or remembering it much later in your life you may in fact switch the order of the two events because the more canonical order, the more typical order of the script is to first interview and then be admitted. You might actually make this error, and it would seem plausible to everyone including you. It would just also happen to be false.

A final piece of evidence that scripts are real is that when people are asked to generate a script, or to draw inferences about what happens next in a story, they're more likely to choose something that's pretty central to the script, rather than something that's more peripheral or could be left out.

So, if I ask you to generate a script for eating out in a restaurant, you'll include items like being seated, reading the menu, choosing something, waiting for the food, and asking for the bill. But you probably won't things like visiting the bathroom or assessing the quality of the chairs and silverware, because these are things we do when we visit a restaurant, but they're peripheral to that main idea of having dinner out, and leaving them out suggests that scripts aren't just a memory for eating out, but they're actually a list of rules and events that are central to the event of eating out.

What all this means for learning is that we approach any learning situation with prior knowledge and beliefs about categories and scripts, and these influence what we perceive, understand, learn, and later remember from material we're trying to learn. Now, as I said, two of the prominent features of prior knowledge are categories and scripts, although there are other kinds of prior knowledge. There are prior knowledge about body movements, scripts for muscle movements for example, that also qualify as kinds of schemata and that also affect learning.

In this lecture, we have emphasized the ways in which purposes and prior learning influence current learning. Now, you may be thinking, as I was when I first learned about the powerful role that scripts play in learning, you may be thinking "But, but, but, where do we learn scripts?" Well, the next lecture, we'll ask where and how we acquire categories and scripts, as surely, these are also learned.

Categories, Rules, and Scripts
Lecture 5

In the previous lecture, we discussed how our minds are not a tabula rasa—that the way in which we learn is influenced by our prior understanding of categories and events. We also learned that those prior understandings can be called schemata, and scripts are one kind of schemata. This begs the question of how those things are learned and what precisely we're learning in the first place. This is the topic we're going to take up in this lecture on categories, rules, and scripts.

Categories and Perceptual Learning

- Categories are critical well beyond the role they play in learning. For example, knowing whether something is edible or whether a person can be trusted are category judgments.

- One of the first demonstrations of category learning occurred in the area of perceptual learning, which is a very important type of learning. For example, perceptual learning is what permits children to distinguish between the letters d, b, p, and q—all of which look pretty similar, especially to a child learning to read.

- Initially, perceptual learning was thought of as a memory-based process. However, in the 1950s, James and Eleanor Gibson argued that what we learn through perceiving—somewhat automatically— is to perceive increasingly more aspects or features of what we're looking at, and as a consequence, we can make more fine-grain distinctions among things we're looking at.

- Discriminating between different things is a fundamental precursor to being able to understand categories, which exist because certain distinctions matter while others don't. Furthermore, prior learning about categories has many implications for what we learn.

- Initial work on perceptual learning that was done by the Gibsons showed that just looking at material over and over again increases the extent to which we can perceive differences in those materials. Because judgments of similarity and difference are fundamental parts of category learning, perceptual learning is a basic step in acquiring categories.

- The results of perceptual learning studies show that all age groups improve at the task over time. They also show that once you're an adult, your ability to quickly acquire perceptual categories is significantly improved. In addition, the learning that people do isn't in response to rewards.

- Human beings and monkeys appear to acquire categories in stages. First, we master what's typical, and then we seem to learn the strange examples. The fact that we do this in stages leads to the question of how we are managing our learning.

Early Theories of Category Learning
- Early views in the area of category learning were called exemplar theories, and they focused on memorizing each example of a category individually as a member of that category. This would be like learning the association between each individual fish and the overarching category of trout.

- The prototype theory account stated that we first have an experience with a category—for example, fish—and from that experience, we form a representation of the prototypical category member. Then, when we encounter a new fish, we match it up with the prototype of fish that we have formed in order to decide whether the thing we're looking at is a fish.

- These accounts turn out not to be very helpful, in part because they really don't correspond to how the brain processes information. In addition, categorization is so important for us that we're likely to go about it in different ways.

- More recent theorists believe that there are at least two broad routes to category learning. One is a very deliberate, verbal, rule-based approach. The other approach involves simply guessing about category membership.

- In the rule-based approach, we operate like scientists: We have a guess about the rules for the category, and the rule we're guessing about can be used to make a prediction about whether a new example belongs to the category. Then, we try out our guess, get some feedback, and revise the rules and the guesses for the next round. One example of this approach is learning to differentiate between letters of the alphabet.

- The second route involves making a guess and finding out whether that guess is correct. At some point, we become very good at guessing, but we don't know precisely how we become so good at it.

- Some research suggests that we rely on different routes depending on the kind of category or the nature of the category when learning.

- In some situations, it would be difficult to describe a simple set of rules for making certain judgments accurately without having more experience with the subject area. This type of category is called a nonlinear category, and researchers now think that it is learned by a process of information integration.

- In other words, instead of explicitly testing a rule and keeping your working rule until you find that it doesn't work on a particular occasion and then revising it, people's minds just track the feedback they receive on a more implicit and less conscious level until they can categorize objects well and accurately, even though they're not quite able to tell you how they do so.

Acquiring Scripts

- We acquire scripts in many of the same ways that we acquire categories. There are two ways that we acquire scripts: One is to very deliberately collect information that leads to the rules for a script, and the other is a more tacit approach that involves good guessing after amassing a lot of experience.

- Early in childhood, the process of verbally working through the rules that constitute a script can be seen vividly in a famous case study. Katherine Nelson, a New York–based child development researcher, examined the tape-recorded monologues of a young girl named Emily.

- The recordings were taken between the ages of 21 months and the time that Emily turned about three years old; they were begun very soon after Emily acquired the ability to speak. Each night, after she was put to bed, Emily would lie in her crib and talk to herself. Parent-child dialogue also played a role in these recordings.

- Emily engaged in talk that resembled the kind of explicit rule-based self-talk that we might do to extract a rule about a concept. Not only did Emily focus heavily on the routines of her life, but it's interesting to note that the emphasis on figuring out scripts actually changed over time. Later in her recordings, Emily focused more on unique experiences, and she started to engage in less self-talk about routines.

- This is important because one of the major findings from this area of research is that early in our lives, we seem more attuned to using everyday events to extract scripts rather than trying to actually learn about a specific experience.

- In fact, Emily's monologues are one of the pieces of evidence that suggest an explanation about why we can't recall specific events from very early in our lives. In fact, researchers think that we can't remember specific personal experiences very well until we've actually learned scripts with which we can understand those events.

- This early childhood acquisition of scripts has actually helped to explain a phenomenon termed early childhood or infantile amnesia, which refers to the fact that virtually all adults can't recall specific life experiences from prior to about age three or four years. This is puzzling because many researchers have shown that babies have fully functioning memory abilities.

- The consensus is that those early experiences are not recalled as singular events; rather, what we're really trying to learn from events that occur prior to age three or four is how things usually go. As such, we focus on the pieces of our experiences that get repeated across time. We don't focus on the distinguishing features that make a particular event unique. Until we have scripts, it's difficult to learn from events in general.

- Emily's recordings also showed that we sometimes learn, or try to learn, scripts from a single event. Given that scripts are complicated and multidimensional—in ways that aren't easily described by rules—you might expect that we only learn scripts through repetition. Therefore, one question is how we pull this learning from a single experience off and whether we can do it as adults.

- Researchers Woo-kyoung Ahn, William Brewer, and their colleagues examined this by giving college students some specific stories about Native American potlatch ceremonies, and they assigned students to have different learning experiences.

- The most efficient way for people to learn the script for a potlatch ceremony was to be told the script directly, but people were also able to learn the script from a single story about a specific potlatch ceremony, provided that two things happened: They needed to be given some background knowledge, and they had to use that background knowledge to explain the single story to themselves.

Children who are given a script about the zoo before visiting it learn and remember more than in the reverse scenario.

- An interesting feature of this is students did not spontaneously take the background knowledge and try to explain the event to themselves. They only did it when the experimenters told them to do it. This suggests that we have a large capacity to learn scripts from just a single event, but we probably don't try to do so very often. Perhaps in most cases, we reserve our effort for things that are going to happen repeatedly.

Goals for Learning Scripts
- As children, the data from Emily's recordings and from more controlled studies suggest we're actively engaged in a process of script extraction—that is, we're experiencing events and actively trying to explain those events to ourselves in terms of what we already know about the world, however minimal that might be.

- In childhood and beyond, others are engaged in helping us to do so, too. Emily talked with her parents and her caregivers, and we often talk with one another about the events of our lives to try to figure out what usually happens.

- As adults, the extent of our background knowledge is typically much broader. We've spent a couple decades at least on script extraction, and we're probably less likely to need to develop new scripts. We can therefore remember our daily experiences as distinct events rather than using them to figure out the script for how things usually happen.

- Under some circumstances, we are vitally interested in acquiring new scripts. These circumstances include new jobs, moving to new towns, and taking on new social roles. Depending on the extent of the changes, the old scripts may be useful to us, but the capacity to acquire new scripts is there when we need it.

- Jobs often provide explicit training in the scripts that are important for doing a job well. Other new experiences can leave us with much less explicit training in scripts to draw on. In these cases, the self-explanations and deliberate thought that Emily was relying on may actually be our best adult tools for navigating a new world.

Suggested Reading

Ashby and Maddox, "Human Category Learning."

Nelson, *Narratives from the Crib.*

Questions to Consider

1. In what contexts do people have to learn categories without feedback? In what contexts do they get substantial feedback about whether they are correct? Based on thinking about these examples, does getting feedback speed up category learning? Can feedback have a negative side?

2. Ideas about scripts can also be applied to how we make sense of and perceive more emotionally laden events. Consider how scripts might involve sequences of events such as: "I try something new. It is difficult at first, but then I become able to do it well. Later, it is an important, enriching, and fulfilling part of my life." Or, alternatively, "I try something new. It is difficult at first, and I become frustrated. I give up but later regret that I did not try harder." Are scripts one way to think about personality?

Categories, Rules, and Scripts
Lecture 5—Transcript

In the previous lecture, we discussed how our minds are not a tabula rasa—that the way in which we learn is influenced by our prior understanding of categories and events and those prior understandings can be called schemata, and scripts are one kind of schemata.

Now, as I noted, this begs the question of how those things are learned and what precisely we're learning in the first place. And this is the topic we're going to take up in this lecture on categories, rules, and scripts. Later in this course, we'll return to issues of purpose and script learning as well.

Now, let's start with categories. How do we learn categories? Categories are really important, even beyond learning. For example, knowing whether something is edible or not is a category judgment. Knowing whether a person can be trusted or not is also a category judgment. So categories are critical well beyond the role they play in learning.

One of the first demonstrations of category learning occurred in the area of perceptual learning. Perceptual learning is a very important type of learning. For example, perceptual learning is actually what permits young kids to distinguish between the letters d, b, p, and q, all of which actually look pretty similar, especially to a child learning to read.

Initially, perceptual learning was thought of as a kind of memory-based process. In other words, the idea was that kids were memorizing b, d, p, and q and then recalling them later on, and the process of reading depending on memory and recognition. But, James and Eleanor Gibson, in the 1950s, made some important arguments about perceptual learning that were not related to memory. Specifically, they argued that what we learn through perceiving, and what we learn actually somewhat automatically, is to perceive more and more aspects or features of what we're looking at, and as a consequence we can make more and more fine-grain distinctions among things we're looking at.

So it's isn't memorizing p, b, d, and q. It's that after we look at those letters over and over and over and over again, we learn to notice that the little stick on the side of the circle is changing its orientation.

Another lovely and more pleasurable example might be to think about wine. On my arrival in Palo Alto, California as a graduate student, I could distinguish between white and red wine on the basis of color and taste, but I had no idea of differences in different varietals within white wines, say, and I couldn't tell the difference when I was tasting wines.

After living for five years in some proximity to the Napa and Sonoma valley wine regions, and accumulating many perceptual experiences of taste and smell and color, I was actually able to make varietal distinctions. On the other hand, my Austrian friend and officemate, who had been a wine fanatic for most of his adulthood, was already able to discriminate many flavors and actually to categorize wines by growing regions, and so on. So, some of what we think of as wine expertise is based on this kind of perceptual learning process.

Why does this matter? Well, discriminating between different things is a fundamental precursor to being able to understand categories. Categories exist because we're saying that certain distinctions, like where the tail is on the b versus the d, matter, while others distinctions, whether the tail is longer or shorter, whether it is a serif or sans serif typeface, don't matter. And, as we already discussed, prior learning about categories has a lot of implications for what we learn.

Some initial work on perceptual learning was done by the Gibsons in the 1950s. The Gibsons presented participants of various ages with drawings of squiggles, and these were sort of badly drawn spirals. Now, there was a target squiggle—sort of the squiggle you were supposed to focus on—and this squiggle had four coils visible on the left side of the drawing, and there was some space between each of the coils.

Now, the Gibsons also showed participants 17 other types of squiggles. And these other squiggles varied in the number of coils they had and whether the coils were on the left or their right side and then how closely or widely spaced the coils were. Now, the variations were pretty subtle, but if you were told which details to look for and you were shown all of the squiggles at the same time, you could immediately see the differences. The trick happens when you're shown the squiggles one at a time and you're not sure of the dimensions or the ways in which the coils can vary, and you're asked is this like or unlike the target squiggle. That's a harder task.

So, the Gibsons presented the target squiggle along with the non-target squiggles—the sort of squiggles that participants were asked to categorize— on cards, and they did this one at a time, to participants. And participants had to look at each new squiggle and say, "Is it the same category as the first squiggle, or is it a different category?" Participants didn't learn whether they were right or wrong, and the Gibsons made them continue to make these judgments until the point at which they got to be 100 percent accurate. Now, at that point, they can be viewed as having learned the rules by which a squiggle gets classified as the same or different from the target squiggle.

The Gibsons tested three groups in this experiment. They tested adults. They tested older children between 8 and 11 years and younger children between six and eight years. Now, the adults were very capable of discriminating the squiggles from the beginning. They made only three errors, on average, on their very first try, and they only needed those three tries to get to perfect classification. The kids took a bit longer. It took them nearly five times through the cards to reach perfect identification. And that younger group needed longer to get it right, even more than five times through, and most of that younger group never really got it perfect.

Now, another difference between the age groups was that adults' and older kids' mistakes were subtle. In other words, they made mistakes at first with squiggles that were pretty close to the target squiggle but only a little bit different. Little kids actually made lots of mistakes, even with squiggles that were very different.

What we need to take from this work, and subsequent work—and actually Eleanor Gibson went on to work with children's ability to recognize letters as they learn to read—is that just looking at material over and over again increases the extent to which we can perceive differences in those materials.

Now, since judgments of similarity and difference are a fundamental part of category learning, this kind of perceptual training, this perceptual learning, is a basic step in acquiring categories.

So, what the results of the studies show us is that all age groups get better at the task over time. They also show us that once you're an adult, your ability to quickly acquire perceptual categories is significantly improved. Now, the second thing that the study shows us is that people didn't get feedback about whether they were right or wrong—ever. They just had to keep making judgments until they were getting it right. And so, the learning that people did wasn't in response to rewards. It wasn't even a response to the reward of the experimenter saying, "Right, good job."

Now, of course, being able to make same and different judgments among squiggles isn't quite the same as fully learning a category. So, consider our category of birds: You might consider robins and sparrows as a kind of prototype of bird. These are the kinds of birds we usually think of when we think about the category of birds. Now, there are however, other birds that are part of this concept or this category, like parrots, hawks, eagles, and vultures. All of these birds that I've mentioned so far share the features of feathers, beaks, wings, egg laying, and flight.

But what about penguins and ostriches? These are also birds. Bird is a complicated category even for the non-ornithologists among us. Over time though, we've come to acquire the idea of birds and the idea that these more atypical birds also are part of that category. Now, how did we do that? To pull back momentarily to the Gibson's initial work, we'd say this is like learning that the target squiggle category includes all four coil squiggles, regardless of distance, and the occasional three coil squiggle because of some bizarre exception. So, how do we pull that off?

In fact, we—and monkeys—appear to acquire categories in stages. First we master what's typical, and then we seem to learn the sort of wacky examples. So, we first figure out that robins, sparrows, and starlings are all birds, then we move a bit farther afield for hawks and raptors, and then we finally get around to mastering the weird examples like penguins and ostriches. But the fact that we do this in stages actually begs the question of really how we manage it. And so, what is it that we're really learning here? And how are we doing it?

Well, category learning is so important. It actually looks like we have a number of different ways of learning about regularities in our environment.

Early views in this area were called exemplar theories, and they focused on memorizing each example of a category individually as a member of that category. So, this would be a little bit like learning the association between each individual fish and the overarching category of trout.

Now, another idea, the prototype theory account, goes like this: First we have an experience with a category. For example, fish, and from that experience we form a representation of the prototypical category member. Then, when we encounter a new fish, we match it up with the prototype of fish that we have formed in order to kind of decide whether the thing we're looking at is a fish or a fowl.

But these accounts turn out not to be very helpful, in part because they really don't correspond to how the brain processes information. And, categorization is so important for us that we're likely to go about it in different ways. In engineering they would say it's likely to have some redundancy.

So, more recent theorists believe that there are at least two broad routes to category learning. One is a very deliberate, verbal, rule-based approach. In that approach, we operate a bit like little scientists. We have a guess about the rules for the category, and the rule we're guessing about can be used to make a prediction about whether a new example belongs to the category or not. And, what we do is we try out our guess, we get some feedback, and revise the rules and the guesses for the next round. A lot of the category learning we do in school works this way. And you can consider how you learn to differentiate between letters as one example of this.

As another example of this rule-based approach, children learn to make the plural of a noun, in English, by adding an s. So one cat, four cats. Now, initially kids actually try this rule out on things where it doesn't work. They say, "sheep" and "sheeps," "mouse" and mouses." They have an idea about the rule, and they try to use this rule all the time. Gradually they learn when the rule does apply and when it doesn't. They learn the categories of regular and irregular plurals.

Now, I said there were two routes. The other route is simply guessing about category membership—just saying, "I think that's an x," and finding out whether we got it right. Now, at some point, we get very good at saying, "Yes, that's an x," but we don't know precisely how. So you might be thinking, "What's the difference here?" Well, let me give you an example.

Here's a good example. We're very good at guessing whether someone is male or female from the way they walk and from a pretty wide distance. Now, for the most part, none of us can explain exactly how we make this categorical judgment. We don't actually know the rule we're using to make the guess. There are differences in walking gait by gender, between men and women, along a lot of different dimensions, and we are somehow able to sum up all these small variations and to make a call, to make a category judgment, male or female, well before we can see other gender differentiating features like clothing or hair or body shape.

So, if we have these two routes for categorizing, rule-based and good guessing, what do we know about them? Some research actually suggests we rely on different routes depending on the kind of category or the nature of the category when learning. So let's think this through for a moment.

Imagine you need to learn categories of fish. Now, these fish could be categorized in two different ways. In one way, the fish are simply categorized by size. So, if the fish is in the large enough group, you may keep the trout. If the trout is too small, you have to release it again. The category distinction that you're trying to learn here relies on one dimension (size) and there's a very simple rule for determining which category a fish belongs in. In fact, the Division of Wildlife's rule in my state is that you can keep a fish over 40 inches for some species.

Now, to learn this kind of category from scratch—let's say you don't actually know the 40 inch rule and you don't have a ruler—you might do the following. You might catch fish after fish, and in each case you think is it long enough or is it not long enough and you decide based on your judgment of how long the fish is whether you're going to keep or release the fish. Now, the ranger meanwhile standing by gives you either a nod or a citation. Over time, you're going to figure out this rule and you're going to be able to successfully classify fish as a keep or release size.

But, as a fisher, you may also encounter a lake that contains both a permissibly catchable variety of trout and a number of other fish that are restricted—in my home state, various chubs and suckers that are considered endangered. Determining whether a fish is a permissible or non-permissible fish can no longer be described with a simple, single rule about length. Now you have to integrate a number of different dimensions along which a fish can vary—and this includes fin size, fin placement and number, gill placement, body shape and size, color, and so on.

It would be hard to describe a simple set of rules or a couple straightforward rules for making this judgment accurately. It's going to take you more experience with looking at fish to be able to do it. This type of category is what's called a nonlinear category and it is learned, researchers now think, by a process of information integration, putting together all those different dimensions that operates more tacitly. That is, instead of explicitly testing a rule, like the fish has to be long enough, and keeping your working rule until you find that it didn't work for you on a particular occasion, and then revising it—instead of doing that, people's minds just track on a more implicit and less conscious level the feedback they receive until they can categorize objects well and accurately, even though they're not quite able to tell you how they can do so, just as we can tell someone's gender from the way they walk, without really being able to tell you exactly what we're paying attention to in order to make that category judgment. So, two ways of categorizing: rules and guessing.

Now, as with perceptual learning, feedback about correct guessing isn't always needed. For example, one study examined kindergarten children's understanding of the category or the concept of science and how this concept developed across the school year. So to do this they interviewed kids about what science is prior to a program in the fall of the school year, mid-way through the school year in December, and then again in spring.

Now, in the beginning, before the kids did any kind of activities related to science, all the kids had some interesting ideas about science that scientist themselves probably wouldn't endorse. In particular, what kids thought is that science was what involved science-type stuff. Science is about lasers and rockets and chemicals and explosions. Or, kids thought about science as fixing things—science more as engineering.

Then, some of the kids participated in the science program, and this program involved kids over the school year engaging in a bunch of different activities, all of which were referred to as science by the teacher. The activities included things like figuring out the density of liquids, figuring out differences between different types of insects, and many other kinds of hands-on, science activities.

After exposure to this program, it turned out kids had learned to think about science much more the way that grown scientists think of it. They thought about science as a method for answering questions, as a way of finding things out, rather than involving a specific content or being about fixing things.

Now, here's the key. This change in kid's category understanding only happened when kids were given lots of exposure in activity of a science-oriented nature. In other words, kids didn't get told science is about finding things out; they worked that out on their own when they were given a lot of exposure to science activities. Now, children who didn't receive that exposure did not in fact change their understanding of what science was over the course of that kindergarten year.

The idea of science as a category brings us to more complicated kinds of prior knowledge, and this takes us to the subject of scripts. Recall that we also talked last time about scripts and we discussed the script for eating a meal in a restaurant as an example. So how do we acquire scripts?

Now, the short answer to this question is that we do so in many of the same ways that we acquire categories. Two ways: One is to very deliberately collect information that leads us to the rules for a script; the other is a more tacit approach that involves good guessing after amassing a lot of experience. And in fact, early in childhood, the process of verbally working through the rules that constitute a script can be seen really vividly in a famous case study. Katherine Nelson, a New York-based child development researcher, examined the tape-recorded monologues of a young girl named Emily.

The recordings were taken between the ages of 21 months and the time that Emily turned about three years old. So, they were begun very soon after Emily acquired the ability to speak. Each night, after she was put to bed, Emily would lie in her crib and talk to herself. Here are some excerpts from these monologues. This first one comes from 23 months of age, and Morm in this quote is Emily's grandmother: "One morning … when Emmy go Morm in the daytime … that's what Emmy do sometime. Sometimes Emmy go sleep and have read … daddy no."

What you can hear in this excerpt is that Emily is doing something a lot like that explicit rule-based kind of self-talk that we might do to extract a rule about a concept. As she does so, she's working on identifying the key elements of her script for her mornings. And these mornings were somewhat complicated in variable because they involved working parents, care by a nanny, and sometimes by her grandmother, and midway through the recording period a shift to attending a preschool.

Now, parent-child dialogue also plays a role in this. Recordings of Emily talking with her father during the same timeframe actually show very similar patterns of emphasis on routines and scripts for daily events. Figuring out what happens usually.

Not only did Emily focus heavily on the routines of her life, it's interesting to note that the emphasis on figuring out scripts actually changed over time. Later in her recordings, Emily's actually focused a little bit more on unique experiences that were one-of-a kind, and she starts to do a little bit less self-talk about what happens usually.

This is important, because one of the major findings from this area of research is that early in our lives, we seem more attuned to using everyday events to extract scripts rather than trying to actually learning about a specific, one of a kind experience. In fact, Emily's monologues are one of the pieces of evidence that suggest an explanation about why we can't recall specific events from very early in our lives. In fact, researchers think that we can't remember specific personal experiences very well until we've actually learned scripts with which we can understand those events. So, this part of script learning, this early childhood acquisition of scripts, has actually helped to explain a phenomenon termed early childhood or infantile amnesia.

This term refers to the phenomenon that most, and in fact virtually all adults, can't recall specific one-time life experiences from prior to about age three or four years. Now, this is puzzling because many other researchers have shown that babies, even eight and nine-month-old babies, have fully functioning memory abilities. They can learn from experiences. They can remember what's happened to them. And so, this makes it actually kind of puzzling that we don't remember earlier experiences than about age three or four.

The consensus is actually that those early experiences are not recalled as singular events. Rather, when we experience things prior to age three or four, what we're really trying to learn from those events is how things usually go. And as such, we actually focus on the pieces of our experiences that get repeated across time. We don't focus on the distinguishing features that actually make a particular event one of a kind and unique. And, until we have scripts, it's actually hard to learn from events in general. More recent research actually shows that kids recall new experiences much better if they first get a script for it. So, for example, if kids are first told what generally happens when you take a trip to the zoo and then they go to the zoo, they learn more on that trip, they remember more of their experiences than if things are done in the reverse order (if they go to the zoo and then talk about what generally happens).

Now, before we leave Emily, I want to highlight one other feature of script learning that can be gleaned from her monologues because it relates to the last point that I want to discuss about script learning in adults.

In another excerpt, somewhat later in the recording period, Emily takes up the topic of air travel. Now, this is an experience she's had only a couple times in her young life. "If we ever go the airport we have to get some luggage. If have to go to the airport, have to take something of the airport, to the airport or you can't go. Need your own special bus and they zoom. Zoom. Zoom. Zoom. Zoom."

Aside from being just deadly cute, this quote of Emily's points to the fact that we sometimes learn or try to learn scripts from a single event. Now, given that scripts are complicated and they're multidimensional, in ways that aren't so easily described by rules, you might expect that we only learn scripts through a lot of repetition. So, one question is how we pull this learning from a single experience off, and whether we can do that as adults.

So, researchers Ahn and Brewer and their colleagues actually examined this, and they did it in kind of an interesting way. They gave college students some specific stories about Native American potlatch ceremonies. These ceremonies are large, family feasts, and they're generally held for the purpose of redistributing a family's wealth. So, students in the study were unfamiliar with the cultures from which the stories were drawn prior to being in the experiment.

Now, in this series of experiments using these materials, Ahn and colleagues assigned students to have different learning experiences. So, some students received a written description of the script itself. Others received a single story, and still others got two stories—more consistent with kind of learning a script from being exposed to events on multiple occasions. Some students were asked to just read the passages. Others were asked to figure out the potlatch ceremony. And finally, some students were given background information on Native American northwestern cultures, not about the potlatch ceremony at all, but about power relationships and hierarchies and family dynamics.

Now, it turned out that the most efficient way for people to learn the script for a potlatch ceremony was to be told the script directly. And, if we think about many approaches to employee training, this is a feature of such training. Many times as employees people are taught in this situation for this kind of event this is what needs to happen and it needs to happen in this order.

But, people were also able to learn the script from a single story about a specific potlatch ceremony, provided two things happened. First, they needed to be given some background knowledge—that is, they needed to understand the culture within which the event was taking place. And second, they had to use that background knowledge to explain the single story to themselves—that is, they had to put together what they already knew with the event in order to extract a schema from a single instance.

Now, an interesting feature of this is students did not do this spontaneously—that is, they didn't spontaneously take the background knowledge and try to explain the event to themselves. They only did it when the experimenters told them to do it. And what this suggests is that, we have a lot of capacity to learn scripts from just a single event, but we probably don't try to do so very often. And my guess is that in most cases we reserve our effort for things that really are going to happen repeatedly. So, if you think about these college students, in their real lives, their lives outside the experiment, understanding and learning the potlatch script wasn't very important because they weren't going to have to do a potlatch any time soon.

Let's now consider the ways in which we learn scripts more broadly, and with a little more attention to our everyday lives, and how those lives look. And it's here that we're going to return to ideas about purposes or goals for learning scripts.

As children, the data from Emily and from other more controlled studies suggest we're actively engaged in a process of script-extraction, a lot like the one Ahn, Brewer, and their colleagues pointed towards—that is, we're experiencing events and we're actively trying to explain those events to ourselves in terms of what we already know about the world, however minimal that might be. Further, in childhood and beyond, others are engaged in helping us to do so, too. Emily talked with her parents and her caregivers about this. We talk with one another about the events of our lives to try to figure out what usually happens.

Now, as adults, the extent of our background knowledge is typically much, much broader. We've spent a couple decades at least on script-extraction and maybe more. We're probably less likely to need to develop new scripts. Most of the daily events of our lives fit within our existing scripts. And, we can therefore remember our daily experiences as distinct events, rather than using them to figure out the script for how things usually happen.

But under some circumstances, we are vitally interested in acquiring new scripts. These circumstances include, although they're not limited to these situations, but they include new jobs, moves to new towns, and taking on new social roles. And under those circumstances, we return to an active engagement in script construction. Now, depending on the extent of the changes that we're experiences, the old scripts may be more or less useful to us, but the capacity to acquire new scripts is there and waiting for when we need it.

How we do it when we need to do so is also going to be variable. So, as I mentioned, jobs often provide explicit training in the scripts that are important for doing a job well. Other new experiences can leave us with a lot less explicit, available training in scripts to draw on such as holding and carrying for a newborn, navigating the politics of a local school system on behalf of our children, or figuring out the social norms of a new culture or even a new workplace. And in these cases, the kinds of self-explanations and deliberate thought that Emily was relying on in her crib, may actually be our best adult tools for navigating a new world.

But in all those cases, we have something to build from in acquiring a script or a category. Emily had language to use, for example. What about babies? Babies have to start from nothing, so aren't they the real tabula rasa? But I've told you many times there's no such thing. So, in the next lecture, we will consider just how babies manage the overwhelming amount of learning they have to do. And we'll think about what their management of learning has to do with the way that grownups learn.

What Babies Know
Lecture 6

So far, we have suggested that we learn for the sake of learning and as we pursue other goals. In addition, we learn by connecting new experiences to what we know already in the form of categories, scripts, and other schemas. Research on early infancy, which makes use of habituation and dishabituation as well as other approaches, tells us that infants are far from a tabula rasa. They come with sophisticated, innate categories and physical scripts that help them make sense of the world.

Habituation versus Dishabituation

- From birth, babies have particular motor reflexes that are so fundamental that their presence is used to indicate whether a baby is healthy. These behaviors are very important for a baby's survival, and they also help tune a baby's motor system by building connections in the neurons in the brain and peripheral nervous system nerves in the limbs.

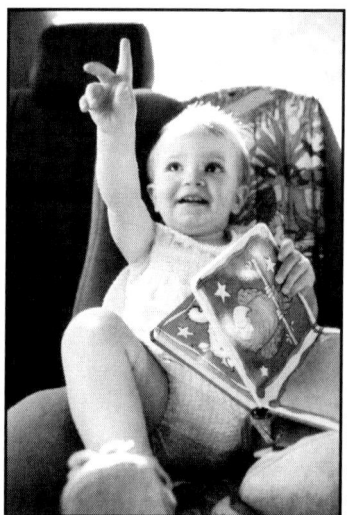

- An aspect in which we appear to have initial schemata involves physical objects. Six-month-old infants already expect a visually presented object to have three dimensions, to take up space, to fall when it's dropped, and other concepts that we know are true of physical objects in our world.

The combination of habituation and dishabituation has given us a window into the learning of babies.

- Habituation is defined as decreased responding after a repeated presentation of a stimulus. Early work on habituation looked at whether rats respond to a loud noise by startling and showed that if you repeatedly play the loud noise, eventually rats stop reacting to the noise. In other words, the rats habituated to the loud noise.

- Without habituation, you could never distinguish between the old and the new or the expected and the unusual. Because habituation is a fundamental prerequisite for many more complex forms of learning, it's not surprising that it occurs across all species and is evident even in human beings as young as newborn babies.

- Habituation is not quite as simple as it seems because it involves a decrease in responding over time, and that means we have to consider at least two other explanations before we decide that habituation is about someone's experience with a stimulus and before we can be sure that habituation is a kind of learning.

- In ruling out these alternative explanations, researchers discovered the phenomenon of dishabituation, and it is the combination of habituation and dishabituation that has given us a window into the learning of very young babies.

- Those alternative explanations are that habituation might be caused by sensory or motor fatigue. If fatigue of either sort is an explanation, the only thing that would allow the rat to start responding again is resting the ears or resting the muscles. It's that startling again that we call dishabituation.

- In fact, if you give the rat a break—if you rest the rat's ears and muscles—and then you play the loud noise again, the startling comes back. The rat dishabituates. However, this kind of finding is a problem because dishabituation after a rest is consistent with the notion that the problem is fatigue and that it's not learning.

- The presentation of a new stimulus—a light or a different sound, for example—can cause dishabituation without any rest. In other words, if you play a different tone to the rats and then go back to the original tone, they will startle again. Because there was no rest, this is powerful evidence that habituation is learning—not just fatigue.

- Babies habituate and dishabituate. What this tells us is babies come equipped with a brain that can determine what is old versus new. For researchers, this means that we can also look at what babies know and learn by figuring out whether they habituate and dishabituate to a stimulus.

- We can use habituation logic to test what babies expect and what they don't expect because a habituated infant will look less at something in the environment. Dishabituation in infants is reflected in increased looking time. Therefore, we can interpret the looking behavior of young infants as what they view as old versus new, unexpected, and interesting.

Inborn versus Learned Knowledge

- Renee Baillargeon is one of several infant researchers whose work has revolutionized our view of infants. Baillargeon and her colleagues presented simple demonstrations of movements with physical objects to young babies to show that infants expect objects to be supported in space.

- Other studies show that infants expect that a hidden object stays still while it's covered up. If an object is covered up and then the covering is removed and the object is still there, infants remain habituated. However, if the object is covered up and then when the covering is removed the object is gone, infants respond with dishabituation to the disappearance of the object.

- Infants also appear to expect that nothing can go through a solid object. If they're shown a different object that appears to be moving through a solid object, they stare at it for an extended amount of time, signifying dishabituation.

- These examples imply that the kind of learning that infants do can be built on the inborn assumptions of objects as three-dimensional, solid, and needing support to be off the ground.

- Another arena in which we have interesting inborn capacities— that are also shared with other species—is in our grasp of numbers. The concept of numbers we start out with as infants is not quite the same as the one we learn in childhood when we attend school, and it's not quite the same as the one that later allows us to do complex computations. It's a foundation on which later understanding can be built.

- Babies and animals don't appear to discriminate different numbers of objects in a strict numerical sense. For adults, the difference between one item and two items is the same as the difference between three and four items. In both cases, one pile of items has one more than the other.

- Infants can discriminate between visual displays of a pile of eight dots versus a pile of 16 dots, for example, and as they get older, they're able to make finer discriminations. They can begin to tell the difference between 12 dots and 16 dots, and they share with adults and animals some of the features of how they make those discriminations.

- The critical point to understand is that even newborn infants have some working assumptions and capacities that are based on an evolutionary heritage, and they can bring these working assumptions to the new world in which they find themselves.

Imitation and Cooperation
- Much of what infants come equipped with appears to be shared with other species, specifically the evolved heritage of land-dwelling mammals on Earth. However, the desire and capacity to share understandings with other human beings and to engage in cooperative actions are especially developed in human beings.

- One example of this is that infants appear to have the capacity to imitate other people from virtually hours after birth. Researchers in this area have argued that what this means is that infants are born with the assumption that other people are like them and that imitating someone is an early way of taking somebody else's perspective. It's also the case that imitation is one of the major ways that human babies and children learn about the world.

- More recent evidence about young infants' abilities to take perspective and focus on shared understandings with others has been carried out by Michael Tomasello and his colleagues. They have concluded that even very young human infants try to influence the mental states of other people and that these attempts are pro-social. Infants often try to help other people, even when there isn't going to be any benefit for them.

- Furthermore, some studies look at whether young children communicate only to get what they want as opposed to whether they care that they're being understood. Researchers in this area have found that young children care rather intensely about being understood, even when they're already getting what they want.

- In fact, by 18 months, children already show evidence that they care as much about being understood as about receiving desired objects. Children this young also showed that they could wait to get what they wanted, as long as they were confident the experimenter had understood what they wanted.

- In a series of studies, Tomasello has shown that as soon as they're capable of it, infants will help adults by picking up dropped objects along with other actions aimed at helping. As it turns out, young chimpanzees also do things like this.

- Young children share food with other humans pretty readily, and when they share, they actually share the good food. According to Tomasello, chimpanzees are not the same. In some studies, chimpanzees are uninterested in another chimps' benefits when deciding whether the other chimp should receive food. However, human children respond to collective benefit.

- Humans communicate constantly; they share information. When chimps share information with other chimps, it's largely to get the chimp to do something desirable, such as share their food.

- Furthermore, studies of language-trained apes suggest that they use their language abilities mostly to get the people that they are surrounded by to deliver food, attention, walks, or other rewards.

- The human capacity to cooperate with others, which is richly evident in young children, is widely evident in both problem-solving activities and in games. Chimpanzees cooperate with a human adult, and they do so fairly readily to solve a problem—but not during games.

- In addition to the reflexes and sophisticated knowledge about objects, infants come with an innate capacity and desire to cooperate with other people and to imitate others. These capacities lay the foundations for allowing us to use imitation of others as a learning strategy and for predisposing us to be able to collaborate in learning about our worlds and achieving our purposes.

The Critical Period of Development
- The idea that infants may need to have certain types of experiences in order to retain and further develop initial knowledge structures is the notion of critical periods in development, which suggests that the presence or absence of some experience at a specific time in our lives has a dramatic influence on later development.

- Critical periods in perception are periods in infancy in which the absence of the right types of experiences cause a failure in important developments of the brain, and the results involve lasting limitations on perception and, by extension, learning.

- Humans process faces less well if, during infancy, they had congenital cataracts, which impair vision during an early critical period for development. Infants who had congenital cataracts but had them removed later in life go on to successfully function like normal adults with a few exceptions: They have deficits in the ability to differentiate among faces based on small differences in the spacing of facial features and difficulties in judging depth due to the discrepancy between the images that strike the two eyes.

Suggested Reading

Baillargeon, "How Do Infants Learn about the Physical World?"

Pinker, *The Blank Slate.*

Questions to Consider

1. There are limits to how young an infant can be tested using habituation paradigms. Is it possible to explain the kinds of concepts of objects infants seem to have with early experience and learning rather than with innate knowledge? How does evidence from other species support the innateness idea?

2. If researchers could figure out the right way to expose adults to perceptual input, could we discover ways to help fix the deficits associated with people who had congenital cataracts?

Lecture 6: What Babies Know

What Babies Know
Lecture 6—Transcript

So far, we have suggested that we learn for the sake of learning and as we pursue other goals, and that we learn by connecting new experiences to the old hat—to what we know already in the form of categories, scripts, and other schemas. But if there's no tabula rasa, what about very young infants? Aren't newborns really learning on a blank slate?

In this lecture, we'll consider what babies come pre-packaged with—the prepackaging that allows learning to take place right away. We'll also look at the fascinating and really clever ways people have figured out to study learning in babies.

What could come with us as babies? It turns out, a lot. From birth, babies have particular motor reflexes, and these motor reflexes are so fundamental that their presence is actually used to indicate whether a baby is healthy or not.

For example, one well-known reflex is called the stepping reflex. If you hold a newborn's feet against a hard surface, the newborn will actually kind of engage in a stepping-like action. Another newborn reflex is called the rooting reflex. If you stroke a newborn's cheek, he or she will turn toward that side and begin to make a sucking motion. And these reflexes actually help babies very quickly learn what are slightly more complicated motor behaviors, such as nursing. And those behaviors are very important for a baby's survival. These reflexes also help to tune a baby's motor system by building connections between neurons in the brain and peripheral nervous system nerves in the limbs.

Another place where we appear to come with some initial schemata involves physical objects. In fact, interestingly, it doesn't look like we learn all that much, in our lifetimes, about physical objects. Why would I say this? I'm saying this because six-month-old infants already expect a visually presented object to have three dimensions, to take up space, to fall when it's dropped, and other kinds of things that we know are true of physical objects in our world.

Now, you might be wondering how I can say that a six-month-old knows these things when a six-month-old can't talk and certainly can't answer my questions about what he or she expected to happen when I let go of the ball. So how we know this is a fascinating story, and it actually capitalizes on a phenomenon called habituation.

Habituation is defined as decreased responding after a repeated presentation of a stimulus. It's a very basic kind of learning because experience is changing how you respond to an event in the world. Early work on habituation looked at whether rats respond to a loud noise by startling. And this work showed that if you keep playing the loud noise over and over again, eventually rats stop reacting to the noise, and then we might say that the rats have habituated to the loud noise.

Now, you may be thinking, "This sounds really minimal as learning goes." Because after all, those of you in the audience have learned to read, to do math, to make complex decisions, and to carry out complex sequences of motor behavior, like when you drive a car.

So, what on earth is so important about habituation? Without habituation, consider you could never distinguish between the old and the new, the irrelevant background, and the important foreground, the expected, and the unusual. Habituation is a kind of prerequisite for all of those more complex forms of learning. And, because it's a fundamental prerequisite, it's probably not surprising that habituation happens across all species, and is evident even in very, very young babies, as young as newly born babies.

And when we start to look at habituation more closely, we'll actually see that it's not quite as simple as you might think. That's because habituation involves a decrease in responding over time, and that means we have to consider at least two other explanations before we decide habituation is really about your experience with the stimulus—before we can be sure habituation is a kind of learning.

What is additionally important is that in ruling out these alternative explanations, researchers discovered the phenomenon of dishabituation, and it is the combination of habituation and dishabituation that has given us a really fabulous window into the learning of very young babies.

So, what are these alternative explanations, and what is dishabituation? Well, those alternative explanations are that habituation, that decreased responding, might be caused by sensory or motor fatigue, right? That is, it's not that learning about the stimulus is causing me to stop responding or the rat to stop startling. It's that the rat's ears are getting tired or that the rat's muscles are too tired for the rat to startle. Now, if fatigue of either sort is an explanation, the only thing that would allow the rat to start responding again is resting the ears or resting the muscles. And it's that startling again that we call dishabituation.

So, in fact, if you give the rat a break, if you rest the rat's ears and the muscles, and then you play the loud noise again, the startling comes back. The rat dishabituates. But, as I've just explained, this kind of finding is actually a problem. Dishabituation after a rest is consistent with saying the problem here is fatigue. It's not learning. So, what now?

Well, now we try to figure out what else might cause dishabituation, but which wouldn't involve resting the animal. And, it turns out that presentation of a new stimulus, say, a light or a different sound, can actually cause dishabituation without any rest—that is, if I play a different tone to the rats and then I go back to the original tone I will see startling again. I'll see dishabituation. Now, since there was no rest, this is powerful evidence that habituation is learning, not just fatigue.

Why does habituation matter? Well, one thing that turns out to be true is that babies habituate and they dishabituate. What this tells us is babies come equipped with a brain that can say, "old news" and "whoa, that's new." This is a great bonus for researchers because it means that we can also look at what babies know and learn, very early on, by figuring out whether they habituate and dishabituate to a stimulus.

More broadly, we can use habituation logic to test what babies expect and what they don't expect. This is because a habituated infant will look less at something in the environment, and they'll look less at a display we're showing them. And, dishabituation in infants is reflected in increased looking time. So with habituation and dishabituation, we can interpret infants' looking behavior, something that even very young infants can do, as telling us what they view as old hat versus what they view as new, unexpected, and interesting.

So let's consider some of what we learned about babies' apparently inborn knowledge of physical objects, along with some evidence about what babies do have to learn. Renee Baillargeon is one of several infant researchers whose work has revolutionized our view of infants. Baillargeon and colleagues set up very simple demonstrations of movements with physical objects, and they show these demonstrations to young babies—sometimes as young as two-and-a-half months of age.

Baillargeon and colleagues showed that infants expect that objects have to be supported in space. They did this by showing infants images of a box on a platform, and tracking what infants watched and how long they watched. So, as the infants viewed the display, the box was pushed along the platform, and there were one of two outcomes of this pushing. Now, in one ending, what infants saw was the box pushed just to the edge of the platform and then it stopped moving. Infants were shown this version of events until they became habituated—they stopped looking, they looked quickly, they looked away, they were bored.

In the second ending the box was pushed all the way over the edge so that it no longer contacted the platform. It just hung in midair. Infants responded to this with dishabituation. They started paying attention again. And this suggested that the box being in mid-air without falling was not what they expected.

Other similar studies show that infants expect that a hidden object stays still while it's covered up. So, if the object is covered up and then the covering is removed and the object is still there, infants remain habituated. If the object is covered up and then when the covering up is removed the object is gone, infants respond with dishabituation to the disappearance of the object. Infants also appear to expect that nothing can go through a solid object. If they're shown a different object that appears to be moving through a solid object they actually look long and hard, and it's almost as though that baby brain is saying, "That's just not how the world works."

Now, I don't want to imply with these examples that infants don't learn anything. For example, infants do have to learn over time that having only part of a box on a platform won't guarantee that it'll stay supported. They start then to respond to images of the box being pushed almost off the edge of the platform but not falling as also being surprising. But what I'd like to show or like to point out is that that kind of learning can be built on the inborn assumptions of objects as three-dimensional, solid, and need support to be off the ground.

Another arena where we have interesting inborn capacities, again, shared with other species, is in our grasp of numbers. Now, it is interesting to learn that the concept of numbers we start out with as infants is not quite the same as the one we learn in childhood when we attend school, and it's not quite the same as the one that later on lets us do complex computations and matrix algebra. It's a foundation on which later understanding can be built. This foundational understanding of numbers lets infants discriminate between different numbers of objects.

So, babies and animals don't appear to discriminate different numbers of objects in what you might think of as a strict numerical sense. So, for adults, the difference between one item and two items is the same as the difference between three and four items. In both cases, one pile of items has one more than the other. Now, from a ratio standpoint, the first difference between one and two reflects a doubling. That's quite a bit proportionally. So, one quarter versus two quarters; I've doubled my money. The second difference from three quarters to four quarters is a lot smaller proportionally. It's an increase of a third.

Infants can discriminate between visual displays of a pile of eight dots versus a pile of 16 dots, for example. And as they get older, they're able to make finer discriminations. They can tell the difference between 12 dots and 16 dots. But they share with adults and animals some of the features of how they make those discriminations. For example, they're more easily able to make the distinctions when the ratios of the numbers are larger. And as an aside, this ratio-like built in programming seems to apply to a lot of perceptual distinctions for human beings.

The critical point to understand here is that even newborn infants have some working assumptions and capacities that are based on an evolutionary heritage, and they can bring these working assumptions to bear on the new world in which they find themselves. Now, we actually share these assumptions with many other species, but we go on to use our learning capacity to build gravity-defying 3D objects like skyscrapers to create algebra and other complex mathematical systems.

In fact, much of what infants come equipped with appears to be shared with other species, and it's the common, evolved heritage of land-dwelling mammals on planet Earth. But some of it, as we'll consider next, is perhaps a little bit specially developed in human beings, and that's the desire to share understandings with other human beings and to engage in cooperative actions, as well as our capacity to do so. In other words, what's uniquely human may be the desire to learn and engage socially.

One example of this is that infants appear to have the capacity to imitate other people from virtually hours after birth. One researchers interested in this area is Andrew Meltzoff. I'm not quite sure how he was able to do this, but he was able to go into delivery rooms in hospitals and test newborn infants, really babies within hours of birth. And what he would do is he would walk into the room, or the experimenter that was working with him would walk into the room, and they would look at this newborn and they would get within visual range for a newborn, which means you have to get pretty close. And then they would do: They would stick their tongue out. And then they would look at what the baby did. And somewhat surprisingly, even newborn babies would actually respond to this by also protruding their tongue.

Now, researchers in this area, including Meltzoff, have argued that what this means that even newborns can do some basic kind of imitating of others, what it means is that infants are born with the assumption that other people are like me. And Meltzoff and others have argued that imitating someone is a kind of early way of taking somebody else's perspective. It's also the case for our purposes that imitation is one of the major ways that human babies and children learn about the world. And there's actually evidence that young children all over the world imitate other people's actions. And that imitation of others is a really critical strategy for learning about the world and for learning how to do things within the world.

Now, at this point though I want to consider some of the more recent evidence about young infants' abilities to take perspective and focus on shared understandings with others. And much of this work has been carried out by Michael Tomasello and colleagues.

In one study, Tomasello's group showed that 12-month-old infants will point to an invisible object that they want in order to get an adult to understand what it is they're wanting. That is, they appear to know that the adult can't see the object, and they're trying to direct the adult's attention to the object. It's a cooperative gesture.

In another study, 12-month-olds who were shown an adult who was looking for something will actually point to an object that they know the adult doesn't know about. They don't point to an object the adult does know about. So, already by 12 months they want to help the adult find the object, and they make a good guess about what the adult's knowledge is.

Now, what Tomasello's group concludes, based on this and other research they've conducted, is that even very young human infants are trying to influence the mental states of other people. And these attempts are actually pretty prosocial. Often infants try to help other people, even when there isn't going to be any benefit for them.

Further, some studies actually try to look at whether young children communicate only to get what they want, as opposed to whether they care that they're being understood.

In one early study in this area, Helen Shwe and Ellen Markman, had two-and-a-half-year-old children make requests about one of two possible objects. In a typical and kind of mean grownup experimenter way, the experiment was such that there were two objects and one was a very cool toy duck, and the other object was something boring—in one case it was a sock. So, kids would of course ask for the duck, and the experimenter could respond in a variety of ways. Now, in the experiment they responded sometimes with, "You wanted the duck; I'm going to give you the duck." This is a win/win situation. If you were the kid you've been understood and you got what you wanted. You got the right toy.

However, in other cases, the experimenter said "You wanted the sock; I'm going to give you the sock." You might think of this as the lose/lose situation. You've not been understood and moreover you got the sock. In other key cases for the study, the researcher either acknowledged the request, but then gave the wrong object ("You've been understood and you have been denied"), or the experimenter misunderstood the request but gave the right object ("You wanted the sock; I'm going to give you the duck"). Now, this last condition is important because there is where we can see whether young children care about being understood, or only about getting what they want. And, the researchers found that young children care rather intensely about being understood, even when they're already getting what they want.

Tomasello and colleagues recently retooled this study so that they could use it to look at somewhat younger children. And they were able to show that already by 18 months children show evidence that they care as much about being understand as about getting their desired objects. And, children this young also showed that they could wait to get what they wanted, as long as they were confident the experimenter had understood what they wanted.

Now, the desire to be understood by others is not the same as the desire to cooperate. Understanding is sort of a foundation on which we can build cooperation. So, what about cooperation?

Well, in a series of studies, Tomasello and colleagues have shown that as soon as they're capable of it, infants will help adults by picking up dropped objects and they'll do other actions aimed at helping. As it turns out, young chimpanzees also do things like this.

But there are some differences. Young children also share food with other humans pretty readily, and when they share they actually share the good stuff. According to Tomasello and colleagues, chimpanzees are not quite like that. In some studies, chimpanzees or young children are asked to pull a board in order to get food for themselves. And in some cases, they'll get food for themselves and food for someone else, right. In some cases, cooperating or getting the food helps somebody else also benefit. Well, chimpanzees don't try any harder whether another chimp will also get food or won't get food. They're uninterested in the other chimps' benefits. But human kids are different. Human kids actually pull harder when the other person also gets something. Human kids respond to collective benefit.

And finally, humans communicate all the time—they share information. When chimps share information with other chimps it's largely to get the chimp to do something desirable, like share their food. In fact, studies of language-trained apes suggest that most of what they do with their language abilities is to try to get the humans beings that they are surrounded by to deliver the goods—that is, they're trying to get their human caretakers to deliver food, attention, walks, or other rewards.

Now, finally human capacity to cooperate with others, which is so richly evident in such young kids, is widely evident in both problem-solving activities, and in games. And chimpanzees actually cooperate with a human adult, and they do so fairly readily to solve a problem. They don't do so for games. So for example, in studies where a gall tossing game is initiated between a group of humans, only kids try to keep that game going when the adult stops the game. Chimpanzees, when the game stops just stop.

So, what does all this mean for learning? Well, in addition to the reflexes and sophisticated knowledge about objects, infants come with an innate capacity and desire to cooperate with other people, and this capacity and desire is there in infancy for normal infants.

That capacity to cooperate and imitate lays the foundations for several important facets of learning. So first, it allows us to use imitation of others as a learning strategy, and in fact, it orients us to look towards others to learn. Second, it predisposes us to be able to collaborate in learning about our worlds and achieving our purposes.

Thus far, we've focused on what infants come equipped with. We focused on the categories and the kinds of schemata and the inborn motivations that allow infants to make sense of initial experiences in the world. Before we leave infancy, however, we need to consider a further set of issues, and that's the fact that infants may need to have certain types of experiences in order to retain and further develop those initial, starting knowledge structures. This is the idea of critical or sensitive periods in development.

The basic idea behind a critical or a sensitive period is that the presence or absence of some experience at a specific time in our lives has a dramatic influence on later development. Now, this broad definition covers a number of potential critical periods, including some that are less critically linked to our focus on learning.

For our purposes, today we'll focus briefly on critical periods in perception. These are periods in infancy where the absence of the right types of experiences causes a failure in important developments of the brain, and the results involve lasting limitations on perception and by extension learning.

Now, as I mentioned previously, some of the data on this look at animals because we have the capacity to control their early environments and early experiences. And you may recall that we talked earlier about the fact that kittens who don't get exposed to horizontal lines early in their lives have difficulty perceiving those lines later on, and can't learn anything that would require them to see horizontal lines. But, similar effects can be seen in the way that humans process faces less well if, during infancy, they happened to have congenital cataracts, which impair vision during an early critical period for development.

Infants who had congenital cataracts, but had those removed later on, go on to successfully function like normal adults with a few exceptions, and these exceptions can be actually teased out in laboratory settings. So, one deficit these adults have is in the ability to differentiate among faces based on small differences in the spacing of facial features. This is a kind of deficit in the ability to process faces holistically.

Now, processing faces holistically means that when we look at someone's face, in order to recognize them, we pay attention to fine details of their features like specific shapes of lips or eyes, but we rely very heavily on how widely spaced their eyes are, how their eyes, nose, and mouth are related, how the face is distributed. That's holistic face processing, and it's critical for face recognition. So adults who had congenital cataracts during a critical period of infancy have difficulty with that kind of face processing.

Now, this particular aspect of critical periods has a distinctly personal feel for me, and I'm going to close by talking about another perceptual ability that's linked to early visual experience, in part, because it can also be clearly linked to learning.

Now, you may know that humans have a variety of ways that we can judge depth—the distances between objects or the location of an object in the sky relative to ourselves. And this capability is relevant to all sorts of everyday and non-everyday tasks.

Some of the strategies for judging depth involve using what are called linear depth cues. So, one example of this is that if you're looking at a street it diminishes in apparent width as it goes farther away. A major source of depth perception in most two-eyed animals, however, is the discrepancy between the images that strike the two eyes. And you can see this discrepancy when you shut one eye, and then the other—the objects around you shift slightly in your visual field. Now, in infancy, one aspect of perceptual learning is how to judge depth based on this difference, which is called binocular disparity. And having one eye blocked visually during that sensitive period impairs the capacity to use binocular disparity to judge depth.

As a child, I was cross-eyed. So, my early visual experience was essentially like having only one eye—my right eye. As a toddler I got corrective lenses and I went on with life, blissfully unaware that there were any long-term consequences to this experience. Then, while taking a college sensation and perception course, we were all have a little field trip to a laboratory and we were looking through a machine called a tachistoscope. This is a machine that presents one image to each eye, a different image to each eye. For people with normal abilities to merge the two images, these two images actually get merged, and what they see is a single image. When we all took turns looking through the tachistoscope, it was clear that others saw something I didn't. My two images weren't merging and I didn't see the full picture that I was supposed to see.

What does this mean for learning for me? Well, to put it bluntly, it means that there are a couple of things that I have tried to learn, and I've been unable to learn, despite investing serious effort and time. One was to serve well in tennis. I played tennis in high school. I was a competent, but not by any means a good player, in most ways, but I was never good at returning a lob—a high shot—or at serving. In fact, I was disastrously bad at serving. Now, why would this be? When you serve in tennis, you toss the ball up and you look up at it in the sky and hit it with a downward stroke. And to do so you have to judge the location of the ball in the sky. The ball isn't on the court which has many lines that help to establish how far the ball is away from a person. When the ball is in the sky I'm unable to judge the ball's position relative to myself. And as a result, I can't learn to serve very well, and despite hundreds and hundreds and hundreds and hundreds of practice efforts I still can't serve very well. For similar reasons I also cannot learn to play volleyball.

A more recent example occurred when my husband and I learned to sail. Again, I was reasonably competent at many elements of sailing, but I have difficulty figuring out if I'm on a collision course with another boat once we're in open water because away from the shoreline binocular disparity becomes a more important cue to depth and trajectory. So, those of you who sail will be happy to know I don't captain a boat. I don't command a tiller any longer.

To summarize today's coverage, research on early infancy, which makes use of habituation and dishabituation as well as other approaches, tells us that infants are far from a tabula rasa. They come with sophisticated, innate categories, and physical scripts that help them make sense of the world. Next in the course, we'll begin to move into specific kinds of learning. But we'll begin with a bridging topic from babies to specific kinds of learning, and that's learning our mother tongue.

One of the most profound achievements of learning and development in human infancy is the acquisition of a native language. This achievement, which really combines learning and development in interesting ways, is fundamental to our ability to cooperate and communicate with one another, and it's also an achievement of learning that raises issues about a critical period because any one of us who's learned a second language well after early childhood knows how different and difficult that can seem. So next time, we will examine the acquisition of a first language.

Learning Your Native Tongue
Lecture 7

A s we move into discussing specific types of learning, we'll begin by considering how babies acquire a first language. One of the most profound achievements of learning and development in human infancy is the acquisition of a native language. This achievement, which combines learning and development in interesting ways, is fundamental to our ability to cooperate and communicate with one another, and it's also an achievement of learning that raises issues about a critical period. People who learn a second language after early childhood know how different and difficult that can seem.

First-Language Learning
- At birth, babies don't have the vocal capacity to generate most human sounds. By age two, they are capable of understanding and communicating using a rather large selection of words and phrases. By age five, they can tell simple stories, and by adolescence, they can tell their parents many complex things. All of this learning appears to just unfold, as though there were a program in the brain.

- Learning your first language is, in fact, learning. In addition, first-language learning relies on some innate assumptions and capacities that infants and children bring to that task. Furthermore, the consequences of that first language may be greater than you think because those consequences include the fact that learning your native tongue also means you are losing some capabilities along the way.

Early Language Acquisition Theories
- Initial ideas about language acquisition were grounded in behaviorist theories about learning. The idea was that we learn to speak through rewards and punishments, but that doesn't explain much about language.

- A concept called universal grammar, which was proposed by Noam Chomsky, has been at the heart of most of the work on language acquisition by infants in the past decades. The basic idea behind universal grammar is that babies are born with an implicit knowledge of some deep and basic principles of language.

- According to the idea of universal grammar, children tune this basic structure to the specifics of their own language in early childhood, but they aren't truly learning; rather, they're tuning an already-present, full-blown language capacity.

- The problem with the idea of universal grammar is that studies of human languages are making it increasingly difficult to keep around this idea that there are fundamental, universal properties of all known languages.

- In fact, recent work suggests there's no real universal grammar; there's just too much variability in human languages. Rather, there are some general learning mechanisms that are present at birth, and those permit babies to take all of the language to which they are exposed and to make out of it a native tongue.

Learning Words

- If you plotted a graph of vocabulary development over early childhood, you'd see a slow start in infancy followed by a huge spurt into toddlerhood—a spurt that involves learning more than a word a day and that continues into adulthood. The rate is amazing.

- Phonology is the sound structure that languages have. The important element for sounds in language is contrast, or phonetic distinction. Even very young infants learn phonemes—the basic sound units of their native language.

- Babies figure out how words sound in their native language by listening to speech around them and then figuring out some basic rules for deciding where words start and end. These rules are based on repeated patterns in the speech streams that they hear. From these basic rules, they begin to divide up speech streams into sound units before they know what words mean. Once they have some words, they then use those words and the patterns those words come with to figure out some additional words. This process is often called bootstrapping, which involves working with the little pieces you do know to figure out the things you don't yet know.

Mastering a language requires babies to segment a stream of sounds and pauses into meaningful units.

- Because languages are not random, the probability of certain kinds of transitions of sounds within a word is quite high, and the probability of transitions between words is lower. This is because one word can be followed by many possible words involving many possible sounds, but within a word, one sound has a smaller set of possible following sounds.

- In English, our words tend to stress the first syllable. This regularity helps babies decipher the beginnings of words. Intonation and pitch also help babies distinguish word boundaries.

- When we talk to babies, we tend to use a type of speech that's often called "motherese," which exaggerates word boundaries and other features of our language to make sure that babies can see, hear, and experience those boundaries.

- The central problem for examining the process by which babies learn words is that babies can't talk, and it takes a while before their larynx, tongue, and vocal apparatus even approach adult function. Therefore, how can we know whether a baby knows a word before the baby can speak that word?

- It is unlikely that babies are actively trying to figure out the process of language in the way that adults might; rather, their learning of language is incidental to the task of trying to understand what's happening around them.

- It is interesting that the capacity to extract words from speech streams is preserved in adults. Work by Jennifer Saffran and her colleagues showed that the innate ability to track transition probabilities in sounds combined with exposure to one's own native language makes it possible for babies to figure out words from very early in their lives.

- By high school, adolescents know 30,000–50,000 words. Once children begin to acquire and produce words, their vocabulary size explodes. Children acquire new words so quickly by building a basis of words from phonetic bootstrapping, and then it becomes easier for them to acquire additional words.

- However, young children's word acquisition is so fast—sometimes involving only a single exposure to a word—that other explanations are needed. As with phonetics rules, these often consist of biases in interpreting new words and, in particular, biases that reduce the number of possible meanings that the word could have.

- Some biases are social; for example, infants use gesture and eye gaze from speakers to help decode what a word is referring to. Another bias is not social, but it involves the assumption that new words refer to whole objects instead of parts of objects.

- A further assumption that children may use is referred to as mutual exclusivity, which is the assumption that objects have one label only—so if a known object is given a new label, the new label must refer to some part of the object. Constraints such as mutual exclusivity, along with capitalizing on social understanding, allow children to acquire words very rapidly over childhood.

- There are differences among children in the process of language acquisition that are related to how much parent-child language interaction there is. Children learn more words in speech-heavy, high-vocabulary households than in households that are more taciturn or that use smaller vocabularies. In later childhood and adulthood, vocabulary acquisition is also related to reading habits.

- A lexicon is a collection of words, or a vocabulary. Part of being a native speaker means not only having a lexicon, but also understanding the rules of grammar in ways that let us generate new sentences and understand the differences among sentences that use the same words but in different orders.

Losses of Language Learning

- The process of word acquisition is believed to be largely incidental—that is, babies don't deliberately try to learn a grammar or a new vocabulary—and it's also powerful. A person's vocabulary increases from 0–60,000 in under two decades.

- The contrast with learning a language in later childhood or adulthood is profound. We often experience second-language learning in adulthood as effortful—as requiring intention and deliberate learning of vocabulary—and the end result is usually far short of native fluency and native lexicon size.

- To some extent, this difference is partly due to the losses that learning our first language involves. We often think of learning as a purely gain-oriented experience, but learning changes us, and sometimes the changes involve losses as well as gains. Language is a particularly useful and interesting place to consider these losses.

- At birth, babies have an amazing capability to distinguish between different sounds; in fact, they can distinguish between all the known sounds in human languages, including clicks and unusual phonemes. Unfortunately, this early linguistic brilliance quickly gives way to a more tuned and focused competence.

- In one study, researchers looked at whether young babies and adults who were native English speakers could distinguish between two "t" sounds that are irrelevant to English but that in Hindi mark important word contrasts. Infants between six and eight months of age can hear the difference in these three "t" sounds, including the English "t" sound. Adult English speakers are not able to differentiate.

- Phonetic losses are important because they help tune the brain for the native language. When an infant is potentially growing up bilingual, the brain is tuning for two languages from the beginning.

- Phonetic losses are not all that's lost with first-language acquisition. More conceptual losses also occur, and this is because languages have an important role in marking which conceptual distinctions matter in the worlds we live in.

- After we learn our native language, Elizabeth Spelke and her colleagues have shown that, as with phonemes, we become less sensitive to the differences that our languages treat as less important.

Language and Culture
- Does our first language shape the way we think? One of the most prominent researchers in this area is Lera Boroditsky, who has suggested that some of the most fundamental aspects of human experience involve our experiences of time and space.

- These are crucial categories that affect how we divide the world into past, present, and future and into near versus far. Language is used to represent, think about, and communicate about space and time, and Boroditsky argues that this has some important implications for how we think—and, via an extension of her work, what we can and cannot learn easily.

- In much of Boroditsky's work, she looks at how communities that speak different languages think about space and time. For example, in aboriginal communities in northern Australia, five-year-old children are able to accurately and immediately point north, no matter where they are or whether they can see the sky.

- Boroditsky argues that the reason for this is that this community's language has a very particular, compass-oriented way of talking about relationships in space—rather than using directions such as left, right, in front of, and behind.

- It's probable that this type of absolute orientation might help people learn a new spatial environment more quickly because the model that they're building is less relative to their own position and has more to do with their surroundings than themselves. This may be a more flexible approach to building a model of one's surroundings.

- Just as your native language is an enormous, impressive achievement of learning—learning done almost with no effort at all—your native language is also an arena of tuning your mind to distinctions and concepts that are deemed important by your culture.

Suggested Reading

Boroditsky, "How Language Shapes Thought."

Hansen and Markman, "Children's Use of Mutual Exclusivity."

Swingley, "The Roots of the Early Vocabulary."

1. Relatively little research addresses the development of language pragmatics in early childhood—that is, our knowledge of how language should be used to accomplish our aims in the real world. Imitation alone cannot explain babies' acquisition of syntax. Can imitation explain how we acquire pragmatic rules of language use?

2. Language clearly influences our thinking in many ways. Do you think language is required for thinking? Why or why not?

Learning Your Native Tongue
Lecture 7—Transcript

Last time, discussed the ways in which babies are not tabula rasa creatures but rather come fully equipped with all sorts of innate skills that facilitate learning. In this lecture, as we move into specific types of learning, we'll begin with language. We'll start by considering how babies pull off one of the most impressive feats of learning around, at least in my view. And, we'll see that as in last lecture, again, babies are not a tabula rasa.

At birth, babies don't even have the vocal capacity to generate most human sounds. By two, they are capable of understanding and communicating using a rather large swath of words and phrases. By five, they can tell simple stories, and by adolescence, they could tell their parents many complex things if they felt like it—which they often don't.

Now, all of this learning appears to just unfold, as though there were a program in the brain. How does that happen? I want to make several points in this lecture.

First, learning your first language is learning. Second, first-language learning relies on some innate assumptions and capacities that infants and children bring to that task. And third, the consequences of that first language may be greater than you think because those consequences include the fact that learning your native tongue also means you are losing some capabilities along the way.

To the first point: What does it mean to learn a language? Mastery of language requires a lot of different and more specific capacities. For example, you need to be able to segment a stream of sounds and pauses into meaningful units—recognizing boundaries between words and integrating sounds that are uttered together into words. You have to know the lexicon, the vocabulary, and what it refers to. You have to know the rules for combining words, the grammar, and you have to be able to use those rules to make new sentences that can be understood by others. You also have to know how the language is to be used—the rules of communicating, how you show that you want a turn at talk, how to wait for a pause to begin your contribution, how different words can have more than one meaning.

Despite how crazily complex this all sounds, learning your native tongue feels, at least in retrospect, effortless and automatic. You're doing much of what I said in that complex list right now as you hear my voice, and it probably feels more or less easy to do. So how do babies actually learn to talk and to listen?

Initial ideas about this were actually grounded in those behaviorist theories about learning. Remember those old ideas about associative learning and operant conditioning? So the idea was that we learn to speak through rewards and punishments. Well, this obviously didn't work out well because it doesn't explain much about language.

The next big idea involved a concept called universal grammar. This concept was proposed by Noam Chomsky, and it's been at the heart of most of the work on language acquisition by infants in the past decades. The basic idea behind universal grammar is that babies are born with a kind of implicit knowledge of some deep and basic principles, or rules, of language.

What happens in early childhood, then, according to the idea of a universal grammar is that kids tune this basic structure to the specifics of their own language, but they aren't really learning anything per se—rather, they're tuning an already present, full blown language capacity. Now, the good thing about universal grammar is that it explains some things that learning theory didn't. The problem with this idea is that studies of human languages are making it harder and harder to keep around this idea that there are fundamental, universal properties of all known languages.

And in fact, more recent work actually suggests there's no real universal grammar. There's just too much variability in human languages. Rather, there are some general learning mechanisms that are present at birth, and those permit babies to take all this language to which they are exposed, and to make out of it a native tongue. In this lecture, we'll consider what those mechanisms might be, and how they work to help us to go from no words, to about 60,000 words, along with complex knowledge of syntax and grammar, by adulthood.

To begin, let's consider how we learn words. If you plotted a graph of vocabulary development over early childhood, you'd see something like the following: a kind of slow start in infancy, followed by a huge spurt into toddlerhood; a spurt that involves learning more than a word a day, and which continues into adulthood. How can this happen? The rate is absolutely amazing. How do we start, and how do we go so fast?

Well, how we start begins with phonology. Phonology is the sound structure that languages have. And the important element for sounds in language is contrast: dog is not bog, and dog is dog no matter how loudly we say it. And, it's those phonetic distinctions that make us know whether someone is telling about their pet, or about an undesirable encounter with swampy ground.

Now, work by a number of researchers shows that very young infants are already learning phonemes—the basic sound units of their native language. Babies use a kind of bootstrapping technique to figure out how words sound in their native language. What they do is, from listening to speech are them, they figure out some basic rules for dividing where words start and end, and those rules are based on repeated patterns in the speech streams that they hear. From those basic rules, they begin to divide up speech streams into sound units, and they actually do this before they know what words mean. Once they have some words, they then use those words and the patterns those words come with to figure out some additional words. This process is often called bootstrapping. It means working with the little pieces you do know, to figure out the things you don't yet know.

Now, in English, first of all, some sounds tend to occur together in words, and other sounds almost never occur together within a single word. So, the statistical probabilities that a syllable will be followed by another syllable are something babies and adults can monitor very well—both in language and in non-linguistic sound streams, like music or just computer-generated noises. Because languages are not random, the probability of certain kinds of transitions of sounds within a word is quite high, and the probability of transitions between words is lower. And this is because one word can be followed by many possible words involving many possible sounds, but within a word, one sound has only a smaller set of possible following events or sounds.

Another thing about English is there are also some distinct stress intonation patterns. My father used to say that sometimes we put the "em*pha*sis on the wrong syl*la*ble." In English, our words tend to stress the first syllable. This regularity also helps babies decipher the beginnings of words.

Intonation and pitch also help babies distinguish word boundaries, and we tend to talk differently to babies. We use a kind of speech that's often called "motherese," and it exaggerates word boundaries and other features of our language for babies to make sure that they can see, hear, and experience those boundaries. Now, here's the central problem though for examining the process by which babies learn words. Babies can't talk, and it actually takes a while before their larynx and tongue and vocal apparatus even come close to adult function. How can we know whether a baby knows a word before the baby can speak that word? To answer this I want to tell you about a clever set of studies by Dan Swingley and Richard Aslin.

In their studies, babies look at pairs of pictures, and they hear words that actually go with only one of the pictures. And they look at how much time the baby spends looking at the correct picture—the picture that corresponds to the word the baby's hearing. Now, what they were able to show is that by 18 months, babies are actually already showing that they know words because they're looking at the right picture when they hear the word. But you can ask, "How good or how accurate is a baby's phonological understanding of that word?" And to test this, Swingley and Aslin provided babies with subtly mispronounced versions of words. So they might say "opple" or "tog" or "vaby" instead of apple, dog, and baby. Now these are subtle mispronunciations, but they're linguistically meaningful. None of you listening to this tape heard the mispronunciations and thought they were the words apple, dog, and baby.

It turns out even 15-month-old babies behave differently with the mispronunciations as compared with the correct pronunciations, and some evidence suggests this is already evident by six months of age. So way before babies can talk, they're already learning the correct sounds of words, and they're linking those words to images.

Now, babies are unlikely to be actively trying to figure these things out in the way that adults might. Rather, their learning of language is incidental to the task of trying to understand what's happening around them.

It is really interesting that this capacity to extract words from speech streams is preserved in adults. Jennifer Saffran and her colleagues played a 20 minute tape of phony speech sounds from a fake language system to adults and children who were asked to engaged in a coloring task. So, the adults and children are sitting there and coloring and in the background is this tape of phony speech sounds. And the speech sound tape lacked gaps between words and the only cues to word boundaries were these statistical transition probabilities—that is, words were composed of sounds that had a high transition probability. In normal English, what that means is that words are consisting of sounds that almost always occur together. Non-words in this phony speech stream were sounds that wouldn't occur together.

Now, after the coloring task, adults and children were asked to listen to sets of sounds on tape, and they were asked to indicate which set of sounds was more like the tape they'd been hearing in the background. Now, both sets of sounds they heard were actually from that tape, but one set was comprised of sounds that would have made up words. The other set would have been non-words, based again on those transition probabilities.

Both adults and six to seven-year-old children were able to do better than chance at this task despite the fact that the tape played only once, only for 20 minutes, and only in the background while they were actually engaged in a different task. In other words, both adults and children were sensitive to the statistical probabilities of the tape they had heard, and in particular, to the statistical probabilities that indicated word boundaries. So the innate ability to track transition probabilities in sounds, combined with exposure to one's own native language, makes it possible for babies to figure out words from very early in their lives.

By high school, kids know 30,000–50,000 words. Once children begin to acquire and produce words, their vocabulary size literally explodes. So, a second question is how can children acquire new words so quickly? Now, one piece of this puzzle is what we've just been talking about. They build a basis of words from phonetic bootstrapping, if you will, and then it becomes easier for them to acquire additional words.

However, young children's word acquisition is so fast, sometimes involving only a single exposure to a word, that other explanations are needed. As with the phonetics rules, like first syllable stress patterns, these often consist of biases in interpreting new words, and in particular, biases that reduce the number of possible meanings that the word could have.

Some of the biases are social. Infants use gesture and eye gaze from speakers to help decode what a word is referring to. It's worth mentioning that this reliance on a speaker's gestures or eye gaze is absolutely connected to the kinds of social, cooperative, and understanding of other's orientation that we talked about in the last lecture.

Now, another bias is not social, but it involves the assumption that new words refer to whole objects. So, if an adult labels an object for the child, the child assumes the label refers to the object rather than its parts.

But then how do we learn labels for parts? A further assumption kids may use is referred to as mutual exclusivity, and this is the assumption that objects have one label only, so if a known object is given a new label the new label must refer to some part of the object.

In one example study, Mikkel Hansen and Ellen Markman showed young kids an object—either a familiar hat which they presumed most kids would have seen before, or an unfamiliar tea strainer—an object the kids had not seen. Two to three-year-old children, who are in the midst of what is called a vocabulary explosion, were shown the object, and the experimenter then introduced them to a new word—brim or mesh. In both cases, the experimenter traced the relevant part of the object while saying the new word. So, the experimenter would trace the brim of the hat while saying "brim." And afterwards, kids were asked to identify what the word referred to.

Now, if kids only needed social cues to determine whether a word was a part- or whole-object reference, the tracing should suffice, but if kids need to also assume mutual exclusivity, then they should get this task correct for the hat because they know "hat" refers to the whole object, and they can then assume brim must be a part. But they should get it wrong for the tea strainer where they're encountering the object for the first time. They hadn't learned tea strainer, and so they can't be sure if they object they were looking at was a mesh or not. And in fact, this is exactly what happened. Children needed both a gesture from the adult—they needed that tracing gesture—but they also needed mutual exclusivity to learn the new word for parts of an object.

Constraints like mutual exclusivity, along with capitalizing on social understanding, let kids acquire words very rapidly over childhood. There are differences between kids in this process, and those differences are related to how much parent-child language interaction there is. Kids learn more words in speech heavy, high vocabulary households than in households that are more taciturn or which use smaller vocabularies. And in later childhood and adulthood, vocabulary acquisition is also related to reading habits.

But that's just a lexicon. That's the collection of words. It's the vocabulary. Part of being a native speaker also means understanding the rules of grammar in ways that let us generate new sentences and understand the difference between dog bites man, and man bites dog.

These rules of order are at the heart of grammar, and to study this process, people sometimes look at the acquisition, or the learning, of a false, simplified grammar. So, for example, babies might be presented with syllables like "ga" and "ti," and these syllables can be organized into threesomes that follow different sequences (for example, ga-ti-ga). Then, infants get tested with new syllables such as "wo" and "fe" organized into either a familiar pattern (so, for those who saw ga-ti-ga, they would see wo-fe-wo), or organized into a dissimilar pattern (wo-fe-fe). It turns out the infants learn the rules for putting different proto words together very easily, and they can learn them for language-like stimuli, like wo-fe-fe and ga-ti-ga, but they can also learn these rules for non-linguistic stimuli. For example, they can learn rules of order for how you might array pictures of dog breeds.

So far, we've seen how babies begin with a very few general, inborn capacities, like being able to monitor statistical frequencies in a sound stream, being able to extract some initial words and understandings of order rules, and being able to use those minimal rules and initial words to identify and learn additional words and rules.

Now, this process is believed to be largely incidental—that is, babies don't sit around deliberately trying to learn a grammar or a new vocabulary—and it's also powerful. It goes from 0–60,000 in under two decades.

The contrast with learning a language in later childhood or adulthood, which we'll consider next time, is profound. We often experience second-language learning in adulthood as effortful, as requiring intention, and deliberate learning of vocabulary, and the end result is usually far short of native fluency and native lexicon size. Now, to some extent, this difference is partly due to the losses that learning our first language involves.

Losses, you say? But yes. We often think of learning as a purely gain-oriented experience. But, learning changes us, and sometimes the changes involve losses as well as gains. And language is a particularly useful and interesting place to pause and to consider the losses.

So what are those losses? Well, first of all, at birth, babies have an amazing capability to distinguish between different sounds. In fact, at birth, babies can distinguish between all the known sounds in human languages, including some of the clicks and unusual phonemes that you may have seen only on a *National Geographic* episode.

Now, unfortunately, this early linguistic brilliance gives way quickly to a more tuned and focused competence. So, in tests of this, a baby would sit on a parent's lap and face an experimenter, and the experimenter sort of shows the baby toys and this keeps the baby paying attention. Now, while this is happening, the baby hears a series of phonemes (sound units) repeated over and over. For example, "ta-ta-ta-ta-ta-ta." And what happens is that the baby gets taught to turn his or her head when the sound changes, at which point the baby gets to see a new bunch of toy animals moving around in the display. This is a really nice little reward for babies, so they're very happy to do this kind of task.

In one study, Werker and Desjardins looked at whether young babies and adults, native English speakers, could distinguish between two "t" sounds that are irrelevant to English—that for English speakers kind of seem the same, and don't mark any important word distinctions, but which in Hindi mark very important word contrasts. Now, the two "t" sounds in Hindi can be made as follows for those of you who are Standard English speakers: For the Standard English "t," English speakers put their tongue on the ridge behind their front teeth and say "t." In Hindi, one "t" is made by putting the tongue on the roof of the mouth, and the other by putting the tongue against the front teeth. If you try this, your mouth will feel different as you try to make a "t" sound, and a Hindi-speaker will hear a different sound. You may or may not be able to hear a difference. Both ways of saying "t" will sound like "t."

Infants between the ages of six and eight months actually hear the difference in these three "t" sounds very well. In that experimental set up that I just described they turn their head when the way the speaker is making the t changes. But adult English speakers are actually pretty bad at doing this. They don't turn their heads or do the equivalent. They can't hear those sounds as being different. And, these losses in the ability to tell the difference in different sounds are actually evident already by 12 months of age. For infants who are learning English and living in North America, but who are also exposed to Hindi in their homes, the distinction remains.

Now, these phonetic losses are important because they help tune the brain for the native language. When an infant is potentially growing up bilingual, the brain is tuning for two languages right from the get go.

Phonetic losses are not all that's lost with first language acquisition. More conceptual losses also occur, and this is because languages have an important role in marking which conceptual distinctions matter in the worlds we live in. For example, in Korean, language marks a difference between the tight and loose fits of one object into another, but this is not a difference we mark in language in English.

Now, we can understand this distinction between a tight and loose fit immediately when I describe it. It's part of that understanding of physical properties of objects that we seem to share with many other species, and with which we're born. However, after we learn our native language, Elizabeth

Spelke and her colleagues speculated that, as with phonemes, we might become less sensitive to the differences that our languages treat as less important.

Spelke and her team used habituation paradigms and they showed infants and adults a series of actions and objects that could be categorized as tight or loose fitting. So, one set of objects might consist of a set of tubes, with one tube inserted into the other, and some pairs of tubes might be tight, while others would be more loose.

After being shown a series of images that represent tight fits, If babies dishabituate to a new scene involving loose fits, it means they view it as being in a different category compared to those they've been looking at. And, five-month-old infants readily made this distinction of loose versus tight fitting object relationships.

By contrast, English-speaking adults do not make this distinction spontaneously when asked to categorize images. They actually ignore the tight versus loose fit dimension. Now, because adults can make this distinction when it's pointed out to them, Spelke and her colleagues believe that what language does at the conceptual level is not to eliminate sensitivity, but to diminish or enhance it.

And, this brings me to the largest issue of all with respect to language acquisition. Does our first language end up shaping the way we think? One of the prominent current researchers in this area is Lera Boroditsky. Boroditsky has suggested that some of the most fundamental aspects of human experience involve our experiences of time and space.

These are crucial categories that affect how we divide up the world into past, present, and future, and into here versus there, near versus far. Now, language is used to represent, think about, and to communicate about space and time, and Boroditsky argues, this has some important implications for how we think, and via an extension I'll make about her work, what we can and cannot learn easily.

Now, in much of Boroditsky's work, she looks at how different language speaking communities think about space and time. For example, she has worked in northern Australia with aboriginal communities, and in those communities, she can ask a five-year-old girl to point north, and that girl will be able to do so accurately and immediately, no matter where she is or whether she can see the sky.

Now, most of us outside that community—well-educated researchers—are not able to do so at all. And in fact, Boroditsky occasionally enjoys herself at presentations by trying it out on her audiences. Now, Boroditsky argues that the reason for this is that that girl's language has a very particular, compass-oriented way of talking about relationships in space. That is, rather than left, right, in front of, behind and so on, the way we might talk about relationships in space, speakers of *kuuk thaayorre* locate objects in cardinal directions. Cups are northwest of plates, or the guy to the west of Joe is his uncle.

Does this matter? Well, as Boroditsky points out, first of all, you can't even talk about things in this language without staying oriented to where north is. And then it may be less surprising to learn that people who speak such languages are very good at knowing where they are, even inside buildings they don't know or in unfamiliar environments. It's probable, in my view, that this type of absolute orientation might help people learn a new spatial environment more quickly because the model that they're building is less egocentric. It's less to do with relative to their own position, and it has more to do with their surroundings than themselves, and it may be a more flexible approach to building a model of your surroundings.

Languages differ in a vast array of ways, including in how they represent number. For example, some languages offer better grounds for learning numbers and base 10 arithmetic than others. Some languages, like Tamil, may offer better clarity about place value because of the way that numbers are represented in that language. In fact, even German may offer better place value insight than English because it amounts to representing 21 as "1 and 20," rather than the English "21."

So, just as your native language is an enormous, impressive achievement of learning—learning done almost with no effort at all—your native language is also an arena of tuning your mind to distinctions and concepts that are deemed important by your culture. And that tuning entails some losses as well. Now, those losses are perhaps nowhere better evident than when we look at the acquisition of a second language, which we will do in the next lecture.

Learning a Second Language
Lecture 8

In the last lecture, we talked about the amazing and effortless way in which infants acquire a first language. Learning a second language, though, feels anything but effortless. In this lecture, we're going to look at whether and how other species have been able to learn human language systems—or systems very like human language. In addition, we'll look at how the experience of human adults learning a second language is both like and unlike the case of babies learning a first language and how it is like and unlike animals learning an alien way of communicating.

The Language of Primates

- Some of the ways human beings learn languages have to do with general abilities to monitor statistical relations in perceptual experiences: the ability to track which sounds go together often and which sounds almost never go together, for example. We share these abilities with other species.

- We share much of our genetic heritage with primates, but human speech requires special properties of the vocal tract that most other species don't share. Therefore, we are talking about the ability for primates to acquire symbol systems, such as sign languages or other artificial systems for communication.

- Apes that use these systems have been trained in one of two ways. In one way, animals are trained using rewards—operant conditioning— to link symbols, such as signs or pictograms, with objects. With this approach, training begins relatively late in the ape's childhood and occurs exclusively between the ape and other human beings.

- In the second way, animals are exposed to symbolic communication early in their lives and learn alongside their mother, for example. In this case, apes appear to have more sophisticated skills and to use the symbols with each other as well as with other humans.

- With extensive training, apes acquire up to 500 distinct symbols, but they don't have the kind of takeoff that happens for younger children, and acquisition is certainly not effortless. Instead, it requires fairly intense training efforts from human caregivers.

- Grammar and syntax seem to be absent in animals that have been trained with symbol systems. It's rare for them to combine more than two symbols, and the combinations they make are simple and constrained.

- Some studies show that more than 90 percent of the communication that trained apes engage in with their human caregivers is in the form of imperatives—that is, once animals acquire speech-like capacity, they use that capacity to get what they want.

- In fact, although there is some significant disagreement about the nature of animals' achievements in language, researchers have observed that humans use language to represent their thoughts and to communicate about those thoughts, while apes largely use language to communicate their desires.

The Language of Parrots

- Language studies with animals have not been done only with apes. In fact, parrots can be taught to speak. Alex the Parrot was taught to speak by a researcher named Irene Pepperberg, who used a very interesting technique that is different than the techniques used with primates.

- In this approach, while Alex watches, two human beings interact around an object that Alex has already shown some interest in or some curiosity about. One human might ask questions about the object, and the other human responds to the questions. The human is praised when he or she gives a correct answer and receives disapproval when he or she gives an incorrect response.

- In this case, disapproval involves scolding, removing the item from view, or asking the human to try again. With Pepperberg's method, the correct word is rewarded with the object itself, so the parrots can use language to get what they want in a more direct way, as is the case with human children. With primates, rewards, such as bananas, are often not the objects that are being discussed, which results in confusion.

- Alex the Parrot can make requests, label 50 different objects, and identify shapes, colors, and quantities. However, Alex doesn't use language like human children do. Although his experiences were in some respects more like those of human children, they were still more intensively focused on training language using principles of operant conditioning.

- These methods are somewhat analogous to the methods that we sometimes use to acquire a second language later in our childhoods or as adults. In addition, they're more disappointing in their outcomes, which to some extent may also be true for our efforts to learn second languages.

Human Adult Second-Language Learners

- Even animals appear to be better off if their language training starts very early in their lives. Is there something unique about language acquisition and babies? Is there a critical period for learning language, and is that why learning a second language as an adult is so much more difficult than learning a first?

- Along with evidence from case studies of children reared without language exposure, whose adult attainment of language is never quite normal, research suggests that if you don't get early exposure to a second language, you can never achieve native-like capabilities in speaking or using that language. There is a biological constraint on learning a second language.

- It is possible for adult onset learners to obtain virtually native competence, but for the most part, researchers acknowledge that second-language acquisition for adults is difficult, and it produces a lot of variability among people. On average, second-language acquisition has poor outcomes.

- Many languages mark nouns by gender so that there are male nouns, female nouns, and sometimes even neutral nouns. English doesn't do this, so it may be difficult to reacquire this conceptual category system if you did not develop it in infancy and early childhood. In addition, we use stress and intonation patterns to decode speech that are not the same from language to language.

- Attempts to train people to recognize phonemes—the smallest sound units in a language—that they don't need to distinguish in their native language have not been successful, although this is an area of active research today.

- The incidental learning of words that we seemed able to do as children doesn't always happen with second languages; it appears that sometimes we need to be more intentional in order to acquire new vocabulary.

- Learning a second language is a goal for many adults and others beyond early childhood—despite all the negative information about language learning. There are obvious reasons why it's useful to be able to speak other languages, including giving us benefits during later life by protecting us from cognitive declines that occur in aging.

- Many general learning principles apply to learning languages, such as engaging with the material deeply and using elaborative encoding, which means linking new material to what we already know to enhance our ability to learn and remember the new information.

Tips for Learning a Second Language

- An important technique for learning a second language is immersion, or being immersed in a language. One major predictor of second-language learning outcomes—of how well people learn that second language—involves learning in the second-language country versus in the home country.

- Research suggests that people are equally accurate at grammar when they learned in their home country and when they learned in the second-language country. However, learning in the second-language country appears to improve your lexicon, vocabulary, and grasp of the pragmatics of a second language, which include politeness phrases, slang, and other kinds of nuances of how a language gets used.

- Immersion is better than learning in your home country. First, sheer exposure to language is much greater if you're immersed in the country where you're trying to learn the language than if you're at home taking classes. In addition, in a foreign country, the language is critical for living, and this can make acquisition feel quicker and more efficient than learning in the classroom.

- In addition to immersion, you want to choose the language you're going to learn carefully. The issue is not in the specific language, but rather it's in the distance between your native language and the one you're trying to learn. Studies suggest that the greater that distance between your native tongue and your second language, the slower you are to learn the second language, the harder it is to acquire it, and the worse you will do at the same point compared to those learning languages closer to their own.

- In addition, differences between people in how well they learn a second language aren't just a function of who gets immersion and who spends more time and effort. There are real individual differences in language learning capacity, and studies of twins suggest this ability is highly heritable.

When in a foreign country, learning the language often feels more purposeful and efficient than learning in a classroom.

Being Truly Bilingual

- In the continuum of language learning—from babies (effortless and perfect) to other species (highly effortful and poor outcomes)—second-language learning by adult humans is somewhere in the middle. Unlike other species, we can, given the right situation and good luck on genetically based aspects of ability and hard work, approach perfection.

- However, like other species, we may not be able to learn in quite the same way as we once did. We may need more explicit, deliberate learning strategies, and there are some limits to how perfectly we can learn based on our native language.

- The exception to this rule is learning a second language during the critical period in early childhood. In that case, people have a chance to be truly bilingual—proficient in two languages.

- The issue of being bilingual raises a common concern about language learning: that if we learn two languages, we'll somehow be behind in both or be adversely affected in one of our languages by virtue of learning the second. There is no reason to worry about this for children, and there's every reason to encourage bilingual experience in childhood.

- However, operating in two languages involves the ability to inhibit competing responses. If you want to use one language, you need to be able to push away the vocabulary and words of the other language. The more languages you try to learn, the more potential competing responses you have—and the more experience and more possibilities to link prior knowledge to new vocabulary and grammar you have.

- Research suggests that the capacity to inhibit responses in general gets strengthened when we consistently have to operate in more than one language, and improved inhibition can help our learning much more broadly in many other areas.

- Learning a second language is effortful, and it's difficult in part because of the way in which a brain tuned to our native language misses important information in the new language, making it difficult to acquire particular sounds, concepts, and grammatical structures in that new language. This difficulty means that in second-language learning, we have to employ more deliberate and effortful strategies to achieve mastery of that language.

- However, we're far from being as badly off as nonhuman species in learning a new language, and the ceiling on our second-language acquisition—while perhaps lower than the ceiling for our first language—is still pretty high.

Suggested Reading

Hyltenstam and Abrahamsson, "Maturational Constraints in SLA."

Savage-Rumbaugh, Segerdahl, and Fields, "Individual Differences in Language Competencies in Apes."

Questions to Consider

1. To what extent do adult learners of a second language face similar or different learning problems as nonhuman animals?

2. In what ways can immersion-like experiences be created in one's own country?

Learning a Second Language
Lecture 8—Transcript

Last lecture, we talked about the amazing and effortless way infants acquire a first language. Learning a second language though, feels anything but effortless. Why might that be? Why is learning a second language so much harder than learning our native tongue?

In this lecture, we will consider this question from a couple of angles. First, we're going to look at whether and how other species have been able to learn human language systems, or things very like human language. Second, we'll look at humans learning a second language. We'll look at how that is both like and unlike the case of babies learning a first language on the one hand, and how it is like an unlike animals learning an alien way of communicating on the other.

So, can other species learn human language? And if so, how? These are important questions for us because how other animals learn a language suggests something about how languages might be learned by us, and it also forces us to think about what it means to have language.

Remember that some of the ways we learn languages as babies have to do with general abilities to monitor statistical relations in our perceptual experiences. (our ability to track which sounds go together often, and which sounds almost never go together, for example). And we actually share those abilities to track statistical properties of our perceptual experience with other species.

In considering other animals, we're going to begin by looking at primates because we share so much of our genetic heritage with them. And because of this, we won't begin with speech, which requires some special properties of the vocal tract that most other species don't share with humans.

And in fact, this is actually why we're vulnerable to choking on our food. The anatomy that lets us make so many different sounds is also the anatomy that kind of screws up and combines eating and breathing in ways that allow choking to happen

So, we're not really talking about language here. We're actually talking about acquiring symbol systems (sign languages, modified, or other artificial systems for communication by using computer keyboards and sets of symbols, for example).

Apes that use these systems have been trained in one of two ways. In one way, as with many of the early studies on Koko the gorilla, and Lucy the chimpanzee, the animals are trained using rewards, using operant conditioning, to link symbols like signs or pictograms, kind of stylized pictures, with objects. So the apes are shown a picture of a dog, and given the sign or the symbol that means dog in their false language, and then they're asked to generate that symbol for dog whenever they're shown the image. If they get that right they'll get some kind of treat. With this approach, training begins relatively late in the ape's childhood and training happens exclusively between the ape and other human beings.

In a second way, and this is the way employed by Sue Savage-Rumbaugh and her colleagues, animals are exposed to symbolic communication early in their lives and they learn alongside their mother, for example. In this case, apes actually appear to have more sophisticated skills and to use the symbols with each other as well as with other humans. But to say that apes acquire some symbols and use them doesn't really answer the question of how well they do.

Thinking back, we talked about how babies acquire a vocabulary or a lexicon that ends in adulthood, at some 60,000 words or so. Now, with extensive training, apes acquire up to 500 distinct symbols, but they don't have the kind of take-off that happens for younger kids, and acquisition is certainly not so effortless. It doesn't happen automatically. It requires fairly intense training efforts from human caregivers.

We also talked about the rules of combining words to form complex thoughts and ideas—grammar and syntax. This also seems absent in animals that have been trained with symbol systems. It's rare for them to combine more than two symbols, and the combinations they make are sort of simple and constrained. Further, some studies show that more than 90 percent of the communication these trained apes engage in with their human caregivers is in the form of imperatives—that is, once animals acquire speech-like capacity, they use that capacity to get what they want. Give me banana; Give me a hug, and so on. But apes generally don't use their communication abilities to do more than that.

Now in fact, although there is some significant disagreement about the nature of animals' achievements in language, researchers have observed that humans use language to represent their thoughts and to communicate about those thoughts, and apes largely use language to communicate their desires.

Of course language studies with animals have not been done only with apes. So, let's consider now some work on parrots too. And here recall that parrots can actually be taught to speak. Alex the Parrot, and African Gray parrot, was taught to speak by a researcher named Irene Pepperberg, and they used a very interesting technique that is different than the techniques used with primates.

In this approach, while Alex watches, two human beings interact around an object that Alex has already shown some interest in or some curiosity about. So, one human might show the object to the other human and say, "What is here? What color? What shape?" The human model then responds to the questions. Now, the human model gets praised when they give a correct answer and they receive disapproval when they give an incorrect response. And that's especially true when they give an incorrect response that's a lot like whatever Alex is making at the time in response to those questions.

And what is disapproval? Well disapproval is scolding, removing the item from the sight of the human model, and sometimes the human model is asked to try again. As you can see, this is a real contrast to studies with apes, and it's particularly a contrast to those early ones in some ways. As Pepperberg argues, when you reward correct answers with foods—as in the early approaches with apes—that's confusing. The apes heard "What is this," they said "cork," and they got a banana. With her method, the right word gets you the object, so you can use language to get things that you have requested in a more direct way, as is the case with human children.

And with this clever method, which is more like some aspects of human children's experience, how far does Alex get? Alex can make requests. He can label 50 different objects. He can identify shapes, colors, and quantities. But again, Alex doesn't use language like human children. And, although his experiences were in some respects more like those of human children, they still were more intensively focused on training language using operant conditioning-like principles, and that's not the effortless acquisition that we see in our own infants. However, these methods are worth looking at because they're a bit more analogous to the methods that we sometimes use to acquire a second language later in our childhoods or as adults. And, they're a bit more disappointing in their outcomes, which to some extent may also be true for our efforts to learn second languages.

Let's turn our attention now to human adult second language learners. Are we as bad as animals with as much effort? And if so, why would that be? And even animals appear to be better off with their language training starts very early in their lives. So, is there something unique about language acquisition and babies?

This is a more specific version of the same idea we considered a couple lectures back. Is there a critical period or a sensitive period for learning language, and is that why learning a second language as an adult is so much more difficult than learning a first?

Well, evidence for a critical period would need to go something like this: If you don't get early exposure to that second language, you can never achieve native-like capabilities in speaking or using that language.

Let's get the bad news over quickly. It turns out this is true. Now, to look at this issue, researchers Hyltenstam and Abrahamsson recruited second language speakers of Swedish into their laboratories. And they were particularly interesting in people who had been speaking Swedish for decades, living immersed in Swedish culture, and who were routinely mistaken for native speakers by other native speakers of Swedish.

They presented these people with a series of very difficult language tasks, including what is called a grammaticality judgment test. To give you some perspective on this test, judging the grammatical correctness of a sentence can vary from what is expected for most competent speakers of a language, to very difficult and subtle judgments that are made accurately only by a highly proficient speaker.

What they found with this sample of people who were clearly very good at speaking Swedish is that under extreme circumstances, generated in their laboratory, native speakers and the second language Swedish speakers were different. Along with evidence from case studies of children reared without language exposure, whose adult attainment of language is never quite normal, this work and other work really suggest that there is some kind of biological constraint on acquiring or learning a second language.

But, an alternative way to think about this work is this: This work also shows that it is possible for adult onset learners to get virtually native competence, so much so that they can only be distinguished from native speakers in a very tough laboratory-based language challenge. Now, the near-native competence of these research participants is of course not typical. And for the most part, researchers acknowledge that adult's second-language acquisition is difficult; it produces a lot of variability between people—some people get very good, others don't. On average, second language acquisition has poor outcomes, at least if the standard for comparison is a native speaker.

Why is this? So, recall that in the last lecture we noted two ways in which our native language changes us—in terms of the phonemes we can distinguish, and in terms of the concepts or categories that we emphasize or de-emphasize, and the way we think about the world. Now, we focused on a physical category—tight or loose-fitting—and it was easy to get that category back when adults were asked to focus on it. But other categories may not be so easily re-built.

For example, many languages mark nouns by gender so that there are male nouns and female nouns and in German even neutral nouns. English doesn't do this, and it may be quite difficult to re-acquire this conceptual category system if you did not develop it in infancy and early childhood. Other ways that our native language changes us were also mentioned last time. We begin to use stress and intonation patterns to decode speech from early on, and those patterns are not the same from language to language.

Native English speakers, as we noted, use stress to segment utterances in words in English. Our words are typically stressed on the first syllable as opposed to syllable. So this is a good way to figure out where words start in English. It's a good strategy. English speakers exploited as infants, but if you then learn a new language that doesn't segment using stress in that way, that strategy is going to hurt you.

A different way to think about this is that cues are located in the speech stream, but the segmentation of that stream is something that happens in the person who is speaking and using the language, and sometimes these two are mismatched, and that's more likely for second language learners.

Can you train people to recognize phonemes—the smallest sound units in a language—that they don't need to distinguish in their native language? Attempts to do this have not been successful, although this is an area of active research today.

The incidental learning of words, that we also seemed able to do as children, doesn't always happen with second languages either. And there it appears that sometimes we need to be more intentional in order to acquire new vocabulary. So, in one study for example, participants were asked to read a passage in the second language, and some participants were asked to make special note of the vocabulary words in the passage and others read just for comprehension. In this case, intentional vocabulary study led to better learning of the vocabulary words as indicated by better performance on a later test.

But, learning a second language is a goal for many adults and others beyond early childhood despite all this negative news, and there are obvious reasons why it's useful to be able to speak other languages; these include travel, but they also include required foreign language learning in schools, especially in high school and college years. They include the ability to read books and poetry in their original and untranslated versions. And they even include the capacity to know a broader range of world news than is on offer in our own language. That's not even to mention careers as translators, in anthropology or classics, or any other field involving cross-cultural work, and so on. There are many, many good reasons to learn a second language. Finally, and this something we'll actually return to in more detail later, speaking a second language appears to give us some benefits during later life by protecting us from cognitive declines that occur in aging.

So, given all that, what if you missed the boat on the critical period? How can you fulfill your adult dream to learn Spanish or German or Mandarin Chinese? Many general learning principles apply to learning languages, engage with the material deeply, use elaborative encoding. Remember this means linking new material to things we already know to enhance our ability to learn and remember the new information. But here, let's consider some special features of languages that will give you a few more helpful ideas for learning a second one.

The first important technique is to find a way to what is called immersion—being immersed in that language. One major predictor of second language learning outcomes of how well people learn that second language has to do with where people do the learning. Let me give you a personal example. I grew up in the United States. I learned French in school off and on for several years in two different states. I probably spent up to six or seven years taking French classes in school beginning at the age of six or so. Now, despite all this early exposure and the fact that I'm a fairly diligent and competent student, I was never able to use French effectively to communicate.

By contrast, I spent approximately eight months in formal German instruction, but here's the key difference. I was living in Berlin, Germany at the time. And although my work language was English, I had substantial immersion in German language and culture. I lived in Berlin for three years, and while I would never have been mistaken for a native speaker, I was able to read the major newspapers, to engage in random conversation with people—including on more substantive topics than weather—and I was able to read relatively straightforward novels. And the difference in these two experiences was immersion.

Other research suggests that where you're learning may be relatively unrelated to your acquisition of grammar—that is, people are equally good at learning the grammar of a new language regardless of whether they learn in their home country or in the second language country. But learning in country appears to really improve your lexicon, your vocabulary, and your grasp of the pragmatics of a second language. And the pragmatics means what you say when—politeness phrases, how to say things appropriately versus inappropriately, slang, and other kinds of nuances of how a language gets used.

So, what is it that makes the difference between immersion and learning from the safety of home? There are at least two major reasons why immersion is better. Now, one is simply exposure. Sheer exposure to language is much greater if you're immersed in the country where you're trying to learn the language than if you're at home and taking an occasional class.

The second difference is that issue of purpose. When learning a second language in one's home country, the language is never critical for living except in the context of the classroom. But in a foreign country, the language is required for negotiating everyday life, and this can make acquisition feel not quite effortless, but quicker and more efficient than learning in the classroom.

In addition to immersion, a second thing you want to do is to choose the language you're going to learn carefully. A rumor had it, when I was in high school, that Spanish was an easy language, German was a difficult one, and French was somewhere in between. Is this true? Well, sort of. As it happens, the issue is not in the specific language, but rather it's in the distance between your native language and the one you're trying to learn. And studies suggest that the bigger that distance between your native tongue and your second language, the slower you are to learn the second language, the harder it is to acquire that second language, and the worse you're doing at the same time point compared to those learning language closer to their own. In other words, it's going to take you longer to get the same level of ability.

What makes for linguistic distance? Well, interestingly, there are many ways to go about determining this. So, one is to consider the origins of different languages in a kind of language family tree. For example, the romance languages have evolved historically from Latin, and both the romance and Germanic languages have common roots, along with some other languages, in what is called the Indo-European language family. The idea here is that languages that are closer together historically ought to be easier to learn, so English speakers should have an easier time with, say, German, than with Tamil.

But there could be other ways of thinking about language distance. Another way to think about it is to look at a 200 item database of basic, high-frequency words in about 84 languages and dialects. And this database was developed by Dyen and colleagues. And based on this database, you can figure out whether two languages share more or fewer of these high frequency words. These are words like milk, mother, tree—they're words that nearly every language needs.

A researcher named Van der Slik examined how these two measures of language distance fared in predicting language learning outcomes, and he did this by looking at learning of Dutch by people who had a variety of native languages. Dutch is a really nice language to study, by the way, because unlike English, it is possible to grow to adulthood with no exposure to Dutch until you actually start to learn it. By contrast, English is so ubiquitous in the world that it's actually hard to know when people began being exposed to English, and it makes it very difficult to figure out how long people have been learning or experiencing English.

So, they did this in the Netherlands, and to look at linguistic distance they examined the results of a set of exams that are given to migrants who want to go to college in the Netherlands. The exams test speaking, writing, reading, and listening in Dutch, and they do so all separately, but Van der Slik focused on speaking and writing, and this was expressive language, and it's usually a little bit harder than listening and reading.

So, the tasks on the test are things like responding to questions. So for example, people might be asked, "What is your opinion about advertising on TV?" This is just testing your ability to express yourself in an everyday context. People might be asked to give instructions, to complain—that's my favorite—telling a story, to write about something you've read, and so on. So, judges evaluated people's responses, and the emphasis of the evaluation is functional proficiency. So, it's not important that participants get it perfect; it's that they are able to communicate effectively. Content is more important than form.

Now, because this same test is given to many different migrants, from many different native language communities, this permits a very nice test of the role of linguistic distance in people's language proficiency. So, Van der Slik also looked at the age of arrival in the Netherlands, the length of time people had lived there, the number of hours per week that they studied Dutch, and their prior educational history. What he found was that the distance between Dutch and the native tongue predicted how well people did on the exams, and the closer the native tongue the better the exam performance.

A third important thing is to be lucky in language capacity. Differences between people in how well they learn a second language aren't just a function of who gets immersion and who spends more time and effort. There are real individual differences in language learning capacity. Studies of twins suggest this ability is highly heritable. So if you think, as I do, that language abilities run in your family, or if you think they don't, you're also likely to be right about that to some extent.

Now, this is not a reason to avoid learning a second language. It's more a reason to adjust your expectations a bit about two things: about how competent you will get in a new language, and about how much effort you will have to spend. So, think about all those Europeans who can speak English: Some are fast, some are slow, some are accented, some are really fluent. But if so many people can learn our language well enough to communicate, nearly all of us should be able to learn enough of a second language to function, even if we aren't going to be mistaken for a native speaker.

Before we turn to the last topic of this lecture, let's revisit the continuum of language learning from babies (effortless and perfect) to other species (highly effortful and pretty poor outcomes). Second language learning by adult humans is somewhere in the middle. Unlike other species, we can actually, given the right situation and good luck on genetically based aspects of ability and some hard work, get pretty close to perfect.

But, like other species, we may not be able to learn in quite the same way as we once did. We may need more explicit, deliberate learning strategies, and there are going to be some limits to how perfectly we can learn based on our native language.

The exception to this rule is learning a second language during the critical period in early childhood. In that case, people have a chance to really be truly bilingual—proficient in two languages. Many of my cousins have this type of fluency in both Tamil (my family's native tongue) and Hindi, and they nearly have that level of capability in English as well. But the issue of being bilingual raises a common concern about language learning, and that's the idea that if we learn two languages, we'll somehow be behind in both or we'll be adversely affected in one of our languages by virtue of learning the second. For many of you in this course the concern may not be about yourselves but about children or grandchildren.

Well first, there is no reason to worry about this for children and there's every reason to encourage bilingual experience in childhood however you can. And we'll return to that a little bit later in our course when we discuss how you can enhance some of the basic cognitive capabilities that actually support learning broadly in all kinds of areas.

But second, let's consider this point with second language learning in adulthood. Does learning a second language actually mess up your first? Well, there's this interesting way in which it actually has to do so, at least temporarily, when you're initially learning that second language.

Consider how this might work just for a moment. When you learn a new word in a foreign language—let's say we're learning German, so we learn that in German, a dog is *ein Hund*. Now, we have a bunch of associations we have acquired over our lifetimes, including one between our native term for dog, and now our new German term, *Hund*.

Suppose we're walking down the street in Berlin, and there's a dog. In order to correctly use the German word—*Hund*—you have to actually inhibit your much faster and better learned response, which is "dog." In fact, the better you are at suppressing "dog," the better you'll be able to learn to say *Hund* while in Berlin. But the effect is temporary. Once you learn *Hund* very, very well, you don't need to be as worried about suppressing "dog."

This is precisely what Levy and colleagues found in a recent study of Americans learning Spanish vocabulary. If participants were asked to repeatedly name objects in Spanish, that temporarily slowed down their ability to access those names in English, and this effect was most strongly found for the people whose Spanish was much weaker than their English. Those were the people who really had to push their English vocabulary down in order to get the Spanish vocabulary correct. Now, in this particular case, these were American students and they were located in the U.S., and the inhibition effects of learning a second language were temporary.

The important take-home point here is that operating in two languages involves the ability to inhibit competing responses. If you want to use one language you need to be able to push away the vocabulary and words of the other language. And the more languages, the more potential competing responses you have. Now, of course, the more languages you have it's also the case that you have more experience and more possibilities to link prior knowledge to new vocabulary and grammar.

Research is suggesting that the capacity to inhibit responses in general gets strengthened when we consistently have to operate in more than one language, and improved inhibition is something that can help our learning much more broadly in all kinds of other areas. And we are going to return to this aspect of language learning later in the course. For now, this is just something to add to the list of all those good reasons to learn a second language.

Learning a second language is effortful and it's difficult in part because of the way in which a brain tuned to our native language misses important information in the new language, and it makes it hard to acquire particular sounds, concepts, and grammatical structures in that new language. This difficulty means that in second language learning, we have to employ more deliberate and effortful strategies to achieve mastery of that language. Having said that, however, we're far from being as badly off as non-human species, and the ceiling on our second language acquisition, while maybe lower than the ceiling for our first language, is still pretty high up.

In the next part of the course, we'll be focusing on the what of learning. We'll look at different types of learning with two broader distinctions in mind—the distinction between skills and knowledge, and the distinction between learning on purpose and learning incidentally. Language learning in childhood and adulthood are a kind of miniature version of those distinctions.

In language learning, we learn both knowledge (we acquire vocabulary and grammatical rules) and we acquire skills (the motor ability to articulate new phonetic combinations, the capacity to use the right phrases in greetings, the ability to speak and converse). And, we learn both incidentally, as when we simply hear our native tongue and absorb words and phonemes, as well as deliberately, when we sit down to study a set of vocabulary words in our second language.

Virtually all learning combines skills and knowledge, but as we move through the next section of the course, we're going to move from an initial focus on skill-acquisition, to a more knowledge focus, as we turn to think about learning in the areas of math and science.

Further, as we go, we will consider both tacit forms of learning—that is, learning without words, like when we acquire an understanding of a space by moving around within it—and more deliberate forms of learning, as when we test out a theory about a math problem or study a map.

Learning How to Move
Lecture 9

Virtually all learning combines skills and knowledge, but as we move through the next section of the course, we're going to move from an initial focus on skill acquisition to a focus on knowledge. Furthermore, we will consider both tacit forms of learning and more deliberate forms of learning. In this lecture, we will look at motor learning—or learning how to move in ways that allow us to achieve particular goals—and how it is acquired. In addition, we will consider some important issues for maximizing motor learning, including verbalization, observation, and visualization.

Feedback Systems

- Our days are full of movements large and small, and we take many of the movements we make for granted; in fact, it may not seem like we ever learned some motor skills at all.

- Of course, there are many motor skills that we may vividly remember acquiring—or, perhaps, not acquiring all too well. For example, you might remember learning how to play tennis or to dance.

- As with many types of learning, we need to perform the behavior we're trying to acquire repeatedly with motor learning. The more practice and repetition you experience with a movement, the better your ability to make that movement will be. Furthermore, the more that practice is distributed over longer periods with rest intervals in between, the better your retention of the motor skill will be over time.

- Similarly, there is no tabula rasa with motor movement. In fact, when a baby, animal, or adult human try to learn a new movement, they are usually assembling bits and pieces of movements that they already know how to do.

- In acquiring new motor skills, under most circumstances, we also critically need feedback; we can't just rely on repeated exposures and repetitions of the movement itself without any sense of whether we are doing the movement correctly.

- There are two types of feedback, and they vary depending on where we are in the learning process. One source of feedback is called knowledge of results. For example, consider target shooting or typing; it is very clear and obvious whether the movements you make result in success.

- When babies begin to learn to reach and grasp objects, they make use of knowledge of results to refine and hone their movements. The same is true for standing, walking, and other motor skills that we acquire early in life.

- Not all skills entail obvious knowledge of results. With dance and other kinds of performances, knowledge of results may be less available;

With dance and other performance arts, knowledge of results as a source of feedback is not always clear to the beginner.

it is not always clear to the beginner whether the body has executed a movement correctly. For many kinds of motor skills, it is important to get feedback from others in the initial stages of acquiring those skills.

- Feedback sources also shift across time as people develop more capacity within a given area. As skill improves, people begin to rely more on a second feedback system: the proprioceptive system.

- The proprioceptive system is one of our senses, but it is one we usually ignore unless it malfunctions. It is the system of sensory inputs and sensory processing that tells us where we are, how we're positioned, and even the relative tension or the lack of tension in our muscles.

- Like any of our sensory systems, the proprioceptive system consists of receptors and nerve projections that carry the receptor signals to the brain. Once at the brain, those signals can be interpreted and made use of to help us do whatever motor action we're performing at the time.

- The proprioceptive system involves parts of the inner ear called the vestibular apparatus, receptors called muscle spindles that are located in what is called the belly of our major muscles, and additional receptors in joints and in the junction between tendons and muscles.

- These different receptors take in distinct pieces of information. The vestibular system involves receptors that signal posture, balance, and head movements in relation to gravity. Muscle spindles add different information into the proprioceptive system—such as how tense your muscles are and how quickly they are contracting—and they also help to tell you how your joints are positioned.

- All of these receptors transmit information to the brain, which then integrates all that information so that we have an awareness of where we are, how we're standing, and how we're moving with respect to the world around us. These signals also provide feedback about our performance of motor movement, and it is feedback about the process of making the movement that can help us acquire a motor skill.

Stages of Motor Learning
- Our initial experiences of learning motor movements are often verbal and fairly cognitive. Gains at this stage are very rapid and large—after all, people are starting from almost no skill—but people's movements in this stage are not very smooth, effective, or reliably produced.

- In fact, at this stage of motor learning, there is a lot of variation in how effectively people can produce a movement, and this is the place where feedback in the form of knowledge of results is salient and important. In this stage, we're learning a lot about our motor movement by using visual input and knowledge of results as feedback.

- Next, learning a motor movement goes toward refining and automating a motor movement pattern so that we can do that pattern without deliberate thought. At this point, things begin to vary depending on the kind of motor skill that we're learning.

- Dance moves are considered closed skills because the environment for performing those skills is pretty predictable: You know how the stage will be and how you need to move on that stage, and the idea is to move in the same way each time for a particular dance. The key to motor learning in these cases is to learn the best, most effective movement and to be able to reproduce that movement reliably.

- Many motor skills—such as tennis, driving, and typing—are considered open skills because some basic motor movements may be involved, but you also have to change the movements in response to changing environmental conditions.

- For open skills, the refinement process takes significantly longer, and people also need to make very certain that they practice the motor movements in different conditions because that's the only way they will be able to respond to changing environmental conditions. In fact, if people train under too homogenous a situation, the generalizing of the training to real performance conditions is not going to be very good.

- After this middle stage, people move to what's called by some researchers an autonomous phase of motor development, which is characterized by continued learning—even long after we think we're not improving anymore.

- Improvements at this stage are difficult for people to detect because they are already performing very well, so the amount of improvement is very small in comparison to what they have learned so far. In addition, the learning is not happening at a level where people are attentive to it, and in fact, people may not even notice that their movements are becoming more refined.

- At this phase of learning, almost all of the feedback that's relevant to honing motor skills is proprioceptive feedback within the body and outside our conscious awareness.

Improving Motor Learning

- If learning a motor skill initially is verbal and cognitive, verbalization can be used to help people acquire a motor skill in the first place. An example of an instructor using verbalization to help people learn motor skills is when an artist teaches others to paint by verbalizing brush strokes that achieve a particular technique.

- Verbalizing during early acquisition, as we're just learning a movement, appears to be helpful. Later in the learning process, verbalizing may actually disrupt our motor skills.

- Verbal instructions can be very useful because they direct participants' attention in the right way. The verbalization focuses attention on the movement to be learned at a phase where we can't produce that movement automatically. Where and how we focus our attention during motor learning also turns out to matter a great deal.

- In this arena, an external focus of attention generally means a focus outside the body and self—often, a focus on the goal of the movement. An internal focus means a focus on the self, on one's own thoughts and feelings or movements. An external focus is often a better focus for motor learning than an internal one.

- Gabriele Wulf and her collaborators have analyzed people acquiring a broad variety of sports-related motor skills. While they're learning, some people in these studies are asked to focus internally on the bodily experience of the movement, and others are asked to focus externally on the ball, for example, and its trajectory.

- In Wulf's studies, an external focus improves the speed with which people acquire a motor skill, and it improves their level of performance with that skill. An external focus helps because as we acquire motor skills, our shift from jerky, uncertain movements to smooth, automatic movements happens via feedback loops that involve comparing what we actually accomplished with our movement and what we had wanted to accomplish.

- The feedback loops involved, though, exist at both conscious and nonconscious levels. At a nonconscious level, your proprioceptive system and visual system are interacting with one another, and they're adjusting your movement without your deliberate thinking process.

- Deliberate thinking is effortful, slow, and inefficient compared to the kinds of mental processes we have that are more nonconscious and automated. Therefore, an internal focus when we're learning motor skills can interfere with the more automatic feedback loop that involves proprioception and vision, and it can shift us to the more effortful process of deliberate thought instead.

- As compared with some other types of learning, the distinction between explicit and deliberate processing is very important with motor skill learning.

Observation and Visualization
- When we learn a new motor skill, we often begin by observing others. Physical practice is better than just watching, but research has shown that it is extremely helpful to watch someone engage in a motor skill, practice what that person did, and perhaps talk about strategies in between.

- Although observation is clearly helpful for motor learning, it can be more helpful for some people than for others, and the key difference is in expertise. Depending on the motor skill to be learned, observation may function more effectively for people who already have a little bit of experience with a task.

- Visualizing success in motor tasks is not only highly motivating, but it also might be effective at helping people acquire a skill.

- Imagery is defined as the process of mentally rehearsing a motor act without moving the body. Imagining motor actions involves the same brain regions as doing the motor movements. In addition, imagining motor movements takes about as much time as doing the motor movements, and it can even create the same changes in breathing and heart rate.

- Imagery can help in the acquisition of motor skills in two ways: It can help you gain more with less physical practice, and it can sometimes result in better outcomes.

Suggested Reading

Schmidt and Wrisberg, *Motor Learning and Performance.*

Questions to Consider

1. Are there individual differences in the ability to use observation to learn motor skills? Think about yourself and people you know.

2. If visualizing successful movements facilitates motor learning, what about visualizing failures? Could visualization facilitate other types of learning as well?

Learning How to Move
Lecture 9—Transcript

As we discussed in the last lecture, we are going to begin our tour of different types of learning by looking at more skill-like learning. A second language is, to some extent, one example of that but in this lecture we will look at motor learning, learning how to move in ways that lets us achieve particular goals.

We'll also consider some important issues for maximizing your own motor learning and in particular four questions. What should I pay attention to while learning a motor skill? Can verbalizing a new motor skill help me learn it more effectively? What about learning by watching versus learning by doing? And can I just imagine doing the movement and get any benefit?

Our days are full of movements large and small and we take many of the movements we make for granted like being able to cut a steak or to take a job around the park on a running trail. We've been able to do those things for so long and we can do them so fluidly and well that it may not seem like we ever learned these skills at all.

Of course, there are other motor skills that we may vividly remember acquiring or, perhaps, not acquiring all too well. Many of us may have taken piano lessons at some time in our lives and some of us even acquired considerable skill. Or you might remember learning how to play tennis or to dance.

If you recently watched a child at the table, however, or had a new puppy, you know that even those skills we take for granted have to be learned at some point and if you, yourself, have recently tried to learn a new motor task you're likely all too aware of the gap between beginners and experts.

Some things about motor learning operate exactly like verbal learning. As with many types of learning, we need to perform the behavior we're trying to acquire and we need to do so repeatedly. We need to practice it. Learning to move is not different in this respect and you will find that the more practice and repetition with a movement the better your ability to make that movement will be. We're actually so good at walking as adults because we practice this movement over and over and over again until all the muscle movements and joint shifts required to get us from point A to point B can be performed with virtually no thought from us whatsoever. Further, the more practice is distributed over longer periods with rest intervals in-between the better retention of a motor skill over time will be.

Even more consistent with things we've already outlined is that with motor movement there is no tabular rasa, either. In fact, when a baby, an animal, or an adult human tries to learn a new movement they are usually assembling bits and pieces of movements that they already know how to do.

For throwing a ball we already know how to raise and lower our arm, how to rotate the arm and how to shift body weight and how to grasp and release an object. The throwing of the ball helps us to assemble all those constituent pieces into one coherent whole. That whole is both new but it is also old. So when babies learn to walk basic motor patterns are already in place for them from the reflexive movements that they actually started to practice in utero.

But in acquiring new motor skills, under most circumstances, we also critically need to get feedback. We can't just rely on repeated exposures and repetitions of the movement itself without any sense of whether we are doing the movement correctly.

And there are two types of feedback and they vary depending on where we are in the learning process. One obvious source of feedback is sometimes called knowledge of results. For example, consider target shooting or throwing or typing. It is very clear and obvious whether the movements you made resulted in success or not. For babies when they begin to learn to reach and grasp objects they make use of knowledge of results to refine and hone their movements. The same is true for standing, walking, and other motor skills that we acquire early in life.

But not all skills entail obvious knowledge of results. With dance and other kinds of performances knowledge of results may be less available. It is not always clear to the beginner whether the body has executed a movement correctly. To give a concrete example, when I began to do yoga I found that sometimes I would position my body incorrectly for a given pose and I wouldn't really be aware that I was positioned incorrectly. The only way to get feedback about that was to have the teacher notice and then reposition hips or shoulders so I was correctly in line. So for many kinds of motor skills it is important to get feedback from others in the initial stages of acquiring those skills.

Feedback sources also shift across time as people develop more capacity within a given area so as skill improves people actually begin to rely more on a second feedback system (not knowledge of results anymore, but rather feedback from the proprioceptive system).

The proprioceptive system is one of our senses. It is one we usually ignore unless it malfunctions. It is the system of sensory inputs and sensory processing that tells us where we are, how we're positioned, and even the relative tension or the lack of tension in our muscles.

Like any of our sensory systems, the proprioceptive system consists of receptors and nerve projections that carry the receptor signals to the brain. Once at the brain those signals can be interpreted and made use of to help us do whatever motor action we're performing at the time.

The proprioceptive system involves parts of the inner ear called the vestibular apparatus, receptors called muscle spindles that are located in what is called the belly of our major muscles, and additional receptors in your joints and in the junction between tendons and muscles.

These different receptors take in distinct pieces of information. Many of you will already know that the vestibular system involves receptors that signal posture, balance, and head movements in relation to gravity. If you've ever had an inner ear infection you may recall being dizzy and having trouble with balance, maybe even some nausea, and these symptoms tell you that the vestibular system thinks your posture is not upright even when it is.

Muscle spindles, for example, add different information into the proprioceptive system such as how tense your muscles are and how quickly they are contracting and they also help to tell you how your joints are positioned. All of these receptors transmit information to the brain and the brain, then, faces the task of integrating all that information so that we have some awareness of where we are, how we're standing, and how we're moving with respect to the world around us.

As you may have already figured out as I'm talking, these signals also provide feedback about our performance of a motor movement. It is feedback about the process of making the movement that can actually help us to acquire a motor skill.

So motor learning can actually be described in stages. Our initial first experiences of learning motor movements is often verbal and fairly cognitive. We are trying to figure out how we perform a given movement. We're very aware of how we're moving. And gains at this stage are very rapid and very large because people are starting from almost no skill but people's movements in this stage are not very smooth. They are often not very effective and they are not very reliably produced. And in fact, at this stage of motor learning there is a lot of variation in how effectively people can produce a movement, and this is the place where feedback in the form of knowledge of results is salient to us and it is important to us.

So as you might imagine, in this stage we're learning a lot about our motor movement by using visual input and knowledge of results kind of input as feedback.

But next, learning a motor movement goes towards refining and automating a motor movement pattern so that we can do that pattern without deliberate thought, without being so aware of how we're moving. And at this point, things begin to actually vary depending on the kind of motor skill that we're learning.

Bowling and dance moves might be considered somewhat closed skills because the environment for performing those skills is pretty predictable. You know how the stage will be and you know how you need to move on that stage and the idea, in fact, is to move in the same way for a particular dance every single time. So the key to motor learning in these cases is to learn the best, most effective movement and to be able to reproduce that movement reliably.

But many motor skills, like tennis, white water rafting, some of the motor aspects of driving and even something like typing are considered open skills in that there may be some basic motor movements like a forehand or paddling and weight shifting or changing gears. You also have to change the movements in response to changing environmental conditions.

Here the refinement process takes significantly longer, and for open skills, people also need to make very certain that they diversify their training. That is that they practice the motor movements in different conditions because that's the only way you'll be able to respond to changing environmental conditions.

In fact, if you train under too homogenous a situation the generalizing of your training to real performance conditions is not going to be very good. For example, if you train for typing by typing the same sentence, "The quick brown fox jumped over the lazy dog," you may be very fast and accurate with that sentence and technically you'll have acquired all the keystrokes that you need, but you're not going to be a star typist when you have to actually type something else.

After this kind of middle stage people move to what's called by some researchers an autonomous phase of motor development and this phase is characterized by continued learning, even long after we sometimes think we're not improving anymore at all.

For example, in one classic piece of work Crossman looked at cigar rolling among factory workers over a period of seven years and he focused particularly on how long it took a person working in this factory to finish a cigar. Over seven years people actually continued to improve over the entire length of the study, although the improvements were very tiny. They were incremental. So improvements at this stage are actually hard for people to detect and that's for two reasons. One is people are already performing very well so the amount of improvement is, as I mentioned, very small, much smaller than when people begin to learn a task.

The second reason it's hard for us to be aware of learning at that stage is that the learning that is taking place is tacit or it's implicit. It's not happening at a level where we're attentive to it and, in fact, we may not even be noticing that our movements are getting ever more refined. And at this phase of learning almost all the feedback that's relevant to honing that motor skills is proprioceptive feedback within the body and outside our conscious awareness.

Given these phases many of the questions that I began with about motor learning may involve primarily that early phase of learning. At later phases learning is about repetition and practice and it's not going to be so conscious.

In what remains of today's lecture I'm going to talk about what the science tells us about things we can do to improve our motor learning, especially in the early phases of acquiring a new skill.

First, if learning a motor skill initially is quite verbal and cognitive, does verbalization help us acquire a motor skill in the first place? Now, there are many examples where instructors use verbalization to help people learn motor skills. For example, in a Zumba class, which combines Latin dance moves with the goal of exercising, instructors often have students count or verbalize as they take steps. For example, students might be saying, side, side, front, front, side, side, front, front.

The words correspond to the direction in which students should be stepping. Chanting them together to the rhythm of the music helps to keep the class moving to the music and in unison, and in a crowded gym this is actually important for preventing mishaps.

Other examples of verbalization while learning motor skills are found in many different cases. When people learning to cross-stitch they may verbalize the stitches. Even on painting shows that I watched as a child the artist would often verbalize when demonstrating a brush stroke that would achieve a particular technique.

But none of this answers the question of whether we're faster to learn a motor skill if we do this, and the answer to that question turns out to depend on when we do the verbalizing. Verbalizing during this early acquisition, as we're just learning a movement, appears to be helpful. Later in the learning process verbalizing may actually disrupt our motor skills.

Verbal instructions can be very useful because they direct participants' attention in the right way. The verbalization focuses attention on the movement to be learned at a phase where we can't produce that movement automatically. But exactly where and how we focus our attention during motor learning also turns out to matter a great deal. In this arena, researchers distinguished between an external focus of attention and an internal focus of attention. So what do they mean, exactly?

An external focus of attention generally means a focus outside the body and the self often on the goal of the movement. Remember that knowledge of results. An internal focus means a focus on the self, one's own thoughts and feelings or one's own movements.

If you can, I'm going to give you some instructions to follow right now and you might pause the lecture and try this out. I'd like you to reach out and grab an object near you. It might be a coffee cup or it might be a pencil. And I'd like you to do this twice. The first time I want you to focus on just the object and grabbing the object. Then, I want you to put the object down in the same place and repeat the motion. This time imagine your arm moving incrementally towards the object. Pay attention to how your arm feels and your hand is shifting and how you're actually engaged with grasping.

If you are like most people the second experience of movement was a lot less effective and smooth than the first. In the first case you had an external focus of attention. You were focused on the result that you wanted to achieve. In the second I tried to get you to focus internally as much as possible, and what this demonstration shows you is that an external focus is often a better focus for motor learning than an internal one.

Gabriele Wulf and her collaborators have done a great deal of this work looking at people acquiring a broad variety of sports-related motor skills from slalom skiing on a ski simulator all the way to tennis and golf strokes, and while they're learning, in these studies, some people are asked to focus internally on the internal bodily experience of the movement they're making. Others are asked to focus externally by focusing on the ball, for example, and its trajectory

Time and time again in Wulf's studies that external focus improves the speed with which people acquire a motor skill and it improves their level of performance with that skill. So why might an external focus help? Well, recall that as we acquire motor skills one of the shifts that goes on is from jerky, uncertain movements to smooth and automatic movements and this shift happens via feedback loops that involve comparing what we actually accomplished with our movement and what we had wanted to accomplish.

The feedback loops involved, though, exist at more than one level. Now, at one level you can imagine consciously noticing that your hand is not quite on target for grasping the object and thinking to yourself, oh, I have to shift to the left. But at a much less deliberate and conscious level your proprioceptive system and visual system are interacting with one another and they're adjusting your movement without your deliberate thinking process.

A wealth of research in all areas of psychology shows us deliberate thinking is effortful and slow and inefficient compared to the kinds of thinking we engage in or the kinds of mental processes we have that are more non-conscious and automated. So an internal focus when we're learning motor skills can actually act to interfere with that more automatic feedback loop that involves proprioception and vision and it can shift us, instead, to that more effortful process of deliberate thought. And this is a real distinction about motor skill learning as compared with some other types of learning where that explicit and deliberate processing is very important.

Another difference is that when we learn a new motor skill we often begin by observing others and not surprisingly there is a fair amount of work showing that actual physical practice is better than just watching. But it turns out observing helps, too. For example, in one study people were asked to balance on a balance board. The board is mobile and you have to keep track of the balancing or your lack of balance and you have to continuously adjust your posture to maintain balance. For one-third of participants in this study they just practiced balancing on their own and they were given several practice sessions. The other groups of participants participated in the study in pairs. One-third of them participated by taking turns observing one trial and then trying the task on their own and then observing and then trying and in-between each turn participants were encouraged to talk to one another and share strategies and information.

The final third of participants took turns also but they did it differently. One participant first did all their practice turns and then the other participant did all their practice turns and then the two were allowed to talk. You'll note that this group had the same amount of physical practice, observation and dialogue as the middle group but their experiences weren't interwoven. They were just sort of distinct blocks.

To find out how well participants had learned they came back the next day and they were tested individually on the balance board. So this is a performance measure. Did you, in fact, learn to balance well? If you looked at a figure of the findings in this study what you would see is that all the groups learned regardless of how they practiced. They're all better at that test session than they were when they began. Further, you would see that during the learning itself the individual physical practice people actually started with better performance because they were getting more tries.

By the end of the learning phase at the test, the best group in terms of performance and learning is the pairs who took turns practicing, observing, and talking. So something was really useful in that experience of watching someone do it and then practicing what they did and maybe talking about strategies in-between. In fact, when the researchers looked at what kinds of dialogue participants engaged in they actually talked about strategies like bending your knees and focusing attention on a point and these strategies seemed useful.

Both of the paired groups actually had similar suggestions but only that interwoven turn taking group could hear a suggestion and immediately try it out and that may be what was key to helping observation be so effective for those individuals. Although observation is clearly helpful for motor learning one further and very interesting set of findings here suggests that observation can be more helpful for some people than for others and here the key difference is in expertise.

So one study that was looking at this kind of issue actually looked at brain activity in people observing piano playing. For the pianists, watching piano playing movements involved different brain activity than did watching other finger and hand movements, so pianists' brains actually looked like they were simulating the kind of activity involved in playing the piano when they were watching movements of another pianist or just hearing the soundtrack of pieces of music.

What this suggests is that depending on the motor skill to be learned, observation may function more effectively for people who already have a little bit of experience with a task. And it also brings us to the last topic of today's lecture, which is the topic of imagining or visualization in acquiring a motor skill.

Those expert pianists' brains looked like they were imagining the physical movements that would be required to generate the piece being played, and you may have also heard, in learning motor skills yourself, exhortations to visualize yourself making the basket or imagine yourself clearing the pole or other similar admonitions.

These kinds of statements are based on the idea that visualizing success in motor tasks is not only highly motivating but it also might actually be effective at helping people acquire the skill. So could visualization actually improve your movements? Let's take a closer look at this with a really cool study.

First, imagery is defined as the process of mentally rehearsing a motor act without moving the body. So imagining motor actions turns out to involve the same brain regions as doing the motor movements. It also turns out that imagining motor movements takes about as much time as doing the motor movement and it can even create the same changes in breathing and heart rate so it makes sense to think that imagining motor acts might actually help people learn them.

Now, to investigate this one team of neuroscientists in France looked at a grasping task. They asked participants to reach out and grasp an object with only the thumb and index fingers and then to take that object and insert it into a base. They moved the object around as the participant continued to perform the task so it might be here and then here and you'd have to change your movements a little bit each time to accommodate that. The object was also built in such a way that you had to grip it very precisely or you wouldn't be able to successfully do the task.

In this study participants were grouped into five distinct groups so one group was the physical only group. This was a kind of control group and they only did the task physically. And what this control group did was allow the researchers to know how many trials it takes to learn the task to perfection, and it turns out to be a lot of trials. It turns out to be 240 trials.

So three additional groups in the study did a combination of physical and imagine trials and they always began by imagining themselves doing the task a number of times and then they completed an additional set of physical trials until they got to 240. So these three additional groups ranged from imagining 25 percent of their trials to imagining 75 percent of the trials.

Finally, the researchers added one more control group for comparison purposes and this was a control group that imagined a totally unrelated motor task and then did the target grasping task 60 times. And what this group does is it helps us know whether just imagining any movement is what is helpful or whether it really is about visualizing the specific movement you're trying to learn. So these participants imagined rotating a dial to align with a tick mark.

In the imagery conditions, participants were asked to imagine executing the grasping task from beginning to end with themselves doing the task. And this was important. They were not visualizing somebody else and kind of an observation thing. They were really visualizing their own body, their own arm.

To look at the results we can do a number of things. What we can do first is to compare how long it takes people in different groups to do the first real trial. So for people in the all physical practice group this is the first trial they do. For the people in the 75 percent imagine group it means trial number 180, so they have imagined the action 179 times and now they are going to try it out for the first time physically. This comparison tells us whether imagining doing the task gives you any benefit in your first attempt at really doing the task. It's really cool. It does. For those people who imagined at least 120 trials, their first real attempt to do the task was significantly faster and better than the first real attempt for the people who did fewer trials.

Second, we can look at that last trial, that's trial number 240, and we can see how imagery and physical practice look in combination, and here we actually see no differences between the groups and what that means in practical terms is that the high imagery groups actually got a lot more learning out of fewer real practice attempts.

So finally, the researchers looked at different components of the movements and they found that overall performance on placing the object into the support base was improved for people who did 50–75% imagined trials. And, in fact, what that means is if you did a lot of imagined trials, you actually ended up having better learning of the second part of the movement. You didn't actually have better learning of the first grasping movement.

The take home message for the rest of us here is relatively straightforward. Imagery, visualizing yourself performing motor movements, can help in the acquisition of motor skills in two ways. It can actually help you gain more with less physical practice, and it can sometimes actually result in better outcomes.

So what we talked about in this lecture is the acquisition of motor skills large and small and we focused on some commonalities in that acquisition, including feedback and knowledge of results, the move from a concentrated focus to relatively non-conscious sources of feedback in the proprioceptive system, and on some issues that are relevant for real world learners like ourselves, the role of verbalization, the role of observation, and the role of imagery or visualization. In the case of visualization, what we go forward knowing is that observation and imagery can help us acquire motor skills more efficiently than simply physically practicing and in the case of observation and dialogue, perhaps, we have a lot more pleasure and a lot of fun via the social exchange.

Of course, once you know how to move, you can ask what sort of space you are moving through. That's also something that we learn and in the next lecture we'll pick up the topic of spatial learning, learning our way around the spaces that we inhabit.

Learning Our Way Around
Lecture 10

From very early infancy, we are equipped for learning about space and objects within it. As we get older, learning our way around happens first through navigation and eventually through the use of maps and other representations. These distinct ways of representing space have implications for what we learn, but in general, we're trying to build a cognitive map over time that allows us to represent space flexibly and with enough—though not necessarily precise—accuracy. Although navigation often involves conscious work, the spatial learning that arises from it is often relatively tacit.

Spatial Learning

- Spatial learning involves some aspects of skill but also some aspects of knowledge—representations of how the world is organized in space. Spatial learning problems are problems we share with all mobile creatures on the planet, most of which do some type of foraging or hunting activity to obtain food and water. Many mobile creatures—as varied as squirrels, birds, and human beings—store and must later retrieve food or other necessities from various locations in their environment.

- Spatial learning allows us to accomplish several important tasks, including orienting, which involves knowing where we are and where desired objects or places are in relation to our current position. In addition, we can navigate using spatial learning by integrating sensory and perceptual feedback into our orientation knowledge on a continuously updated basis.

- Many species have impressive capabilities for using sensory and perceptual information about the position of the Sun or Earth's magnetic pull to orient in truly amazing ways during long migrations across Earth

- For example, homing pigeons can fly directly home after being placed several hundred kilometers away in unfamiliar territory. In addition, honeybees can use magnetic fields to orient and navigate, making their ability to forage and return to their birth hive incredible.

- There are also distinct navigational tasks that vary in their demands, and two of those that matter to human beings are piloting and path integration. Piloting is finding a goal by familiar reference points, so it is a very typical navigational task for most animals and humans. This is the major task in getting to and from work and school.

- With path integration, you might wander around widely. Path integration happens for human beings on a daily basis when, for example, you run a bunch of errands and then return home via the most direct path to your house.

- Human beings can't read magnetic fields, but our spatial abilities are quite good. In fact, what we have in common with honeybees and other species is that we learn cognitive maps of our spaces. A cognitive map is a representation of a new space that will allow you to accomplish many different actions within the new location and to flexibly navigate that space.

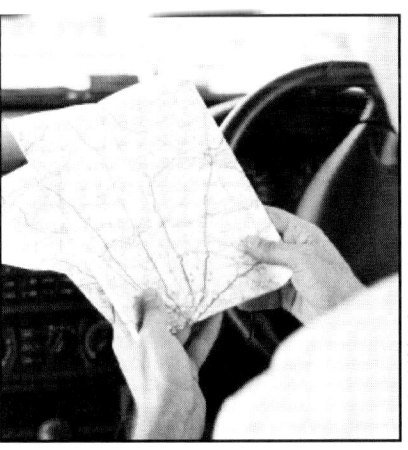

Our ability to build cognitive maps of spaces we observe is present very early in life.

- A good cognitive map shows us where we are, where important objects or landmarks are, and which possible paths we can travel to move around from one point to another within our space.

- For most humans in the modern world, there are a number of ways we encounter spatial information. Perhaps the most primary way is through direct perceptual experience.

- Perceptual experiences are both static—such as when you stand still and look at the array of items in a space—and dynamic— such as when you move around and through a new environment, learning what routes there are and what kinds of objects are within that environment.

- Our ability to make use of static visual perception, to build maps of spaces we're observing, is present very early in life. Research suggests that by three to four months of age, infants are already distinguishing between different areas of a spatial array that they look at. Spatial abilities are almost certainly part of our evolutionary heritage.

- As we get older, we can experience the spatial world in more ways by moving through the world so that we get some dynamic visual experience and by using abstract representations such as maps or verbal descriptions of a space.

Allocentric versus Egocentric Perspectives

- Allocentric perspectives of space are perspectives that are not necessarily specific to your own position within a space. A typical way to represent an allocentric view is to think about a map or to consider a mental model of a space, such as a floor plan of a house.

- One advantage of this perspective is that you can move it around and rotate it in different ways. Another is that you can consider how spaces within the house are related to one another more easily. An allocentric representation of a space does not change when you move to a different vantage point; it is helpful for path integration.

- Egocentric perspectives of space are perspectives that have to do with where you are standing and how you are moving. These are sometimes called route perspectives.

- In an egocentric perspective, what you represent of your house is the experience you have of walking or moving through the house. Egocentric perspectives are less flexible than allocentric ones, but they are one of the central ways that we experience spaces that we're in and arrays of objects that we move through.

- One of the important issues in spatial learning is how we move from what is in an egocentric perspective in our everyday experience to an allocentric one over time and with increased experience.

- There are some specific cases where egocentric perspectives are actually better than allocentric ones, including route knowledge. In addition, egocentric perspectives may be maximally useful for piloting.

- Research suggests that as people experience an environment through navigation, they increasingly build a more allocentric representation, beginning with landmarks that help them to orient, then connecting landmarks with routes, and finally integrating various routes to arrive at something more maplike.

- It is important to note that our cognitive maps are not veridical—that is, they are not precisely accurate in representing the world that we live in. Instead, they're cognitive approximations.

- We do much of our spatial learning without devoting exclusive attention to that process—that is, we pay attention to the immediate problem of getting from point A to point B. Over time, we make use of the experiences of getting from point A to point B and also to points C, D, E, and F. We make use of these experiences of getting around to build a more allocentric cognitive map.

- We often vary in our spatial learning goals. Sometimes we just want to learn the best route from point A to point B, and other times we really want to understand where we are and how different areas are located with respect to one another—other times, we really do want to have a map.

- Adults often use maps to learn more information about areas in addition to navigation, so to learn about these issues with adults requires us to look at how they use map-related information in learning in addition to using maps for navigation.

- If you're engaged in learning a new area, maps serve one set of needs. For example, if you want to get a sense of the layout of the entire space and how places in that space are related to each other. Navigation serves a different set of needs, such as getting from one point to another. Over time, navigation contributes to the building of an allocentric model, a more maplike model.

- This is probably because allocentric models are more effective for being able to navigate flexibly from any point to any other point. That is, for a specific navigation task, you may not need the layout of the entire space, but when you want to have options, the layout—the allocentric model—is a critical thing to have.

Spatial Learning and Gender
- Stereotypes about spatial functioning and gender abound, and there are a number of studies that show that men outperform women at spatial learning. Moreover, these gender differences are evident across multiple studies and even across multiple species.

- However, not all research supports the existence of a general male spatial advantage; it may depend on what the task is. Pierre Lavenex and Pamela Banta Lavenex suggest that we need to think about several things before we conclude that women are poorer at navigation and spatial learning than men.

- They suggest that we need to make sure we don't confuse spatial learning with other tasks that involve spatial abilities but aren't necessarily critical for developing a cognitive map. For example, rotating objects mentally is a common spatial ability task—and it's one in which men show a very strong advantage—but it's not critical for spatial navigation.

- In addition, they suggest that women typically show distinctive strategies for exploring an environment, even when they perform similarly well. Women are more likely to explore an environment extensively, which might result in poorer performance—depending on what counts as good performance.

- If you take a longer-term perspective, then getting lost has some longer-term value in terms of building a more complex and thorough map. This is true for both genders, even if one gender gets lost a bit more than the other.

Spatial Learning and Designing Spaces

- Planned complexity for a building has several features. One feature that makes buildings more or less complicated is the number of choice points, or hallway intersections. The more choice points you have, the more complicated the building is to learn. Another feature is how many signs there are and how visible they are.

- A broader array of issues affect learning to navigate a building, including visual access—how well you can see one part of the building from another—and architectural differentiation, which is how distinctive the different areas of the building are from one another.

- Research on the complexity of different buildings, which is determined by analyzing planned complexity, shows that buildings higher in complexity cause problems for people in navigating and make it take longer for people who work in those building to acquire a good allocentric map of the building.

- For buildings that are designed primarily for use by insiders, high planned complexity is fine because there is no need for a stranger to walk in and be able to navigate the building immediately with speed or accuracy. In other buildings—such as libraries, hospitals, and hotels—lower planned complexity is needed.

- Buildings requiring low planned complexity should be organized along one central axis, which makes them simpler to understand and reduces the number of choice points. In addition, these buildings need to maintain visual access. Finally, these buildings need to keep different areas distinct in color and form to help people figure out quickly where they are.

- In addition to properties of buildings, some of the problem is in human beings in general, but other aspects of the problem are specific to individuals. People bring assumptions when constructing a cognitive map, and they also tend to simplify and, therefore, distort their cognitive maps. In addition, some people are simply not good at navigation while others are, and researchers are only beginning to understand why that might be and what it means.

Suggested Reading

Allen, ed, *Human Spatial Memory.*

Carlson, Hoelscher, Shipley, and Dalton, "Getting Lost in Buildings."

Taylor, Naylor, and Chechile, "Goal-Specific Influences."

Questions to Consider

1. Given the research findings reported in this lecture, how might one best give directions to a stranger to an area? What about to a person familiar with the city?

2. How do you think the increasing prevalence of GPS and other technological solutions for navigation might influence our spatial learning in the future?

Learning Our Way Around
Lecture 10—Transcript

Imagine yourself in a new city. You've relocated and you have to figure out how to get to your office building from your new house. Or consider a different problem. As you have unpacked and put objects away in your new kitchen you've made a number of decisions about where your things will live. But now, facing the task of preparing a first meal you have to remember where in the kitchen you've placed the items you now need.

Last lecture we talked about motor learning, which is important for how you will flip that omelet you're about to make in your new kitchen. This time we're going to consider how you learn where things are in that kitchen or how to get from that kitchen to work.

These two sets of problems are problems of spatial learning. Spatial learning involves some aspects of skill but also some aspects of knowledge, representations of how the world is organized in space.

Spatial learning problems are problems we share with all mobile creatures on the planet. Most mobile creatures can be viewed as doing some type of foraging or hunting activity to get food and water and many mobile creatures, as varied as squirrels, birds and human beings, store and then later have to retrieve food or other necessities like a cell phone from various locations in their environment, and spatial learning allows us to accomplish several important tasks.

Orienting, which involves knowing where we are and where desired objects or places are in relation to use and our current position, but we can also navigate using spatial learning by integrating sensory and perceptual feedback into our orientation knowledge on a kind of continuously updated basis.

If you think about how complex these tasks are, it is rather magical, especially navigation, and many species have really impressive capabilities for using sensory and perceptual information about the position of the sun or the earth's magnetic pull to orient in truly amazing ways during long migrations across the earth.

For example, the Arctic tern spends summers breeding in the Arctic and then goes for the winter towards the Antarctic for feeding. Homing pigeons can fly directly home after being placed several hundred kilometers away in unfamiliar territory. Experienced pigeons can do this even when they were under anesthesia during their outbound journey.

Honeybees can also use magnetic fields to orient and navigate and that makes their ability to forage and return to their natal or birth hive incredible. They have, actually, a lot of flexibility. Some work by Fred Dyer has shown that when a bee colony fissions—that is, when it splits to form a daughter colony with a new queen—honeybees are able to very quickly learn their new hive location, even if it's close to the old hive, making that a difficult discrimination task. If the hive is removed they go back to that original birth hive and that tells us that they haven't forgotten their old route and location; rather, they learned new ones in a very quick and very efficient way.

There are also distinct navigational tasks that vary in their demands and two of those that matter a lot to human beings are piloting and path integration. Piloting is finding a goal by familiar reference points, so piloting is a very typical navigational task for most animals and humans. This is the major task in getting to and from work and school and play.

Path integration is a little bit different. In path integration you might wander around widely. For example, you might be wandering around in the forest hunting deer, but when it's time to go back to camp you take the straightest path home. This is also called dead reckoning. Path integration also happens for human beings on a daily basis when, for example, you run a bunch of errands and then you return home via the most direct path to your house.

Human beings can't read magnetic fields but our spatial abilities are not terrible. We are actually quite good. In fact, what we have in common with honeybees and other species is that we learn cognitive maps of our spaces. A cognitive map is a representation of the new space that will let you accomplish many different actions within the new location and to flexibly navigate that space.

A good cognitive map shows us where we are, where important objects or landmarks are, and the possible paths that we can travel to move around from one point to another within our space. A good cognitive map is a good thing, indeed, but where and how do we get one?

For most humans in the modern world there are actually a number of ways we encounter spatial information. Perhaps the most primary way is through direct perceptual experience. Perceptual experiences are both static, like when you stand still and look at the array of items in a space, and they are also dynamic, as when you move around and through a new environment and you learn what routes there are and what kinds of objects are within that environment.

Our ability to make use of static visual perception, to build maps of spaces we're observing, is present very early in our life. Research suggests that already by three to four months of age infants are distinguishing between different areas of a spatial array that they look at. Researcher Paul Quinn showed infants a very simple spatial array in which they looked at a screen that was divided by a horizontal or a vertical bar into two halves so some infants saw an up/down half and others saw a left/right half.

He then habituated the infants, got them used to and a little bit bored with a diamond shape that would be located on, for example, the left half of the display so this means, again, he showed them the image until they're bored and they're kind of looking away. They're not very interested anymore. Then, Paul Quinn shows them the diamond in a new location, and he did that in one of two ways: He either showed those babies who had been looking at the diamond on the left, he either showed them a diamond on the lower left when it was in the upper left, or he showed them a diamond on the other half of the vertical bar that is in a different part of the spatial array the babies were looking at.

Infants showed a preference for looking at the diamond. They showed greater dishabituation when that diamond had moved to the opposite half of the space. What this means: If very little infants are able to distinguish between different halves of space, what it means is that babies are already learning where stuff is. They are already using just a static visual to build a cognitive map of the space that they're looking at. That map they're building includes different halves, so a left and a right half or an up and a down half. It also includes ideas about where objects are in the space the baby has mapped; that is, where is the diamond located? And this makes sense because spatial abilities are almost certainly part of our evolutionary heritage and as such we'd expect to see them very early in our lives.

As we get older we can experience the spatial world in more ways by moving through the world so we get some dynamic visual experience, and by using abstract representations like maps or verbal descriptions of a space. We can also ask is it better for me to devote time to driving around my new city or wandering around my new office building or is it better and more efficient to study a map of the city and how well do we make use of those descriptions people give about how to get to a specific place to add and extend these kinds of cognitive maps?

Let's first introduce a little bit of terminology to help us think about these issues. One important distinction in this research is between two different perspectives that you might have on space. Allocentric perspectives are perspectives that are not necessarily specific to your own position within a space. A typical way to represent an allocentric view is to think about a map or to consider a kind of mental model of a space. For example, if you were thinking about your house, you can do so in an allocentric way by imagining the floor plan.

If you do this you can see that this perspective has a number of advantages. One is that you can move it around and rotate it in different ways. Another is that you can consider how spaces within the house are related to one another more easily. You can see multiple possible routes by which you can move from point A to point B within your house. You can also make judgments more easily about how far apart two areas of the house are or where one object is in relation to another object in the house.

An allocentric representation of a space does not change when you move to a different vantage point and it is an allocentric view that's helpful for path integration.

Egocentric perspectives are a different way of thinking about space and these are perspectives that have to do with where we are standing and how we are moving. These are sometimes called route perspectives.

In an egocentric perspective what you represent of your house is the experience you have of walking or moving through the house. Egocentric perspectives are less flexible than allocentric ones but, importantly, egocentric perspectives are one of the central ways that we actually experience spaces that we're in and arrays of objects that we move through. So one of the important issues in spatial learning is how we move from what is in an egocentric perspective in our everyday experience to an allocentric one over time and with increased experience.

And there are some specific cases where egocentric perspectives are actually better. One of them is route knowledge. Egocentric perspectives can be very useful and may be even maximally useful for piloting.

Now, early work by Barbara Tversky and her colleagues, including Holly Taylor, suggested that people attempt to build an allocentric representation from their experiences regardless of how those experiences unfold. So for example, in one study they gave people either a route-based description or a survey-like description. The route-based description might sound something like this. To find the laboratory as you enter the building turn left. You will pass the main departmental office, the office of the Chair, the office of the Associate Chair and two additional faculty offices. At the end of the hallway turn right. You will see two classroom doors on the left and then a large wooden door on your right. That door leads to the reception area of our laboratory.

In contrast, a survey-like description would sound like this. The building is rectangular with rectangular hallways that are situated between a central core of rooms and an additional rectangular layout of rooms around the outer walls of the building. Faculty offices and the main office are situated on the southern hallway along both sides of the hall. Classrooms and laboratory rooms are situated on the western hallway with classrooms along the outer walls and laboratories on the inner walls. Our laboratory is the first laboratory door on the west hallway.

Afterwards, participants were queried about various aspects of the spatial layout that they had learned to assess what kind of cognitive map they had created. Participants were equally quick and accurate in responding to questions regardless of whether they received a route-based description or a more survey-like allocentric description.

What Tversky and Taylor concluded is that people actually attempt to build a survey-like allocentric representation immediately, even when they are getting information from a more egocentric perspective.

Other work suggests that as people experience an environment through navigation, they increasingly build a more allocentric representation beginning with landmarks that help them to orient, then connecting landmarks with routes and finally integrating various routes to arrive at something more map-like.

It is interesting and also important to note that our cognitive maps are not veridical—that is, they are not precisely accurate in representing the world that we live in. Instead, they're cognitive approximations; they're representations that work well enough.

Here's an exercise in using one of your cognitive maps. Without consulting a real map, which city lies farther east, New York City or Chicago? How about Reno, Nevada and San Diego, California? Many people incorrectly respond that Reno is east of San Diego and this happens, actually, to not be the case. We make this error because our cognitive maps of the United States are not veridical representations of maps we have seen; rather, they are organized along various geographic boundaries like state boundaries and country boundaries and the Pacific Ocean. When we are asked to answer questions based on our map, that organization leads us astray. The states of California and Nevada and the inland versus coastal location of these two cities leads us to make an incorrect prediction. That prediction actually shows us that our maps are often more regular and more squared off than real spaces.

As implied by early behaviorist work that shows tacit learning of mazes by rats, we do a lot of our spatial learning without devoting explicit attention to that process—that is, what we pay attention to is the immediate problem we have of getting from point A to point B. Over time we make use of the experiences of getting from point A to point B and also to point C, D, E and F. We make use of these experiences of getting around to build a more allocentric cognitive map.

In some more recent work Taylor and colleagues got interested in the issue of whether our goals for learning a spatial environment were relevant to how we represent the environment in cognitive maps. So it is the case that we often vary in our spatial learning goals. Sometimes we actually just want to learn the best route from point A to point B. Other times we actually really want to understand where we are and how different areas are located with respect to one another. Other times we really do want to have a map and might these different goals actually affect the strategies we use in spatial learning and our spatial learning outcomes.

Consider the following example study. In this study children were actually asked to learn the layout of a fun house or they were asked to learn the best route through the fun house, and kids did very different things to learn about the environment depending on which goals they were asked to pursue.

So kids who were asked to learn the layout of the fun house spent more time in more rooms and they also used a slide in the fun house to help them get a bird's eye perspective. And those kids, actually, then had better knowledge about how rooms were related to one another within the fun house.

But adults often use maps to learn more information about areas in addition to navigation, so to learn about these issues with adults requires us to look at how adults use map-related information in learning in addition to using maps for navigation.

To do this, Taylor and colleagues asked people to do one of two learning tasks. They were either asked to learn the layout of the Psychology Department at Tufts University—that is, form an allocentric map of the psych department—or they were asked to learn the fastest routes between rooms and complexes, and this would make use of a more egocentric cognitive map of that same area.

Participants were then assigned to either learn by wandering around the department by actually engaging in navigation or by studying a map. So you have two goals, a layout versus a route goal, and you have two types of information, a route-based navigation experience or an actual map.

After the learning phase, participants were tested in a variety of ways to see what they had learned about the spatial layout. They were asked to estimate the distances between two locations. They were asked to describe how different rooms were related to other rooms, and they were challenged to figure out the fastest route between the rooms.

For tasks that required route-based knowledge participants with a route goal were more accurate and in some cases learning through navigation was superior. So remember the idea of transfer-appropriate encoding where how well you learn is affected by how similar your encoding is to the way in which you're going to need to use the knowledge you've acquired? This is a prime example. People who had had a route goal assigned learned through navigation ended up being better at the route-based knowledge task.

For tasks that assessed survey or allocentric perspective knowledge, like describing how different rooms in the building were related to one another in space, goals didn't really turn out to matter but the learning method mattered a lot and in this case maps were superior at helping people learn that allocentric map.

So the take home message here is that if you're engaged in learning a new area maps serve one set of needs. For example, if you want to get a sense of the layout of the entire space and how places in that space are related to each other. Navigation serves a different set of needs best. That is, of course, navigation needs, getting from one point to another, but over time navigation is going to contribute to the building of an allocentric model, a more map-like model.

This is probably because those allocentric models are more effective for being able to navigate flexibly from any point to any other point. That is, for a specific navigation task you may not need the layout of the entire space, but when you want to have options, the layout, that allocentric model, is a critical thing to have.

It is hard to address spatial learning without considering gender. Stereotypes about gender, wayfinding, willingness to ask for directions and spatial functioning abound and there are a fair number of studies that show sex differences in spatial learning and these studies usually show that men outperform women at spatial learning. Moreover, those differences are actually evident across multiple studies and even across multiple species.

Having said that, it may depend on what the task is. Not all research supports the existence of a general male spatial advantage. Looking only at human studies, like the study described above in which people were given spatial information in different ways and were asked to achieve different goals while learning a space, in those studies no gender differences in performance were observed.

Another study by Lavenex and Lavenex asked men and women to learn a real environment, one that included various landmarks and had rewards positioned around the space. They also found no gender differences. It's instructive to look at how they make sense of their findings versus previous work on navigating spaces for rewards. They suggest that we need to think about several things before we conclude that women are poorer at navigation and spatial learning.

First, we need to make sure we don't confuse spatial learning—what we've been talking about in this lecture—with other tasks that involve spatial abilities but aren't necessarily critical for developing a cognitive map. For example, rotating objects mentally is a common spatial ability task. It's one in which men show a very strong advantage, but it's not critical for spatial navigation and wayfinding of the type we've been emphasizing here.

Second, they suggest that women in their study show some distinctive strategies for exploring the environment, even when they did similarly well. So most importantly, women were more likely to explore the environment extensively, and Lavenex and Lavenex suggests this may result in poorer performance depending on what you count as good performance. If you're going for efficiency women will be viewed as doing badly if they engage in excess exploration. That's not critical for solving the task.

If, on the other hand, you take a longer-term perspective then, as I say when I've recently moved, getting lost has some longer-term value in terms of building a more complex and thorough map, and that's true for both genders, even if one gender gets lost a bit more than the other.

Finally, I want to consider some issues about designing spaces in relation to our spatial learning. When I finished my Ph.D. I did postdoctoral research at the Max Planck Institute for Human Development, which is located in Berlin, Germany. It's a beautiful building to look at. When you enter the building, you're in a large spacious lobby area and you have diagonally oriented staircases that go up to various hallways, and the hallways are also diagonally oriented and have offices to one side with central gathering areas placed periodically around the hallways. The building itself has this odd and irregular shape that surrounds an internal garden area, and you can enter that garden area from the ground floor cafeteria.

Here's the catch. The three staircases that appear to all take you to one location and one level but that turns out not to be true and the hallways all look exactly the same. This means that when you begin to work in this building it's very easy to get lost and actually it happens to virtually every new employee for at least one or two months.

Most of us have encountered at least one such building in our lifetimes. There's another building of this sort on my current campus and I haven't had to learn that building, so whenever I have to go to a meeting there my strategy is to wander around looking disoriented until a staff person from the building takes me and walks me directly to my destination. There are buildings that may be deliberately designed to keep us wandering around merchandise shelves because more time in the store means more dollars at the register. So you can ask is it me and my lack of spatial learning ability? What makes buildings like this? We could say they're just complicated, but that seems a little bit like sidestepping the issue because what does it really mean when we say a building is complicated?

So it turns out researchers have actually tried to address this and planned complexity, as they call it for a building, has several features. So one feature that makes buildings more or less complicated is the number of choice points or hallway intersections. The more choice points you have the more complicated the building is to learn.

Another feature related to planned complexity is how many signs there are and how visible they are, so both of the buildings I have mentioned lack any signs that can help people figure out where they are in the building and where they might need to go.

A broader array of issues affect learning to navigate a building and these include visual access, how well can you see one part of the building from another, and architectural differentiation, which is a fancy way of saying how distinctive are different areas of the building from one another?

Thinking about these three features suggests that my most difficult building is, indeed, a very difficult building. Visual access to the hallways from the main entrance area is poor. The hallways have corners that impede visibility of the more distinctive commons areas. The hallways all look exactly the same and the complexity of the plan is generally large. There are a lot of nonlinear hallways and in many offices the floors also slant into one another so it's difficult to keep track of what floor you're on.

Research on the complexity of different buildings using this way of counting up planned complexity shows that buildings higher in complexity cause problems for people in wayfinding and make it longer for people who work in those building to acquire a good allocentric map of the building.

For buildings that are designed primarily for use by insiders, like the building where I did my postdoctoral work, this is fine. There is no need for a stranger to walk in and be able to navigate the building immediately with speed or accuracy. But in other buildings, like libraries, hospitals and hotels, you need lower planned complexity because you need strangers to be able to quickly come in and navigate the building and acquire a sense of a plan.

So what should these buildings have in terms of design with this idea in mind? Well, one idea is that these buildings need to be organized along one central axis. That makes them simpler to understand and it reduces the number of choice points.

A second idea here is that those buildings need to maintain visual access. You need to be able to see different parts of the building from other parts of the building. And finally, one idea is that these buildings need to keep different areas distinct in color and form and other properties that help people figure out quickly where they are.

In addition to properties of buildings, of course, some of the problem really is in us and some of it is in human beings in general but other aspects of the problem are specific to individuals. So a general human problem is that people bring assumptions to bear on constructing a cognitive map and so, for example, people tend to assume that every floor in a building is similarly structured whether or not that is the case.

People also tend to simplify and therefore distort their cognitive maps, and in some more complicated buildings this distortion will actually be a problem in ways that our Reno and San Diego confusion generally isn't such a big deal.

Finally, some of us really are not so good at navigation while others are and researchers are only beginning to understand why that might be and what it means.

To summarize, we come into the world equipped for learning about space and objects within it from very early infancy and as we get older learning our way around happens first through navigation and eventually through the use of maps and other representations. These distinct ways of representing a space have implications for what we learn, but it looks like in general, over time what we're always trying to build is a cognitive map that lets us represent space flexibly and with enough, though not necessarily precise, accuracy.

Although wayfinding often involves a lot of attention and conscious work, the spatial learning that arises from it is often relatively tacit meaning we don't know we have that knowledge until we have to call on it.

This is somewhat distinct from some of the types of learning we have talked about so far, and we'll turn next to another type of learning that is often also relatively tacit and that's learning to tell stories. Even though that kind of learning, too, is often acquired without conscious attention it's very distinct in other ways from spatial and motor learning.

Learning to Tell Stories
Lecture 11

Storytelling is an area of learning that is acquired in the service of other activities with repeated practice and assistance from adults and others. In this way, learning to tell stories is similar to learning our way around a new town. The stories we learn to tell reinforce our membership in such groups as our family, subculture, economic class, and larger culture. We start out learning to tell stories, and then we use storytelling as a way to learn, which brings us to a shift from learning a skill—telling stories—to learning knowledge.

The Importance of Storytelling

- Storytelling is a crucial way that we connect with other people. It is also an important learning mechanism for learning about ourselves and about the social world across our lifespan. It's also an important way that we teach other people.

- People first learn to tell stories and then they're able to learn from stories, and through storytelling, we can represent experiences that are displaced in time and space. Unlike other species, we can talk about what happened there and then, and we can make it part of our here and now.

- The flexibility we have in being able to talk about there and then allows us to keep drawing on past experience to make sense of the present. In this way, stories are a fundamental mechanism for learning—they're a fundamental way that we can engage in elaborative encoding.

- Learning to tell stories is an important way in which we become members of our culture because part of learning to tell stories is learning to tell them in the culturally appropriate way, which varies from place to place.

- What all of us learn through storytelling is to narrate our own experiences in a way that is ordered in time, communicate the essential details of what happened in those experiences, and make it clear enough to our audience why they should listen.

- The experiences we have are rich in sensory and perceptual details, so to translate that effectively into a verbal form isn't an easy task. Storytelling also requires adaptation to the audience— to what the audience does or does not know and to what the audience is interested in or not.

Storytelling helps us to bond with other people; it is also an important learning mechanism.

Features of a Good Story

- A good story has at least four features, and children learn to employ these features across childhood and even into adulthood and middle age. Two of these features were named by Jerome Bruner as the landscape of action and the landscape of consciousness.

- An adequate story has to communicate what happened, which is the landscape of action. However, a story that communicates only what happened isn't sufficient; a good story also conveys the landscape of consciousness—the thoughts, desires, and emotions of the people involved in the event.

- Stories also do two additional things that we have to learn to do: They convey the way events happened in time, and they make an experience coherent, sensible, and meaningful by putting all the action and consciousness elements in order and by presenting them in such a way that the story has a point, or larger meaning.

- We're not born with the capability to tell stories that are good along these four features. From early childhood and into adulthood, our stories become longer and convey more of the landscape of action and consciousness.

- As we get into adulthood and middle age, we continue to sharpen our ability to convey the landscape of consciousness, which changes in its nature over time.

- For young children, the landscape of consciousness is reflected in how the child felt, which emotions were experienced, and what the child wanted. By middle age, we're still talking about how we feel and what we want, but we're also talking about what an event signifies about our values and morals.

- From early childhood into adulthood, we become more sophisticated at conveying the sequence of our experiences and at telling our stories in ways that have more meaning. We even acquire the ability to tell stories with flashbacks and more complex structures.

- These developments in personal storytelling about our own experiences are mirrored by age-related changes in the ability to narrate fictional experiences as well. However, these findings come from studies of age differences in how people tell stories—what they don't reveal is how we learn to tell those stories.

- Particular developmental changes allow us to acquire new storytelling skills, but this process also involves learning.

- The developmental precursors for learning to tell stories in the way that we do as adults include language, memory, and self-awareness. The emergence of language is a critical factor.

- A second developmental factor involves memory function. Basic capacities for memory function are in place by the end of a baby's first year, but memory systems mature up until about age eight, which is when these systems function the way they do in adults.

- A third factor is that learning to tell stories about our experiences also requires a sense of the self that is thought to emerge by about the age of 18 months.

- Once those factors are in place, the major learning process for storytelling is immersion in learning. Just as with motor learning and spatial learning, a major force in learning this task is to just do it.

- In addition, the task involves a relatively implicit way of learning. Children come home and tell a story about their day to share information, seek comfort, or share a laugh. Through the pursuit of those other goals, they simultaneously are learning how to structure a story.

- Early in the process, children need help from adults and older children to build a structure in which they can tell a story. This process is called scaffolding by developmental psychologists.

- For young children learning to tell stories, scaffolding from parents often looks a lot more like parents telling a story around a child's minimal contribution.

- Over time, children's stories develop into elaborated and more sophisticated stories that are more accessible to an uninformed audience. As children get older and show more capability at telling stories, parents pull back and ask their children to put more of themselves into the story.

- Children also learn how to gauge from a listener whether they are paying attention, how to shift their story to get attention, how to recognize that the listener looks confused and provide clarification, and how to note the facts and also include the larger point of a story.

- Parents differ in the ways that they scaffold their children's storytelling, and those differences shape what children learn about how to tell a story.

The Elaboration of Stories

- Some stories are told with rich detail and vivid emotion, and others are told more sparsely or in a more taciturn way. Robyn Fivush, Elaine Reese, and their colleagues have looked at how parents conarrate stories with their children from very early in life. Broadly speaking, they find that there are two kinds of mothers: elaborative and repetitive.

- Elaborative mothers encourage their children to express a broad range of information about the event, including what happened; who was there; why the event occurred; and what the child and others thought, felt, and wanted. By contrast, repetitive mothers emphasize accuracy; they're interested in a few key details but not in a broad, elaborative approach.

- Fivush and Reese have found that by elementary school age, children of elaborative mothers include more detail and vividness, and they talk more about emotions and about meaning than children whose mothers are repetitive.

- Importantly, the act of telling stories is fundamentally an act of learning about our own experiences and history. Therefore, when we tell a story, we are retrieving and re-encoding the experiences of our lives.

- As a result, elaborative children may end up remembering more of their own experiences because their ways of learning those events through telling them were more elaborate. They used deeper encoding strategies to learn about their own lives.

- The way we tell stories about our experiences has lasting effects on how we remember those experiences and what we learned from them. Furthermore, telling yourself a story of what you learned can be an effective reinforcement for learning in many contexts.

- A more close-grained study of elaborative mothers has suggested that they are warm and affectionate, provide encouragement and support to a child as the child attempts to tell a story, and provide clarity and assistance on how to search memory and how to reconstruct an event.

Storytelling and Culture
- Within psychology, Chinese and American cultures are viewed as varying quite a bit in their relative emphasis on individual distinctiveness, which is emphasized more in the United States, versus relationship obligations and duties, which are emphasized more in China.

- Qi Wang and her colleagues looked at mother-child storytelling about the child's experiences in Chinese and American families, and they found that Chinese mothers focused less on lengthy and elaborative rehearsals about the way the event highlighted the child's unique characteristics.

- In addition, they found that Chinese adults had shorter and less detailed personal memories that had themes of duties and relationships when compared with American adults.

- Recent proposals by Dan McAdams have focused on what he views as a characteristically and peculiarly American way of telling stories called redemptive storytelling, in which we talk about how the bad, negative, traumatic, and tragic were made good, somehow, by a more optimistic ending.

- We all belong to multiple cultures and subcultures, and in fact, some findings suggest that the kind of story that works within one part of our lives could be less effective in other contexts.

- Shirley Brice Heath examined language use in low-income European-American and African-American communities as well as in a middle-class white community. She found that low-income African-American children were gifted storytellers. By contrast, the European-American groups seemed to focus on the function of stories to inform, resulting in a push for accuracy.

- The implications for school are potentially problematic: The creative storytelling rewarded in one's community may not be an easy fit with the school's orientation toward accuracy, and the creative talent of the more entertainment-oriented storytelling may be underappreciated in some school settings.

- One of the least understood aspects of learning to tell stories is how we learn to adapt our stories for different social contexts. One of the things we have to learn over time about telling stories is how to successfully craft the story for different audiences and different purposes.

- Many studies show that by the age of three, children know the difference between reminiscing, telling stories together with other people who experienced the event, versus recounting—telling a story to someone who wasn't there and therefore needs more background information and explanation.

- For the children studied, children who are middle class and predominantly white or Asian appear to be more oriented toward recounting—telling to share information rather than for entertaining.

- By adolescence, we know that we should edit versions of stories to not offend parents or other people around us. However, how we learn to use narratives in context-specific ways represents an open question in this area of learning.

Suggested Reading

Brice-Heath, *Ways with Words.*

McAdams, *The Redemptive Self.*

Questions to Consider

1. Elementary teachers often speak of a shift from learning to read in kindergarten and first grade to reading to learn in the later elementary years. Might a similar shift characterize learning and stories—from learning to tell stories to learning from or through telling stories?

2. Stories aren't always true, as entertainment-oriented storytelling shows. If stories are not true, does this undermine the notion that we are learning from them? Are we learning wrong information from stories? Why or why not?

Learning to Tell Stories
Lecture 11—Transcript

Last lecture we discussed how we learn our way around both by actually navigating spaces and by looking at maps and other representations. Today we'll talk about learning to tell stories, and this is one of my primary research interests.

On the surface this seems like a totally different thing to learn. It's all talk no moving. But as we'll see we actually learn to tell stories by doing it, and in that way it's a little more like learning our way around or learning to move than you might have thought. But first, why would we worry about learning to tell stories? Why is this even important to understand? Well, it turns out there are a few reasons.

First, storytelling is a crucial way that we connect with other people. Storytelling helps us to bond with other people. It also helps us to learn about ourselves what we can and cannot do, what we like and do not like, and even to figure out how we can be the same person now as ten years ago in spite of a vast array of changes in our lives.

Storytelling is also an important learning mechanism for learning about yourself and the social world across your lifespan. It's also an important way that we teach other people, and some of this we already talked about a little bit earlier. Recall that Emily's childhood monologues in her crib were a kind of early storytelling and what that storytelling helped Emily to learn were scripts about everyday events in her life.

In other words, people first learn to tell stories and then they're able to learn from stories, and through storytelling we can represent experiences that are displaced in time and space. We can talk about what happened there and then and we can make it part of our here and now.

This is not something animals appear to do when they're trained with human symbol systems. They use those systems to talk about the here and now only and the flexibility we have in being able to talk about there and then allows us to keep drawing on past experience to make sense of the present, and in this way stories are a fundamental mechanism for learning. They're a fundamental way that we can engage in elaborative encoding.

In this lecture we'll consider how we learn to tell stories over our lifespan and how this very different task has more in common with learning to dance or navigate than you might think.

Also, learning to tell stories is an important way in which we become members of our culture because part of learning to tell stories is learning to tell them in the culturally-appropriate way and that's going to vary from place to place.

To begin with I also need to make another important note for you. We need to consider in thinking about storytelling what is learned by all of us rather than to focus on unusual or impressive storytelling abilities like those of comedians, scriptwriters, film directors, novelists and other people who actually make their living by telling stories. So we're going to be focusing today on what all of us learn, which is to narrate our own experiences in a way that is ordered in time, communicates the essential details of what happened in those experiences, and make it clear enough to our audience why they should listen.

To do this is a complex task because the experiences we have are rich in sensory and perceptual details. They're visual. They are visceral and they have a lot of detail and to translate all that richness effectively into a verbal form isn't going to be an easy task, and storytelling requires adaptation to the audience. To what the audience does or does not know, which means providing enough background information but not too much and to what the audience is interested in or not. Shortening the parts of the story that the audience will find less interesting or which are known and therefore not important to highlight.

A good story has at least four features and children learn to employ these features across childhood and even into adulthood and middle age. Two of those features were named by Jerome Bruner as the landscape of action and the landscape of consciousness. An adequate story, a decent enough story, has to communicate what happened. Who was there? When and where things occurred and so on, and this is the content that Bruner called the landscape of action.

But a story that communicates only what happened isn't sufficient so Bruner noted that a good story also conveys what he called the landscape of consciousness. A good story tells us what it felt like and it conveys the thoughts and desires and the emotions of the people involved in the event.

Stories also do two additional things that we have to learn to do. They convey the way events happened in time. They don't always do so by telling events in sequential order but they give us enough information to reconstruct that order. They also make an experience coherent and sensible and meaningful, and they do that by putting all those action and consciousness elements both in order and also presenting them in such a way that the story has a point or a larger meaning.

We're not born with the capability to tell stories that are good along these four features. From early childhood into adulthood our stories get longer and they end up conveying more of the actions and more of the landscape of consciousness, as well. I'm going to have you consider two examples and these come from my own research in conjunction with collaborator Cecilia Wainryb and the examples are from a seven-year-old and a 15-year-old participant in a series of studies we did.

> Me and Julie were laughing. And then, … then, um, Ariel and Jasmine, they pushed me. And they're like, "Sorry, I didn't mean to." But, it was on purpose 'cause I saw them do it. And I heard them say that and then, we were hiding so they don't hit us and hurt us, and then, um, then we got out 'cause we forgot.

Here's a second story.

> It's not very bad but um … the other, I think it was like a week ago. I have a friend named Lisa, and lately she's not as close of friends as we used to be because we don't have as many classes together this year. And she was talking with me and she came up to me in the hall and she was acting really excited because she's one of those

people that likes to, you know, come up and say, "Oh, how are you doing?" and give you a big hug. And, she came up and she started talking with me, and I started talking with her. But then this girl came up who she has lately been becoming friends with.

These two examples, even though one is only the beginning of what's a quite long and elaborated story, showcased differences in the way that children of different ages represent actions and represent consciousness, and they also showed differences in how children of different ages can show you clearly in a story the order of events and can make a story meaningful and understandable, can make a story have a point. In all cases the adolescent story has more facts. It has more of the landscape of consciousness. It is more ordered and it also is better at conveying the larger point of the story. The meaning the story held for that adolescent.

As we get into adulthood and middle age, we continue to sharpen our ability to convey the landscape of consciousness and that landscape actually changes in its nature over time. For young kids the landscape of consciousness is reflected in how the child felt, the emotions that were experienced, and what the child wanted, the child's desires.

By middle age in adulthood we're still talking about how we feel and what we want but we're also talking about what an event signifies about our values and our morals. In other words, the landscape of consciousness begins to have a much more long, temporal scope. It involves things that are true of us over a long time.

From early childhood into adulthood we become more sophisticated at conveying the sequence of our experiences and in also telling our stories in ways that make a point, that have more meaning. And we even acquire the ability to tell stories with flashbacks and more complex structures. We don't have to follow a linear time order sequence anymore.

These developments in personal storytelling about our own experiences are actually mirrored by age-related changes in the ability to narrate fictional experiences, as well. But these findings come from studies of age differences in how people tell stories, and what they don't really reveal is how we learn to tell those stories. How do we go from the kind of story that a seven- or eight-year-old tells to the kind of story that a 40-year-old tells?

Now, some of that story is developmental and by that I mean particular developmental changes allow us to acquire new storytelling skills but some of that story is also clearly learning.

Early in childhood at least three things have to be in place before we can learn to tell stories so there are three developmental factors. One critical factor and very obvious factor is the emergence of language. It's very hard to tell a story as we understand that act without having language.

A second developmental factor involves memory function. I told you that basic capacities for memory functioning are in place by the end of a baby's first year but the fact is also that memory systems mature up until about age eight and it's only by about age eight that you see memory systems functioning the way they do in adults.

A third, perhaps, more striking and interesting factor is that learning to tell stories about our experiences also requires a sense of the self that is thought to emerge by about the age of 18 months. That's not to say that little babies don't have a sense of self earlier than that but rather by 18 months what babies can do is they can recognize their own image in a mirror and so this is something like the understanding that you can talk about yourself as an object of regard. So these three things, language, memory and self-awareness or self-recognition, appear to be developmental precursors for learning to tell stories in the way that we do as adults.

Once those things are in place the major learning process for storytelling is immersion and involvement in learning, in telling stories. So just as with motor learning and spatial learning, a major force in learning this task is to just do it.

Also, because the task is learned by doing it's going to involve a relatively implicit way of learning. That is, it isn't that little kids come home and tell a story about their day with this goal that they're going to learn to tell a story about their day. Rather, children come home and tell a story about their day with some other purpose in mind: They want to share information; they want to seek comfort; they need a parental advocate; they want to share a laugh. Through that action of pursuing those other goals they also simultaneously are learning how to structure a story.

Early in the process kids can't do this alone. They need help from adults and older kids and that help is called scaffolding by developmental psychologists and what it means is that adults help children to build a structure in which they can tell a story. And scaffolding, which we'll actually come back to in the last lecture, is one of the important ways that other people, coaches and teachers and experts, help someone learn to do a difficult task.

For young children learning to tell stories, scaffolding from parents often looks a lot more like parents telling a story around a child's minimal contribution, and to give you some idea of what this looks like I'm going to give you an example from my own life. This is an event, which we often label as my son's first story, and it happened when he was around 18–20 months of age. My son entered the bathroom and he had his teddy bear with him and the teddy bear was sopping wet and leaving a trail of liquid behind it and I said to him, "Thomas, what happened to Teddy? Goodness," and Thomas looked at me and he gave me a huge triumphant grin and he said, "Plop."

Now, let me fill in the gaps in the story for you because it is likely that you are thinking that's pretty cryptic, so my son had dropped his teddy bear in the dog's drinking water bowl and he was really thrilled by the sound that it made and then he went to find me in the bathroom to tell me what had happened.

As I said, my son was 18–20 months old or so when the story was told and his contribution, though it was the punch line, was pretty minimal, and you can also see that the story or understanding the story requires a lot of filling in for someone who wasn't there and wasn't part of the experience. So even with help there's no story here as we conventionally understand it, but what did happen in this event is that in that interaction what Thomas learned was that he needed to explain what happened up until that end point.

He didn't learn it based on one try but several years later he's fully able to tell a story with drama and still he can pull off the punch line.

Now, based on the findings I reported earlier, we know that over time kids' stories develop into the kind of lengthy and elaborated and more sophisticated stories that are more accessible to an uninformed audience. In other words, kids figure out how to tell stories for real and they do so because kids are repeatedly involved in conversations like that minimal one and from that involvement they learn what to include in a story and how to organize it for other people. As children get older and show more capability at telling stories, parents pull back and they actually do less and they ask their children to put more of themselves into the story.

Children also learn some other important things like how to gauge from a listener whether they are paying attention and how to shift their story to get attention, how to recognize that the listener looks confused and provide clarification, and how to make sure that they both say the facts of what happened and also include the meanings and the larger point of a story.

Differences in the behavior of parents around storytelling with their kids turn out to really matter in this process. That is, parents turn out to differ in the way that they scaffold their children's storytelling, and those differences shape what children learn about how you tell a story.

To look at this let's consider the elaboration of stories. Some stories are told with rich detail and vivid emotion and others are told more sparsely or in a more taciturn way. Robyn Fivush, Elaine Reese, and their colleagues have looked at how parents co-narrate stories with their children from very early in life. In some studies they begin with 18-month-olds, and what they find is that broadly speaking there are two kinds of mothers and they label these moms elaborative and repetitive.

I want to note that these differences are probably evident in fathers and other people, as well, but in this area of research it's mothers that have been the most thoroughly studied. Elaborative mothers do a variety of things to encourage their kids to say more about an event. That's why they're called elaborative. They encourage their kids to express a broad range of information about the event. They encourage their kids to talk about what happened, who was there, why the event occurred, what the child thought and felt and wanted, what others thought and felt and wanted, and so on.

Repetitive mothers, by contrast, they appear to look at this job of telling a story with their child with the idea of getting the right few details, so they emphasize accuracy and they're interested in a few key details but not in this kind of broad and elaborative approach.

A couple interesting things about these styles among mothers is that they're stable over time. That is, elaborative moms tend to stay elaborative if you bring them back over and over again and look at how they tell stories with their kids. These differences are also somewhat specific to personal storytelling. That is, moms who are elaborative about personal stories are not necessarily really elaborate, vivid readers of fictional books to their kids; rather, they're really about how we tell stories about our own lives.

Over time Fivush and Reese and their colleagues and collaborators have followed children whose mothers were initially classified as elaborative or repetitive and they find some interesting things. By elementary school age children of elaborative mothers are telling stories quite differently than children of repetitive mothers. Children of elaborative mothers include more detail, more vividness. They talk more about emotions and they talk more about meaning than children whose mothers are repetitive.

A different way to think about those from the perspective of this class is that mothers' scaffolding of children's early storytelling helps to teach children how to tell stories about their experiences, and for elaborative mothers they're teaching their children to talk about their experiences with rich detail, and for repetitive mothers they're teaching their kids to not put too much detail into those stories.

Importantly, telling stories serves as a way of rehearsing or practicing the experiences of our lives, and in other words the act of telling stories is fundamentally an act of learning about our own experiences and our own history so when we tell a story we are retrieving and re-encoding the experiences of our lives.

So it shouldn't surprise you that those elaborative kids may end up remembering more of their own experiences because their ways of learning those events through telling them were more elaborate. They used deeper encoding strategies to learn about their own lives.

In fact, my own research has shown that the way we tell stories about our experiences—which is, by the way, something we usually do within a day or two that events happen—this has lasting effects on how we remember those experiences and what we learned from them. You could extend this logic telling yourself the story of things you learn can be a really effective reinforcement for learning in many contexts and we'll see more of that in upcoming lectures.

A more close-grained study of what elaborative mothers do has suggested three things. First of all, they're warm and affectionate. They provide encouragement and support to a child as a child attempts to tell a story. They also provide clarity and assistance on how to search memory and how to reconstruct an event and they do this by cuing the child effectively by asking "Wh" questions to get the child to insert certain kinds of information in the story. So mothers and likely other caregivers help children to learn how to tell personal stories early in childhood and this process differs across mothers.

Interestingly, this process also differs across class and culture in some important ways and to think about this for a moment let's consider Chinese versus U.S. American cultures. Within psychology these are viewed as cultures that vary quite a bit in their relative emphasis on individual distinctiveness, which is emphasized in the United States, versus relationship obligations and duties, which is believed to be emphasized more in China.

Qi Wang and her colleagues wondered if these different cultural orientations might be evident in the way that parents scaffold their children's stories. More sweepingly, what Wang was wondering is could it be that the way we learn to be Chinese or to be American is by learning to tell American or Chinese stories about our lives?

To examine this possibility Wang and her colleagues looked at mother-child storytelling about the child's experiences and they did so in Chinese and American families, and they found some rather compelling cultural differences in the emphasis that members of these two cultures brought to personal storytelling.

American mothers were focused on the child's distinctive emotional experience and events and in getting the child to elaborate the experiences that they had, and by contrast Chinese mothers were focused on relationships between the child and others and on responsibilities and moral obligations, so less on lengthy and elaborative rehearsals about the way the event highlighted the child's unique characteristics.

When Wang and colleagues then went on to look at adults what they was that Chinese adults had shorter and less detailed personal memories and they had personal memories with different themes, themes of duties and relationships when compared with American adults. So Wang's findings showcase how we become members of a particular culture by learning to think about and talk about our past experiences in culturally-appropriate ways.

Some recent proposals by Dan McAdams have focused on what he views as a characteristically American way of telling stories that he terms redemptive storytelling. In redemptive storytelling we talk about how the bad, the negative, the traumatic, and the tragic were made good somehow by some more optimistic ending or outcome. For example, we may talk about traumatic childhoods as fostering our strength of character or the loss of one job as opening the door to a new career path. In general, these ways of telling stories about difficult, emotionally negative experiences look like they're very adaptive, at least in the American samples McAdams has studied.

People whose stories are characterized by redemption themes also report higher levels of psychological well being. What that means in more everyday terms is that people whose stories about negative experiences are redemptive also say they're happier, less depressed, less anxious, and that they have a stronger sense of purpose and meaning in life.

People whose negative stories are also redemptive also report a greater interest in and involvement in giving back to their communities, a quality psychologists call generativity. So redemptive themes are good for the person who tells the story and they're also may be good for the rest of us.

What this has to do with learning is two-fold. First, we may learn to tell stories in this way because we're exposed to redemptive storytelling in our families as our parents ask us what we learned from a bad experience or to consider the good qualities even our worst hours may reveal.

We also learn to do this from our broader culture via fictional stories and even autobiographical accounts. It's worth noting that celebrity memoirs in the United States are often structured in a redemptive way with trauma and depravation and despair that are ultimately transcended by a now wiser, healed and deeply happy narrator.

But remember, we first learn to tell stories and then we learn from the stories we tell, so as we tell stories in redemptive ways we are learning from our experiences. Redemptive lessons, broadly speaking, tell us that what doesn't kill us makes us stronger. That what seems terrible now may bring unexpected or unforeseeable good consequences in the future and that we can endure suffering and go on to thrive. Although the details of those lessons are unique to each event and each person telling their story, the broader message is an optimistic and reassuring one and so it's not so surprising that people who tell redemptive stories also report greater happiness and greater well being.

McAdams has argued that this way of telling stories may be peculiarly American with other parts of the world a bit less concerned with making lemonade out of lemons. As yet, redemption themes have only been examined within American samples and mostly within adults so some of the important research questions in this area really are about how culturally bound versus universal redemptive storytelling may be and about how people come to tell redemptive stories or not as they grow into adulthood.

But certainly an American mother-child reminiscing one can see the seeds of later redemptive themes. Mothers are often really trying to help children turn bad events into learning experiences or opportunities for growth, and that's really the heart of redemptive storytelling.

You might think we all belong to multiple cultures and subcultures and you'd actually be right about that and, in fact, some findings suggest that the kind of story that works within one part of our lives could be less effective in other contexts. One example of this is work by Shirley Brice-Heath, an ethnographer who examined language use over a broad spectrum. She was interested in many ways that we use language, including written language and various kinds of oral communication but also in storytelling, and she looked at storytelling in low-income European and African-American communities, as well as in a middle-class white community.

One of Brice-Heath's findings was that low income African-American children in the community she studied were gifted storytellers. In contrast to European-American homes, regardless of class, the African-American children were surrounded by storytelling from early on and they weren't actually encouraged to participate in storytelling until they could do so more or less as well as the adults. The emphasis within that community was also on telling a good story and a good story in a particular sense: dramatic, entertaining, fun, playing with language and dialogue in interesting ways.

Doing this well requires a tenuous relationship with truth because the point of a good story isn't always truth in the sense of accuracy. Sometimes it's to highlight a deeper message, to illustrate something, or to entertain. By contrast, Brice-Heath found that the European-American groups were focused on the function of stories to inform and this really results in a push for accuracy. Brice-Heath pointed out that the implications for school could be problematic. The kind of creative storytelling rewarded in the African-American community may not be an easy fit with a school's orientation towards being truthful and accurate and the creative talent of those entertainment-oriented storytelling children may be actually underappreciated in some parts of the school setting.

This brings me to the last point and probably one of the least well understood aspects of learning to tell stories, which is how we learn to adapt our stories for different social contexts. At the beginning of this lecture we considered how stories are told for multiple reasons, for sharing of information to seeking emotional support and comfort and to having fun and entertaining one another. One of the things we have to learn over time about telling stories is how to successfully craft the story for different audiences and different purposes, and some basic elements of this ability are acquired or learned by the age of three so by the age of three children in many studies show that they know the difference between reminiscing, telling stories together with other people who experienced the event and also, therefore, know how the story should go versus recounting, telling a story to someone who wasn't there and therefore needs more background information and explanation.

So they appear, at least for the kids studied, who are middle class and predominantly white or Asian, more oriented towards this latter kind of retelling. That is, kids appear more oriented towards recounting—telling to share information, rather than telling for entertaining.

By adolescence we know that we should not tell the laugh out loud version of the party to our parent but rather the heavily edited and sobered up thoughtful version, if we tell them anything at all. But how we learned to use narratives in those context-specific ways represents an open question in this area of learning.

Summing up, I want to highlight how learning to tell stories is an area of learning that is tacit or implicit. It's acquired in the service of other activities with repeated practice and assistance from adults and others. As I said in the beginning of today's lecture, this is a way that learning to tell stories is like learning our way around a new town. A lot of the learning happens on the way to somewhere else, and stories we learn to tell are one way that we become members of our family, subculture and economic class, and larger culture. In other words, we start out learning to tell stories and then we use storytelling as a way to learn, and that brings us to a shift from learning a skill, telling stories, to learning knowledge.

Next time we're going to consider learning in the areas of math and science where there are certainly skills to be acquired but there's also a body of knowledge.

Learning Approaches in Math and Science
Lecture 12

L earning in math and science domains combines a focus on the facts we know about the world with a focus on a process that people can use to identify and solve new problems. Like storytelling, once we learn the skills within these domains, we are able to also use those skills to generate and acquire more knowledge. When learning math and science, it is important to have clear and explanatory feedback and to engage in self-explanations because it is the process of explaining errors to ourselves that can lead to real learning—of new strategies or even new problems.

Learning Strategies in Math and Science

- Strategy acquisition in math has been studied by a variety of researchers, but the work of Robert Siegler and his group stands out. They have focused on a number of types of problems in math. Some of their work looks at how children learn the counting on strategy for solving addition problems, for example.

- Initially, young children use their fingers and counting to solve addition problems, but this doesn't work well when they realize they don't have enough fingers. Eventually, children learn that they can begin counting from the larger of the two numbers in the problem, and that expands their counting options significantly.

- Class-inclusion problems involve reasoning about wholes and parts. As an example, John has three cats and four dogs. Does John have more dogs or more animals? You can solve this by counting—which is an empirical strategy—or by reasoning about sets and subsets—which is a logical strategy.

- Although adults can continue to have trouble with class-inclusion problems of a relatively sophisticated sort, most of us acquire a basic understanding of these problems in early to middle childhood—by the end of the elementary years.

When they begin adding, young children count on their fingers to solve addition problems.

- Microgenetic designs make many observations of people learning something over a short period of time. Generally, such studies show that right before people discover a new strategy or approach to a problem, their performance becomes more variable.

- The discovery of a new strategy is followed with a period in which the new strategy coexists with older ones, even when children know the advantages of the new strategy. Adoption of new strategies is slow.

- Variability across different children is high. In addition, solving class-inclusion problems is something we learn to do; it doesn't require special maturation that only happens magically by a certain age.

- Class-inclusion problems can be learned quickly, given a few conditions: many opportunities to try out the problems, feedback about whether we are right or wrong along with an explanation about why our wrong answers are wrong—specifically, an explanation that highlights the correct, and most efficient, solution strategy.

Self-Explanation Research

- In her work on science learning, Michelene Chi and her collaborators have noted that self-explanations play a critical role in determining how well people learn aspects of physics and other sciences.

- A feature of science is the role played by models of how things work; to understand many aspects of science is to understand something about the model that is supported by existing data.

- Chi's work focuses on how people learn and update their models of how something works—with a few key assumptions. First, Chi and her colleagues assume that everyone brings an existing understanding, for example, of electricity—although it may be flawed.

- For Chi, science learning is a process of changing an existing model to a more accurate one based on readings or other experiences that expose students to facts. Chi and her collaborators focus on self-explanations as a key factor that can improve this process.

- They define self-explanations as the occasions of talking yourself through a difficult problem or text in which you explain what you do know, try to think of related knowledge, and try to identify what you don't know.

- This process is similar to elaborative encoding, but it's oriented toward grappling with difficult-to-understand material and toward making sense of that material.

- While people sometimes engage in self-explanations spontaneously, they can also be instructed to do so—particularly beginning in middle childhood, or at around age eight. If you instruct people to engage in self-explanations, the result is better problem solving and better comprehension of texts.

- When you ask people to talk to themselves while working on learning material, some of the things they say are not self-explanations, such as "I'm confused" or "I am feeling exhausted." These don't concern the material to be learned directly, and they are not linked to better learning.

- Other things that people say are part of self-explanations and include restarting and summarizing what is in the problem or text.

- Some of what people say are what Chi and colleagues call self-explaining inferences, which are statements that go beyond what is in the problem or text and make inferences about it.

- It is specifically these latter types of statements that are associated with increased learning and, more importantly, with changes in people's models—from the naive models that are inconsistent with scientific findings to the more science-supported models.

- Siegler's and Chi's findings highlight the process of explanations in the learning of strategies and in the updating of mental models. They also point to the way that people do very well—given a lot of exposure to problems and a little support—at self-directed learning and acquisition of knowledge.

Teaching to Promote Self-Explanation and Strategy Discovery
- Discovery-based learning involves the notion that the learner should be the center of action and that the learner should be engaged actively in trying things out and making his or her own discoveries about the material to be learned. This type of learning is viewed as being most effective in the long term and as preserving the learner's own motivation.

- Discovery-based learning is contrasted with explicit teaching, or traditional instruction, which is described as focused on the authority—often a teacher, who presents material for the student to learn and directs how things unfold. Proponents of discovery-based learning argue that traditional instruction leaves students passive and unmotivated.

- A middle ground between these two extremes emphasizes guided discovery or elicited self-explanations, and the work of both Siegler and Chi would point to this middle ground as ideal. Entire educational systems have been built on these types of principles.

- On the surface, discovery-based learning sounds great, but it has some potential pitfalls.

  o First, it is labor intensive and cannot, especially at younger ages, be done with large class sizes.

  o In addition, it can be costly in material terms, though computer-aided instruction may change that.

  o Furthermore, it may take a naive student a long time to discover things that are foundational, so it may slow down the educational process.

  o Finally, at what age can we be sure that children can systematically explore an area rather than simply do a bunch of disorganized and random actions that don't teach them much at all?

- Because there has been a great deal of work in this area over the last several decades, a meta-analysis, which is a technique for synthesizing findings from many different studies to draw a general conclusion is considered more reliable and trustworthy than analyzing individual studies.

- A recent meta-analysis of about 108 studies of discovery-based learning shows that if we compare purer forms of discovery-based learning to explicit, traditional forms of instruction, explicit instruction is more effective for learning outcomes in many domains—including math and science.

- This is also true across childhood and adulthood—but the advantage of explicit instruction is particularly strong for adolescents as compared to adults—where the two forms of instruction aren't so different.

- The same meta-analysis also looked at enhanced discovery learning, which is more like the moderate approach, and found that two forms of it are generally better than other forms of instruction—and particularly so for adults and adolescents. Those better forms of instruction are elicited explanations, which is very much like Chi's work, and guided discovery, which is more like Siegler's studies.

- One feature that all forms of discovery-based learning have in common—whether they are the pure, and apparently less effective, forms or the more moderate and highly effective forms—is a focus on solving problems rather than on hearing a lecture.

- Problem-based learning is another kind of approach that is used to teach areas where people will need to engage in a reasoning process rather than simply recall facts.

- Problem-based learning is effective in arenas such as ethics, medical school, business school, and science and math—particularly where problem-based learning, as with discovery-based learning, is scaffolded by more expert individuals.

- Evaluations of problem-based learning versus more traditional approaches generally show that people are more motivated by it, but the outcomes in terms of actual learning are more mixed. It doesn't seem to do harm, and in some cases, people may be better at thinking through procedures when they have been engaged in problem-based learning.

Identifying Good Problems in Science
- While learning in science, math, and many other fields can be viewed as the process of solving problems, science is an arena where people also need to learn how to identify a good problem.

- A good problem in science is one that isn't already resolved but that can be resolved using available scientific methods and techniques and that is viewed as being important to resolve.

- Despite the ironic fact that most graduate training of scientists in various fields is aimed at teaching people to both identify and solve important scientific problems, relatively little is known about how people learn to do so.

- Creativity research based on examining the biographies of eminent individuals suggests that to produce great works, people need to first acquire a relatively high level of expertise in their field.

- Expertise provides a basis or a foundation from which to create novel works for at least two reasons: Without a basic, foundational knowledge of the area, it is difficult to avoid repeating old ideas or concepts, and that foundation provides people with a set of rules and assumptions within which creative work can emerge.

- Within a given area of science, for example, there are widely understood phenomena, and any new question will generally assume these phenomena to operate as currently understood. As someone's knowledge develops, he or she has a greater chance of being able to notice an arena where there is too little knowledge or where there is some conflict or contradictory result.

- Because science involves having guesses about how data will look and then testing your expectations, or hypotheses, against data, we learn a great deal from having our expectations violated.

- Being able to analyze and learn from the cases where our findings did not come out as we expected may be an important source of finding new questions in science.

Alfieri, Brooks, Aldrich, and Tenenbaum, "Does Discovery-Based Instruction Enhance Learning?"

Siegler and Svetina, "What Leads Children to Adopt New Strategies?"

Questions to Consider

1. Why might adolescents and adults benefit particularly from enhanced discovery learning relative to younger children?

2. Is it possible that discovery-oriented learning methods promote students' interests and desires to learn better than explicit instruction, even if they are not as efficient in promoting student knowledge?

Learning Approaches in Math and Science
Lecture 12—Transcript

This lecture we will be talking about learning in math and science. What is unique about learning in math and science domains is that they combine a focus on what, the facts we know about the world within various science and math domains, with a focus on a process, a kind of how, that people can use to identify and to solve new problems within science and math domains.

Like storytelling, once we learn the skills within these domains we're able to also use those skills to generate and acquire more knowledge. On the one hand, the learning of what, like acquiring the multiplication times tables or memorizing the periodic table of elements in chemistry, that has a lot in common with information processing approaches and verbal learning research.

What I mean by that is using elaborative encoding strategies and repeatedly testing yourself are going to be good strategies for acquiring those facts. If you think about it, especially for the multiplication times tables, that is how schools help kids learn those parts of math and science.

But how do we learn a process of problem solving within these fields? Today we'll first look at how people learn strategies in math and physics, and then we'll move out to the broader issue of discovery or inquiry-based approaches to learning in math and sciences. This has been a fairly hot topic within education for the last decades.

Strategy acquisition in math has been studied by a variety of researchers but the work of Siegler and his group actually stands out in this regard. They've looked at a lot of different kinds of problems in math, and some of their work looks, for example, at how children learn what's called the "counting on" strategy for solving addition problems.

When they begin adding, young children use their fingers and they use counting to solve addition problems. But this strategy falls apart when you don't have enough fingers, so as soon as you're trying to do something like add eight and eight you run into trouble.

Eventually, kids learn that they can begin counting from the larger of the two numbers in the problem. They can start with 8 and go 9, 10, 11, 12, 13, 14, 15, 16. That expands their counting options significantly and that strategy is called adding on.

Siegler's work examines how children learn strategies like adding or counting on and more importantly how children learn to use them well. You might be thinking, "Duh, you tell the kid what to do and then he or she practices." But oddly, it's not always so simple. And just to give you one example of this I've been attempting to show my five-year-old daughter the counting on strategy for some time now. Now, she understands the strategy when I show it to her. It makes sense to her, but she finds it difficult to figure out how to start it when she's on her own and she hasn't adopted it herself, yet. As I'm giving this lecture I've demonstrated the strategy to her about three times and I've had no apparent success so far.

Let's consider a different type of math problem. There's a type of math problem called class inclusion, and class inclusion problems involve reasoning about wholes and parts of wholes. Let me give you an example problem. John has three cats and four dogs. Does John have more dogs or more animals?

Now, you can solve this by counting, which is an empirical strategy, or you can solve it by reasoning about sets and subsets, reasoning about class inclusion. That's what we would call a logical strategy. Now, if you choose the logical strategy here, you didn't even need to bother with the numbers. You know that because both cats and dogs are animals John has to have more animals than dogs.

This is a pretty easy example and adults can continue to have trouble with class inclusion problems that are sophisticated and complicated, but most of us can acquire a basic understanding of class inclusion problems in early to mid-childhood, by the end of the elementary school years, say by age ten or so.

But earlier on we do have trouble. Five-year-olds, for instance, when presented with this kind of problem respond that there are more dogs because there are more dogs than cats and that confuses them.

As I said it's not until age nine or ten that the majority of children in the United States correctly respond to a standard class inclusion problem of this type. Knowing that there are age differences, though, doesn't really explain how kids come to understand these problems and learn to solve them correctly, and to do that researchers need to use what's called a microgenetic research design.

Microgenetic designs make a lot of observations of people learning something and they do that over a short period of time so generally studies like this show that right before people discover a new strategy or a new way to solve a kind of problem, their performance gets more variable. So a child who is about to discover a logical way of solving class inclusions might begin to get some problems right and others wrong shortly before he or she first gets to that logical strategy.

Often, discovering a new strategy is followed with a period in which the new strategy coexists with older ones, so even when kids know the advantages of the new strategy, remember that I mentioned my daughter understands that the new strategy works for bigger problems, but even when kids understand that they are sometimes slow to fully adopt the new strategy.

Variability across different kids is also pretty high and what that means is different children's acquisition of strategies looks different, happens at different times in the process, and the acquisition of strategies doesn't always look all that orderly, the way we might imagine it in the abstract.

This isn't always the case. Sometimes when kids get a strategy it's like an Aha! moment and they just get it and they go with that, and that happens to be the case for class inclusion and I'm going to illustrate this with an example study.

In this particular study Siegler and his collaborator Svetina were interested in children's learning of logical versus empirical strategies for class inclusion. Now, remember, empirical strategies involve doing the counting and comparison of the relevant numbers, and logical strategies involve simply reasoning about the groups, saying they're all animals, therefore, more animals.

As we saw in the example, a logical strategy is more efficient. You don't have to do any addition. So in this study, five-year-old children saw 30 different class inclusion problems like the one I just told you about and they saw them on three separate occasions so on each occasion the kids would see 10 problems. The researchers randomly divided the kids into four different groups.

Now, one group received explanations about why they were getting it wrong and, remember, these are five years olds and so they get the problems wrong. So one group received explanations that were empirical explanations. The experimenter would say, "No. That's wrong. The correct answer is more animals," and then the experimenter would show the child the exact number of animals there were versus how many dogs there were by actually counting it out for the child, so the experimenter would explain using an empirical strategy. A second group got logical explanations about their wrong answers. The experimenter would talk about how there had to be more animals than dogs because all of the pets were animals but only some of the pets were dogs. A third group received both types of explanations in response to their wrong answers, and a fourth group simply were told whether they had the right or wrong answer but they weren't given any explanation at all about why.

If you looked at the results of this study, what you would see is that by the third session children who had received logical explanations, whether or not they had also seen an empirical explanation, were successfully solving eight out of the ten problems.

Children who were given no explanations were still only solving about 40 percent of the problems correctly and that's about the same as where they were when they started. And kids who got empirical explanations where the experimenter showed them how to count also didn't get much better.

The second thing you can see when you look at the findings here is that performance didn't get better gradually, rather, as soon as kids discovered how to use the logical strategy and started using it their performance skyrocketed. So in this case, learning to solve the problems is really about learning the best strategy for doing so.

Now, I wanted to tell you about this study in particular for a reason because there was a different part of the study that makes it, for me, one of the coolest studies that I've read in this area. Siegler and Svetina also checked how performance on class inclusion problems changed with age in a different group of kids, and in that group of kids the children ranged from five to ten years of age. Over that timeframe performance on the class inclusion problems goes from about 30–40 percent correct in the five-year-olds to 90 percent correct in the ten-year-olds. So what Siegler and Svetina did with three sessions of ten class inclusion problems each plus some explanations was to take five-year-olds and teach them to perform like ten-year-olds in the space of 30 problems.

What this means is solving class inclusion problems is something people learn to do. It doesn't require some sort of special maturation, special developmental changes that only happen by the age of ten.

The other thing that's cool about this study is that it shows class inclusion problems can be learned really fast, given a few conditions, one of which is just having a lot of opportunities kind of massed together to try out the problems, getting some feedback about whether we're trying the problems and getting them right or getting them wrong, and getting a good explanation about why the wrong answer is wrong and an explanation that specifically highlights the correct, most efficient solution strategy.

We've hinted around about the idea of self-explanations before as little Emily worked out scripts in her crib through telling stories and when we discussed adults explaining the potlatch ceremony to themselves in order to learn the potlatch script.

In her work on science learning, Michelin Chi has noted that self-explanations play a critical role in determining how well people learn aspects of physics and other sciences. To understand where she's coming from you need to consider that one feature of science is the role played by models of how things work. So to understand many areas of science is to understand something about the models that exist in those areas and the way those models are supported by the data scientists have collected.

Chi's work focuses on how people learn and update their models about how something works with a few key assumptions. First, they assume everyone brings to the table an existing model, say, of how electricity works, although that existing model may be flawed. For example, it's common for people's naive models of gravity to include the idea that differently weighted objects will fall to earth at different speeds, and it's also not unusual for a novice model of electricity to be focused on the idea that electricity is a substance rather than a process. It's common for novice models of the circulatory system to be inaccurate about how blood is oxygenated or to be mistaken about the role of the lungs in oxygenating blood.

So for Chi, science learning is a process of changing students' existing models to more accurate ones based on what students read or their experiences that give them additional facts.

As a science teacher you can ask, "How can we do this better?" Or as a science learner you can say, "How can I do a better job changing or modifying a naive model towards one that's going to be more accurate, more consistent with what scientists know?"

Chi and her collaborators focus on self-explanations as a very important factor in that process. What's a self-explanation? Well, a self-explanation is the occasion where you talk yourself through a difficult problem or a difficult text. You explain to yourself what you do know. You try to connect what you're reading about to related knowledge and you try to identify what it is about the text that you're not really understanding yet.

This process should sound a lot like what we were earlier referring to as elaborative encoding or deeper processing but it has a bit of a twist. It's oriented towards grappling with difficult to understand material and towards making sense of that material, towards making an accurate model.

People sometimes engage in self-explanation spontaneously but they can also be instructed to do so, particularly beginning in middle childhood, around age eight or so and if you instruct people to engage in self-explanation the result is better problem solving and better comprehension of texts.

Of course, when you ask people to talk to themselves while they're working on learning something they say many things and some of these things don't count as self-explanations. People also say things like, "I'm confused." "I'm feeling exhausted." These don't concern the material to be learned directly and they're not linked to better learning at all, so it's not just anything you say to yourself while you're trying to learn, it's explaining things to yourself as you're trying to learn. It's focused on the content.

Self-explanations include things like restart, restating, summarizing what's in the problem or the text, and other ways of bringing together what's in the text with what the person already knows.

Finally, some of what people say are what Chi and colleagues call self-explaining inferences, and these are particularly good. These are statements that go what's beyond in the text and make inferences about it. These are statements that say, "Oh, so if blood then goes to the lungs it has to come back through the heart in order to get pumped out to the body." Statements like that are associated with increased learning and more importantly they're associated with changes in students' models from the naive models that are actually inconsistent with scientific findings to the models that are more supported by the available data.

Now, Siegler and Chi's findings really highlight this process of explanation in the learning of strategies and the updating of mental models and they also point to the way that people can do quite well at self-directed learning and self-directed acquisition of new knowledge as long as they're given a lot of exposure to problems and a little support in the way of feedback and explanations.

So if self-explanations and trying out strategies is so important to how learn in a problem solving domain like math and science then one of the most obvious questions to ask is are there ways of teaching that kind of material that are likely to promote those activities or likely to promote people explaining things to themselves and trying out strategies.

Well, since the 1950s educators, researchers, and even parents have proposed movements in favor of what is called discovery-based learning. Discovery-based learning means many things but specifically it involves the notion that the learner should be the center of action and that the learner should be engaged actively in trying things out and making his or her own discoveries about the material to be learned.

This type of learning is viewed as being most effective in the long-term and it's also viewed as good because the idea is that this kind of learning really preserves the learner's own motivation. That is, it's exciting and engaging to learn by doing and trying things out yourself.

Within this kind of area and within this kind of thinking discovery-based learning is contrasted with explicit teaching or traditional instruction. Explicit teaching and traditional instruction are described as focused on an authority figure, often a teacher, and the authority figure presents material for the student to learn and directs how things will go, what's going to be covered when, how students should understand what they're hearing.

Proponents of discovery-based learning argue that traditional instruction leaves students passive and unmotivated. Of course, as is always the case when you have two extremes there is a middle ground and a middle ground between these two extremes emphasizes what's called guided discovery or elicited self-explanations. And you may be thinking—and you'd be right—both the work of Siegler and Chi that we just discussed would point towards this middle ground as the ideal.

In fact, entire established and successful educational systems have been built on these kinds of principles. Montessori education is probably one of the best known examples and it's probably best conceived of as involving guided discovery.

On the surface, discovery learning sounds great. It has a lot of catch words that we really like, engaged, motivated, discovery, inquiry, but before we get too enthused we need to think about some of its potential pitfalls.

First, it is labor intensive and it can't, particularly for younger kids, be done with large class sizes. A teacher can't provide individualized feedback and individually tailored explanations for a class of 30 or 40 children.

Another issue with discovery-based learning is it can be costly in material terms. That is, kids need materials that they can work with for discovery-based learning, again, especially when they're younger. Now, computer-aided instruction may change that in that it makes it less expensive to create situations for kids to explore.

A third problem is that it may take a naive student a very long time to discover things that are foundational, things that we've known for so long and that we need to take for granted before we can move to the next step in an area, and because of that discovery-based learning could slow down the educational process.

And finally, developmental psychologists would say you really need to think about the age at which we could be sure kids could systematically engage in inquiry-based learning rather than simply do a lot of disorganized and random actions with their materials that end up not teaching them very much at all.

So how does research suggest that this type of learning stacks up? Well, there has been a great deal of work in this area over the last several decades. It's been published in many of the major journals in educational psychology and when we have that fortunate circumstance as scientists one of the best ways to make sense of everything is called a meta-analysis. A meta-analysis is a technique for synthesizing findings from many different studies in order to be able to draw some general conclusion, and when there's a large body of research findings, it represents a way to pull together all the findings. Because of that it's considered much more reliable and trustworthy than a single individual study. It's kind of a picture of everything we know.

To do a meta-analysis researchers first collect all the individual study reports then for each study something called an effect size is computed. An effect size represents the difference between different groups in the study. In our present case that would mean the difference in how students do with discovery-based learning and traditional instruction.

Once each study gives an effect size, we put the effect sizes together across all the studies and we can use some statistical tests to say whether that effect size, in general, across all the studies, is different than zero. An effect size of zero would mean there's no difference between the two types of instruction. It doesn't matter for student learning whether they have discovery-based or traditional instruction.

Now, beyond just that, beyond just asking is there a difference and what is the difference we can also look at what factors from different studies look like they're related to the size of the difference. We can look at factors like the age of the people who are learning. For example, we can ask, "Does discovery-based learning work differently for children than adolescents than adults?" and so on.

So a recent meta-analysis of about 108 studies of discovery-based learning shows us that if we compare what I'm going to call purer or you can think of it as more extreme forms of discovery-based learning, if we compare those to explicit, traditional instruction explicit instruction is more effective for learning outcomes in many domains and that includes math and science domains.

This is also true across childhood and adulthood, and the advantage of explicit, traditional instruction is particularly strong for adolescents as compared to adults. In adulthood, the two forms of instruction are not so different. This is disappointing news for that positive, exciting sound of discovery-based learning, but the news isn't all bad. The same meta-analysis also looked at enhanced discovery learning, which is something like the kind of middle ground approach that I mentioned above and it's the kind of approach that would be consistent with Siegler's findings and with Chi's findings on self-explanations.

In that comparison, two forms of kind of moderate discovery learning, guided discovery, were better than other forms of instruction. They were better than pure discovery learning and they were better than traditional instruction, and this was especially true for adults and adolescents.

Now, those better forms of instruction are elicited explanations, that's exactly like Chi's work where instructors get students to generate self-explanations, and guided discovery, which involves an adult or expert providing informative, meaningful feedback and structure for students' own discovery-based learning and that's quite a bit more like Siegler's studies.

One feature that all forms of discovery-based learning have in common, whether they are the pure and apparently less effective form or the more moderate and highly effective form, is a focus on solving problems rather than on hearing a lecture.

Problem-based learning is another kind of approach that's used to teach areas where people will need to engage in a reasoning process, a kind of how rather than to simply recall facts. Arenas where problem-based learning has been used include: ethics, where people are presented with ethical dilemmas and asked to reason about how they can be resolved; medical school—in particular with issues of diagnosis—medical students are presented with symptoms and asked to engage in the process of diagnosing; in business school, students read case studies about different businesses facing different kinds of dilemmas and they think about how the business might strategically respond to those dilemmas, and then they're often able to look at how the business did respond and what the consequences were and in science and math.

Problem-based learning is effective in many of these cases and what problem-based learning consists of is really giving people a problem to solve and, again, as with what we've just discussed problem-based learning, just like discovery-oriented learning, is best when it is scaffolded or assisted by people with greater expertise.

Evaluations of problem-based learning versus more traditional approaches in those fields also show that people like it more. They're more motivated by it.

Sometimes, however, the outcomes are kind of mixed and that, again, is also a little bit like what we saw with the meta-analysis. Problem-based learning never seems to hurt people and that's different than the meta-analysis we discussed. In some cases people actually may be better at thinking through procedures when they've been engaged in problem-based learning and certainly people feel more confident in problem-based learning environments. They feel more certain of their abilities to go through the real aspects of their jobs.

Finally, while learning in science, math and many other fields can be viewed as both learning what and learning how or the process of solving problems the sciences are an arena where people also need to learn how to identify or to find a good problem.

A good problem in science is one that isn't already resolved but it's one we can resolve or we can answer using available scientific methods and techniques and usually a good problem also needs to be one that we think is important to resolve.

So a final question in this area could be how do scientists learn to identify good problems in their fields? Well, despite the ironic fact that most graduate training of scientists in various fields of science is actually aimed at teaching people to both identify and to solve important scientific problems, remarkably little is known about how people learn to do so.

But we can draw from work on creativity and innovation to make some guesses about how people learn to find problems. Creativity research, based on examining the biographies of eminent individuals like Beethoven, for example, suggests that to produce great works and in science that would be great questions, people first need to have a relatively high level of expertise in their field. They need to know what is known in their field. That expertise gives people a foundation from which they can create novel and creative works, and this happens for at least two reasons.

First, without a basic foundational knowledge of the area it's very hard to avoid repeating old ideas or concepts so scientists who don't have a foundational knowledge ask questions that we already know the answers to. Now, second, though, that foundation of expertise gives people a set of rules and assumptions within which creative work can emerge or really important new questions. So within a given area of science, for example, there are things we know a lot about and any new question will build on the understanding of those phenomena that we currently have. But as someone's knowledge develops he or she has a greater chance of being able to notice an area where we don't know enough or where there's some conflicting findings and it would be good to figure out what's really going on.

Finally, because science and many other endeavors involve having guesses about how your data will look and then testing your expectations or hypotheses against the data you actually get we learn a lot in science from having our expectations violated. In other words, we learn a lot from being wrong, just like Siegler's five-year-olds.

So being able to analyze and learn from cases where our findings didn't come out as we expected may be one of the most important sources of finding new questions in science and, again, that really brings us right back to those five-year-olds learning class inclusion problems. Failing and having failures explained was a crucial way that they made it to the next level.

In summing up, research and learning in math and science emphasizes a body of knowledge, a what, and a process for solving problems and generating additional knowledge, a "how." Because of this latter component, the how, people learn math and science partly by solving problems and so some of the important questions in the area have really been about how people learn more effective and more broadly applicable problem solving strategies and how they're able to change their models or understandings of something from less accurate models to more accurate models.

As we've seen in this lecture, as people acquire new strategies they may initially become more variable in their performance before they settle on the newer and better strategy. People also need clear, explanatory feedback about their performance for this type of learning and when they engage in self-explanations about what they're learning that really helps them move from incorrect to more accurate models.

In fact, the process of explaining errors to ourselves that can lead to real learning, explaining errors is something like the way telling stories help us figure out scripts for events in the world but it applies more particularly to math and science. In explaining errors people consider their own answer to the math problem versus the correct answer or they consider what they expected or believed to be true about, say, electricity and what turns out to be true.

This is the core of theory testing in science more broadly, contrasting our expectations with our actual observations, and as it happens, some approaches to learning view all learning as being a kind of theory testing and the argument is that what people do when they learn is they develop and express expectations and then they look at whether their expectations prove to be accurate.

Is this a good way to understand learning? Next lecture we'll see how that way of thinking about learning, the idea of learning as theory testing, looks. We'll ask how well this idea of theory testing does at explaining what we do know about learning, and finally we'll discuss whether theory testing itself is something we have to learn over time how to do.

Learning as Theory Testing
Lecture 13

W hat is behind discovery-based learning is the notion that learning proceeds like science and that people are like intuitive scientists—that they explore their environment, generate ideas about how the world works, and test those ideas. On testing, they adopt altered models that account for the results of the tests. The questions we will address in this lecture are as follows: What do we mean by saying that people are like intuitive scientists? Is that thinking true of the way nonscientists learn about their worlds? Is that thinking process something that has to be learned—and if so, how?

Distinguishing Theories and Evidence

- What is common to scientific thinking as a way of accumulating knowledge is the coordination of theories and evidence. Theories are interrelated ideas or models about how a system works, including causal relationships within the system. They are based on a body of evidence garnered from observations.

- Working scientists can articulate their working assumptions or theories, describe the evidence that would support those theories—and the sort of evidence that would raise problems for those theories—and explain the process by which they have come to endorse a particular theory, given the available evidence at any time.

- Scientific progress in understanding a phenomenon is made by positing models of the phenomenon and then coordinating such models with evidence.

- Deanna Kuhn described two ways in which we can speak of people as being like scientists in their learning. One way is to say that learning proceeds as people's models are supported or challenged by new evidence and are accordingly confirmed or revised.

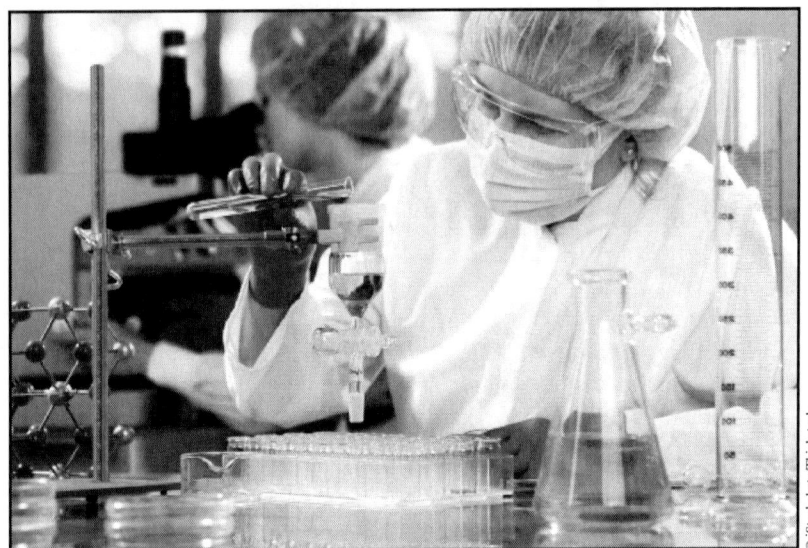

Discovery-based learning suggests that learning proceeds like science and that people are like intuitive scientists.

- The second way people might be like scientists is that they deliberately and consciously examine their theories or assumptions and the available evidence. This is more like the way that scientists work, testing their models against evidence.

- The idea of self-explanations makes it seem that when people update their ideas about the world based on new experiences, they do so like a scientist. However, Kuhn and her colleagues looked more closely at the process of reasoning about theories and evidence, and they found that this is an acquired skill—and one that is quite difficult.

- To investigate these issues, Kuhn and her collaborators often follow a relatively simple strategy: They elicit people's starting theories about a situation, and present them with evidence, and ask them to put theory and evidence together.

- Kuhn and her colleagues observed that people did not do well at distinguishing theories and evidence. However, working scientists had no difficulty distinguishing their starting expectations from the evidence.

- After making the distinction between theories and evidence, people need some way to resolve contradictions between the two so that they gain knowledge. In Kuhn's work, sometimes people simply ignored evidence that didn't fit theories they held.

- This might not be such a bad strategy. Often, a working theory that we hold is something we believe because of past evidence, so we should not just toss out a good model of the world after a single instance of disconfirming evidence.

- Working scientists don't treat all evidence as equal; they consider the way the evidence or data was obtained. This is a deliberate decision to weigh new evidence differently than established evidence and to be conservative about theory revision.

- However, for Kuhn's participants, there was little sense of awareness of the distortion of evidence; participants seemed not to choose to discount some evidence but simply to ignore evidence without awareness.

- People presented with disconfirming evidence might also revise their theories to fit the evidence. However, in Kuhn's work, participants seemed to engage in this revision process not in a reflective way but, rather, in an unaware fashion. They simply shifted theories to match the evidence.

- Kuhn's findings in her early and more recent work suggest that people do get better with age at distinguishing theories and evidence, in part because of changes in basic information-processing capacities. Children are particularly weak at making the theory-evidence distinction, and adolescents are capable of doing so at more adultlike levels.

- Perhaps discovery-based learning works better for adults because they are more likely than children to be able to distinguish beliefs or theories and evidence and, thus, benefit from experimenting directly and on their own. Children and adolescents may need help with drawing distinctions between theories and evidence and coordinating the two.

- Even adults retain some significant weaknesses in distinguishing theory and evidence, particularly in more complex circumstances, where the evidence is mixed and the number of variables involved in a system are higher.

- Kuhn suggests that the cost of failing to distinguish theory and evidence is that our learning is dominated by one or the other—and although sometimes people are overly data driven, it may be more often the case that they are overly theory driven.

- In other words, this is an area of learning where prior knowledge and belief doesn't simply help us learn new information; it distorts that learning toward maintaining our existing beliefs. Often, we cannot even imagine the evidence that would contradict our beliefs.

Confirmation Biases

- Kuhn's findings and concerns point to a phenomenon called confirmation bias, which is the tendency for prior knowledge, beliefs, or theories to be maintained in the face of contradictory evidence.

- Considering the different types of learning discussed thus far, confirmation biases are relevant primarily to learning information and updating models of the world that are not purely linked to our direct experience, perhaps especially in various areas of science. Self-explanations can certainly function to support or maintain our theories.

- In the 1970s, Charles Lord, Lee Ross, and Mark Lepper found that exposing people of different initial beliefs to the same body of mixed evidence leads them to become more polarized in their opinions. Later work suggests that this is because people selectively apply their reasoning capabilities to evidence against their preferred theories.

- Confirmation biases are also evident in the arena of learning about ourselves, which is often explicitly modeled as a process of theory development and revision.

- Broadly speaking, we develop theories about what we are like—and about what others are like—during adolescence, although these initial theories draw on experiences from infancy through childhood as well.

- Thereafter, new experiences offer us evidence that either confirms or contradicts those theories based on the information offered by those new experiences. That is, new experiences offer us an opportunity to either learn that our existing views of ourselves are correct or that those views need revision.

- However, we are anything but objective and dispassionate about ourselves and our self-beliefs. One general bias is that we all like to think well of ourselves and often have a self-enhancing bias in the way we interpret evidence from our experiences. Thus, researchers note that we explain bad things by appealing to circumstances or other factors and gladly take credit for good things ourselves.

- The analogous bias to confirmation biases has been examined more extensively by Bill Swann, who correctly points out that the most compelling evidence for confirmation biases about oneself is found in people who view themselves negatively.

- In various studies, Swann has shown that people with negative self-views engage in a wide variety of strategies to ensure that their negative beliefs about themselves are confirmed by the available evidence. Swann points out that for self-views, it is easy to become trapped in the negative image of self that some people have.

- There are many studies that look at problems with people's ability to modify theories in response to evidence, and they are overwhelmingly conclusive: We maintain our strongly held beliefs in spite of contradictory evidence, and we are not highly aware of how we are doing this. Worse yet, we tend to view others with contradictory opinions as wrong.

- Where things are particularly fraught are the arenas where public decision making and science intersect, such as climate change and health care policies. These are arenas where at least some aspects of our decision making should be informed by scientific evidence, which means that the public and their elected officials need to be able to coordinate theories and evidence.

- Beyond those issues are the intergroup conflicts that are exacerbated by both sides believing that they are right and that the other side is deluded. Naive realism is the tendency we have to see our own theories and beliefs as corresponding to reality—that is, not as theories but simply as facts.

- Naive realism is in accordance with Kuhn's findings that people don't distinguish very well between theories and evidence because they view their theories as facts, and facts are, after all, a form of evidence. Furthermore, if your theories aren't theories, but are actually facts, then it doesn't make sense to change your theory in response to conflicting facts.

- Bias blind spot, on the other hand, is the tendency we have to see others as biased. (Based on naive realism, we are completely unbiased.) In fact, we are rather good at spotting other people's mistakes in reasoning and biases in interpreting evidence.

Teaching People to Avoid Bias

- There are strong links between education and the ability to better coordinate theories and evidence. Furthermore, as trained scientists generally can do this, it seems possible to train people to think like scientists about theories and evidence, and it seems plausible that people could adopt strategies to prevent confirmation biases.

- However, scientific training and acumen in one arena don't always generalize, so trying to help reduce confirmation bias tendencies won't be easy. Different proposals about how to do this target different issues. One of the most obvious is to educate people about confirmation biases.

- To some extent, educating people about biases reduces their likelihood of falling prey to them. Paul Klaczynski argues that participants in his studies within this area do not learn the skills of scientific reasoning, but rather, they learn information and techniques to ensure that they employ those skills generally—rather than only in the face of evidence they want to refute.

- Other attempts at helping people to avoid bias include encouraging them to consider the opposite. In this approach, you ask people to imagine the opposite of what they believe or the opposite of what their own findings suggest. This has had moderate success in some studies.

- A different direction might be to enhance training in scientific thinking applied to everyday issues at educational levels from kindergarten to high school. Currently, our approach is concentrated more heavily in the advanced and collegiate settings and is quite domain specific—it occurs within disciplines such as chemistry, psychology, or biology.

- A general understanding of how to think like a scientist might be useful to people more broadly if taught in a way that involved application to everyday life. This may be especially important with increasing exposure to opinion, evidence, and mixtures thereof in our multimedia, information-overloaded age.

- All of these types of intervention share an effort to move people from low-effort reliance on prior beliefs to a more deliberate and rule-oriented evaluation of evidence and theory.

Suggested Reading

Kuhn, "Children and Adults as Intuitive Scientists."

Swann, *Self Traps*.

Questions to Consider

1. Are there situations in which being right doesn't matter and confirmation biases are acceptable?

2. One issue for learning about self and others in an Internet age is the sheer amount of information that is available about one's own and others' past and present behavior. Do Facebook and other social media make it easier or harder to engage in self-confirmation?

Learning as Theory Testing
Lecture 13—Trancript

Last time we considered the role of self-explanations in learning about math and science, and we ended up with a somewhat skeptical look at the idea of discovery or inquiry-based learning. In this lecture, we will continue to look critically at this approach to learning. It is a very popular idea and it is worth, therefore, a bit of a continued critique.

One reason that these approaches to learning, that emphasize people doing their own theorizing, and their own testing of their theories, may fail or fall short of our expectations has to do with the model that they have about how learning proceeds.

What is behind discovery-based learning is the notion that learning proceeds like science and that people are like intuitive scientists, they explore their environment, they generate ideas about how the world works, and then they go on and test those ideas. After they test those ideas, they might adopt an altered model of how the world works, but takes into account the results of the tests they have made.

Well, what does it really mean? In science, broadly speaking, the accumulation of knowledge is hugely varied, and the way that I, for example, engage in science is not the way that the physicist down the hall does so.

Really, there are three questions here. First, what do we mean by saying that people are like intuitive scientists? Second, do nonscientists really learn about their worlds by acting like intuitive scientists? Third, is thinking like an intuitive scientist something that itself has to be learned, and if so, how do you learn to think like that?

To begin with, what is common to scientific thinking as a way of accumulating knowledge is the coordination of theories and evidence. Theories are interrelated ideas or models about how a system works, and they including ideas about causal relationships within the system. Theories are based on a body of evidence that we get from making observations.

At a minimum, working scientists can articulate their working assumptions or their theories. They can distinguish between what is a theory and what is evidence, they can describe the kind of evidence that would support their theories, and the sort of evidence that would support their theories, and they can describe the kind of evidence that would raise problems for their theories. In other words, scientists can explain the process by which they have come to endorse a particular theory, given the available evidence at any particular time in their field.

Scientific progress and understanding a phenomenon, a phenomenon like learning for example is made by positing some sort of model of the phenomenon, a theory. One example would be associative learning theories, which we discussed in the lectures on classical and operant conditioning, so this is the idea that learning is about forming associations, for example, between pushing a lever and receiving a pellet. Then coordinating models of associative learning with the evidence we see when we observe actual learning taking place. In other words, we have models about how learning works, and then we test that model by making systematic observations and we update the model based on those observations.

As we saw, that early associative learning model did not pan out so well when we looked at the evidence that was accumulating. There were observations of learning in animals and people that were not explained by associative learning theories.

Given this description, are people like scientists? Do they coordinate theories and evidence? Is learning like the accumulation of scientific understandings?

One thing to note here is that this idea of people-as-scientists is stunningly different compared to that model of associative learning. That is because everything about a notion that we are everyday scientists is at odds with associative learning. The metaphor of people-as-scientists involves us as being active creators of our own learning experience, and it relies heavily on an internal mental phenomena, expectations we have about the world.

A researcher named Deanna Kuhn, in a very influential contribution to this area, laid out the main assumptions of the "people-as-scientists" theory of learning. From her perspective, there really are two ways in which we can talk of people as being like scientists in the way they learn.

One way we can do this is to say that learning proceeds as people's models, the way they understand things to work, are supported or challenged by new evidence, and after that confirmed or revised. This would mean science is a metaphor for the way people's understandings change. It does not actually necessarily assume that people act like scientists as their models are being shifted. In a way, what Kuhn meant with this understanding is that if learning works this way, science-like-learning would happen without necessarily involving deliberate thinking or awareness on the part of the person who is doing the learning. This is important. That is, it doesn't necessarily mean that the person actively goes out, formulates expectations, tests them, and then changes their understandings.

That may seem somewhat confusing. Let me give you a concrete example. In my field, we admit graduate students to our program on a yearly basis. As we do so, we look at evidence about that student's potential in the form of their prior grades and their test scores and their entrance essays. We base our theory about how that student would be as a researcher on the available evidence to us at the time. Some students are admitted and they join our program. After they join our program, we have a lot of opportunities to gather new evidence about whether that student is a talented scientist or not. They conduct new research under our supervision. They write papers and so on.

We might in the face of that new evidence revise our theory about whether the person is qualified to be a scientist or not over time. Some students come to the program and they do not do as well as we might have expected based on their entrance data. With this model of our understanding changing and response to evidence, but not in the way that is conscious and deliberate, what we mean is that we might say, "So-and-so is kind of a bad student." But we wouldn't be aware that when so-and-so was admitted, we thought that he would be the next Einstein. Rather, we would just say, "Well, so-and-so is a bad student," and if someone were to ask us, "Well, what did you think when you admitted him?" we might say, "Well, I had some doubts; I had some concerns."

In this way our understanding is changing in response to facts, but we are not aware of it, we are not aware of that process of model revision, and we are not actively consciously engaging in that process.

The second way people might be like scientists is that they deliberately and consciously examine their theories or assumptions and the available evidence. One example of this comes from Chi's work, where people engaged in self-explanations that sometimes deliberately called up what they used to think, and what they were seeing now, in their class material. This is also more like the way that real scientists work. They attempt to deliberately and consciously test their models against evidence.

When people update their ideas about the world based on new experiences, do they do it like a scientist? The idea of self-explanations would certainly make it seem so. Participants in Chi's studies articulate explanations to themselves. They say, "Oh, I used to think that. Oh, really." Then they proceed to adapt their models to those provided in a textbook. Their self-explanations are a way of examining both the new evidence and the models they hold in their head in light of this new evidence.

When Kuhn and colleagues, as well as others, have looked more closely at the process of reasoning about theories and evidence, they found this is an acquired skill, and it is one that is quite difficult. Kids may have models of the world that change over time, with their experience, but it does not necessarily occur in a conscious and scientist-like manner because to change a model like a scientist does is to take a fairly sophisticated approach to both evidence and theories.

To investigate these issues, Kuhn and her collaborators often follow a relatively simple strategy. They elicit people's starting theories about a situation, and then they present them with evidence, and ask them to put theory and evidence together.

Sometimes they give participants confirmatory evidence, evidence that supports their preexisting theories, other times with disconfirming evidence, evidence that goes against their current theories. The situations that they use involve things like whether variations in a tennis ball's color or coating cause better hitting, whether different foods cause people to get colds. They are relatively simple and straightforward scenarios.

The evidence that they present participants with can vary from evidence that is completely consistent or inconsistent with a theory, to more complex probabilistic evidence where sometimes you get some support for your theory and sometimes you do not, something a little more typical of real science. They look at participants who range in age from third graders, so eight, nine-year-olds through adulthood, and, and this is kind of important, they also asked some working scientists to engage in the tasks as well.

First, to think like a scientist, people have to distinguish between what is a theory and what is evidence, and then, they have to coordinate the two in some way. One of the first things Kuhn and her colleagues observed in these initial studies was that people do not do well at distinguishing theories and evidence. For example, children asked about their theories in light of evidence might refer only to the evidence. They might say, "Well, some people who ate cake got colds," or they might refer only to the theory, "I think cakes caused colds." They seemed unaware that those were distinct things.

For simple scenarios, where all the evidence is consistent or inconsistent with the theory, 9th graders and college students did better. As soon as evidence becomes only partially supportive, they also had difficulty distinguishing between theories and evidence.

You may be thinking, "Not me, this is a problem for less-than-brilliant people and children," but I am going to give you a kind of example of a failure to distinguish theory and evidence that we engage in all the time. When you go out to a park and you see people smiling, and laughing, and tossing a ball, you probably assume that those people are happy. But the fact is, what you are seeing is smiling, laughing, and tossing around a ball. You can't see happy. Happy is a theory about what those pieces of evidence mean. In this example, it is a pretty safe theory. It's a theory that is probably right, but it's still a theory, and what I hope you can see through this example is that we all blur the difference between theories and evidence a lot in our everyday lives.

Fortunately, working scientists had no difficulty distinguishing their starting expectations from the evidence. That's important because it tells us that what we think is true about scientists is in fact true, and it further highlights the fact that what most of us are doing most of the time is not quite like what working scientists are doing.

After making this critical distinction between theories and evidence, people need some way to resolve contradictions between the two so that they can gain knowledge. In Kuhn's work, sometimes, people just ignore evidence that does not fit theories they hold. For example, a participant who thinks the dark-colored balls produce better tennis strokes, when confronted with evidence that an equal number of dark balls resulted in poor hits versus good hits is going to focus on the balls that resulted in good hits as confirming his or her theory as supporting what he or she already believes.

This might not be so bad, because often, a working theory that we hold is something we believe because of past evidence, and we do not really want to just toss out a perfectly workable model of the world after a single case where we got some evidence against our theory, even if it happened in Deanna Kuhn's lab, right.

It is true that working scientists also do not treat all evidence as equal, they also consider the way the evidence or the data were obtained and how these new pieces of evidence stack up against accumulated evidence. What I just described about what working scientists do involves a deliberate decision to weight new evidence differently than established evidence and a deliberate tendency to be conservative about revising theories. That is not what Kuhn saw.

For Kuhn's participants, there is little sense of awareness that evidence is getting distorted. Participants actually seemed not to choose to discount some evidence by saying, "Well, I am not sure that player was hitting right," rather they decided to just ignore it without seeming to be aware that they were ignoring conflicting evidence.

People presented with disconfirming evidence might also revise their theories to fit the evidence, and this sounds like the right thing, that is, we should revise our theories in light of new evidence. In Kuhn's work, participants seemed to engage in this revision process not in a reflective way, rather, in a kind of not-very aware fashion. They simply shifted theories to match the evidence. What participants did not say, for example, was, "I guess I was wrong, I expected that the color of the ball would matter, but it does not." Rather, participants said, "Oh, color does not matter. Look, both dark and light balls got good hits," with no awareness that they previously had a different theory. This is a lot like that example of what happens in my department when we admit a graduate student, get new evidence, change our minds about whether the person is a good or a bad scientist, and forget that we ever thought differently.

Kuhn's findings in her early and her more recent work suggest that people do get better with age at distinguishing theories and evidence, and partly this appears to happen because of changes in their ability to process information at a pretty basic level, and we will talk about those changes in more detail in a few lectures. Children are particularly weak at making the theory-evidence distinction, and adolescents are capable of doing so at somewhat more adult like levels.

We also discussed last lecture that inquiry based learning or discovery based learning works better for adults. This may be because they are more likely than children to be able to distinguish beliefs and theories from evidence, and that helps them to benefit more from experimenting directly and on their own. Children and adolescents, on the other hand, may need help drawing distinctions between theories and evidence, and they may need help to put the two together.

Even adults retain some significant weaknesses in distinguishing theory from evidence, and this is particularly the case in more complex circumstances, where the evidence is mixed or the number of variables involved in a system is higher.

Kuhn suggests that the cost of failing to distinguish theory and evidence is that our learning gets dominated by one or the other—that is, we are dominated by what we believe to be true or we are dominated by what we are seeing, and we do not do the hard work of putting them together. As we will consider next, although sometimes people might be overly data or evidence driven, it seems like it is more often that they are overly theory driven.

In other words, this is an area of learning where prior knowledge and prior beliefs do not just help us learn new information or engage in deeper processing, in fact, our prior knowledge and especially our prior beliefs can also distort our learning toward maintaining those beliefs. Even in the face of very good evidence, often we cannot even imagine the kind of evidence that would change our beliefs. There is a question we do not ask ourselves, "What would show me I am wrong," and if we are asked this question by others, we have a hard time coming up with an answer. We are very good, however, at articulating the reasons why we are right, and that is not the way a scientist—a good scientist—thinks.

Kuhn's findings and concerns actually point to a phenomenon out of social psychology called confirmation bias. Confirmation bias is the tendency for prior knowledge, beliefs, or theories to be maintained even the face of contradictory evidence. Considering the different types of learning we have discussed so far, where might we find the strongest tendency for confirmation bias? Confirmation biases are relevant primarily to learning information and updating models of the world that are not purely linked to our direct experience, perhaps especially in various areas of science. It is important to consider that self-explanations can certainly function to support or maintain our theories. We are good at holding on to understandings and models we already have and already endorse.

A classic piece of work on confirmation biases was done in the 1970s by Lord, Ross, and Lepper. They recruited participants whose views on capital punishment differed. Some participants favored capital punishment because they believed it had a deterrence effect. Their theory was that having capital punishment led to lower rates of crime. Others participants were against capital punishment because they believed it had no such deterrent effect.

The researchers presented these participants with fictitious study results that supported a deterrent effect, for example, scientists have shown that murder rates in 8 of 10 states with capital punishment are significantly lower than in states without capital punishment, and they presented participants with studies that showed no evidence for deterrence.

They asked participants to evaluate the quality of the studies, and to report whether their own opinion changed as a result of reading both studies, the studies against and the studies for their preferred theory. The overall effect of reading the evidence in the study should have been null, or even maybe have moved participants' beliefs to be more moderate and more close to one another because everyone in the study read evidence in favor of their belief and evidence against their belief.

If we think about the findings of Kuhn, we can suspect that was not the case. We would be right. Participants were likely to interpret the evidence given to them in biased ways, such that both sets of participants came away with their prior beliefs strengthened. In other words, exposing people of different initial beliefs to the same body of mixed evidence, led them to become more polarized in their opinions.

Later work suggests that this is because people selectively apply their critical reasoning capabilities to evidence against their preferred theories. Paul Klaczynski and his colleagues looked at strongly held theories in high school and college students, and then presented them with confirming or disconfirming evidence. The theories, for example, might concern studying to music versus silence, and let me tell you this is something that young adults and adolescents have strong opinions about. When presented with confirming evidence, participants simply accepted the evidence. They did not really think hard about whether that evidence was good or whether it was poorly done.

When they were presented with disconfirming evidence, evidence against their preferred beliefs, participants engaged the full weight of their reasoning faculties to discount the evidence. They explained why the study was faulty, badly done, had too small a sample size, used the wrong music, used the wrong media player and so on.

What changed from high school to college in Klaczynski's work was the sophistication of these reasoning strategies. Alas, what did not change was participant's selective use of those reasoning strategies to discount problematic evidence, to discount evidence that they did not want to deal with, rather than to critically evaluate all the evidence, perhaps especially confirming evidence.

My favorite example of this tendency comes from a paper by three judgment and decision-making researchers. I am going to spare you the gory details, but suffice it to say that two of the researchers had opposing theories about a decision-making process and how it worked. They decided to figure out a study that would provide evidence about which camp had the correct theory. They asked a third person to serve as a collaborator and mediator because their relationship was actually somewhat hostile. They conducted the study, and as is often the case, the data were somewhat complicated and the evidence wasn't clearly favoring one theory over the other. In the end, the collaborators each interpreted the study findings as supportive of their own view.

The paper they published is called an exercise in adversarial collaboration. The larger point is that even highly trained scientists, when they are strongly committed to a theory, have a desire to interpret ambiguous data as supporting their own perspective. I should note that these researchers are working scientists and they are good scientists, and they did shift their theories somewhat to accommodate the evidence, so they are not quite as biased as untrained college students.

Confirmation biases are also evident in the arena of learning about ourselves, even though learning about ourselves is often explicitly modeled as a process of theory-development and revision. Broadly speaking we develop theories about what we are like and what others are like during adolescence and into young adulthood. These theories we have about what we are like draw on our experiences from infancy and our childhood as well of course. Thereafter, when we have new experiences they offer us evidence that either confirms what we believe to be true of ourselves, or that contradicts what we think is true of ourselves based on information in those new experiences. That is, new experiences offer us an opportunity to learn that our existing views of ourselves are correct, or that they need revision.

We are anything but objective and dispassionate about ourselves and our self-beliefs. One general bias is that we all like to think well of ourselves, especially here in the United States, and so we often have a self-enhancing bias in the way we interpret evidence from our experiences. Researchers have documented that we explain bad things that happen in our lives by appealing to circumstances or external factors, and we are very happy and very easily take credit for good things that we do as coming from us and who we are.

The analogous bias to confirmation biases that I have been talking about has been actually examined more extensively by a researcher named Bill Swann. Swann rightly points out that the most compelling evidence for confirmation biases about oneself is actually found in people who view themselves negatively. In a variety of studies, Swann has shown that people with negative self-views tend to selectively ignore positive feedback about themselves, they prefer romantic partners who view them similarly negatively, and they actually stay with such partners longer then they stay with partners who view them positively. If they enter college and have a roommate, over the first year that they are with that roommate, they get the roommate to view them negatively, and so on. They have a variety of ways in which they end up maintaining their negative beliefs about themselves. They would rather be right than feel good.

Swann points out that for self-views, or theories about ourselves it is easy to become trapped in the negative images of self that some people have if you think about all these strategies for ignoring feedback that you are actually not such a bad person. Beyond the self, confirmation biases are a real obstacle for learning more broadly. Further, they are a legitimate issue of concern to policy makers. There are many, many studies that look at problems with people's ability to modify their theories and beliefs in response to evidence, and they are overwhelmingly conclusive. We maintain our strongly held beliefs in spite of contradictory evidence, and unfortunately, we are not highly aware of how we are doing this. Worse yet we tend to view those with contradictory opinions as wrong.

Where things are particularly fraught, from my perspective, are the arenas where public decision-making and science intersect. Areas like climate change and health care policies. These are all arenas where at least some aspects of our decision-making should be informed by scientific evidence, and that means that the public and their elected officials need to be able to coordinate theories and evidence.

Beyond even those issues are the intergroup conflicts in the world that are exacerbated by both sides believing they are right, and the other side is deluded. This is because confirmation bias goes along with some other pernicious biases, known as naive realism and bias blind spot.

Naive realism is the tendency we have to see our own theories and beliefs as corresponding to reality. That is, not as theories at all, but simply as facts. In fact, naive realism goes exactly along with Kuhn's findings that people do not distinguish very well between theories and evidence because they view their theories as facts, and facts are, after all, a form of evidence. Further, if my theories aren't theories but are actually facts, then it does not make sense to change my theory in response to conflicting facts at all.

Bias blind spot, on the other hand, is the tendency we have to see others as biased based on naive realism; of course, we are completely unbiased. In fact, we are actually rather good at spotting other people's mistakes in reasoning and other people's biases in interpreting evidence.

This brings me to the last issue for today's lecture, can people learn to better coordinate theories and evidence, and if so, how? There are strong links between education and the ability to do so. As trained scientists generally can do this, it seems possible to train people to think like scientists about theories and evidence more broadly, and it seems plausible that people could adopt strategies to prevent confirmation biases.

Notably, however, scientific training and acumen in one arena do not always generalize. Not everyone with scientific training applies that training to her aspects of their lives. Linus Pauling had some crazy ideas about vitamin C, for example. Trying to help reduce confirmation bias tendencies will not be easy.

Different proposals about how to do target different issues, one of the most obvious is just to educate people about confirmation biases. Does educating people about the biases reduce their likelihood of falling prey to such biases?

Well to some extent, yes. One approach, developed by Klaczynski, involves a kind of cognitive therapy–like approach. Participants are shown their biases in reasoning, and they are educated about the general phenomenon of confirmation bias and some of its pitfalls. They are then asked to try to reason about evidence from the opposing viewpoint.

Following this intervention, participants are asked to reason about a different issue to test the generalizability of what they learned. Preliminary results are encouraging. Klaczynski argues participants did not learn the skills of scientific reasoning, but rather, they learned some information and techniques to ensure that they employed those skills generally, rather than only when they want to argue against evidence.

Other attempts at de-biasing people include a "consider the opposite" approach. In this approach, you ask people to imagine the opposite of what they believe, or the opposite of what their own findings suggest. This has had some moderate success in some studies.

A different direction might be to enhance training in scientific thinking applied to everyday issues, at the K–12 educational level. Right now, our approach to training in scientific thinking is concentrated more heavily in the advanced and collegiate settings, and it is quite domain specific. It happens within disciplines like chemistry, psychology, or biology. A general understanding of how to think like a scientist might be useful to people more broadly, if it was taught in a way that involved application to everyday life. This may be especially important in light of the increasing exposure to opinion, evidence, and mixtures thereof in our multi-media, information-overloaded age.

A healthy skepticism about our own ability to judge our own and other's beliefs is probably a good thing to cultivate. If you really want to think like a scientist, in an ideal way, cultivate a habit of asking yourself, "How might I be wrong? What fact or observation would show me that my idea here, is actually not correct?"

All of these types of interventions that have been examined recently by researchers, have in common an effort to move people from what might be called lazy, low-effort, reliance on their prior beliefs to a more deliberate, rule-oriented evaluations of evidence and theory. In fact, the idea that there are two modes of thinking, a lower and a higher effort version will be something we will return to in the next lecture, where we will weigh some commonalities and differences across different types of learning that we have examined in this part of the course, and will think about broader implications for how we learn.

Integrating Different Domains of Learning
Lecture 14

In this lecture, we will consider how different domains of learning can be integrated—and where they are distinct—by way of some broad dimensions along which different types of learning can be considered. In addition, we will discuss some theories about learning as involving two types of mental processes, along with the interplay of those processes and some evidence for those theories. Finally, we will discuss strategies for learning that appear to generalize, and we will address sleep as a behavior that has been shown to facilitate learning in many different domains.

Themes for Different Domains of Learning

- On the surface, it may seem like the way we learn motor skills and the way we learn to speak have little in common—and even less in common with how we learn about science or storytelling. However, there are some ways in which learning across different content areas is similar and ways in which learning may be distinct.

- First, repetition is critical to learning in most cases. People learn by either repeatedly being exposed to information, co-occurrences, or repeatedly making efforts to do something.

- In addition, learning can be more specific and limited than we'd like. For example, when we learn motor skills, it is important that a variable skill, such as catching a ball, be practiced with varying conditions; otherwise, we can get pretty good at catching a very specific type of throw. If we need to make use of our ability to engage in good scientific reasoning, we don't always appear to do that in areas where we would rather not revise our opinions.

- Furthermore, learning depends on prior knowledge; this is true in virtually every domain we have examined, regardless of whether this notion was emphasized. In addition to its use for babies in learning about their worlds, prior knowledge can also lead us astray, as in the case of confirmation biases, and it can render it difficult or impossible to learn new things, such as particular phonemes in a second language.

- Finally, learning can happen with and without our awareness, and that is true in virtually any domain we have discussed, but different domains of learning may differentially emphasize one versus another process.

Two Systems of Learning

- Theorists have proposed two different sets of processes by which people perceive and learn about their worlds. The first type of process is a low-effort, often unconscious or implicit process that tracks associations between events. The second type of process is a deliberate, conscious, and somewhat effortful one, and it will be known as system two.

- The first type of learning process will be known as system one; it is fast, intuitive, and can process a whole lot of information without a thought or care from us. System one is related to the idea of intuition, knowing or having a hunch without knowing quite why. Recent work shows that this is not just a single system but likely a host of different systems that operate similarly—and, importantly, operate outside conscious awareness.

- System two is often discussed as being slow and has what is called low capacity. That is, there are limits to how much we can learn at any one moment in time within this system—and, again, it is possible to think of this as multiple systems as well.

- These two processes are not unique to learning; rather, they have been proposed across an enormous range of activities in which human beings and other species engage, including memory, attention, social cognition, reasoning, and decision making.

- Evidence for the two systems comes from a variety of areas, but we will consider only two: visual perception and memory.

- In visual perception, system one provides for broad attention to the environment and for picking up various stimuli while system two looks at a scene in a goal-driven way, noting and recognizing specific, desired objects or pieces of information.

- This has been shown with neuroimaging studies and also by looking at people who have specific lesions in their brains that damage areas related to one system but not the other.

- In studies of recognition memory—in which the task is to say whether something has been seen before or is new—people's judgments of recognizing something can be based on a system one feeling of familiarity and a system two actual recall of having seen the item. Both types of information—familiarity and recall—contribute to saying that we recognize something.

- When researchers look at the different contributions of the two systems differently, some revealing information can be gained. Restricting recognition only to items that people actually remember results in lower performance, so system one does appear to let us recognize more information than system two.

- In addition, looking at people or circumstances that make deliberate recall difficult suggests that deliberate recall and familiarity are two distinct systems. The two systems involve different areas of the brain in neuroimaging studies as well.

- One proposal from reasoning and decision making is that when these two processes result in different outcomes, we have a chance to override our default intuitions, which are based on system-one thinking, via deliberate and effortful involvement of system-two processing. In essence, this is what is required to overcome confirmation biases, but these systems also interact all the time.

Enhancing Learning

- It's no surprise that practice and rehearsal support learning. If you consider spatial learning, motor learning, and even learning to tell stories, it's important to practice and rehearse in particular ways.

- In general, practice and rehearsal that are spaced over time—that is, not all right before you have to show your learning, but occasionally in small increments—is more effective. This is true for reviewing vocabulary words, learning to play a musical piece, and developing a map of a new town.

- Researchers such as Robert Bjork think that our brains evolved to learn and retain skills and information that we have to use over time—not to waste energy retaining what we only use once. Therefore, spacing rehearsal over time appears to make it clear to our brains that we can't lose track of a skill or ability because we will continue to need it.

- In part, the fact that elaborative encoding works means that we connect to what we already know—either deliberately, by thinking about how information connects to past knowledge or personal experience, or implicitly, as when we learn a motor skill and our body makes use of past movement patterns to acquire a new one.

- It is not surprising when studies find that we learn better with information presented in more than one modality—if we both see and hear information, for example, or if we experience both motor and spatial learning.

- Practice and rehearsal that are variable, rather than precisely the same, work better for learning in most cases because variable practice means you learn material in ways that are more easily available in a variety of situations. Therefore, studying and retrieving vocabulary words in different contexts and settings, and in different ways, is important.

- Variable practice and rehearsal allows you to really learn things—not just temporarily memorize them for a test. Sometimes, this type of variation has unanticipated benefits. In fact, a recent study of category learning promotes this idea of variability even in the area of category learning and for children as young as 18 months.

- Practice and rehearsal that correspond to how you need to use your learning are likely to be more effective than if they are not relevant to how you will use your learning. In most cases, this means that you need to practice in ways that are similar to use. For motor learning, for example, you can practice by visualizing and observing, but you'll eventually have to actually do the task to get better.

- You can also be strategic about the interplay of the two learning systems. For example, immersion probably aids second-language learning because it involves that implicit statistical tracking system, even when you don't think you are actively learning the language.

- Some situations call for more use of system two than seems to occur naturally. For example, when grappling with new evidence, you want to bring system two fully on board because it allows you to distinguish theory from evidence and to evaluate the quality of each piece of evidence.

Sleep and Learning
- After you rehearse and practice, one of the best things you can do for learning may be to sleep because sleep allows your brain to finalize the various neuronal connections you forged through learning and practice.

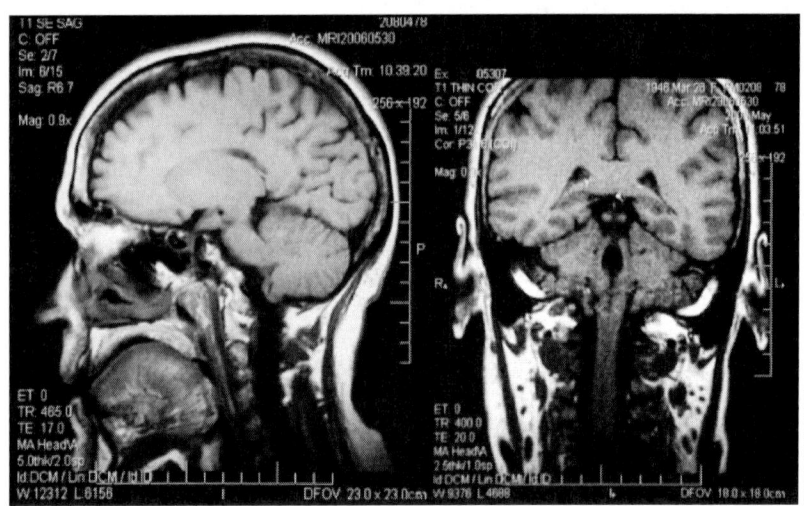

Images of the brain's activity during sleep suggest that it might be replaying learning during the REM stage.

- Sleep involves a change in people's states of consciousness, and it is divided into stages: REM sleep is characterized by rapid eye movements and a lot of brain activity along with muscle paralysis; stages one and two involve relatively light sleep with rapid brain waves; and stages three and four involve deep sleep characterized by slow brain waves.

- People cycle through these stages in 90-minute intervals, with REM sleep occurring throughout the night. In the early half of the night, we spend more time in slow-wave sleep while in the latter half of the night, we spend time in stage two and REM sleep.

- REM and slow-wave stages of sleep may be critical for learning. Studies have looked at people trying to learn under conditions of sleep deprivation, and it seems that learning is impaired under these circumstances. Therefore, you should try to rest before you learn.

- Far more studies have looked at the role of sleep in consolidating learning—in other words, whether sleep helps you retain learning longer or improve memory. This can be studied by looking at a participant's memory for what they have learned after a delay that either included or did not include sleep.

- Across an enormous range of learning domains, sleep appears to improve retention of foreign vocabulary, motor-sequence learning, and even discrimination learning. In addition, at least with motor and visual learning, short naps during the day enhance performance compared to not napping.

- Research suggests that your brain might be replaying learning while you are engaged in REM sleep. This is documented by comparing images of brain activity during learning with brain activity during REM sleep, and some findings suggest that for motor learning, these relationships can be seen fairly clearly. In this way, sleep acts as an extra rehearsal.

- Recent evidence indicates that the belief that people don't make new neurons as adults—that people have all their brain cells at birth—may not be true. In particular, the hippocampus is a location where new neurons are generated in adult mammals.

- The hippocampus is an integrally important part of the brain for learning and memory. Sleep deprivation—during both REM and stage four sleep—may reduce the extent of building new neurons in the hippocampus after learning and disrupt the ability of those cells to develop into mature cells. Without building those neurons, and letting them mature, you are hampering your memory capabilities.

Suggested Reading

Evans, "Intuition and Reasoning."

Perry, Samuelson, Malloy, and Schiffer, "Learn Locally, Think Globally."

1. Can you think of recent experiences where you have had to correct an initial intuition or judgment based on deliberate reasoning? How did you realize you needed a correction?

2. There are concerns about the rising use of Ritalin and other stimulants by college students to reduce their need for sleep. What might the use of such medications mean for learning?

Integrating Different Domains of Learning
Lecture 14—Transcript

At this point in the course, we have just spent about seven sessions talking about the way we learn different "whats," languages, motor skills, spatial layouts, storytelling, and knowledge in math and science domains.

In all of these cases, the whats combine both skills and knowledge, but they emphasize one or the other more so. For example, in language and motor skills, skills like being able to speak or being able to dance or move are emphasized a little bit over knowledge, and in math and science, we might emphasize knowledge a little bit over the skill of how to actually do, say, science. And, in all cases, learning the skills and the knowledge involved both deliberate efforts, conscious efforts at learning, but also more subconscious processes in learning.

What I would like to do in this lecture is to consider how these different domains of learning can be integrated and where they might be distinct. We will do this in two ways. First, we will consider some broad dimensions or principles along which different types of learning can be considered.

Second, we will discuss some theories about learning as involving two types of mental processes along with the interplay of those processes. We will look at some of the evidence for those theories. Finally, I will close with strategies for learning that appear to generalize, that is, strategies that will be effective in different types of learning tasks. I will also cover one additional behavior that has been shown to facilitate learning in many of these different domains: getting a good night's sleep.

On the surface, it may seem like the way we learn motor skills and the way we learn to speak have little in common, and even less in common with how we learn about science, or storytelling. But here are some organizing themes. These are ways in which learning across different content areas is similar, and some ways in which learning may be distinct.

First and this is probably not going to shock you, repetition is critical to most types of learning in most cases. People learn by repeating things. They learn by being repeatedly exposed to information or by repeatedly making an effort to try out a movement or to find their way from point A to point B.

Learning can also be more specific and limited than we would like. For example, when we learn a motor skill, it is important that a variable skill like being able to catching a ball be practiced under varying conditions. Otherwise, we can get pretty good at catching a very specific type of throw, but not the wide range of throws that might occur during a dynamically evolving game. If we need to make use of example of the ability to engage in good scientific reasoning, we can do that maybe in our domain of science, but we might not always do it in an area where we would rather not revise our opinions or expend the effort.

Learning also depends on prior knowledge, and this is true in virtually every single domain we examined, whether or not we emphasized it at the time. We talked about how babies use built in, evolutionarily based prior knowledge about objects, about space, and they even use evolutionarily based prior knowledge about how muscles move to begin to make sense of their worlds and to begin to move within those worlds. They do this from birth and maybe even earlier on through adulthood.

Prior knowledge can also lead us astray as we discussed in the case of confirmation biases. It can make it difficult or less easy to learn specific new things like particular sounds in a second language. This issue of prior knowledge is really critical, and we are going to be revisiting this issue in other ways throughout the rest of the course.

Learning can happen with and without our awareness, and this is also true in virtually any domain we have discussed. Here is a place where different domains of learning might differentially emphasize one kind of process versus another.

As it turns out, theorists have proposed two different sets of processes by which people perceive and learn about their worlds. I am going to talk about these as two processes, but remember that in each case, we may be talking about a set of similar processes, not just one kind of process.

The first type of process is a low effort, often unconscious or implicit process that tracks associations between events. It is this kind of process by which babies recognize regularities in the way sounds happen in the way sounds happen in their language, and it is this kind of process by which the motor system makes fine-tuned corrections to your movements as you learn to play a particular piece on the piano. This is also the kind of process by which basic aspects of learning to tell stories are likely to be learned. By doing stories over and over again, with expert partners, you come to just know how a story ought to be told under varying situations.

It is also this kind of process that may be involved in updating your map of your city when you do not really try to do so. You are not really effortfully trying to learn your city. You only realize that you have learned it this way when suddenly you know there is a shortcut you can take. It is this kind of nonconscious process that nods and accepts when we hear confirming evidence about our theories of the world and that does that accepting without thinking, "How good is this evidence really?"

Let us call this kind of process "system one" for learning. System one is fast, it is intuitive, and it can process a whole lot of information without a conscious thought or a deliberate care from us. System one is related to the idea of intuition, of knowing or having a hunch without knowing quite why we have that intuition. Again, recent work shows this is not just a single system, it is likely a host of different systems that operate quite similarly, quickly, efficiently, and importantly for us outside conscious awareness.

The second process is a deliberate, conscious, and somewhat effortful one. Every time you furrow your brow to try to figure out what a word means, or how the model of the circulatory system that you are looking at in this textbook figure actually doesn't fit with what you thought was true, in those cases, you are engaging this learning process.

Every time you sit down to study a list of foreign vocabulary words, you are engaging this process. When you try to think through a route you took and your existing model of how your city is laid out and put them together to describe to yourself in fact how your city is laid out and how the route fits within that model. You are using this process to learn about your surroundings.

We will call this one "system two." It is often discussed as slow, and it has what people would call "low capacity." What I mean by that is there are limits to how much we can learn at any given moment in time within this system. Again, it may be possible to think of this as multiple systems, as well.

These two processes are not unique to learning. Rather, they have been proposed across an enormous range of activities in which human beings and other species engage. They have been proposed to occur in memory, attention, social cognition, reasoning, and decision-making.

What is the evidence we have about these two processes? What I want to do next is to consider some of that evidence by moving out from learning a little bit and talking about a couple other areas. Then we will bring it back to learning and consider the merits and costs of each of these systems. We will also think a little bit about where they intersect.

Evidence for the two systems comes from a variety of areas, but let us consider just two, visual perception and memory. In visual perception, system one provides for attention to the environment, broadly, non-specifically, and it allows us to pick up a lot of different stimuli in that environment. By contrast, system two looks at a scene in a goal-driven way. It notes and recognizing specific, desirable objects or pieces of information.

Consider driving. System one lets you generally monitor other vehicles and traffic flow without consciously paying a lot of attention to that. In fact, you are generally not aware of paying attention to traffic flow unless something gets disruptive and you need to respond to it. System two in the mean time is looking for signs for your desired exit, and considering whether there is going to be traffic problems on Foothill Drive at this time of day.

These two systems have shown with neuroimaging studies—that is, different areas of the brain are involved in those two different kinds of visual attention. Also, if we look at people who have specific damage to particular areas in the brain, damage in areas related to one system disrupts that system, but not the other system.

Another example comes from recognition memory. In studies of recognition memory, the task is to say whether or not something has been seen before or whether something is new. People's judgments of recognizing something can be based on a type one system feeling of familiarity—a sense that that is familiar to me. They can also be based on a type two system actual recall of having seen the item. I remember the moment where that word flashed on the screen.

Both types of information, familiarity and recall, contribute to when we say that we recognize something. Yes, I have seen that before. However, when researchers look at the different contributions of the two systems for example by asking people who say they recognize a word, do you remember seeing the word or do you just kind of know that you saw it. They get some revealing information.

As one example, in the false memory studies that we talked about earlier when we talked about hearing a list of words like bed, night time, brushing your teeth and things like that and how people often falsely remember seeing the word sleep. What actually happens is that for many people they just kind of know that they saw the word sleep, but they do not actually remember seeing it there, so system one is actually fooling you in that case. System one is telling you sleep must have been there.

If in fact on a recognition test you restrict yourself to items that people say I actually recall seeing that word in the list, you will get lower performance. One way to think about this is system one lets us recognize a lot more information then system two does, but at some cost.

Looking at people or circumstances that make deliberate recall hard also tells us that deliberate recall system two and that familiarity system one are two distinct systems. For example, age differences in recognition memory can be teased apart by using this approach. What researchers find is that people's familiarity, their system one memory, is preserved, but their ability to engage in system two recall is diminished with age and adulthood; that is, older adults are not as good at that kind of recall as younger adults are.

As with visual attention, these two systems involve different areas of the brain in neuroimaging studies as well.

How do these two systems or kind of processes interact? Well one proposal from reasoning and decision-making work is that, when these two processes would result in different outcomes in a different decision, we get a chance to override default intuitions based on system one by engaging in deliberate effortful involvement of type two processing. In essence, this is the kind of way that people can overcome confirmation biases of the sort we discussed in the last lecture.

I think it is safe to say these systems also interact all the time in many other contexts. When you try to make a new sentence in a foreign language, if you've been immersed, many of your errors will be apparent to you in part because of type II processing, but in part because of type I learning that tells you what sounds right and does not sound right. It is type II processing that then comes into play as you deliberately and effortfully correct your sentence.

As we move on to the next section of the course, we will more often look at factors like how we are learning, and why. In some cases, these factors, the how and why of learning involve precisely the kinds of system two processes and the way they can be engaged in our learning experiences to hopefully enhance our learning.

Let us turn now into the idea of putting all of this into practice. What have we already seen that we can use to help us in learning? Well, practice and rehearsal support learning and that is probably not news to you, but you can also be smart about how you use practice and rehearsal. If you consider spatial learning, motor learning, and even learning to tell stories, it is important to practice and rehearse in particular ways. So, here I want to talk about some ways of practicing that are good across many types of learning.

Practice and rehearsal that is spaced in time, that is, not all right before you get tested on your learning, but in small increments and happening every so often with space in between turns out to be more effective. This is true for reviewing vocabulary words. It is also true for learning to play musical piece or developing a new spatial map of a new town.

Why this works is actually pretty interesting. Researchers like Robert Bjork think that our minds and brains have evolved to learn and retain skills and information that we have to use over a longer period of time. That is, we have evolved not to waste a lot of energy retaining what is going to be used only use one time. Spacing rehearsal over time with days in between appears to make it clear to the brain and the mind that we cannot lose track of a skill or ability, because we are going to keep needing it in the future.

We also know that elaborative encoding works, but what does that mean about learning and practice? Well in part, it means connecting to what we already know either deliberately by thinking about how information connects to past things we have learned or to personal experience, or also implicitly as when we are learning a motor skill and our body automatically makes use of past movement patterns to generate and learn a new movement pattern.

The role of prior knowledge also means that it is not surprising when studies find that we learn better with information presented in more than one modality. If we both see and hear information, for example, or in motor and spatial learning if we see our movements on a map and also experience our movement in real time, with sensory-perceptual feedback we learn better. This is part of elaborative encoding and it increases the prior knowledge connections that we can make.

It also means that practice and rehearsal that is variable rather than precisely the same is going to work better for learning in most cases. Variable practice means you learn material in ways that are more easily accessible across a variety of situations.

Studying and retrieving your vocabulary words in different contexts, different settings, and in different ways, is important. You do not always want to review your Spanish at the kitchen table by going over flash cards. You want to try telling a friend the words you are learning while you are waiting to be seated at dinner. You want to try recognizing or finding familiar words in a Spanish novel. You want to look at the words in the morning but also at night. Variable practice and rehearsal let you really learn things, not just temporarily memorize them for one kind of test.

Sometimes, this type of variation has unanticipated benefits. In fact, a recent study of category learning really promotes this idea of variability even in the area of category learning, where we didn't actually talk about it and for very little kids, in this case 18-month-olds.

Perry and colleagues had 18-month-old kids learn categories by showing them examples and teaching them which examples went with what category. Half of the kids learned examples that were all very similar to one another. Half were taught with examples that varied quite a bit and weren't so similar to one another. Over time, all the kids in the study learned the categories for the examples they were shown. They were good at that, and human beings are good at that. The kids who learned with examples that were more variable were better able to generalize the categories to new examples; that is, when they got a new example, they were better able to say which categories it belonged to.

They were also better able to use the categories for word learning over the same timeframe. In the end, their greater flexibility in the learning phase—seeing more variable examples—actually let those same kids learn more vocabulary words over the course of the study.

The point here is that variable learning helped kids learn the category itself better; that is what we know from the fact that they were able to correctly classify new examples. It potentiated a number of other effects on their learning. It actually gave them some new ways of thinking about solid objects in terms of different shape categories than what they would normally have known. It sped up their vocabulary learning because they had prior knowledge. They had these shape categories and they could attach new labels, specific names of objects to those category names.

We also need to remember transfer-appropriate encoding. Practice and rehearsal that correspond to how you need to use your learning are going to be more effective than if you are practicing in a way that is not related to how you will use that learning. In most cases, this means you need to practice in ways that are like use. For things like motor learning, it means that although you can get some benefit from visualizing and observing, eventually you really are going to have to do the motor movement in order to get better, in order to learn it.

You can also be strategic about the interplay of the two learning processes. For example, immersion probably aids second language learning because it involves that implicit, statistical tracking system, system one learning. Even when you do not think you are actively learning the language because you are wandering around thinking your English language thoughts in an environment where everyone around you is speaking another language, you are still picking up elements of that other language.

To consider another example, Suzuki violin instruction involves having students listen to the pieces they are learning to play over and over and over and over again. Interestingly it is not that the child has to sit down and listen and pay attention like it is a homework assignment, rather the teacher says just have it playing in the car when you are going to school. This is because that kind of background listening uses system one to train the child's sense of the rhythm of the pieces and the melody of the pieces without having to force the child to pay lots of attention and invest hours and hours a day with more effortful system two like processes.

I just focused on a couple of times when we may not use system one enough, and when we ought to make more use of system one. Other situations call for more use of system two than might seem to happen kind of naturally. For example, when engaged in grappling with new evidence, should you stop eating gluten in order to lose weight, for example? You want to bring system two fully on board because it is only system two types of thinking that is going to let you distinguish theory, the idea that gluten is somehow related to weight gain. From evidence, the actual findings of studies that look at this question, and it is only system two that will let you evaluate the quality of the evidence and make appropriate changes to your theories.

Finally, after you learn and practice, make sure that you sleep on it, because it turns out that it is sleep that allows your brain to finalize various neuronal connections that you forged through learning and practice. And this seems as good a point as any to end on.

We have not talked about sleep thus far, but one of the best things you can do for learning may be to sleep before and also after you rehearse or practice or otherwise engage in learning. Sleep involves a change in people's states of consciousness, and you probably know that researchers have divided sleep into stages. REM sleep, characterized by rapid eye movements and a lot of brain activity, along with muscle paralysis. Then stage 1 and 2 being relatively light sleep that involves rapid brain waves, and stages 3 and 4 sleep involving what is called deep sleep and being characterized by quite slow brain waves.

People cycle through these stages of sleep in roughly 90-minute intervals, and REM sleep occurs throughout the night as well. Research shows that in the early half of the night, we spend more time in slow wave sleep, and in the latter half of the night, we spend time in stage 2 and REM sleep a bit more.

It turns out that REM and slow wave stages of sleep may be critical for learning. Some studies have looked at people trying to learn under conditions of sleep deprivation. For example, they ask people to learn lists of words after they have not slept in 36 hours as compared to a group of people who learn the same words but after having had a normal night's sleep.

You are probably not surprised to know that learning is impaired under these circumstances. It takes people longer to acquire the words in the sleep-deprived group. If you look at words that vary in how emotional they are it turns out it is especially difficult to learn neutral and positive words when you are tired. These findings suggest that you should try to learn when you are well rested if possible.

Far more studies have looked at the role of sleep in consolidating learning. For example, once you have learned words, does sleep help you retain your learning longer? Does it improve memory? This can be studied by looking at a participant's memory for what they have learned after a delay and comparing participants where that delay includes a night of sleep or does not.

In these studies, we find that everything favors sleep. This is true across an enormous range of learning domains. Sleep appears to improve learning and areas as diverse as the retention of foreign vocabulary, the retention of learning motor sequences and it even seems to improve people's ability to learn to discriminate between two different textures by touch. Also, and I found this particularly interesting myself, even sleep during the day can help at least for motor and visual learning. These findings come from studies, which compare participants whose delay includes short naps versus not including a nap.

One way this works is that your brain might be replaying learning and particularly while you are doing REM sleep. The way that researchers document this is that they look at images of brain activity during learning and then they look again at images of the brain's activity during sleep, and particularly REM sleep. Some findings actually show that for motor learning you can really see the relationship pretty directly. In other words, what happens is while you are learning a motor task and practicing it, your brain shows certain patterns of activity and this is activity in the motor cortex and in the visual cortex that is related to actually performing the motor action that you are trying to acquire. Then, during REM sleep, the brain replays those patterns. Remember you are paralyzed during REM sleep and that turns out to be kind of important because otherwise you would be sort of doing the motor movement in your sleep, because in REM sleep you are paralyzed, the brain can actually replay those motor patterns without you engaging in the movements. It is quite like sleep is an extra rehearsal at the brain level.

Finally, you may have heard that you never make new neurons as an adult, that you get all your brain cells at birth. This is another myth. Recent evidence really suggests his is not true. There is pretty good evidence that many animals generate new neurons well into old age and human beings are not likely to be an exception; that is, it is pretty likely that we also do this. We may be generating new neurons throughout our lives, and in particular, we may be generating new neurons in a location of the brain called the hippocampus. Why does the hippocampus matter so much here? Well the hippocampus is an integrally important part of the brain for learning and memory. It appears to be involved in initial learning, and it is also involved in the transfer of our initial learning into lasting changes in the brain—that is, in the retention and storage of learning.

As it turns out, sleep deprivation, and that includes depriving people of both REM and stage 4 sleep, what you do by watching brain waves on a monitor in a sleep laboratory and running in and waking people up when they hit a particular stage. This kind of sleep deprivation reduces the extent of building new neurons in the hippocampus after learning. It also disrupts the ability of those new neurons to develop into mature cells. Without building those neurons, and without letting them mature, you are actually hampering your brain's ability to retain the things you are trying to learn.

So, to sum it up, space your rehearsal, spread it out. Make it variable, mix it up. Make it elaborative, draw the connections. Make it transfer appropriate, learn the way you are going to use your learning. Then sleep on it!

Today we have really focused on common factors across different "whats" in our emerging picture of learning. These common factors actually suggest something about how we might learn best. The lecture today has attempted to integrate and summarize those principles along with some examples.

Next we are going to turn our attention to the circumstances of learning, with a particular focus on how we learn, where, when, using what strategies and approaches. We will begin by considering attention, working memory, and executive function. These are capacities to focus your perceptual system on specific parts of the environment, and to think about those parts of the environment, while not thinking about other things going on. They are, for example, related to your ability to focus on my voice, make sense of what I am saying, and ignoring the sound of the telephone ringing in your neighbor's house.

Recall that we considered system two thinking today as one way we learn. We will see that system two thinking depends critically on attention, working memory, and executive function.

In the next lecture, we will learn what those terms mean in more detail and how they contribute to learning. In later lectures, we will move on to consider the strategies and monitoring that abilities like attention, working memory, and executive function permit. We will move from that discussion to an exploration of motivation and emotion in learning.

Cognitive Constraints on Learning
Lecture 15

In this part of the course, we are shifting from looking at specific types of learning to looking at factors that can influence learning more broadly and across different types of learning. One of these sets of factors involves three interrelated, interconnected abilities: attention, working memory, and executive function. In this lecture, we'll consider the evidence for the importance of these capacities in supporting—or limiting—learning. We will also talk about whether and how these capacities can be improved or supported to enhance our learning abilities over our lifespan.

Attention

- Attention is the focus of your conscious awareness. Sustained attention is the capacity to keep paying attention to something over an extended period of time. Divided attention is the act of switching back and forth between two different tasks. Selective attention involves focusing on one thing among many competing, distracting items.

- Usually, we assess these distinct capacities for attention in laboratory tasks that, for example, look at how well we can identify one item within an array (selective attention), how long we can track a particular image as it moves around (sustained attention), or how well we can switch between two competing tasks (divided attention).

- These ways of measuring attention show that attention is a limited resource; we cannot pay attention to everything within our visual field, everything we hear, or everything we feel.

- Attention plays a very important role in learning because what we do not attend to is often not learned. However, there are some exceptions to this that involve tacit learning.

- Attention is so powerful in ensuring that we learn things that attention researchers have discovered a series of phenomena, including inattentional blindness and change blindness. Essentially, if you are not attending to something, even if you are looking directly at it, you don't see it, and what you do not see you cannot learn.

Working Memory

- Once you've paid attention to something, in most learning situations, that's not the end of it; rather, when you engage working memory in the service of learning, it is within working memory that you are actively connecting new material—material to be learned—to what you already know. This is a process that is similar to the idea of elaborative encoding.

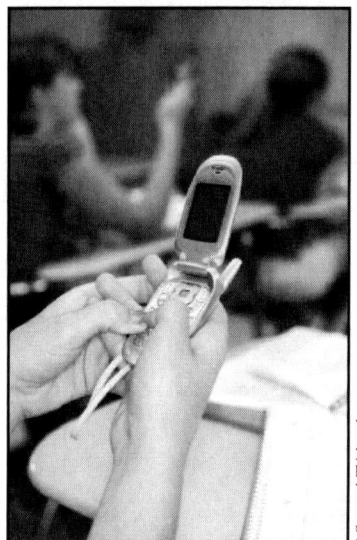

© Comstock/Thinkstock.

Divided attention involves switching focus between two different tasks, such as text messaging and doing schoolwork.

- Furthermore, and perhaps most importantly, the use of working memory need not be focused specifically on learning. In fact, you are likely to learn what you engage with in working memory even if the reasons you are engaging with it are not explicitly about learning.

- While intending to learn or not learn information may not matter, intentions do influence what you pay attention to and how you engage with it in working memory.

Executive Function

- Executive functions are the array of abilities that comprise planning, flexibility, and inhibition; they are connected to the ways in which we deliberately employ, shift, and focus our attentional capacity and make use of working memory capacity in the service of our goals.

- Planning is the capacity to think through a complicated task so that you don't make early errors that are costly. One way that planning gets assessed involves tasks with various rules or constraints, and you have to find a solution that does not violate the rules.

- An example of a planning task is the Tower of Hanoi problem. In this problem, you have two platforms with three pegs that hold various disks, and the general task is to match one platform to another platform in terms of disks and configurations. This task requires people to visualize moves ahead in order to avoid being in a situation where they cannot follow the rules of the game

- Flexibility is the capacity to change from one set of rules to another. For example, a researcher might ask you to sort a series of cards with shapes of different colors on them; first, the researcher might ask you to sort them by color and then by shape. The more errors you make when you have to switch tasks, the lower your cognitive flexibility is.

- Inhibition is the ability to ignore distracting information. For example, in what is called a Stroop task, a researcher might ask you to look at a series of color words printed in different ink colors. In some cases, the words are printed in the same color that they name, but in other cases, the word "red" might be printed in blue ink, for example. Your task is to name the ink color—not to read the word. In this task, the word meaning becomes a distraction; it interferes with your task, which is to pay attention to the ink color.

- By measuring how quickly you respond in those conflicting cases versus the congruent cases, where name and ink color match, the researcher has a measure of how effectively you can inhibit the distraction of the word meaning. The bigger the discrepancy—the more that conflict slows you down—the more trouble you have with inhibition of distracting items.

Executive Function in the Brain
- Executive functions are housed in the prefrontal cortex of the brain, and there is a way in which this is a more-is-better situation. Some of the best illustrations of this come from cross-species comparisons.

- Different species of primates have different amounts of prefrontal cortex, and this matters for how well they perform on executive-function tasks. For example, the reverse reward task is a difficult task for animals in which they are shown two different piles of food and are allowed to point to one. The trick is that they receive the pile that they do not point toward, and consistently choosing the smaller amount of food requires inhibition.

- Different species of monkeys perform differently on such a task, and the differences between them depend on the size of their prefrontal cortex. Different ages of humans also have different amounts of prefrontal cortex, which is one of the latest-maturing parts of the brain that is an area of significant age-related decline in later adulthood.

- Attention and working memory are critical for learning, and executive functions allow you to direct and control these processes—and, more broadly, your behavior. These abilities help to determine what gets perceived and encoded and to retrieve information or engage in a skill at a later point in time.

Enhancing Attention, Working Memory, and Executive Function
- Researchers are identifying ways to improve the capacities of attention, working memory, and executive function and, therefore, to make learning more effective and efficient for people.

- The main way that executive function and attentional processes can serve learning is by allowing us to strategically focus on different aspects of the material to be learned and also to manage both what we are trying to learn and other competing demands on our time and attention.

- In variable priority training, which was developed as a method of improving people's ability to do two things at once, people are asked to learn to do two different tasks at the same time, shifting their priorities of the tasks at various points in time.

- Variable priority training is performed in laboratories with laboratory-like tasks, so one of the major issues with these approaches is what is called transfer, which refers to whether learning one type of task—the one used in variable priority training—will actually benefit you in some other task, such as executive function or even learning capacity.

- In one study, Art Kramer and his colleagues asked older and younger adults to learn to simultaneously perform an alphabet-arithmetic task and to monitor a set of six gauges that changed continuously. The results showed that variable priority training was better than fixed priority training; this was true for both older and younger adults and for both being able to perform the training tasks and being able to perform quite different tasks.

- Variable priority training is being built into software packages for improving cognitive function among adults and for better preparing young children for school. However, these products are often untested, and they often depart from the types of laboratory tasks that have been evaluated in order to create a more marketable and appealing product.

- Mindfulness meditation is a practice that originated in Buddhist traditions and is geared toward increasing people's mindfulness, which is characterized by two major features: full attention to the current, moment-to-moment experiences—both internal to oneself and external—and an attitude of being open and nonjudgmental.

- Mindfulness meditation has been incorporated into a number of psychological treatments and is linked to many positive outcomes for people who practice it: higher well-being, more control over substance use, lower blood pressure, less emotional distress, and benefits for chronic pain and other disorders.

- Because mindfulness encourages people to focus their awareness in the present rather than being distracted by concerns about the past or future, it could also help to expand attentional capacity.

- A recent review of a number of studies suggests that asking people to engage in mindfulness meditation practices appears to be linked to improvements in attention, working memory, and executive function. Furthermore, long-term meditators show better performance on these types of abilities.

- Another way to improve mental capacities is bilingualism. Ellen Bialystok and her collaborators have been studying bilingual individuals for many years, and they consider people bilingual if they regularly use two languages.

- Bialystok has found that people who are bilingual show above-average performance on working memory capacity and executive function—particularly regarding inhibition of distractions and flexibility.

- Bialystok speculates this is because in order to switch back and forth effectively between two languages, people need to use executive abilities. In addition, she and her colleagues have shown the same effects across different languages.

- These advantages for bilinguals actually grow larger over time; in other words, the way that bilingualism enhances executive function seems to be increasingly evident as people grow older—a time when executive function is often on the decline. Some evidence suggests that bilingualism may even protect against dementia.

- However, it isn't clear if people who learn a language later in life will experience benefits, and it isn't clear what happens if people once were functioning as bilinguals but now largely function as monolinguals.

- Another intervention to improve executive functions is called dramatic play. There are many computer games that are being developed for these purposes, but they aren't well tested for the most part.

- Work done by Adele Diamond and her collaborators has shown that getting young children to engage in dramatic play—role-playing and pretending, for example—improves executive functions. This is probably because such play requires children to take turns, wait to talk, inhibit some actions, and focus their attention on what is happening around them.

- These findings apply to at-risk children, whose initial executive function in preschool was not great. In addition, they underscore the value of a broad curriculum for children. Finally, they suggest that as adults, we might maintain and even optimize executive function by playing more often.

Suggested Reading

Diamond , Barnett, Thomas, and Munro, "Preschool Program Improves Cognitive Control."

Hertzog, Kramer, Wilson, and Lindenberger, "Enrichment Effects on Adult Cognitive Development."

1. Are there ways of structuring a learning experience so as to avoid demands on attention, working memory, or executive function?

2. What might be adult analogues of dramatic play in childhood? How might such activities enhance or help to maintain executive function in adulthood and later life?

Cognitive Constraints on Learning
Lecture 15—Transcript

Throughout our discussions of specific types of learning, we have mentioned issues like attentional focus, for example, or elaborative encoding and their role in better retain new material we are learning. In this part of the course, we are shifting from looking at specific types of learning, to looking at factors that can influence learning across different types of subject matter.

One of these sets of factors involves three inter-related, interconnected abilities that are studied under the terms attention, working memory, and executive function. In this lecture, we are going to delve a bit deeper into some features of attention, working memory, and executive function that are useful for understand for our own learning experiences.

We will take these terms in turn, because they are nested within one another in some important ways. We will consider the evidence for the importance of these capacities in supporting, or limiting, learning. We will close by talking about whether and how attention, working memory, and executive function can be improved or supported to enhance our learning abilities over the lifespan.

What are these things? Attention is really about the focus of your conscious awareness. Attention researchers consider several aspects of that awareness For example, sustained attention—this is the capacity to keep paying attention to something over a longer period of time. Divided attention involves switching your attentional focus back and forth between two different tasks. Selective attention means focusing on one thing among many competing and distracting items, so for example listening to your spouse's voice in a crowded, noisy restaurant.

Usually, we assess these distinct capacities for attention in laboratory tasks that look at how well we can identify one item within an array of distracting items (that would be selective attention), how long we can track a particular image as it moves around (that would be sustained attention), and how well we can switch between two competing tasks—like watching a dot move around on a screen and identifying the shape it is tracing—while simultaneously responding to questions about whether words are spelled correctly (and that would assess divided attention).

These ways of measuring attention show us that attention is a limited resource. We cannot pay attention to everything within our visual field, everything we hear, or for that matter, everything we feel. Unless you are wearing particularly uncomfortable clothes right now, you are probably not paying attention to the many tactile sensations from your clothing.

For our purposes, attention plays a very important role in learning, because what we do not attend to is often not learned. There are some exceptions to this and they have to do with tacit learning which we have mentioned earlier. Right now, I want to give you an illustration.

Take a piece of paper right now, and try to draw an accurate picture of a penny. Get out a real penny and take a look. Did you get anything wrong? When I did this exercise, I reversed the direction of Lincoln's face, I forgot the word liberty, and I put the date of the penny's minting on the wrong side of Lincoln's profile.

For most of us, despite countless exposures to pennies, we have never really learned what a penny looks like in any detail. Why? You never had to pay attention to the kinds of details that let you draw a penny accurately from your memory. In fact, what you have to attend to with a penny for everyday use is very minimal. The penny differs a little bit in size, and very much in color, from our other coins. To recognize a penny, unless perhaps you live near the Canadian border, you do not need to pay attention to how it looks in any detail because those minimal cues of color and size suffice.

In fact, as an aside, it might be that Americans get more details right about their paper money than Europeans, whose currencies have always provided a bunch of size and color cues that go with what amount the paper money has. By contrast, our U.S. currency has always been more similar. All our greenbacks look like one another, so we have had to pay at least some minimal attention to the illustrations on the face of a bill in order to distinguish them by amount.

Attention is so powerful in ensuring that we learn things that attention researchers have discovered a series of phenomena which they label with terms like "inattention blindness" and "change blindness," and so on. Essentially, if you are not attending to something, even if you are looking right at that thing, you do not see it. What we do not see, we often cannot learn. For example, in one study conducted by David Strayer and his colleagues, participants drove a high-fidelity driving simulator. That means it is very similar to normal driving. You are sitting in a seat. You have a windshield around you and so on. They drove in the simulator on a course that was populated with billboards just like some of our highways.

Some participants merely drove the course, and others did so while talking on a cell phone. This latter condition it represents a situation where participants' attention is divided. Remember, I told you attention is limited. What this means is people cannot pay as much attention to their driving and to the course that they are on.

As you may already know from the enormous media attention that Strayer's work has garnered, using a cell phone while you are driving is a truly dangerous act. For our purposes today, what is interesting to ask is whether people learned anything about the billboards they saw while they were driving.

After participants finished driving, they were actually given a recognition memory test for those billboards to see if they had learned them. They were shown billboards from their drive, but they were also shown similar billboards that were not on their simulated drive. What this does is it tests whether they are simply guessing. If they only had to say yes or no, they would have a 50% chance of responding accurately even if they guess on every turn.

As it turns out, people's ability to recognize the billboards declines significantly if they drove the course while talking on a cell phone. By using an eye tracker device, which can document where people's eyes are looking while they're engaged in some task, these researchers were able to show people were actually looking right at those billboards, even though later they were not able to recognize them. In fact, this is actually directly analogous to the penny example, because despite looking at pennies over a lifetime, we still haven't actually learned the details of their features.

Once you have paid attention to something, in most learning situations, that is not the end of it. Rather, we want to do something to the item that we are paying attention to. We are going to think about working memory as the kind of metaphorical mental space where you actively engage with material. For example, imagine that you really are trying to learn what a penny really looks like. You begin by looking at that penny more carefully than you have before. You focus your attention on the way that the face of a penny is designed.

You might ask yourself questions, like what are the features of a penny's face? Where are they located with respect to one another? As you think about these questions, you are engaging working memory capacity to learn the face of the penny. As you use this capacity, what you are doing is that you are making use of knowledge about measurements. You might estimate distances between the perimeter of the penny and the date, or consider whether the nose of Lincoln faces the date or not.

If this sounds suspiciously like the idea of elaborative encoding, it should. When we engage working memory in the service of learning, a few things are happening. First, it is within working memory that we are actively connecting new material, material we are trying to lean, to things we already know. Second, and maybe most important, the use of working memory need not be focused on learning, specifically. In fact, we are likely to learn what we engage with in working memory even if the reasons we are engaging with it are not explicitly for learning. Recall that the intention to learn mattered less in studies of wordless learning than how people thought about what they were learning and how they knew the material later. If you are planning to draw another penny picture, you will be likely to learn the penny's face better than if you are not.

What we are likely to learn about our penny are the features we focus on in working memory? In this example, you have already seen that you probably have not ever tried to estimate how far from the perimeter the date is located or which way Lincoln's face is turned. This is because while intending to learn or not learn information may not matter, intentions do influence what we pay attention to, and how we engage with it in working memory.

This idea of our intentions or goals brings us to the last and the broadest capability we are going to address today, and that's something we call "executive function." Executive functions are the abilities that comprise planning, flexibility, and inhibition. They are connected to the ways in which we deliberately employ, shift, and focus our attentional capacity and make use of working memory capacity in the service of our goals. Let us discuss each of these executive functions planning, flexibility, and inhibition.

Planning means the capacity to think through a complicated task so that you do not make early and costly errors. You plan according to the rules of the task, so planning involves assessing the rules and the constraints on what you can do, and figuring out a solution that is not going to violate those rules.

An example of a typical laboratory task is called the Tower of Hanoi problem. In this problem, you have two platforms with three pegs on each and they hold disks. The rules are that you may move one disk at a time. Disks must always be on pegs. That is, you cannot put a disk on the table while you figure something out, and you can't put a larger disk on top of a smaller disk. The task you have is to match your task platform to a demonstration platform in terms of disks and how they are configured. As you can see, the task requires you to visualize moves ahead. In other words, you have to plan your moves in order to avoid being in a situation where you cannot actually follow the rules of the game.

Flexibility is the capacity to change from one set of rules to another. For example, I might ask you to sort a series of cards with shapes of different colors on them. You could sort the cards by shape, or you could sort them by color. You could sort them by both. In a flexibility task, I might first ask you to sort in one way, and then later you have to switch. The more errors you make when you have to switch, the lower your cognitive flexibility.

Inhibition is the ability to ignore distracting information. For example, in what is called a Stroop task, I might ask you to look at a series of color words printed in different colors of ink. The words would be blue, red, yellow, green and they would be printed in blue, red, yellow, and green ink. In some cases, the words are printed in the same color that they name, so you see red printed in red. In other cases, red might be printed in blue. What I am going to ask you to do is to the ink color, not to read the word. In this task, the word meaning can becomes a distraction. It interferes with your task, which is to pay attention to the ink color.

If I measure how quickly you respond in those conflicting cases versus the congruent cases, where name and ink color match, I have a measure of how effectively you can inhibit or push away the distraction of the word meaning. The bigger that discrepancy, the more conflict slows you down, the more trouble you are having with inhibition of distracting items.

In terms of the brain, executive functions like planning, flexibility, and inhibition are housed, if you will, in the prefrontal-cortex. There is a sort of way in which this is a kind of "more is better" situation. More prefrontal cortex or a larger prefrontal cortex is typically better.

Some of the best illustrations of this actually come from cross-species comparisons. Once I saw a talk given by a neuroscientist named Art Shimamura, who is a professor at Berkeley. He began his talk by talking about how difficult it is to train a cat, versus a dog. For example in my household, we want to train pets to stay off the kitchen table. What Shimamura suggested is that, even when you are very sure that both the cat and the dog understand that you very are displeased when they get on the table, and they stop doing it while you are standing there in your kitchen, your cat is probably only following the rules while you are physically present. In my household, there are telltale paw prints to confirm Shimamura's conjecture. The dog actually might be trustworthy all day by himself, my dog is. The difference, according to Shimamura, is the prefrontal cortex. Dogs have more than cats.

As it turns out, different species of primates have different amounts of prefrontal cortex. This actually matters for how well they do on executive function tasks. Consider for a minute the ability of inhibition and something called the reverse reward task. It is going to sound simple, but I assure you, it is a hard task if you are an animal, and it is also a hard task if you are a young child or if you are very hungry.

In the reverse reward task, I am going to show you two different piles of food, and you are allowed to point to one. In fact, you have to point to one. Here is the trick. You will get the pile you do not point toward. If you are a lab monkey, and you do this task, the way to win it is to consistently point to or choose the smaller pile of food. To do so, you need some serious inhibition, because everything in your little monkey mind is telling you to look at and point at and want the big pile. Different species of primates do differently on a task like this, and the differences between them actually end up depending on the size of their prefrontal cortex. Chimps do well, for example, and lemurs not so well.

For the parents or the people in the audience who have a lot of experience with children and teenagers, this probably will not shock you. Different ages of human beings also have different amounts of prefrontal cortex. The prefrontal cortex is one of the latest maturing parts of our brains. There is clear evidence that this part of our brain is still maturing into the mid-20s. It is also an area of significant age-related decline in later adulthood.

A person's ability to plan and shift strategies and inhibit distracting, extraneous information doesn't fully form until he or she is over 20 years old. From my perspective, this can explain an awful lot of about frustrating exchanges parents have with adolescents.

Why do executive functions matter? Well, if attention and working memory are so critical for learning, and executive functions let you direct and control attention and working memory processes, and more broadly, they let you direct and control your behavior, you can see why these abilities probably matter for learning. It is these abilities that help to determine what is perceived and encoded and also how well you can retrieve that information or engage in that skill later on.

The evidence that executive function abilities matter for learning, and beyond, is easy to come by. To give you just one example, Clark and colleagues conducted an important longitudinal study of kid's mathematics learning in the early elementary years. They were interested in how well kids did with math learning as a function of the level of executive function they displayed prior to school, at the pre-school years, so maybe age four or so.

To look at this they used an assessment of math that involved basic addition and subtraction problems. For six-year-olds, this is kind of the bread and butter. This is what math is.

Clark and colleagues found that executive function skills at age four were strongly predictive of math performance at age six. This was true regardless of the kids overall IQ and reading ability, both of which are related to early math abilities. Specifically, children's ability to shift kid's flexibility and their ability to inhibit distractions were quite important for predicting how well they would do on addition and subtraction when they were six years old.

How does this work really? The role of executive function here could operate in at least two ways. First, in a test of addition and subtraction, just being able to do the problems is going to be affected by your ability to inhibit distractions and to shift tasks. You have to shift from one to another strategy in solving the problems, and you have to inhibit distracting elements both on the test and around you in the room. For example, the fact that a test might have multiple problems poses some distractions.

Importantly though in this case, the associations that the researchers were finding were not between executive functioning and math performance at the same age. Rather, they looked at executive functioning when the kids were four and they were using that to predict how they would do on math at age six. In this case, the researchers argued that executive function abilities in preschool influenced how well children were able to learn math. In other words, it is difficulties in being flexible about strategies and inhibiting distractions that affect kids learning of mathematics, not necessarily a native ability or inability to learn the principals of math, and not necessarily the ability to do well at the test in one point in time.

All this makes it important to ask whether we can enhance attention, working memory, and executive function? How we might do that. As it turns out, researchers are identifying ways to improve these capacities, to make people's learning more effective and more efficient. Today, I am going to focus on four approaches that are yielding at least some preliminary success. In looking at these four approaches, we are going to move from what I think is the most obvious to what I think is the most surprising and the most fun.

Strategy one is to get yourself something called variable priority training. Variable priority training was developed as a method of improving people's ability to do two things at once. If you think about it, the main way executive function and attentional processes serve learning is by allowing us to focus on different aspects of the material we are learning, and also to manage what we are trying to learn, and other competing demands on our time and attention. It could well be that variable priority training is a way to enhance executive function.

Here is how it works. In variable priority training, people are asked to learn to do two different tasks at the same time, but they are asked to shift their priorities around so that at some points in time, task 1 is more important, and at others, task two is more important. Variable priority training is performed in laboratories with laboratory-like tasks. That means that one of the major issues with these approaches is what is called transfer. Transfer refers to whether learning one kind of task, like the one that was used for variable priority training, whether learning that task is actually going to benefit you in some other task. Fr our purposes, what this means is if you learn variable priority training with one pair of tasks, is it really going to help you with executive function more broadly, and learning capacity in everyday life. We do not yet know for sure whether variable priority training can improve executive function and learning.

In one study, Art Kramer and his colleagues looked at older and younger adults and what they asked them to do for variable priority training was to learn to simultaneously perform what is called an alphabet-arithmetic task, and—hold onto your seats here—to monitor a set of six gauges that changed continuously. Periodically participants had to reset a gauge when it entered the red phase. If they did not do this after a little bit of time, the computer would reset the gauge and that was counted as an error.

While they are monitoring the gauges, participants are asked to do the alphabet arithmetic task, and this consists of problems like $k - 3 = ?$, and the answer to that problem is H. These problems always involved adding or subtracting two or three letters. The participants also had to tell whether the answer was lower or higher than the letter from the previous trial. It was self-paced. The measure of success in this particular task in the alphabet arithmetic task is how many problems you solve over the course of the task period.

If your head is not spinning yet, you also had a bar on the screen, and the bar on the screen would let you know two things. The first thing the bar let you know depending on where it was divided was how much you should prioritize the alphabet arithmetic task or the gauge-monitoring task. Sometimes you were to place high priority on the gauges, and at others, you were supposed to place higher priority on the arithmetic task.

The second thing the bar did was it showed you how well you were doing at the two tasks. Perfect performance would color the entire bar in on both sides of the dividing line. When the bar was not completely colored in, it showed you that you were getting things wrong.

Kramer and colleagues gave people two kinds of training on this dual task. In one type, people were always asked to place equal priority on the two tasks. That bar was always divided right in the middle. In the other type, people were asked to place different priorities on each task at different times. They then looked at whether people got better at doing both tasks, and, more importantly—this was the transfer issue—they looked at whether people also showed improvement when given a different set of dual tasks to do and this different set involving scheduling and memorizing pairs of associate words.

To cut to the chase, variable priority training produced better results than fixed priority training, and this was true for older and younger adults. It was also true for both being able to perform the training tasks, alphabet arithmetic and gauge monitoring, and for being able to perform the quite different tasks of memorizing words and scheduling.

Unless you were completely horrified by my description, you might be asking where you can get access to variable priority training. Well, variable priority training is being built into software packages for improving cognitive function among adults and for better preparing young children for school. I am going to have to caution you however because these products are not always tested and you probably are not surprised to learn that they depart from the kinds of laboratory tasks that have been well evaluated in order to create a more marketable and appealing product, so caveat emptor.

Variable priority training seems to work, but it is very hard work. The tasks are absolutely non-appealing and it requires you to draw on motivational resources. Fortunately, research is suggesting there are some other options.

A second strategy, and one I like a little better is mindfulness meditation. Mindfulness meditation is a practice originating in Buddhist traditions and it is geared toward increasing people's mindfulness. What is that? Mindfulness is characterized by two major features. One is full attention to the current, moment-to-moment experiences that you are having both internal and external. Second mindfulness involves an attitude of openness and non-judgment.

Mindfulness meditation has been incorporated into a number of psychological treatments for mental disorders and physical disorders. It is linked to many positive outcomes for people who practice it. People who practice mindfulness meditation report higher well-being, they report more control over substance use, lower blood pressure, they have less emotional distress, and there are clear benefits for chronic pain and other physical disorders.

However, mindfulness could also help to expand attentional capacity because it encourages people to focus their awareness in the present, rather than being distracted by concerns about the past or the future. A recent review of a number of studies suggests some evidence for precisely that. Mindfulness meditation practices appear linked to improvements in attention, working memory, and executive function. Long-term meditators show better performance on these types of abilities as well.

Quality variable priority training and mindfulness meditation are two strategies for improving executive functioning for improving your ability to plan, to switch from unsuccessful strategies to more useful ones and to improve your focus and your ability to inhibit distractions.

Two other cool strategies specific to improving and maintaining executive function and so potentially to strengthen learning are bilingualism and dramatic play. These are also relatively recent lines of investigation. Let us start with bilingualism. Ellen Bialystok and her collaborators have been studying bilingual individuals for many years. Broadly speaking, they think of someone as bilingual if the person regularly uses two languages.

Their initial work focused on the implications of being bilingual for language development. Subsequently, they expanded their work to begin looking at how bilingualism influences non-verbal aspects of cognition. Their findings were very surprising. As it turned out, people who were bilingual show above average performance on working memory capacity and executive function. They are particularly good at inhibiting distractions and at switching between tasks or flexibility.

Bialystok speculates this is because in order to switch back and forth effectively between two languages, people need to use those executive abilities. They have been able to shown the same effects across a lot of different languages. It does not matter which two languages people are speaking, only that they are speaking two languages.

These advantages for bilinguals get bigger over time. That is, the way that bilingualism helps executive function gets more and more evident as people grow older and enter an age where executive function is often on the decline. Some evidence actually is suggesting that bilingualism may even be a protective factor against dementia. These are more good reasons to study second languages.

There are some caveats however. First, it is just not clear if people who learn a language later in their lives will experience the same benefits as people who have been bilingual from early in their lives. It also is not clear what happens if people once functioned as bilinguals as I did in Germany for my post-doctoral years. Largely function as monolinguals, as I do now that I have returned to my native country.

My favorite strategy to improve executive functions is to play! There are a lot of computer games that are being developed for these purposes, and those are not really well tested for the most part. Some more trustworthy and really beautiful findings have emerged from work done by Adele Diamond and her collaborators.

What they have done is they have shown that getting young children, very elementary school aged four, five, six-year-old children, to engage in dramatic play. By dramatic play, I mean the old school, role-playing and pretending kind of dramatic play, playing house. This improves executive functions. This is probably because this kind of play requires kids to take turns, to wait to talk, to inhibit some of their actions and to pay a lot of attention to what is happening around them, to what their friends are doing so that their responses make sense within the game.

I love these findings for a few reasons. First, they apply to at-risk children. Diamond and her colleagues were studying kids whose initial executive function when they got to preschool was not very good. We know already that is a risk factor for academic performance later on. The second thing they do is they underscore the immense value of having a broad curriculum for children, not a narrow specialization early on. Finally, they suggest to me that as adults, we might maintain and even optimize executive function by doing a little more playing ourselves. I think this is a low risk thing to try because even if it does not really help executive function for adults, it probably will make your life a lot more fun!

Attention, working memory, and executive function are important in supporting learning. Variable priority training, mindfulness meditation, learning another language and playing more may help us sharpen and maintain those abilities. What attention, working memory, and executive function also let us do is to monitor our learning, and next lecture, we will think more about monitoring learning and choosing strategies.

Choosing Learning Strategies
Lecture 16

In this lecture, we will discuss how our attention, working memory, and executive function allow us to monitor our learning. In any learning situation, we need to be able to devote some attention, working memory, and executive function to whether we are learning effectively, and judging our own learning is an important part of the process. If they are accurate, judgments about our learning can be very helpful. Knowing how to effectively use your judgments of learning will allow you to become an active, purposeful, engaged learner rather than a passive recipient of learning.

Judgments of Learning

- Judgments about our learning can tell us what we know and what we don't know, which also tells us what we need to focus on in a learning situation, whether we have learned something well enough to remember it later or perform it well, and whether we need to invest more time and effort in learning something. This is monitoring our learning progress.

- Additionally, if we need to invest more time and effort, our understanding of our own learning also encompasses the best strategies for how to invest that time and effort so that it pays off.

- The accuracy of our judgments of learning and choices about strategies is complicated by the issue that there are many different types of judgments and choices that we might be making.

- Judgments of learning are assessments of the extent to which you feel you have learned something. Often, in the laboratory, these judgments are studied in relation to learning a list of words or word pairs.

- In these settings, we can ask a couple of questions. First, how accurate is someone at predicting whether he or she has learned a word pair? This is a measure of absolute accuracy. You can also ask whether a person's judgments help differentiate between what they did and did not learn. This is a measure of relative accuracy.

- Generally, both types of accuracy are important, but in terms of allocating study time and employing study strategies, relative accuracy is a more important outcome.

Factors That Influence Judgments of Learning

- The accuracy of people's judgments of learning depends on a variety of conditions, and we are vulnerable to getting tricked in a variety of independent ways—that is, we can be inaccurate under some predictable circumstances.

- One important contribution to accuracy is when you're asked to make the judgments. If you are asked to judge your learning immediately after you have studied some items, you tend to overestimate your learning. Accuracy is enhanced if you wait a while and then ask how well you learned something.

- This is likely because in the immediate moment, your new learning is very accessible and feels very real; after a delay, you have a more accurate sense of whether you learned material because you don't have that immediate illusion that you really know it.

- We also base judgments of learning on irrelevant things. One of those things is the ease of processing the information in the first place—not the ease of learning, but the ease of just seeing the stimulus.

- For example, if you are presented with words, and some are presented very loudly while others are presented very softly, you will judge the loud words as better learned than the soft words. In fact, loudness of presentation has no bearing on recall; softly presented and loudly presented words are just as easily learned and remembered later.

- Researchers felt this might have to do with a sense of effort—that is, the more effortful it is to process information, the less well we think we have learned that information, regardless of whether that is true.

- Another factor that influences judgments of learning is how much time we've spent studying, but this factor is much more complicated than the others. In some cases, the more we study something, the more we judge we've learned it. However, in other cases, the more we study something, the less we judge that we've learned it.

- This only makes sense if you think about two different factors underlying study time: We study things longer if they are more important to learn and then view them as better learned, but we also study things longer if we think they're harder and then give them lower judgments of learning.

- Through their research, Asher Koriat and Ravit Nussinson showed that judgments of learning depend on our sense of effort and on our interpretation of that sense of effort. Specifically, when we interpret the effort as related to item difficulty, we downgrade our sense that we've learned the item. When we interpret the effort as related to us investing in learning, we upgrade our judgments of learning.

Using Judgments to Guide Learning Behavior

- A discrepancy reduction account is an approach in which you use judgments of learning to determine what you don't know, and then you invest time and study actions on what you don't know very well yet. Much of this work focuses on study time—not on how people learn.

- This discrepancy reduction account leads to the expectation that there will be a negative relationship between judgments of learning and allocations of study time; the more you think you know it, the less you study it.

Judging your learning involves knowing what you know and knowing the best strategies for maximizing learning.

- Across 16 studies in which researchers measured both judgments of learning and study time, 13 showed a negative relationship between the two, and 3 showed no relationship.

- More broadly, many studies show that people allocate more study time to more difficult items, and they also judge learning of such items as lower. This is consistent with the idea that judgments of learning are associated with strategic allocation of study time. However, the relationship disappears when people are under time pressure and when well-learned items are taken out of the to-be-studied items.

- These types of findings led to a different notion of how judgments of learning influence study behavior—again, in terms of time—and that is the region of proximal learning framework, in which people stop working on studying what they have already learned and then focus on the easiest of the items remaining in the material to be learned, shifting gradually toward more difficult items as they feel they have mastered the easier remaining items.

- We do this in part because the payoff of investing time in the easiest stuff we have not yet learned is likely to be very high. By contrast, a discrepancy reduction model means you could keep investing study time in items that are very difficult to learn—those that might consume your available time. However, there are important possible costs for eliminating easier and already-learned items from the study pool.

- The most effective strategy for learning is to repeatedly retrieve both items that are known and items that are not as well known. In studying, when we choose to recall only the items that we haven't yet mastered, we run into a memory issue that can disrupt learning called retrieval-induced forgetting.

- In retrieval-induced forgetting, people learn a set of items on a list. Then, they selectively practice only some items and are asked to not practice others. Over time, people show forgetting of the unpracticed items that is more than you'd expect; it's as if failing to practice these items makes them unlearned.

- This raises some questions about whether we know what strategies work best even when we use judgments of learning to focus on what we haven't yet mastered.

- Because every retrieval we do of something we learned is another rehearsal opportunity, repeated testing means repeated practice of the thing you're trying to learn to do. In many cases, it is impossible to rehearse something without repeatedly testing ourselves, so studying and testing are the same.

- However, in other cases—for example, when learning foreign vocabulary—you can study words by looking at them rather than by trying to generate them from scratch. The latter is more like testing.

- We know that repeated testing is extremely effective for learning and retention of learning more than simply studying materials that can be studied in non-test-like ways.

Research and Learning Strategies

- A series of experiments by Jeffrey Karpicke suggests that in many cases, we don't make good choices about using repeated testing. To investigate this, Karpicke did a series of four experiments in which foreign Swahili word pairs were studied.

- In the first study, Karpicke found that judgments of learning were highest for people who kept studying all the word pairs—higher than for those who dropped word pairs they had learned and for those who were repeatedly tested on already-learned pairs. Therefore, repeated testing doesn't increase judgments of learning.

- Karpicke also found that people's learning of the vocabulary words, as assessed one week later, was far higher in the repeated testing condition. This shows that people didn't realize that repeated testing was producing better learning.

- In the second experiment, Karpicke found that, given the choice, participants usually chose to drop items they had learned, to repeatedly test words that they were fairly confident of having learned, and to repeatedly study words they were less confident of having learned. Notably, this amounts to using your less effective strategy on the words that you think require the most learning.

- In the two additional studies, Karpicke showed that attempting retrieval early—before people have learned much—substantially improves the effects of studying. In other words, forcing people to take a test well before they are ready meant that afterward, in studying, they learned more. In addition, Karpicke found that people did not make use of this approach; given the choice, they opted to delay testing and to engage in more study.

- Research suggests that our judgments of learning are tightly tied to effort and that they are accurate enough to serve as a guide to where and how to invest learning efforts. Furthermore, we're fairly decent at monitoring what we do and do not know, and we can be subtle and strategic about how we use that information to determine what items deserve our studying effort in terms of time.

- The bad news is that we tend to stop studying and testing ourselves on things we believe we've already learned. However, this is a way to unlearn those things. Therefore, once you've learned something, that doesn't mean you should stop trying to retrieve it.

- Additionally, we tend to make far too little use of testing as a strategy for learning. We don't use repeated testing as often as other, less effective strategies—such as rereading or studying items—and we use it late, when we feel we have learned things.

- Unfortunately, early in the learning process, testing appears to make studying work more; in a way we should begin with testing and then move to studying, but people prefer the reverse order. To increase learning, study by testing yourself, and use repeated testing for material that might not otherwise lend itself to that approach.

Suggested Reading

Weinstein, McDermott, and Roediger III, "A Comparison of Study Strategies for Passages."

Zaromb, Karpicke, and Roediger III, "Comprehension as a Basis for Metacognitive Judgments."

Questions to Consider

1. Why do you think people avoid engaging in repeated testing while trying to learn material? What could be done to encourage students to use this extremely effective strategy?

2. Considering earlier lectures on different types of learning, why do you think repeated testing is so effective as a learning strategy?

Choosing Learning Strategies
Lecture 16—Transcript

In any learning situation, we need to be able to devote some attention and working memory and executive function to whether or not we are learning effectively. Judging our own learning is a really important part of the process. If they're accurate, judgments about our own learning can tell us many things. They can tell us what we know and what we do not know. That is important because that tells us what we need to still focus on in a learning situation, and whether or not we have learned something well enough to remember it later or perform it well, and they can tell us whether we need to actually invest more time and effort in learning something. This is monitoring of our learning progress.

Also, if we need to invest more time and effort, our understanding of our own learning also encompasses the best strategies for how we are going to invest our learning time and effort so that it pays off.

Let me outline a brief example of these two judgments knowing what we know and knowing the best strategies for maximizing learning given the time we have to do so. In earning a new piano piece, by monitoring your learning, you know which parts you can play without music, versus where you need the music, and which parts, even with the music. You really do not have down yet. You do not yet have the motor routines established to play it smoothly and without error. That is the monitoring part.

The strategy part is somewhat more complicated. Should you memorize the music so you do not need to read? Maybe. Should you invest a lot of time repeatedly playing the section of the piece that you do not have well learned yet, and just ignore the part you already know for now? Maybe. If you play that tough part over and over, you may not adequately learn the transition from the easy part to the rough part, so it could be better to just play the whole piece over and over again until the entire piece is learned well enough. Should you add to practicing by actually playing the idea f just reading over the musical notes now and then?

What we can do right away is we can ask how accurate are judgments of learning and how good are our choices about strategies? This turns out to be a somewhat complicated question, because there are a lot of different types of judgments and choices that we could be making. We are going to start with a particular kind of judgment, which is often just labeled "judgments of learning." This is an assessments of the extent to which I feel I have learned something.

Often, in the laboratory, these judgments are studied in relation to learning a list of words or word pairs. For example, I might be asked to learn a set of word pairs of words like chair-window, pillow-table, bed sheet–sofa. At some point after I have seen the word pairs, I am then asked to evaluate whether I am likely to remember or, to put it differently, whether I have learned a given word pair.

Often this is presented something like the following: If you see the word chair how likely are you to recall the correct paired word, the word that goes with chair? Usually I will be asked to rate the likelihood that I am going to remember that word on a 5 or 7 point scale. Then of course, I actually am tested on whether I really do remember this word.

If we are armed with this technique, we can ask a couple questions. The first question we can ask is how accurate are people at predicting whether they have learned a word pair? Imagine that I say I will remember about 75 percent of the words, that is, I give ratings of five or higher to 75 percent of the words I am shown. If I go on, on that recall test to get about 75 percent correct, I have demonstrated pretty high absolute accuracy.

You can also ask whether my judgments help differentiate between what I did, and did not learn. If I gave chair-window a high judgment of learning, and I gave pillow-table a low judgment, and then I go on and I remember window and I do not remember table, I am showing relative accuracy, even if my ratings were not precisely on target.

Generally, we are going to care about both of these, but if you think in terms of how to allocate study time and focus study strategies, it is that relative accuracy that is more important for us, knowing what we have versus what we have not learned.

With approaches like this, we can ask how accurately people are able to judge their learning. It turns out that accuracy depends on a variety of conditions, and it also turns out we are vulnerable to being tricked in several different ways, that is, we can be inaccurate in ways that researchers can now predict.

One important contribution to accuracy is when we are asked to make the judgments. Have you ever sat in a course or another learning situation and thought, yes, yes, wow I totally get this stuff, and then you go home, and maybe you try to work some homework problems and you find that suddenly what you thought you knew, you really had not learned. It does not make sense any more.

If you are asked to judge your learning immediately after you have studied some items, you tend to overestimate your learning. Accuracy is enhanced if you wait a while and then you consider how well you learned something. This is likely because in the immediate moment, your new learning feels very accessible and it feels very real. After a delay, you are going to have a more accurate sense of whether you have really learned that material, because you do not have that immediate "just learned it" illusion of accessibility and understanding.

This all sounds good, but we also base judgments of learning on irrelevant things. One of those things is the ease of processing the information in the first place. Note I am not talking here about how easy it really was to learn the material, but how easy it was just to see it. Consider this example, if I present words to you, I might just capriciously decide to present some words very loudly, and I might decide to do others very softly. If I ask you for judgments of learning, you will judge the loud words as better learned than the soft words.

In fact, the loudness of presentation has no bearing on your learning. Softly presented and loudly presented words are just as easily learned, and they are just as easily remembered later. Some researchers felt this was because people felt a sense of effort in processing the words. That is, the more effortful it is to process information, the less well we think we have learned that information, even if our judgment, our thoughts about whether we have learned the information, aren't accurate.

Another factor that influences judgments of learning is how much time we have spent studying, but this factor is more complicated. In some cases, the more we study something, the more we judge that we have learned it, and that makes sense, right. You have invested more time, and you should therefore have learned something better.

In other cases, the more we study something, the less we judge that we have learned it. These two sets of findings can only make sense if you think about two different factors that underlie study time choices. We study things longer if they are more important to learn, and then we think of them as better learned. We also study things longer if we think they are harder, and then we give them lower judgments of learning. If you want to test whether this idea is correct, you need a very clever way to make people feel like something is harder when there is absolutely no real difference in difficulty. You also need a way to disentangle study time from how difficult the items are.

Some researchers named Koriat and Nussinson did this in what I think is just an absolutely clever way. In a first experiment, they had people study pairs of words. People were told the study was about forehead muscle tension in computer work, and that they would look at pairs of words on the computer and they would simulate forehead tension in one of two ways.

In one condition, participants had to squint their eyebrows, which is a facial expression that is associated with mental effort. In another condition, participants had to raise their eyebrows. This makes people think they not doing anything effortful. Then, people learned paired associates and they judged their learning. People with the squinted eyebrows made lower judgments of learning, although virtually everything about their experience was identical except for that furrowed brow.

In a second study, Koriat and Nussinson wanted to show that if people attributed their sense of effort to the goal of working harder on some items, rather than to the items being more difficult, they could reverse this effect.

In other words it is not just that you feel you have put in effort, it is also important that you think the reason you put in effort was because the items were hard.

To do this, they made people feel time pressure and they told them we want you to selectively allocate study time to only some of the items we are asking you to learn. They asked that people only make their required facial expression, the squinting or the raised eyebrows when studied items, and not to do that when they looked at items that they were not going to actively study.

In this instance, people spent most of their study time on easy items and those who were making squinty eyebrows judged the items as better learned. What people did was to take that squinty-eyed sense of effort, and they connect it to studying hard, rather than to the items being difficult.

What this means is that judgments of learning depend on our sense of effort, and on how we interpretation of that sense of effort. Specifically, when we interpret the effort as related to the item difficulty or to the things we are learning being hard, we downgrade our sense that we have learned the item. We do not feel we have learned as much if that effort is connected to the material being hard.

When we interpret the effort as related to us investing ourselves and learning, we upgrade our judgments of learning. When we belief our effort is due to our goals for mastering learning, we feel we have learned more. In general, we can make judgments of learning and they are actually pretty accurate, even though they are subject to some distortions based on our sense of effort, and we can find ways to trick that sense of effort in the laboratory.

This is only one step. Given that you have judged your learning, do you then make use of those judgments to guide learning behavior? Do you make strategic use of these judgments? If so, how?

One way to think about the use of judgments has been called a discrepancy reduction account. What this means is that you use a judgment of learning to determine what you do not know. Then you invest time and study actions on the stuff you do not know very well yet. Discrepancy reduction account, it means you take account of what you do not know the discrepancy between what you have learned and what you have not learned, and you use that accounting to focus your studying effort on some parts of the material. A lot of this work looks at allocating study time to different material rather than on exactly what people do when they are studying.

This discrepancy reduction account gives us the following kind of expectation. We think there is going to be a negative relationship between judgments of learning and allocating study time. In other words, the more you think you know it, the less you study it.

Across 16 studies where researchers measured judgments of learning and study time, 13, the vast majority of those studies showed a negative relationship between these two, and three showed no relationship. More broadly, many studies show that people allocate more study time to difficult items, and they also judge learning of those difficult items as lower and all of this is consistent that with the notion that when we judge our learning we use those judgments to strategically put study time into the stuff that we do not know yet.

The relationship goes away under some circumstances, in particular when people are under time pressure, and when you take well-learned items out of the items for you to study. Why would this be?

These kinds of findings actually led to a different notion of how judgments of learning effect study behavior, and again, we are still talking in terms of how much time people spend and not what they do. This new account is called the region-of-proximal learning framework. In this framework, people stop working on or studying what they have already learned. What they then do is they focus on the easiest of the remaining items in the material they are learning, and they shift very gradually toward more difficult items after they feel they have mastered those easier.

Why would we do this? Well it is actually pretty smart. We do this because the pay off putting time into the easiest things we have not yet learned is likely to be really high. We think they are pretty easy. We have not learned them yet. Putting in a little time is going to yield payoffs. By contrast, a discrepancy-reduction model means you could keep investing study time in items that are really hard to learn, and that might eat up your available time, and you might still not be able to learn them.

We choose different strategies about time in relation to how much time we have, what we judge to be easy or difficult to learn, and what we think we have learned versus what we think we have not learned.

Having said this, there are some important possible costs for eliminating easier and already learned items from your study pool. This brings us to the issue of how people choose to study, not just how much time they allocate.

The most effective strategy for learning is to repeatedly retrieve both items you have already learned and items that you have not learned as well. When we choose, in studying, to recall and study only the items we have not yet mastered, we run into a different memory issue that can get in the way of learning, and that is called "retrieval induced forgetting."

In retrieval induced forgetting, people learn a set of items on a list. They might learn say a list of types of flowers. Then, they selectively practice only some items, and they are asked to not practice others. Over time, people actually forget the unpracticed items, but they forget them more than you would expect. It is as though failing to practice those items actually makes them get unlearned.

You still have to keep studying the stuff you already know as well as the stuff you think you have not mastered yet if you are going to perform well in a test situation. This raises some questions about whether, even when we use judgments of learning to focus in on what have not yet mastered, on whether we know what strategies work best.

Let us briefly reconsider the importance of repeated testing again here. Remember, every retrieval we do of something we have learned is another rehearsal opportunity. Repeated testing means repeated practice of the thing you are trying to learn to do or learn to remember. In many cases, it is impossible to rehearse something without repeatedly testing ourselves. I can't study a piano piece very well without actually playing it, so studying and testing are the same.

In other cases, say, learning foreign vocabulary, or learning about learning, I can study words or material by looking at them over and over again rather than trying to generate them from scratch. Generating them from scratch is more like testing. One thing we know is that repeated testing is extremely effective for learning and for retaining learning, much more so than simply reading over materials that you can be read over, that you can study in a non-test like way.

A lovely series of experiments by Karpicke suggests that in many cases, we do not make good choices about using repeated testing as a learning strategy. To investigate this, Karpicke did a series of four experiments. In the first, he was concerned with demonstrating two things. First, he wanted to demonstrate that repeated testing was a superior way to learn foreign vocabulary. Second, he wanted to show that repeated testing did not influence people's judgments of learning. That is, people were not aware of how good it was.

In the study, participants learned Swahili words, and they alternated between studying and testing until they had correctly remembered 40 words at least one time. After each test phase, participants judged how well they had learned the words. As soon as they correctly recalled a word, for some participants, that word was completely dropped from future study and test periods. For others, the word was not tested any more, but was on their study lists. For a third group, the word was no longer presented for studying, but it kept being tested. One week later, participants took a test on all of the vocabulary words.

In this initial study, Karpicke found that judgments of learning were highest for people who kept studying all the word pairs, higher than for those who dropped word pairs they had learned, and for those who were repeatedly tested on already-learned words. Repeated testing does not increase judgments of learning. That is, people are not aware that repeated testing is helpful for learning, and that is where that other goal becomes important.

Which group learned best? Karpicke found, not surprisingly, that people's learning of the words was far higher in the repeated testing condition. The other conditions recalled an average of 35 percent of the words. Those in the repeated testing condition recalled nearly 75 percent of the items they had learned; that is a huge difference. The take home picture here is people did not realize that repeated testing was producing better learning. They were not aware of that.

In that first experiment, participants were not given choices about what to do, the experimenter determined whether they were going to repeatedly study words or be repeatedly tested or whether they dropped already learned items. It is not like real world studying, where people make their own choices.

Naturally, a next question is going to be, "What happens when you let people make their own choices?" In the second experiment, Karpicke kept things largely similar, but when people first correctly demonstrated learning a Swahili word, they were asked to determine whether they would drop the word, keep studying the word, or keep testing the word. Participants have to decide how they would proceed with the words. Given their own choice, participants usually chose to drop items they had learned. They only chose to repeatedly test words that they were fairly confident they had learned extremely well. They chose repeated study for words they were less confident of having learned. What I want you to see is that this amounts to using your less effective learning strategy on the words that you think require the most learning.

In the two addition studies, Karpicke went on to show that attempting retrieval testing early before people really have learned much, actually substantially improves how effective it is to studying. Forcing people to take a test well before they are ready meant that afterwards, as they studying, they actually learned more. As with the issue of testing as a form of studying, Karpicke found that people did not make use of this approach given the choice, they always opted to delay testing and to engage in more study.

What might be going on there has to do with anxiety about being tested. Apparently being tested is scary even if we do it to ourselves and there aren't any real risks involved. There is no risk of being wrong or not knowing in studying, so reading over the words is what we prefer to do rather than give ourselves a test.

Why people are so reluctant to do self testing is a question where we really just do not know the answer yet, and it is going to be important to find out why if we want to persuade them to change and to actually make use of self-testing as a better way to learn new material.

A few other studies on learning strategies warrant some consideration here. Many of them come from Henry Roediger and his many collaborators. One involved looking at reading strategies and learning from texts. In this particular study, the researchers examined recall of text passages based on three different study approaches. In one approach, participants just reread the passage. This is what my undergraduate students do routinely when they study material they are learning.

In another condition, participants answered experimenter-generated questions. This is sort of like having to respond to thought questions about a text. In still another condition, participants had to generate and then answer their own questions. Participants were then asked to predict their own performance, which is fairly similar to judgments of learning. Participants thought generating and answering their own questions was related to significantly better learning. As it turned out, answering anyone's questions—theirs or the experimenters—led to improved performance.

Here I think we see some more of that effortfulness leading to higher judgments of learning, even when, in this case, there was no payoff for effort. It was actually more effort to make up and answer questions than just to answer the ones that the researcher posed, but that extra effort did not really help learning.

Another study from this same group of people looked at people's learning of sentences. Some sentences were harder to understand, and you needed a clue in order to make sense of them. To give you an example, one sentence was, "The notes were sour because the seam split." This is not easy to understand unless you have a clue, and the clue in this case is bagpipe.

Other sentences, like, "The colors appeared because the rain stopped," are fairly easy to figure out even when you do not have the clue, and the clue in that case was rainbow. People were shown the sentences in three different ways. They were given the sentences without clues, with the clues given right away, and with the clues given after some delay during which participants tried to figure the sentence out on their own.

They were also asked to make judgments of comprehension and learning. Judgments of learning were lower when people did not get clues at all but they were not lower when they got the clue after a delay. Here is the kind of important piece of that, waiting for the clue, having to try to figure out the sentence on your own before you got the clue actually produced better learning of the sentences, and this is because people had to puzzle a little while. Again, people did not realize this was the case.

Where does all of this leave us? Well first of all judgments of learning are tightly tied to effort and they are pretty accurate. They are accurate enough to serve as a guide to where and how to invest learning efforts. We are pretty descent at monitoring what we do and do not know. We can be subtle and strategic about how we use that information to determine what items deserve our studying effort in terms of time.

Where the good news breaks down is around the issue of how we choose learning strategies once we take into account judgments of learning and identify items to focus our study efforts on. The good news breaks down in several ways. Here, I want to recap those ways and I want to connect them to some everyday examples.

First, we tend to stop studying and testing ourselves on things, we think we have already learned. This turns out to be a way to unlearn those things. Once you have learned that *ein Hund* is a dog, it does not mean you should just stop trying to retrieve *Hund* now and then. In fact, you should occasionally try to say *Hund*.

You will notice that some types of learning are going to have built in protections about this. Musicians often play pieces they already know, and have already learned because it is fun. They may not consider this part of the learning or part of the maintenance of learning but it ends up having the same effect. In other cases, like learning foreign languages while being in your home country, we may be quite vulnerable to the tendency to just stop studying and stop testing what we have already learned.

Second, we tend to make way too little use of testing as a strategy for learning. Again, some types of learning, learning from what we read, and learning lists of vocabulary words are more vulnerable to this problem than others, like motor learning where it's difficult to study without actually testing. We do not use repeated testing nearly as often as we use other much less effective strategies like rereading or studying items.

We also tend to use it late in the game when we feel we have already learned something. People in most of the studies reviewed earlier want to focus self-testing on things they are sure they know, things where they have a lot of confidence.

Unfortunately, early in the learning process, testing makes studying work better, so in a way, we really ought to begin with testing ourselves and then go to studying. Unfortunately, people prefer, on their own, the reverse order. What I encourage my students to do, and you as well, is that if you want to learn something, study by testing yourself.

Sometimes, I actually tell students to do a "blank piece of paper" approach. Once you have encountered material you want to learn, whip out a blank piece of paper and try to write everything you can recall from the material. Then go back and look at the material again and try another blank piece of paper. This is the way we can use repeated testing to enhance learning, for material that might not otherwise lend itself to that approach. Or, to put that slightly differently, this is a way you can use self testing to learn material where it is very easy to become a passive recipient, a passive reader over rather than an active, purposeful, engaged learner.

In this lecture, we have focused on monitoring whether or not we have learned something. Another thing we might want to keep track of is where, when, and from whom we have learned something, because some people and contexts are better and more reliable sources than others. This is an issue we are going to take up in the next lecture.

Source Knowledge and Learning
Lecture 17

It's important to monitor your learning so that you can choose wise strategies, but it is also important to consider the source of your learning—learning where, when, and from whom you are acquiring a piece of information—because not all sources are equally reliable, valid, or trustworthy. Learning source information, also called source monitoring, is a very important part of learning. This lecture is about learning information that helps you decide whether other information is worth learning—or how much weight to give other information when pooling information from many places to learn about a topic.

Source Monitoring

- Source monitoring refers to learning the source and circumstances where we learned a fact, along with the fact itself. Many of the judgments we need to make relatively often in our lives depend on learning the source of a thought, image, or memory as well as the contents of that memory.

- The problem is that we do not appear as well suited to learning the source of our information as we are for learning the information itself. There are separate brain circuits involved in learning source information, for example, and many studies show that our memory for the content of information we have learned is superior to our memory for how we learned that content—where, when, and from whom.

- This divergence in our ability to learn sources versus information first became evident in the context of what is known as the sleeper effect in persuasion. Research on persuasion, in contrast to learning, is focused on how to change people's beliefs or attitudes toward something.

- In a typical persuasion experiment, you are exposed to some type of argument in favor of a particular position, product, or person. Researchers then vary pieces of that argument to see what factors make it more or less effective.

- For example: Does it matter if it is a famous actor endorsing the politician versus a random person? Are complex, elaborated arguments more effective than simple claims? Do those factors depend on something else, such as characteristics of the audience?

- Early on in this area of research, people became interested in what was termed source credibility—that is, if a plumber tells you about a toilet maintenance product, you might take his opinion seriously, but if your mechanically inept friend tells you something similar, you might not.

- Immediately after hearing a message, the credibility of a source matters in this way. However, over time, the low-credibility source message becomes more persuasive. This is what is called the sleeper effect because it is as though the not-very-credible message is just slumbering in your brain until it suddenly pops up as influential.

- The explanation for this effect has to do with the fact that we are fairly good at learning information that is important to our goals and concerns; we often don't have to try very hard for that type of learning. Unfortunately, we are much less good at remembering exactly where, when, and from whom we learned a piece of information. Because of this, the low-credibility source information fades in time and makes space for the message to stick around and influence us.

- There are serious issues that our bad source-learning ability can raise. One is unconscious plagiarism, which happens when we have a brilliant insight or way of expressing an idea that we think is ours but that, in fact, belongs to someone else.

- An issue surrounding eyewitness memory is that we can become confused about whether we saw something happen or heard about it from other eyewitnesses after the fact. Information from the event itself, from discussing it with others, and from reading about it in the news can all get mixed up in ways that are difficult to disentangle later.

- Another issue involves knowing whether we did something or just imagined it. This is called reality monitoring, and it has to do with whether the source of something we have learned is a real source or just the thoughts or imaginings in our head.

Factors Affecting Source Learning

- Age is related to source learning in several ways. Young children are very bad at learning the source of their experiences as compared to young adults, and older adults are also relatively bad at source learning.

- While we can't do much about being young or old, it is worth knowing that age can put us at a disadvantage in terms of learning where, when, and from whom we have learned something because we can choose to be more careful about our source learning.

- A second factor that influences source memory in ways that can help or hurt us is the use of schemas about a source. We usually have pretty well-developed ideas about sources of information; in fact, that is part of what allows us to know whether a source is credible or not.

- We also have expectations about what others might say or think based on our knowledge of them. When we are trying to figure out who recommended a book, for example, we are likely to use constructive processes to try to remember, based on who we discuss books with and who would like this type of book. We want to know who recommended the book because that tells us how much we should consider buying it. However, this type of constructive, expectation-driven way of trying to guess a source is likely to lead to biases.

- When schemas are violated, it is sometimes easier to learn, provided that you are thinking about your expectations in the first place. For example, if your mother has never recommended a book to you and then does, the fact that you are surprised by this might make it easier for you to remember the source. If you're more focused on trying to remember the name of the book so that you can buy it, however, you might be less likely to recall the source of the recommendation.

- As with other aspects of learning, when we fail to learn something well enough, we make use of existing knowledge to create an educated guess about that thing; in the case of sources, our schemas will often be correct, but they will sometimes be wrong.

- A third factor that influences source learning was identified in a meta-analysis of experiments on the sleeper effect in which researchers confirmed that the sleeper effect exists and is not trivial. They also found that the sleeper effect is very much driven by either failing to fully learn or ultimately forgetting the source of information. Additionally, it matters how you process information about the message and about the source of the message.

- In many cases, people apply different approaches to the information and to the source of the information. It is more likely that you don't pay any attention to the source beyond a cursory nod—one that makes more use of what are called heuristic cues about credibility rather than carefully thinking about the meaning of the source for the information that is being presented.

- Work on unconscious plagiarism reveals another factor affecting source learning: When you encounter information and think about it yourself, it complicates the issue of where a thought originated.

© Jupiterimages/Getty Images/Brand X Pictures/Thinkstock.

Recalling the source of a particular fact is sometimes just as important as learning the fact itself.

- In one study, researchers used an idea-generation paradigm to look at how people come to believe that others' ideas belong to them. Participants first generated ideas in a group, but then they were asked to think about their own and others' ideas more, under a variety of conditions. The condition in which participants were asked to think about the idea and how it might be improved upon made it more likely that people later recalled those ideas as their own—even when they were initiated by others.

- Finally, some researchers point out that there are important clues to source in memory phenomenology. When something actually happened—rather than being just imagined, for example—we tend to remember that event with the perceptual and sensory detail that it had at the time it occurred.

- By contrast, when we just imagine something, we may have memories of our thoughts and feelings, but we tend to have less of a sense of sensory and perceptual detail. Likewise, if we saw something occur, we tend to have perceptual and sensory memories, but if we read about it, this is less the case.

- What this line of thinking suggests is that if people are asked to attend to the sensory and perceptual aspects of memories, they may be better at recalling source information than if they are asked to attend to other types of information, such as their own thoughts and feelings, because these are not so good at distinguishing the source that gave rise to them.

- Research findings point to the fact that if we pay attention to source information and think about what it means—if we elaboratively encode source information—we are able to learn it just fine.

- Elaborative encoding includes paying attention to the source when we are learning, thinking about the meaning of the source for the message in an elaborated, and paying some attention to the sensory and perceptual aspects of a learning experience. These features help us to later remember the source of information.

Source Learning and Modern Society

- In today's information-rich society, we can learn about topics from many different sources, so issues of source learning become important for how we integrate that information into our own understanding of a phenomenon. In fact, an understanding of sources and an ability to weigh them appropriately can be critical in determining how well people understand the phenomena they study.

- In learning about climate change, for example, people might consult a wide variety of sources, including news reports from conservative and liberal news outlets, scientific reports, government documents, press releases from universities, blogs on the Internet, popular magazines, and textbooks.

- To draw conclusions across all these sources, people need to be able to put the texts together and make sense of them, and they are likely to conflict with one another. Furthermore, people need to weigh the sources appropriately, giving less credibility and less weight to information from sources that have obvious conflicts of interest— such as oil companies or highly partisan wildlife protection groups.

- Research in this area has shown that better source learning is associated with better integration across different sources of knowledge. Thus, source learning is critical for avoiding influence by information we'd rather not learn. It may also foster better capacities to integrate information from multiple sources in a way that takes into account source credibility.

- There are many circumstances in our everyday lives in which it is important not only to know what we have learned but also to recall the circumstances under which we learned it—perhaps especially the source of the information. Our tendency is to fail to do so, with some predictable consequences, but some findings suggest that we can do better and that doing better improves learning of what we want to know and helps keep questionable information out of influential range.

Suggested Reading

Kumkale and Abarracin, "The Sleeper Effect in Persuasion."

Stark and Perfect, "Whose Idea Was That?"

Questions to Consider

1. When is it critical to focus attention on and attempt to learn source information? When is it less critical to do so? Are there times in the lifespan when source learning is less important?

2. What might be the utility of having a mind that learns the information itself better than when and where the information was learned and from whom?

Source Knowledge and Learning
Lecture 17—Transcript

It is important to monitor your learning so you can choose wise strategies, but it is also important to consider the source of your learning. Learning where, when, and from whom you are acquiring a piece of information. As I'm sure you are acutely aware, not all sources are created equally reliable, valid, or trustworthy.

Learning source information, which is also called source monitoring, may seem like a very odd part of learning, but it turns out that it matters in all sorts of ways. Consider your knowledge about the way our president is elected in the United States. You know that in the United States the president is technically elected by the Electoral College, which is composed of representatives from the states, who allocate their state's electoral votes, which are in tern based on the number of representatives to the U.S. congress to the president typically wholesale,

Do you recall when and where you learned this fact? Do you remember who taught you this fact? For most of us, probably not. You just learned this feature of our government at some point. For this example, it really does not matter where, when, and from whom you learned about the Electoral College, because in fact, that is an accurate description of the Electoral College.

How about this: Imagine that you learned that newly discovered Herbal supplements can prevent or treat type two diabetes and this is something South Asians have known for centuries. At this point, it becomes rather critical to remember whether you read this on the website of the Mayo clinic, a trusted source, or on the website of a company dedicated to selling that particular herbal supplement.

In a way, this lecture is about learning information that helps you decide whether other information is worth learning, or how much weight to give other information when pooling information from a lot of different sources to learn about a topic.

Source monitoring refers to learning the source and circumstances where we learned a fact or two, along with the fact itself. Some examples of well-known source monitoring tasks include: knowing who said what; knowing whether you actually remember seeing something on your now-forgotten shopping list, or you just know it was there; knowing whether you actually told your husband about the school play tomorrow, or just imagined telling him; and knowing whether you actually saw that driver make an illegal left turn, or overheard another witness say that same thing.

As you can see, these are judgments we may need to make relatively often, and they all depend on learning the source of a thought, image, or memory as well as the contents of that memory. Here is the problem, we do not appear as well suited to learning the source of our information, as we are for learning the information itself. There are somewhat separate brain circuits involved in learning source information, for example, and many studies show that our memory for the content of information we have learned is superior to our memory for how we learned that content, where, when, and from whom.

This divergence in our ability to learn sources, versus just information from them, first became evident in the context of what is known as the sleeper effect in persuasion. If you are like me, in a few minutes, you are going to find our not-so-fabulous source learning capacity to be pretty disturbing along with the confirmation bias and naive realism phenomena that we discussed in Lecture 13.

What is the sleeper effect? This goes back to early research on persuasion. Research on persuasion, in contrast to research on learning, is focused on how to change people's beliefs or attitudes toward something. As you might well imagine, this is a kind of research companies and politicians are very interested in, because it helps them figure out how to get our money and how to get our votes.

In a typical persuasion experiment, you will be exposed to some kind of argument in favor of a particular position, product, or person. Researchers interested in persuasion then vary pieces of that argument to see what factors make it more or less effective. For example, does it matter if it is a famous actor who is endorsing the politician, or a regular Joe the plumber? Are complex, elaborate arguments in favor of a particular policy more effective, or is it better to go with a simple claim? Does the influence of these kinds of issues depend on something else like characteristics of the audience that you are trying to persuade?

Early on in this area of research, people became interested in what was called "source credibility." That is something like this: If your dad the plumber tells you about a toilet maintenance miracle product, you might well take his opinion seriously. On the other hand, if your dad the incompetent, mechanically inept English professor tells you something similar, a grain of salt, maybe.

Here is the catch: Immediately after you hear this message, this is exactly how the credibility of a source matters—that is, immediately when you hear a message, if it is your dad the plumber you say, "Wow, really?" and if it is your dad the English professor you say, "Maybe, dad." Over time, though somehow that low credibility source message comes to have a stronger effect. That is, over time, it gets more persuasive.

Why would this be? On the surface of it, this makes no sense at all. This is what is called the sleeper effect, because it is as though that not-very-credible message is just sleeping away somewhere in your brain, and then suddenly it pops up as being influential.

The explanation for this effect has to do with the fact that we are quite good at learning content—information that is important to our goals and concerns. Often, as we have noted before in this course, we do not really even have to try all that hard to learn that kind of thing. It is really easy to remember that there exists, out there in the world, a miracle toilet product that will solve all our plumbing issues permanently, forever—fabulous.

Unfortunately, we are quite a bit less good at remembering exactly where, when, and from whom we learned about the miracle toilet product. Because of this, the low-credibility source information, which was preventing us from taking that idea of the product seriously, fades in time and it makes space for the message to actually stick around, and influence us.

There are other really serious issues that our bad source learning ability can raise. One of them is unconscious plagiarism. This happens when we have a brilliant insight or, worse yet, we come up with a fabulous way to expressing an idea and we think the insight or the way of expressing the idea is ours, and in fact, it actually belongs to someone else.

In a typical study of this kind of phenomenon, you might participate with a group of people. Initially, you and all the others would generate ideas about something. Say, one example would be a non-traditional way that you could use a typical object like a paperclip. What can we do with a paperclip other than clip papers? In this situation, there are two things you are learning, one is ideas about crazy things to do with paperclips. The other is who came up with each idea.

Later, if I am the experimenter, I can test you both on whether you remember the ideas your group generated, and also whether you remember correctly which ideas were yours and which ideas actually came from other group members. From a grading perspective, people do okay at this. They get about a C+. They get about 78 percent correct judgments of whether ideas were theirs or other people's. What that means is that they do adopt other people's ideas as their own sometimes.

Another issue involves eyewitness memory. In eyewitness memory research, we can get confused about whether we actually saw something happen when we were eyewitnesses or whether we just heard about it from other eyewitnesses after the fact. Information from the experience itself and also from discussing it with other people, reading about it in the news, being interviewed repeatedly about it by people interested in solving a crime, they can all get mixed up in ways that are hard for us to disentangle later, because we do not remember which information came from which source.

Still another involves knowing whether we did something, or we just imagined it, say, did we close the garage door or not? This is called reality monitoring. Again, it has to do with whether the source of something you have learned, whether or not you closed the garage door, is a real source. Watching the door come down, or is it just the thought or imagination part of that where you sort of imagine that you hit the button and then you drove off without actually doing it.

These difficulties with source memory have nothing to do with how intelligent we are. Rather, they have a lot to do with the limited nature of our effortful processing system, so that system two for learning. Everyone is vulnerable. That means we want to ask what we can do to improve our ability to learn source information.

To address this question, let us consider what factors improve or interfere with source learning. Along the way, we will learn some of the ways that source learning still works quite a bit like other forms of learning. Then we will return to the issue of which of those factors represent strategies we can actually use in our own lives, when we need to do source learning.

First, age is related to source learning in several ways. Young kids are pretty bad at learning the source of their experiences compared to young adults, and older adults are also relatively poor at source learning. For example, in one study, children and young adults were shown eight smells—or I guess they were asked to really smell eight smells—by either a male or a female researcher. Later, the kids were tested on whether they had learned the smells, but they were also tested on whether they knew which researcher had presented a smell, the source for that information.

Children were significantly poorer at recalling the source than were young adults. This is actually consistent with a lot of similar findings from other studies that look at other kinds of learning and other kinds of course.

Older adults, similarly, show somewhat poorer source memory or source monitoring on tasks where they hear statements from two different individuals and they are asked later, "Who said what?" This is also true for tasks where older adults are asked to distinguish between actions they did versus actions they only imagined performing.

We really cannot do much about being young or old. It is worth knowing though that age can put us at an advantage or a disadvantage in terms of learning where, when, and from whom we have learned something. It lets us know when source is important that we may need to be somewhat more vigilant if we are for example entering our later years.

A second factor that influences source memory in ways that can both help or hurt us is the use of schemas about a source. We usually have actually pretty well developed ideas about sources of information. In fact, this is actually part of what lets us know whether a source is credible or not.

We also have expectations about what others might say or think based on our knowledge of them. When we are thinking, "Who said I should read that book?" we are likely to use some constructive processes to try to recall based on who we discuss books with, who would like this type of book, and so on. Remember, we did not really quite learn the source in the first place.

We want to know who recommended the book because that tells us how much we should seriously consider buying it. You may already be thinking this type of constructive, expectation-driven way of trying to guess a source is likely to lead to biases. We are likely to guess that our friend Kate told us about that book, when in this instance, it turns out it was our mother.

There is a funny thing about schemas, when they are violated, that sometimes makes something easier to learn, something that violates your expectations can actually be easier to recall provided you were thinking about your expectations in the first place. Imagine that my mother recommends a science fiction novel to me. In more than four decades of my life, this has never happened. If at that moment, I think about the information, the book recommendation, and I pay attention to the source, my mother, the violation of my schema of my mom is likely to make her quite memorable as the source here.

Of course, I might be more focused on trying to remember the name of the book so that when I am at the store, I can purchase it. In that case, I may be less likely to recall the source of the information. In other words, as with other aspects of learning, when we fail to learn something well enough, we make use of existing knowledge to create an educated guess about that thing. In the case of sources, our schemas will often be correct, but sometimes they are going to be wrong.

Remember, we are not going to unlearn schemas—they are actually really helpful; they are really efficient; they do a lot of good work for us. But again, this is a case where this can help us know when source memory matters one of the things that might lead us astray is our schemas about sources.

This example is related to a third factor that influences source learning, and this is a factor that got identified in a meta-analysis of about 72 different experiments on the sleeper effect. In that meta-analysis, researchers first of all confirmed that the sleeper effect exists and it's not trivial. By that, I mean it is pretty sizable as effects go. It actually matters for people's behavior and purchasing decisions and things of that sort.

The second the meta-analysis showed was that the sleeper effect is very much driven by either failing to fully learn, or forgetting the source of information we have acquired. Third, and more important for our current thinking, it matters how you process both information about the message, that is kind of the what, that is the content, and information about the source of the message, who is giving you this information.

In many cases it turns out, people apply quite different approaches to these two kinds of information. If we go back to this book example, when someone recommends a book to you, you often pay most of your attention. The lion share of your attention on capacity goes to information about the book. What is it about? Who wrote it? Particularly what is the title? Where can I get it? Can I get it for the kindle? Can I get it for the iPad? Is it long? How long is it going to last me? Is it tough reading or is it easy reading?

I know that when someone recommends a book to me, I ask a lot of questions about the book. I am doing elaborative encoding about the book, in fact. As we know time and time again, elaborative processing leads to better learning about the book.

What have I paid almost no attention to? The source. Recall that in my made-up example, the source is my mother. She is recommending science fiction! If I am paying a lot of attention to the source, I may really stop and think about that. She doesn't like sci-fi. Does this mean the sci-fi is atypical in some way? Why would mom like this book when she has utter disdain for the genre? Should I weight her recommendation more heavily because of that? Does that means this is just an exceptional piece of literature and happens to be sci-fi? Or does it mean this is sci-fi that isn't really good sci-fi, and I should really pay less attention to this recommendation?

In most cases, it is more likely that I do not really pay any attention to the source beyond a precursory nod, a kind of look that makes more use of what are called heuristic cues about credibility. A heuristic is a rule of thumb quick and dirty way to go about making a judgment. It is kind of like a good guess rather than precise computation or thinking fully through an issue.

In this case, I made kind of a snap judgment about how I am going to treat source credibility instead of carefully thinking about the meaning of the source for the information they are presenting. I might think mom, not the sci-fi expert, but that is as much thought as I give it. I do not go on to say, "Well, what does that mean? How should I take that into account?" As a result, I might actually initially dismiss this recommendation and I don't buy the book right away. Later though, I am wandering around a book store, I see that title and I think, "I heard that was really good," and I buy it; that's the sleeper effect.

Work on unconscious plagiarism reveals another factor that affects source learning. When you encounter information and think about it yourself, it actually complicates the issue of where a thought came from. In one study, researchers used an idea generation paradigm, a lot like that example of the paperclip, and they looked at how people come to believe that others' ideas belong to them.

As in the standard approach, people first generated ideas in a group setting. Then, people were asked to think about their own and others ideas more, under a variety of conditions. In one condition, people were asked to think about the ideas while adding visual imagery to the, so they are sort of picturing how the paperclip could become a sculpture. In another, they were asked to just read over the ideas repeatedly. In still another, they were asked to think about the idea and how it might be improved on.

As it turns out, and kind of unfortunately, this last condition makes it more likely that people later think others ideas were their own even when the idea really came from a different person. This illustrates a source-learning problem, but it also may clarify a number of work-related experiences that many adults have, and maybe some non-work experiences too. It really is possible that your colleague did not intend to steal your idea, and honestly believes it was his own, and that may be particularly true if it was generated in a meeting and people discussed how to make your initial idea better.

Finally, some researchers point out that there are important clues to source in memory phenomenology, in how it feels to us when we are remembering something. When something actually happened, rather than just being imagined, for example, we tend to remember that event along with all of that perceptual and sensory detail that it had when it occurred. This makes sense because when we go through experiences in our lives, we are paying attention to and we are also learning from the sensations and perceptions that those experiences involve.

When we just imagine something, by contrast, we may have memories for our thoughts and feelings, but we also tend to have less of a sense of sensory and perceptual detail. Likewise, if we saw something occur, we tend to have perceptual and sensory memories of that experience of what we watched. If we read about it, this is less the case.

What this line of thinking suggests is that if people are asked to attend to phenomenal logical aspects of their memories, to how sensory and perceptual the memory feels they may actually be better at recalling source information than if they are asked to attend to other aspects of memory phenomenology like their thoughts and feelings. Thoughts and feelings are not so good at distinguishing the source that gave rise to them. They all come from inside our heads and it is hard to know whether they came initially from something outside of us. We can have powerful thoughts and feelings about imagined events. It is harder to have very vivid sensory and perceptual memories for things that did not actually happen.

Let us pause for a moment and summarize what all this means for learning source information. First, children and older adults (people over 65 years of age or so), they are more vulnerable to source learning difficulties, and we just can't do much about that beyond knowing it and trying to keep it in mind when it matters.

The other findings provide some more optimistic perspective on improving source learning. First, the findings point to the fact that if we pay attention to source information and we think about what it means, if we elaborative encode source information, we are able to learn it just fine. Elaborative encoding includes a variety of features.

First of all, it means paying attention to source in the first place when we are learning. Sometimes we can dispense with that when we know we are learning from an authoritative and trustworthy source, but when we don't know that, we need to pay attention to who is telling us information.

Elaborative encoding also includes thinking about the meaning of the source for the message in a more elaborated way. It means not stopping with mom, not the sci-fi expert, but kind of going forward and saying, well how should that effect the message here? How should that effect how I interpret this book recommendation?

It also includes paying some attention to sensory and perceptual aspects of the learning experience, sort of, what it feels like in the moment while I am learning. Where am I? What are the sounds? What are the smells? What is the kind of ambiance of the learning situation? These things help us to later remember the source of information.

It is completely possible to become skilled at doing this. Working scientific researchers learn to encode source information all the time. When we learn about new research findings, we typically also learn who generated those findings. Why do we do this? It helps us to organize research findings. It helps us keep track of what is going on in a field by knowing what other people's full program of research is about. It helps us keep track of who is doing related research, who are the other experts in our field that we might rely on for advice and suggestions about our own work, and whose work is going to inform our next research project. Source knowledge is actually something that distinguishes experts from novices in many scientific fields, because experts know who is generating knowledge as well as what knowledge is being generated.

Well, many of the problems arising from poor source learning extend way beyond simply learning. Knowing whether we actually lock the door or we just imagined ourselves doing it is not quite learning. At the end of this lecture, what I want to do is bring all of this consideration of source learning and source monitoring back to a consideration of how source learning influences other kinds of learning, more like what we have been thinking about all along in this course.

In today's information rich society, we all learn about topics from many sources. Issues of source learning become actually quite important for how we integrate different pieces of information into our own full understanding of a phenomenon. In fact, an understanding of sources and an ability to weigh them appropriately can be critical in determining how well people understand something they are trying to learn about, say, on the internet.

Consider the example of learning about climate change. In learning about climate change, people might consult a wide variety of sources, news reports from conservative and liberal news outlets, scientific reports, government documents, press releases from universities, and blogs on the internet, Wikipedia, popular magazines, textbooks and so on. There is an enormous wealth of information out there.

To draw conclusions about global warming or climate change across all these different sources, people have to be able to put all of the different sources together and they have to be able to make sense of them. These different sources are likely to say things that conflict with one another. People also are going to need to weight the sources appropriately. They are going to need to be able to give less credibility and less weight to information from sources that have obvious conflicts of interest like oil companies on the one hand and highly partisan wildlife protection groups on the other.

In line with this concern, a set of researchers set out to look at how people learn from multiple documents and multiple sources and they did actually focus on climate change. The participants read seven different texts about climate change, obtained from different sources, including a textbook, a popular science text from a University research center, a science article from a research magazine that was authored by a physics professor, a news article from a liberal daily newspaper, a news article from a conservative daily newspaper, a Norwegian government report, and an oil company project report. The texts contained conflicting information, about causes, consequences, and solutions related to climate change.

Participants were tested on their learning by evaluating their comprehension of the materials. This was done with a series of 25 test sentences that combined information from statements within the text in either valid or invalid ways and then another 20 test sentences that did the same thing but instead of combined information within one texts, they combined information that was present in different texts. These latter sentences were the critical ones, because they are the ones that really address understanding that integrates different sources of information. If we are reading seven texts about climate change, we do not really want to memorize seven separate texts. We want to get a general understanding of climate change and the relevant science.

Participants were also tested on their source memory with sentences from the texts and distracter sentences. They were asked to tell which text the sentence came from. This is a classic source memory test. Participants whose source memory performance was better also learned more from the texts. This was true even when the researchers controlled for how much they knew already about climate change, and for how much difficulty they had with reading text. Better source learning was associated with better integration across different sources of knowledge.

Source learning is critical for avoiding influence by information we would rather not learn, advertising from bad sources. It may also foster better capacities to integrate information from multiple sources in a way that takes into account source credibility.

There are many circumstances in our everyday lives in which it is important not only to know what we have learned, but also to recall the circumstances under which we learned it—perhaps especially the source of the information.

Our tendency is to fail to do so, and this has some predictable consequences. The findings we have just considered suggest that we can do better, and that doing better improves learning of what we want to know, and may help keep non-credible information buried somewhere out of influential range.

In the past three lectures, we have considered aspects of how we learn that have to do with dry facts: where, when, from whom, what strategies we employ, and what we know about what we have already learned, and what we are applying basic cognitive capacities to the act of learning. Part of how we learn also involves how we feel and what we want when we approach learning. In the next lectures, we will move to considering these less dry aspects of learning, how what we are feeling affects what we learn, and how what we want to know might do the same.

The Role of Emotion in Learning
Lecture 18

In the past three lectures, we've considered aspects of how we learn that involve the dry facts of where, when, and from whom—what strategies we employ, what we know about what we've already learned, and what basic cognitive capacities we are applying to learning. Part of how we learn involves how we feel and what we want when we approach learning. In this lecture, we'll move to considering these less dry aspects of learning—how what we are feeling affects what we learn and how what we want to know might do the same.

Studying Emotions

- Emotions are defined as a temporary state of a person that entails coordinated patterns of physiological arousal and mental states that can promote emotionally relevant patterns of behavior. In fact, people can experience the physiology of a particular emotion, and sometimes even the subjective emotional state, by posing their faces in the right way.

- Many researchers believe that emotions have an evolutionary basis, and this is important to consider in thinking about how emotions may affect learning. We share basic emotions with many other animals; for example, rats demonstrate anxiety, and dogs show depression.

- Theorists believe that negative emotions, which are triggered by threatening situations, such as anger and fear served to motivate fight-or-flight responses in our evolutionary history. On the other hand, happiness, pleasure, and joy are less clearly evolutionarily functional.

Researchers often induce particular emotions in participants by showing them certain film clips and images.

Negative Emotions and Learning

- The possibility to induce emotion in the lab is what permits researchers to investigate the impact of emotional states on learning. Researchers do this in a variety of ways—from asking people to remember autobiographical experiences that involved particular emotions to showing them film clips and images or playing musical selections that induce particular emotions.

- Many researchers use film clips and images because these materials allow us to expose everyone to the same event or experience in order to make them, for example, fearful. By contrast, using our own events introduces individual differences as factors.

- When we think about how negative emotions affect learning, we need to consider what they have in common, which is unpleasantness, and where they are more distinct, which involve arousal and specific action tendencies.

- Negative emotions appear to narrow our attentional focus, which allows us to be better at learning details about an emotionally negative stimulus than a neutral stimulus.

- In some of the earliest studies, participants would be asked to learn a series of images from slides. Most of the slides would be neutral, but a traumatic slide in the middle was both learned and later remembered. Interestingly, people were remarkably unlikely to recall the slide immediately before or after the traumatic slide.

- Researchers view this as an adaptive attention and learning phenomenon; things that don't matter much are learned when there is nothing more serious going on, but something that is threatening is what you should pay attention to and remember.

- Elizabeth Kensinger showed people a set of images and then asked them to look at a second set of images. In the second set, some of the objects were identical to those in the learned set, others were similar, and some were new. People had to judge whether the objects were identical, which required memory for details, or similar, which just required memory for having seen a particular image. People's memory for details was significantly better for negative images.

- In subsequent work, Kensinger and her colleagues showed that negative stimuli don't just get better learned in general; in fact, we learn the important and central details of negative things and are more likely to forget the peripheral, less important details.

- One study made participants feel sad or happy and then asked them to learn a neutral task. Then, participants were asked to do new tasks to see whether their learning transferred. Participants in a negative mood when learning performed more poorly than those in a positive mood. Participants in a negative mood while trying to generalize their learning to new tasks needed more time to do the transfer tasks and did more poorly at those tasks.

- While fear might enhance learning of threat-relevant information, sadness might suppress learning performance. It is less clear what anger does, but findings in this area suggest that it operates similarly to fear in narrowing attention toward relevant, central details.

- Although some negative emotions may help to focus attention and improve learning of critical, threat-relevant details in the moment, others have shown that over the long term, negative emotions in academic contexts are linked to lower student involvement and motivation; to students being less likely to use more effective learning strategies, such as elaborative encoding; and to students learning as indicated by their academic performance.

- Negative emotions generally seem to narrow attention and focus it on information that is most relevant to the immediate threat, thus enhancing learning of the most important information for the person at that moment and suppressing learning of less relevant information.

- When there is no immediate threat, negative emotions appear to generally suppress a number of factors that we know promote better learning and, ultimately, to have a negative impact on learning itself.

Positive Emotions and Learning

- Positive emotions really don't involve physiological arousal; rather, they are characterized by a lack of stress-related arousal. Additionally, positive emotions really don't promote any specific actions.

- Given the association of positive emotions with lower levels of arousal, Barb Fredrickson discovered that being encouraged to experience positive emotions after negative ones speeds up our return to a baseline, neutral level of arousal.

- In looking at a variety of research findings on creativity, broad thinking, and even artistic temperaments, she also discovered that the function of positive emotions was to support people in broadening and building; in other words, positive feelings support us in acquiring resources for the long term whereas negative emotions support immediate, focused action in response to important, present threats. These resources might take many forms to establish new social relationships and to affirm existing ones.

- Positive emotion also supports us in exploring our environment, and exploration is fundamental to learning. Attachment theory was based on the idea that babies need a secure relationship to their parents in order to explore the environment, and babies who are afraid don't explore. One way to articulate this idea in a more succinct manner is to propose that positive emotions broaden our focus of attention.

- Some studies of learning and emotion show strong relationships of positive emotions in academic settings to motivation, learning strategies, and actual academic achievement. The problem is that the students who were feeling less positive may have already had difficulties with the material and, hence, ended up with lower grades because of less ability or poorer preparation.

- Therefore, to assess causality, studies need to be able to make people feel positive emotions, and they need a way to examine whether the focus of attention is broad or narrow. Additionally, they need to compare positive emotions to a neutral state and to show that different positive emotions—such as amusement and contentment—work similarly to broaden attention.

- To make people feel positive, one strategy is to use brief two- or three-minute film clips. Film clips of penguins at play, for example, are used by Fredrickson and her colleagues to create feelings of amusement while scenes of nature are used to create serenity and contentment. To create a neutral state, film clips of random patterns can be used.

- To examine whether participants had a broader attentional focus after the positive-emotion film clips, Fredrickson and her colleagues used a task that assesses a preference for global (general) versus local (detail-oriented) processing of visual images after participants first viewed an emotion-inducing film clip. Participants in the positive-emotion conditions had significantly more global responses than did participants in the neutral condition. Furthermore, it didn't matter which positive emotion the person was feeling.

- Importantly, attention is not the same as learning, but having a broader attentional focus might increase the amount of information people are able to take in—in contrast to the effects of negative emotions.

- In addition, positive emotions may help to maintain motivation to learn. Amy Reschly and her colleagues looked at positive emotion and academic engagement in a sample of high school students. Students who reported frequent positive emotion in school also reported higher levels of engagement with learning—although Reschly and her colleagues did not have assessments of whether students actually were learning more effectively.

- In another study, researchers looked at positive emotion over the course of a semester for college students, and students who reported lots of positive emotions in the context of classes ended up using better learning strategies, being more intrinsically motivated by school, and ultimately, performing better.

- There are problems with interpreting such research as definitively showing that emotions cause changes in learning because students with more positive emotion may have simply been more capable, more knowledgeable, or otherwise better prepared—so the emotions might not have played a role in better learning outcomes.

- A more recent study in this arena took an experimental approach and focused more explicitly on category learning. Ruby Nadler and her colleagues used music and video clips to discover that being in a good mood enhanced people's ability to learn complex categories that were rule based correctly.

Negative versus Positive Emotions and Learning

- Good moods lead to broader attention, better category learning, and better longer-term academic learning. However, the more creative, attentionally broad cognitive approach that people in a good mood have is specifically good at enhancing transfer; people who learn a task do better at transferring that knowledge to similar problems when they are in a good mood.

- It's clear that emotions influence learning at many phases of the process: They influence the breadth or narrowness of attention, the extent to which we actively seek information, the way we approach the information we get, the speed with which we learn, and our ability to generalize what we are learning—to apply learned rules or approaches in new circumstances or to new problems.

- One way to think about this in practical applications is that some moods are better for some tasks. A relatively negative mood is optimal for situations where we need to be focused on specific material and learning central aspects of that material.

- Some mild anxiety in studying for a test might actually enhance performance by focusing attention and ensuring that we study enough; this is especially true if the anxiety is not chronically present for us, but only there when we need to focus our studying.

- A relatively positive mood, by contrast, may be more useful for taking in new scenes, getting an overall feel for a new place (global focus of attention), creatively using past learning in the service of solving new problems, and other cases where the point of learning isn't for addressing a current, looming threat but for building up knowledge and resources for a longer-term perspective.

Suggested Reading

Fredrickson and Branigan, "Positive Emotions Broaden the Scope."

Nadler, Rabi, and Minda, "Better Mood and Better Performance."

Questions to Consider

1. Fear tends to focus our attention and enhance our learning for details relevant to a frightening experience—the weapon in an attacker's hand, for example. What might anger focus attention on, and what might anger tend to suppress attention toward? How would that influence what people learn?

2. Are positive emotions always good for learning? Are there some positive emotions that might, at least in your own experience, actually result in less learning?

The Role of Emotion in Learning
Lecture 18—Transcript

We have been talking about aspects of cognition that influence learning and we have been focusing on what psychologists call "cold cognition," things like attention, executive function, judgments of learning, and source monitoring. We are moving to what is sometimes called more "hot cognition," and that is how emotions and motivations change the way we learn.

In this lecture, I will be talking about the role of emotion in learning. In the first lecture, one of the myths I mentioned was the idea that emotion interferes with learning. Here, I want to ask specifically, how does it affect learning when we feel happy or sad? Emotions are a tricky topic, and that is because we talk about emotions a lot in our everyday lives, so we need to start by outlining what it means when psychologists study emotions.

Emotions are defined as a temporary state of the person that evolves coordinated patterns of physiological arousal, and mental states that can promote emotionally relevant patterns of behavior. Let us unpack this definition.

One mnemonic device people use for this is the ABC device. A is for arousal. Emotions involve arousal patterns either increased or decreased arousal, depending on the emotion. B is for behavior. Emotions are linked to specific behaviors and this includes characteristic facial expressions like smiling and frowning, and other kind of behavior like approaching or avoiding a person. C is for cognition and this reminds us that emotions involve particular mental states, feelings, goals, and thoughts.

Happiness is a temporary state that is associated with calm physiology, low arousal, a positive mental state, positive feeling, the belief that good things have happened and that the current situation is one we want to keep going, and it is associated with behaviors like smiles, expressing positivity statement and of course it is generally something we like to feel.

By contrast, anger is a state associated with strong physiological arousal: a racing heartbeat and increased blood pressure. It entails an aversive feeling—something we don't like—along with thoughts that we've been thwarted or threatened or had another person get in the way of what we want. It is associated with furrowed brows and narrowed mouth expressions, flared nostrils, and behaviors like yelling or even physical aggression.

These features of emotion, the ABCs go together. In fact, you can actually get people to experience the physiology of a particular emotion, sometimes even to feel the subjective emotional state, by getting them to pose their face in the right expression. For example, one absolutely hilarious research project involved getting people to make facial expressions with instructions that never give away what emotion they are actually posing. I might give you instructions like lift up your eyebrows a bit, crinkle your nose, and note I did not tell you what face you are starting to make with this method.

Then, the researchers looked at people's physiological arousal patterns while they were making that face and they looked at what emotions people reported feeling. It turned out that people's physiological responses matched the emotion they were (unknown to them) posing. And some participants even reported feeling the target emotional state. If you're curious, I was describing pieces of the disgust expression.

Many researchers believe that emotions have an evolutionary basis, based in part on work by Gottman and Levenson, and this is actually important to consider as we think about how emotions might affect learning. Negative emotions are triggered by threatening situations, situations in which we have lost something or may lose something trigger sadness, and anxiety, and if there is a responsible party, if there is someone to blame they can trigger anger.

Anger and anxiety, in particular, tend to rev the body up for fight or flight responding, and theorists believe that anger and fear served to actually motivate fight or flight in our evolutionary history. It is also not surprising that we share these basic emotions with many other animals. Rats, for example, demonstrate anxiety. Dogs easily show depression, and every cat I have ever owned was excellent at displays of anger.

Happiness and pleasure, and joy on the other hand, they are a bit less obviously functional. I do not want you to get me wrong, I really like positive emotions.

It is just not totally clear if they serve a strong evolutionary function, and this is a kind of mystery that we will return to later in this lecture.

Let us start with negative emotions. What do negative emotions do to the learning process? If we want o investigate this question, we can do at least two different things. One thing we can do is we can look at how well people learn positive versus negative stimuli. We can assume that any differences observed in that learning are reflecting the effects of the emotions that are associated with the stimuli.

A second thing we can do is we can actually induce negative emotions in people, and then we can look at how well they learn. To do this second thing, we have to first be able to create emotional states in people in an experimental setting. The ability to do this, to induce emotion in the laboratory is what permits researchers to actually test the impact of emotional states on learning.

Researchers induce emotion in a variety of ways. They might ask people to recall autobiographical experiences that involved particular emotions, and they might also show people film clips, images, or musical selections that seem to induce particular emotions in people. Many researchers have settled on film clips and images, because these materials let us expose everyone to the same event or experience in order to make them, for example, fearful. By contrast, if we actually use our own experiences, if I ask you to recall a time when you were afraid, it means that you might think about failing to make an important customer contact in your company. If I were a participant, I might think about screwing up a lecture, and my five-year-old might think about the idea that ghosts are real and coming to get her.

Another issue is that we have to consider whether we are going to assume that all negative emotions are the same in their impact on learning, or whether we think different negative emotions might have distinctive effects. Let us consider this a little more closely. On the one hand, negative emotions like anger, fear, and sadness have a lot in common. We do not like to feel those feelings. We often seek to do something to get rid of those feelings. What these feelings share is what researchers call a valence, a position on the dimension that goes from things we like to feel to things we do not like feeling and they are on the negative side?

They are different in terms of the kind of arousal they involve. Fear and anger, for example, involve high levels of physiological arousal, and sadness does not do that. It does not involve such high arousal in general. Finally, there is even more distinctness in terms of what these emotions may get us ready to do. Fear is connected to flight, anger is connected to fighting, and sadness, possibly, is connected to resting and or seeking social support from other people.

When we think about how negative emotions affect learning, we will need to consider what they have in common, that negative valence, and we also need to think about where they are distinct in their arousal and in the specific kinds of actions that they are going to promote.

First, let me give you a general claim. Negative emotions appear to narrow our attentional focus so that we are better at learning details about an emotionally negative stimulus. Let us consider some of the evidence for this. In some of the earliest studies, you might be asked to learn a series of images from slides. Most of the slides would be neutral. You would sit there watching along, while one slide after another comes into view. Then, suddenly, you would see a really awful slide, a scene of carnage and then back to the more standard sort of neutral slides.

Later, to test whether you have learned the images, researchers might ask you which slides you were shown before, and they would give you a mix of slides that you did see and slides that you did not see. It is a recognition test.

Normally, when we see a list of items and we are later asked to remember them, we show a tendency to better learn and remember the initial items in the list, and the last items in the list. We are not so great with the middle items. Well, putting that awful slide in the middle really changes things up, and you are probably not surprised to find that you are very likely to learn the awful slide and remember it later.

Interestingly, you were remarkably unlikely to remember the slide immediately before or immediately after that traumatic slide. Researchers view this as an adaptive attention and learning phenomenon. Things that do not matter much are okay to learn if there is nothing more serious going on around us, but if something is really threatening, that is the thing to pay attention to and remember; and you do not want to waste any resources on the kind of neutral stuff that came around it.

Elizabeth Kensinger took this strategy of looking at learning lists of negative, versus neutral images, a little bit further. In her studies, negative images might be things like snakes, and neutral images might be things like a teakettle. She showed people a set of images, and then asked them to look at a second set of images, using a memory test to evaluate their learning of the first set. In this second set, some objects were identical to those in the learned set, others were similar, and some were new.   People   had to judge whether the new images were identical, which requires memory for little details. For example, you have to remember that the snake was a green python and not a rattlesnake, or similar, and the similar judgment just required memory that you saw an image of a snake. It turns out people's memory for details was significantly better for negative images.

Later, Kensinger and her colleagues showed that negative stimuli do not just get better learned in general, we actually learn the important and central details of negative things, and in fact, we are more likely to forget the peripheral and less important details of those things.

For example, if you see a picture of a snake on the riverbank, versus seeing a picture of a string on the riverbank, you learn what the snake looks like very well, but you do not really learn what the riverbank looks like nearly as well. Well okay, this all seems good and this is consistent with the idea that negative emotions narrow attention for important things and help learning for the important stuff, but, you might say, it is not really the same as feeling negative and trying to learn. This is really about learning emotionally negative stuff, and that is just not quite the same thing. You might also be thinking, well snakes, skulls, and other pictures that seems really like it is about fear, not negative emotions in general.

What happens if you make people feel negative emotions and then you ask them to learn things that are more or less neutral? One study in this area people feel either sad or happy, and then asked them to learn to solve some tower of Hanoi problems. You remember the tower of Hanoi. That is the task with the disks and the platforms and the challenges to arrange the disks without putting larger disks on smaller ones or trying to put them on the table and so on. We mentioned it in the lecture about executive function. What can be learned in this task is a procedure for breaking the problem down into smaller parts that are easier to handle correctly.

Well, once in their mood, participants were asked to do additional problems to see whether their learning transferred to similar problems, like a more complicated tower task, and to related, but less obviously similar problems. Participants who were in a negative mood, who were sad when they learned required more trials in the tower of Hanoi task to learn, and they did more poorly over all.

Participants who were in a negative mood when they tried to generalize their learning to new tasks, they needed more time to do the transfer tasks and their ability to generalize their learning was also less good than for participants who were in a happy mood.

So far it looks like fear might enhance learning of threat-relevant information, and sadness might just suppress learning performance. It is less clear what anger does, but it seems likely that it will operate a little bit like fear in that it is likely to narrowing attention toward relevant, central details. In this case, maybe the face and actions of the person that made you angry.

A broad sweep of the findings in this area actually seems to confirm those kinds of broad conclusions. Importantly though, although some negative emotions help us focus attention and improve our learning of critical and threat relevant details in the moment, others studies have shown that over the long-term, negative emotions in academic contexts like college are actually connected to lower student involvement, to lower student motivation, to students being less likely to use effective learning strategies like elaborative encoding. Und ultimately, they are connected to students learning less well as indicated by their academic performance.

This may seem like a bunch of contradictory findings, but they actually make a fair amount of sense in the context of evolutionary work. Negative emotions do seem to narrow attention, and they focus in on information that's most relevant to an immediate threat, so they enhance learning of the most important information for that person at that moment, but they suppress learning of less relevant information.

Then when there is no immediate threat, negative emotions appear to generally suppress a bunch of things that we know promote better learning, and ultimately they have a negative impact on learning itself. Remember, negative emotions mess up learning of unrelated material.

Okay, well that is negative emotions. Remember earlier I told you there is this kind of mystery about positive emotion and what good positive emotions are anyway? Well, Barb Fredrickson, a social psychologist at the University of North Carolina in Chapel Hill, she was quite taken with this issue. First of all, positive emotions do not really involve physiological arousal. Rather, they are actually characterized by kind of a lack of stress-related arousal. Second, what actions could positive emotions really promote, anyway (I mean sort of sitting around like the saying goes, fat, dumb and happy)?

Given their association with lower levels of arousal, Fredrickson first thought maybe positive emotions help us speed recovery from negative emotional arousal, and they do. Actually being encouraged to experience positive emotions after you have experienced negative ones speeds up your return to a baseline, neutral level of physical arousal. Fredrickson thought there might also be more to the story.

In looking at a variety of research findings on creativity, broad thinking, and even on artistic temperaments, Fredrickson settled on a larger idea about positive emotions. It is the idea that their function is to support us in broadening and building. That is, positive feelings support us in acquiring resources for the long-term. Whereas negative emotions support immediate, focused action in response to important, current threats.

The resources positive emotions orient us to acquire might take a lot of forms. For example, positive emotion encourages us to connect with other people, to establish new social relationships and actually to affirm existing social relationships.

Positive emotion also supports us in exploring our environment. In fact, earlier in this class, we talked about the very basic inclination animals and humans have to explore the environments. Rats explore right away when they are placed into new environments, and people also do this. Here is the kicker, this kind of exploration really only happens for rats that are feeling pretty good—rats that are feeling safe, secure, and happy. If a rat is feeling fearful, for example, it does not explore a new space.

Likewise, attachment theory in developmental psychology was based on the idea that babies need a secure relationship to their parents in order to explore the environment. Babies who do not have that secure relationship are less likely to explore, and babies who are afraid do not explore either. Exploration is fundamental to learning. One way to articulate this idea in a more succinct way is to propose that positive emotions broaden our focus of attention and broaden what we can learn.

How to test this idea stringently in the laboratory? In order to do so, you need to be able to make people feel positive emotions, and you need a way to examine whether our focus of attention is broad or narrow. There are some other important issues as well. You need to compare positive emotions to a neutral state, and you need to show that different positive emotions like amusement and contentment all work similarly to broaden attention. How can we do this?

Well, to make people feel positive, one strategy is to use brief two to three minute film clips. Film clips of penguins at play, for example, are used by Fredrickson and her colleagues to create feelings of amusement, and scenes of nature are used to create serenity and contentment. To create neutral states, films that look like random pattern screen savers can be used.

To examine whether participants had a broader attentional focus after the positive emotion film clips, Fredrickson and colleagues used a task that assesses a preference for global or general versus local, detail oriented, processing of visual images.

Some tests of global and local processing use a letter-naming task. You might look at a capital letter B that is made up entirely of smaller letter As. If you are using global processing to name the letters, you should say that you are looking at a B. If you are using local processing, you will say the letter you are seeing is a bunch of little As.

Fredrickson and colleagues, they wanted to look at a slightly different task, because they wanted a task where there was not a single right answer and where participants answers would give a preference for either looking at details or for looking at the big picture. They chose one that uses geometric shapes, and it has a logic a little bit like that letter task. In this case, you look at an image and it shows you a larger shape that is made up of smaller shapes.

For example, you might see three small triangles arranged on the page in a triangular pattern. Here, there is no conflict between global and local processing; it's all triangles. You are either looking at one big triangle or you are looking at three small triangles. Then, you see two additional figures. One figure is composed of a big triangle that is made out of three small squares. The other figure is four small triangles that are placed in a square pattern.

Participants are asked to judge which of the new figures is the most like the one they started out looking at. People whose attention is globally focused are going to use the general shape of the big figure. They are focused on the big picture. What they will do is they will choose the triangular array of squares, because that looks like a big triangle. Those whose attention is detail focused will choose the four triangles, because they were looking at the smaller figures that were making up the big picture.

Both answers are correct in a way. They reflect a preference for looking at the big picture or for looking at the details. Again, if you look at the big picture, you choose the triangular or ray of little squares because you think the big triangle is what you are matching. If you look at the details, you do the opposite. You are trying to match the smaller individual triangles from the previous image.

People in their study first viewed an emotion inducing film clip, penguins, nature, and screen saver and then they responded to that global/local task. The task had eight items. People got one point for each global response they made. The more points you get the more globally focused your attention is.

Participants in the two positive emotion conditions chose significantly more global responses than people in that neutral condition. They averaged about five to six global choices of eight possible points that they could have gotten, and it really did not matter whether they were amused or contented.

As you know, attention is not the same as learning, but having this broader attentional focus might increase the amount of information people are able to take in. In contrast to the effects of negative emotions if you consider previous lectures on the role of attention.

We have also thought, here and there, about the importance of wanting to learn. This is a topic we will go into more detail on in the next lecture. Not surprisingly, positive emotions may help to maintain our motivation to learn. Reschly and colleagues for example looked at positive emotion and academic engagement in a sample of high school students. Students who reported feeling positive emotions a lot in school also reporting higher levels of engagement with learning, Reschly and colleagues did not have assessments of whether students were actually learning more effectively.

In the study I mentioned earlier, that showed negative effects of negative emotion on student's learning, the researchers also did look at positive emotion. Over the course of a semester, they were able to show that students who report lots of positive emotions in the context of classes ended up using better learning strategies, being more intrinsically motivated by school, and ultimately, doing better. And in this case, it was based on their actual academic achievement—their test scores and their end-of-term grades.

There are some problems with interpreting this work as definitively showing that emotions cause changes in learning, because students with more positive emotion may have been more capable, more knowledgeable, or better prepared to begin with. The emotions themselves might not have played a role in their better learning outcomes.

A more recent study in this arena actually took an experimental approach, one where the experimenters actually control who is feeling what emotions and they are able to rule out prior differences in knowledge as a result. This study actually focused on category learning. Ruby Nadler and her colleagues used music and video clips like a laughing baby and excerpts from Schindler's list to see how emotions might influence learning of complex categories that in some cases were rule based and in some cases were not rule based.

People were assigned to positive, neutral, or negative emotion conditions and they first heard music related to their mood condition and then they watched film clips. The film clips for the negative condition were sadness related, and the ones for the positive condition were often amusing. After this, the researchers asked participants to report their emotional states to make sure that they really got the happy condition folks feeling happy and the sad condition folks feeling sad.

People then learned a categorization task that involved something called a Gabor patch, and it looks a lot like a wrinkled patch of a surface. The wrinkles can vary in how many they are and which way they are oriented. In the Nadler study, the category task was of two types. Sometimes it was a rule-based category where people could explain the rule for classifying a visual image of the Gabor patch using words. In the other cases it was a non-rule described category, so the category was complex and they could not really articulate a rule verbally even though they were able to learn the task and categorize things pretty well.

As it turned out, being in a good mood enhanced people's ability to learn the categories correctly when they were rule based, but not when the category system was that more complex intuitively acquired one. The researchers argue that positive moods are going to be most helpful when people are using that explicit, system two kind of learning approach. The kind of learning approach we use, you might remember, for categories where we can describe them with rules. When you need to use system one for categories that are not easily described by rules, it looks like mood may matter less.

That makes sense because attention in the way we have discussed it is more critical for system two kinds of learning. System one learning is going on under the surface, and it has less to do with that conscious focus of attention. Having said this, so far, good moods sound really good. Broader attention, better category learning, better long-term academic learning

There is more. Transfer of learning is a particularly important issue as we have seen. Transfer is not always so optimal. We cannot always take what we have learned in one setting and apply it in some other situation or to another task. It could be that the more creative, attentionally broad cognitive approach that people in a good mood have is specifically good at enhancing transfer. Indeed, that is also what happens in research that investigates this issue. People who learn a task do better at transferring that knowledge to similar problems when they are in a good mood.

In summarizing where we have been today, it is clear that emotions influence learning at many phases of the process. They influence the breadth or narrowness of attention, the extent to which we actively seek information and the way we approach the information that we do get. Emotions appear to affect the speed with which we learn, and they also affect our ability to generalize what we are learning, to apply learned rules or approaches in new circumstances or new problems.

One way to think about this in practical applications is that some moods are better for some tasks. A relatively negative mood is optimal for situations where we need to be focused on specific material and we need to learn central aspects of that material. The way I think about this is that some mild anxiety in studying for a test might actually lead to better performance, because it helps us to focus attention and it helps ensure that we study enough and that we study the central stuff. This is especially true if we are not chronically anxious but we are only anxious when we actually need to be a little bit anxious to get our studying focus underway.

A relatively positive mood, by contrast, may be more useful for taking in new scenes, getting an overall feel for a new place with that global focus of attention, creatively using past learning in the service of solving new problems. In other cases, where the point of learning is not to address a current looming threat like an exam, but rather to build knowledge and resources for the longer term. For listening to today's lecture for example, positive moods are probably better.

While we do not all have the standardized emotion inducing video clips researchers use in controlled experiments, the study of category learning mentioned earlier actually pulled clips from YouTube. The lead author speculated that viewing occasional funny videos at work might actually enhance employee's productivity and maybe creativity.

As will probably not surprise you, emotions are intricately tied to what we want. We feel good things when we get what we want and bad things when our goals are threatened. Next lecture, we will actually consider the issue of what we want in more detail, and how what we want influences what we learn.

Cultivating a Desire to Learn
Lecture 19

Throughout this course, we have assumed that we have some reason to learn and focused on the process of learning without thinking much about the reason we learn something or whether the reason might matter for how and how well we learn something. How people feel about learning—whether they experience it as something they want to do or have to do—can vary quite a bit. In this lecture, we will consider how those motivations might influence learning material over time and how to foster the kinds of motivation that will help support learning rather than undermine it.

Self-Determination Theory

- Self-determination theory, which was developed by Richard Ryan and Edward Deci at the University of Rochester, is a broad theory of human motivation that focuses on the importance of autonomy for human flourishing in general and motivation in particular.

- In self-determination theory, we can think about our actions—including those involved in learning—as arrayed on a continuum from heteronymous to autonomous.

- Heteronymous actions are those that are controlled externally; they are actions that we experience as being required by external circumstance. On the other end of the spectrum are actions that are autonomous, which are things we choose freely for ourselves and without any coercion—usually, things that are consistent with our larger goals and identities.

- Within the continuum from heteronymous to autonomous are other types of actions, such as introjected actions, which are linked to external concerns about what other people want or need or about rules.

- An identified experience of an action means that you have decided to do something for reasons that may be rooted in external forces, but you have thought through the action and are doing it because you think the action is the right thing to do.

- Moving a step further along the continuum, you can connect this action to your overall sense of who you are and what your values are, making the action integrated rather than merely identified.

- Learning for heteronymous reasons can feel relatively bad, and it can undermine people's desire to continue learning about a topic over the long term. In fact, the more autonomy people report in all domains of life, the better they generally are doing in those domains.

- At least two aspects of a learning situation support autonomy: the ability to make meaningful choices about your learning and receiving informative feedback about your progress in learning.

- Anything that reminds us we are learning because of extrinsic forces might undermine autonomy, such as surveillance—being monitored and evaluated via exams and grades and, of course, being punished.

Rewards, Goals, and Learning

- The origins of self-determination theory were focused on the paradoxical effects of rewards on behavior. It turns out that rewards can really disrupt intrinsic motivation. Rewards may not give people intrinsic, autonomous reasons to do something—including to learn—so when the reward is gone, so is the behavior.

- Rewards are complicated. Rewards for learning are often performance based, including receiving good grades and being on the honor roll. As such, rewards simultaneously provide informative feedback about one's learning progress, which can be good for motivation.

- However, rewards also are external controls on behavior; they are offered to encourage us to behave in particular ways. As such, they are controlling and should undermine intrinsic motivation.

- Numerous studies have shown that people who will be rewarded for an activity later are less likely to choose that activity over other options. If they do choose that activity, they keep at it for shorter periods of time.

- As a consequence, when we reward people for learning with good grades or other types of tangible, material rewards, we are potentially undermining the extent to which they subsequently wish to learn about that topic—and the extent to which they will pursue that topic.

- Offering people positive verbal feedback, by contrast, enhances their autonomy and intrinsic motivation to do a task. However, it is critical that the feedback be offered in a noncontrolling way.

- Educational researcher Alfie Kohn has written about how praise can become controlling and can undermine motivation in insidious ways. However, we can be at least somewhat autonomously motivated by different aspects of learning.

- Researchers distinguish between learning goals and performance goals, and you could conceivably hold both types of goals in an autonomous way. Learning goals are about getting better and mastering a content area while performance goals are about demonstrating that knowledge.

- When researchers have looked at these types of goals and how they influence learning, performance goals often leave people vulnerable to losing motivation. If you hold a performance goal, you need to successfully achieve and demonstrate good performance to keep yourself motivated for longer periods of time. If you fail at a performance, your motivation to continue learning suffers.

- By contrast, when we are learning for the sake of learning, a performance failure may be disappointing, but it does not completely undermine our broader goal—and the broader goal of learning and improvement can sustain motivation in the face of failure.

Types of Theorists, Feedback, and Motivation

- Essentially, we can approach learning as a revelation of our underlying intelligence or as a process of changes that is incremental and ongoing. According to Carol Dweck and her collaborators, the majority of people fall into two groups: incremental theorists, who believe that we grow and change, and entity theorists, who believe that we are who we are.

- People can have incremental theories about personality, for example, while holding entity theories of intelligence. In addition, entity and incremental theorists are often equally capable, which means that differences in people's learning can be linked to differences in their underlying theories. Furthermore, there is evidence that intelligence is somewhat incremental—that it can increase given the right circumstances.

- In a review of over 100 studies, Deci and Ryan showed that positive information about performance enhances people's motivation. We all like doing what we think we're good at; if we're learning well, we like to keep learning.

- However, Dweck and her collaborators have focused on getting feedback about performance that is negative. They have focused on discovering what helps maintain motivation when you actually get feedback that says you are doing badly, and they have found that this depends on what theories you have about intelligence.

- If you are an entity theorist and you get feedback that you haven't learned something very well, you interpret that as indicating a lack of intelligence—the problem is your ability. If the problem is your ability, you lose motivation.

- If you are an incremental theorist, by contrast, you tend to interpret the negative feedback as signaling something about your effort or your strategies—but not something about your innate, nonchangeable ability. If you think the problem is effort or strategy, you have a golden opportunity for revitalizing motivation and trying again.

- Dweck and her colleagues find that incremental theorists cope better with a setback or initial failure and go on to do better long term than entity theorists—both in laboratory studies and in real-world learning contexts.

Revitalizing Motivation for Unpleasant Tasks

- Ryan and Deci's focus on how educators and parents can behave around necessary but disliked tasks in order to not undermine people's capacity to internalize the tasks, or intrinsically motivate.

- Some of the findings from this line of thinking suggest that we should avoid controlling language, create opportunities for meaningful choice whenever they are there, and be careful about praise and other forms of rewards. Lack of choice, excessive reliance on praise or praise delivered in a controlling way, and excessive supervision and monitoring can all delay or prohibit an individual's ability to internalize and to autonomously engage in learning.

- A second form for addressing this issue is how people themselves can regulate their experiences with learning in order to maximize their own intrinsic motivation. Work from this perspective is conducted by Carol Sansone and Judith Harackiewicz and their collaborators, who argue that intrinsic motivation is present whenever people do something because they find it interesting.

- This is consistent with Deci and Ryan's more intrinsic side of the continuum—that is, actions we find interesting to do are typically those in which we at a minimum find the task itself to be valuable because it will be interesting, and often they are things we feel at least somewhat autonomous about doing.

- From the self-determination theory perspective, however, a task might flip around on that autonomy-heteronomy continuum—sometimes feeling intrinsically motivated and sometimes feeling extrinsically motivated.

- Sansone, Harackiewicz, and their collaborators argue that we can actively move ourselves around on that continuum; we can turn play into work and work into play via strategies we employ.

- Consider two types of goals that often operate simultaneously in learning: a what goal, which is the activity itself, and a why goal, which is the purpose in doing the activity—and this could vary across different people.

Engaging in self-testing is a great way to create the circumstances that foster motivation in learning.

- When first engaging in an activity, you determine if you find it interesting. If you do, you probably continue doing it. If not, you have to figure out how to engage with the activity in a way that works for you or decide to stop doing it.

- One of the major findings emerging from this work is that a match between the experience and the why goals leads to stronger interest and more sustained engagement in an activity.

- In several studies, Sansone and her colleagues have looked at people whose why goals often include making social connections—people they describe as high in interpersonal orientation—and people whose why goals seldom involve relationships or connections to others.

- Sansone and her colleagues have found that if the context of learning matches the person's interpersonal goals, that is beneficial for motivation. In other words, social people like to learn with others while relatively less social people prefer to learn by themselves—and both types of people are motivated in those contexts.

- For our own learning experiences, we can try to create the circumstances that foster intrinsic, autonomous engagement with learning. That includes trying to structure learning so that we experience a sense of meaningful choice and trying to find ways for achieving meaningful feedback that is informative about our progress. This might include self-testing but also talking with others, which often results in gaining a clearer sense of what we do and do not understand.

- Additionally, cultivate a belief in incremental theories of intelligence and ability. This belief is consistent with a great deal of data, so this is not about delusion but rather about truly seeing how much people can improve their capabilities with practice and time, and it's about believing this is true of ourselves as well as of others.

Suggested Reading

Ryan and Deci, "Self-Regulation and the Problem of Human Autonomy."

Sansone and Smith, "Interest and Self-Regulation."

Questions to Consider

1. Given how much emphasis on external regulation characterizes most of our early school experiences, could current practices undermine the motivation for lifelong learning?

2. What are strategies people can employ to maintain interest when they encounter challenging material? How might these strategies vary as a function of differences among people?

Cultivating a Desire to Learn
Lecture 19—Transcript

Imagine yourself sitting in a classroom. The teacher is droning on about a series of decisive battles in World War I, complete with dates and geographic locations. You feel like you would like to chew off your arm. You are actually imagining that you are me in my world history class in high school. I was a smart kid, I was good at school, and I did well in this history class. I hated every last second of this experience. After I finished the required history courses in my high school curriculum, I did not think about history, ancient, contemporary, or for that matter, current events that will become our history until at least a decade later.

At that point, I discovered that there was an entire world of history out there that dealt with fascinating questions, at least to me. Like how did we come to think about child rearing the way we currently do? Or how did people with minority sexual identities and orientations manage in historical and cultural eras that differed from our own in openness. I made use of my limited free time to read actual books on these historical topics.

What on earth is different about these two situations? Well obviously one thing that is different is I had changed. Was it simply that I do not want to learn the military history but I do like social and cultural histories? Were there other reasons that my experiences in these two circumstances are so different? You have likely had experiences like this one yourselves, where something that was boring suddenly seems quite interesting.

So far in this course, we have assumed that we have some reason to learn and some reason to be focused on the process of learning more narrowly and we have not thought very much about why we learn something, or whether the "why" of our learning might actually matter for "how" we learn and "how well" we learn. Even in the last lecture, we did not really consider how people feel about learning, rather we thought about how they feel while engaged in learning.

How people feel about learning, whether they experience it as something they want to do, or as something they have to do, can vary quite a bit. In this lecture, we will consider how those motivations influence the learning of material over time, and we will also think about how to foster the kind of motivation that helps to support learning rather than undermine it.

Let us start by thinking about something that is known as self-determination theory. Self-determination theory is a broad theory of human motivation and it focuses on the importance of autonomy for human flourishing in general and for human motivation in particular.

In self-determination theory, which was developed by Rich Ryan and Ed Deci some decades ago, we can think about our actions including the actions we engage in while learning as being on a kind of continuum from something called heteronymous to autonomous.

Heteronymous actions are those that are controlled externally; they are things that we experience as being required by external circumstance. If we think about my high school experience or indeed, experience many of us had during our formal education, we can see immediately that my experience of history learning was heteronymous. I did not and I would not have chosen the course, I was compelled to take it by the requirements of the curriculum.

The teacher chose what material would be covered, and how and he was very interested in battles and dates and he thought they were very important, so that was the material I was required to learn. There were also punishments and incentives in place. There were bad and good grades and those were there for evaluating my learning progress and possibly intended to motivate my learning progress. As I already mentioned, my experience of the class was very bad at the time, and it had some lasting effects in that I made certain to avoid ever taking a history course again.

On the other end of that dimension are actions that are autonomous, these are things we choose for ourselves. We choose them freely. We do not have a sense of coercion, and often they are things that are consistent with our larger goals and our sense of identity.

If we look at my current history learning activities, they fall on the extreme autonomous end of that same dimension from self-determination theory. Let me give you a concrete example. I recently read a history about the ideology of child rearing in America. This is a topic that interests me deeply. I am a parent of young children. I am also a developmental psychologist by training, and so there is no part of my life for which this book is not meaningful.

Also, nobody told me I had to read this book. I did not actually have to read this book. Importantly, I chose to read this book. There were no tests. Nobody monitored whether I was reading the book correctly or incorrectly. I had the freedom to stop or start whenever I wanted. I ended up reading the entire book willingly, even though some portions were actually a bit dry in the way that they were written and were not as exciting to read. This is the epitome of autonomous motivation. My learning behaviors were self-chosen. They were consistent with my goals, my ideals, my interests, and my identity.

Of course, any time you have a continuum in this case from heteronymous to autonomous there are some in-between places on that line. One such place is called "introjected." An introjected action is linked to external concerns, concerns about what other people want or what other people need, or concerns about the rules.

In contrast to a completely heteronymous action, an introjected action is one where you can see something about why that action is necessary. Had I been somewhat older when I was in that history class, I might have experienced that learning event as more introjected. I might have been capable of reflecting on the fact that an educated citizenry needs to have a basic grasp of world history and needs to understand how our current geopolitical world arose from those historical events. It would not have made me joyously want to learn battles and dates, but it might have made the experience a bit less horrible.

Another in between place that is a bit closer to autonomous on the line is called "identified." An identified experience of an action means I have decided to do something for reasons that may be rooted in external forces, but I have thought through the action and I am doing it because I think it is the right thing to do. Beyond introjected where I can see why it might work, now I really, I have committed myself in a certain sense. You can even move a step further and you can connect the action to your overall sense of who you are and what your values are. That would make an action what Deci and Ryan term integrated rather than just identified.

Why would it matter where we are on this continuum with respect to learning? Two important reasons are both implied with the example just seen. First, learning for heteronymous reasons can actually feel relatively bad, and we will say some more about a couple of surprising pieces of that in a moment or two. Second, learning for heteronymous reasons actually undermines people's desire to continue to learn about a topic over the long term. In fact, the more autonomy people report experiencing in all domains of lives, the better they are generally are doing in those domains. Learning is not an exception.

This means that a really important question is what supports autonomy. It turns out there are at least two aspects of learning situation that do that, that support a sense of autonomy. One is the ability to make meaningful choices. To imagine an example from formal educational systems, Montessori schools typically offer preschoolers choices about learning activities. As children get older in a Montessori system, they are offered increasing opportunities to make choices about their curriculum and about their coursework. By the time you become a Great Courses customer, you are exercising complete choice about your learning.

A second thing that supports autonomy is getting informative feedback about your progress in learning. Having a sense of how well you are learning course material and where you are still struggling. Recall that we talked about metacognition and the monitoring of learning a couple lectures ago, and you can think about that as a kind of internal source for informative feedback—feedback about how your learning does not have to come from other people or experts in all cases.

What features of a learning situation might undermine autonomy? Anything that reminds us we are learning because of extrinsic forces, because the situation is compelling us to do it. Surveillance, being monitored, and being evaluated via exams and grades are ways that we can undermine a sense of autonomy and of course, being punished is ultimately undermining of autonomy.

Here is the tricky thing, what about rewards? In fact, the origins of self-determination theory were actually focused on what are often called paradoxical effects of rewards on behavior. As it turns out, rewards can really mess with intrinsic motivation.

You might be thinking whoa, several lectures ago you told us that rewards increase a behavior and this seems totally at odds with what you said before. It is not quite that contradictory. Rewards work as long as they are given. What rewards do not do is to give people an intrinsic, autonomous reasons to do something including learning. When the reward is gone, the behavior goes along with it.

In fact, rewards are even more complicated than that. Rewards for learning are often performance based. These are things like good grades, being on the honor roll, having a place on the demonstration dance team, and so on. In this way, rewards do two things at once. They tell you that someone else wants you to do something, which is a problem for autonomy. They also provide informative feedback about your learning progress, and that should be good for autonomy.

Autonomy is good for motivation. Again, rewards are external controls on behavior. Rewards are meant to encourage us to behave in specific ways, and as such, they are also kind of controlling. That is a problem for autonomy, and therefore a problem for intrinsic motivation.

A typical study in this area would give people a task to perform and would vary whether or not people got a reward for it. In one of the most famous examples, children were asked to make marker drawings. This is something children often do spontaneously. They choose to do it. They get the markers and the paper and they make drawing. In this case, some children were actually given rewards for coloring with markers, and other kids were not. In studies of college students, they might be asked to perform some task either in exchange for a small monetary award or just to choose some task to perform for the duration of the experiment.

Then, following the reward-contingent part of the study, the part of the study where people did some task and got a reward for it or did not, participants are allowed to freely choose from among a variety of activities. The variety of activities offered includes the activity that they were previously given a reward for doing.

Study after study after study of this type shows that when you give people rewards for an activity at one time, later they are less likely to choose that activity over other options. If they choose that activity, they do not engage in it for very long. They do not persist.

The consequence of all of this is that when we think about rewarding people for learning with tangible material rewards, what we are potentially doing is undermining the extent to which they later want to learn about that topic, and the extent to which they are going to persist when learning about that topic.

Offering people positive verbal feedback, by contrast, turns out to enhance their sense of autonomy and their intrinsic motivation to do a task. It is rally critical that this kind of positive verbal feedback or praise is offered in a non-controlling way. Educational researcher and commenter Alfie Kohn has actually written quite eloquently about how praise can get controlling and it can undermine motivation in a kind of insidious way. What kinds of things does Kohn think it takes to make a piece of praise controlling? Well just adding the phrase "as you should" to a statement like "you did well."

This brings me to my next point. We can be at least somewhat autonomously motivated by different aspects of learning. Researchers also distinguish between what are called learning goals and what are called performance goals. You could conceivably hold both kinds of goals in an autonomous way.

Learning goals are about getting better and mastering a content area. By contrast, performance goals are about demonstrating your knowledge, doing very well on a test, being able to expound at the dinner table with professorial authority. When researchers have looked at these types of goals and how they influence learning, performance goals often leave people vulnerable to losing motivation.

If you hold a performance goal, you have to successfully achieve and demonstrate good performance in order to keep yourself motivated for longer periods of time. If you fail at a performance, your motivation to keep learning and therefore keep performing actually suffers.

This is in sharp contrast to learning for the sake of learning—that is, those learning goals. When you are learning for the sake of learning, a performance failure may be disappointing—it's disappointing to do badly on a test—but it does not completely undermine pursuing that broader goal of learning. The broader goal of learning and improvement really turns out to sustain motivation pretty well in the face of failure.

There are some other important features of how we respond to feedback, to success and failure and those go beyond whether our goals are oriented toward performance or learning. Some of the most interesting work in this arena has been done by Carol Dweck and her collaborators, it concerns different theories people can hold about themselves and others, and how those theories play out when we apply them to our own learning. Essentially, everyday people (we) can approach learning as a kind of revelation of our underlying intelligence or as a process of changes that is incremental and ongoing.

To make this a little more concrete, imagine how you might respond to the following statements on a scale that runs from I completely disagree with this to I completely agree with this. You have a certain amount of intelligence and you really cannot do much to change it. Your intelligence is something about you that you cannot change very much. You can learn new things, but you cannot really change your basic intelligence.

According to Dweck, the majority of people fall into two groups, those who disagree with these statements and she labels those people "incremental theorists," and those who endorse these statements, and she terms those individuals "entity theorists." Entity theorists believe that we are who we are, and incremental theorists believe that we grow and change. You may notice right away that this likely corresponds a bit to learning versus performance goals.

Before we move on, let us also just make a couple important points about who is an entity and who is an incremental theorist and we will talk a little about how this material fits with what we have discussed earlier. First, people can have incremental theories. That is, people can believe that people grow and change in, say, personality while simultaneously having an entity theory, believing people are what they are with little chance for change of intelligence or vice versa. In other words, people's theories can be specific to a particular aspect of themselves rather than global across all aspects. We focused in my example items on theories of intelligence because those are the ones most tightly linked to learning.

A second point is that entity and incremental theorists are often equally capable. That is, they do not differ in IQ and a host of other qualities. There are smart people who accept entity theories of intelligence, and there are smart people who accept incremental theories of intelligence. This is really important because it means if we see differences in learning between people who hold these different theories, that the differences are better able to be connected to those theory differences rather than being a function of some other ability.

Finally, as we are going to see in the next lecture, there is some evidence that intelligence is at least somewhat incremental, that it can increase under the right circumstances. Incremental beliefs may correspond better to the data we have.

What do our beliefs in intelligence have to do with learning, and the motivation to learn? As it turns out, a lot. That is mostly with respect to how people experience feedback and how feedback affects motivation. Deci and Ryan showed, in a review of over 100 studies, that positive information about performance enhances people's motivation. We all like doing what we think we are good at. If we are learning well, we like to keep learning.

Dweck and her collaborators have focused on getting feedback about performance that is negative. In other words, they are asking, "What helps to maintain your motivation to keep you going when you actually get feedback that says you know what, you are doing well at this, and you are doing badly?"

As it happens, this turns out to depend on the theories you have about intelligence. If you are an entity theorist and you get feedback that you have not learned something very well, let us say you fail a test you interpret that as indicating a lack of intelligence. The problem is your ability.

Well, if the problem is your ability, and your ability cannot be changed what happens in motivational terms? You lose motivation because there is no reason to keep trying. The test has revealed that you are just not very capable in whatever domain you are working in.

If you are an incremental theorist, by contrast, you tend to interpret the negative feedback as signaling something about your effort, or your strategies, but not as telling you something about an innate, unchangeable ability. When we think the problem is effort or strategy, we have a golden opportunity to revitalizing our motivation by trying a new strategy or investing greater effort.

You would expect from a theoretical standpoint that incremental theorists cope better with setbacks or initial failures, and go on to do better long-term when compared with entity theorists. This is precisely what Dweck and her colleagues find. They find this in laboratory studies of people doing tasks on a single occasion over the space of an hour, but they also find it when they follow students across school transitions in real-world learning contexts. If you believe you can learn and change over time, you will. If you believe that what you have it not going to change, it may in fact not change.

So far, we have emphasized how great it is to be autonomously motivated to learn and how much more effective and helpful it is to view intelligence and learning as incremental rather than entity qualities.

Often we have to do things we do not want to do. I really could not just decide not learn the military history that was required by my high school. Even for those of us who are engaged in a largely autonomously motivated lifelong learning experience, there are always moments when the material is hard, or the course turns to a topic we are just not so thrilled with. Another question we can ask is whether there things we can do to revitalize our own or other's motivation under those not so ideal circumstances.

Researchers haven't fully addressed this problem, and it is a big one and an important one. I am going to talk about this problem in two different ways. One issue is what teachers, parents, and other people responsible for getting people to learn can do. Another issue is what we can do for ourselves as individuals.

That first issue is something that Ryan and Deci have begun to address it. They have been working to understand how educators and parents can behave around a necessary but disliked task, so as not to undermine children's capacity to internalize that tasks and just sort of make the task their own, to experience a little more autonomy. If I put it less academically, what can parents and teachers do or not do that will allow kids to become more intrinsically motivated in learning, even the tough stuff.

We will not fully examine this literature but there are a few important conclusions already from it. Some of the findings really suggest that we need to avoid controlling language. One general way you can do this is you focus on your child or your student's own happiness at having done well or their sense of satisfaction at working hard rather than your own pleasure that they did so. You note for them you are really happy. That is just great.

Another thing you can do is you can create opportunities for meaningful choice whenever they are there. Fr just one example you can ask a child to make choices about when he or she will study or do the homework, or you can give students the opportunity to choose a particular topic to focus on for one portion of the course that otherwise requires them to learn material you have dictated.

Finally, praise and other forms of rewards, we need to be really careful about those. Lack of choice, excessive reliance on praise or controlling praise and excessive supervision and monitoring can all delay or interfere with a kid's ability to come to autonomously engage in learning in an intrinsically motivated way. These same issues apply to employees that you are trying to train, because we do not just stop being interested in having autonomy because we are all grown up.

I promised you that another way of asking this question had to do with how people themselves can regulate their own experiences with learning so that they can maximize their own intrinsic motivation. Here there is also some informative research for that purpose.

A good bit of work from this perspective is conducted by Carol Sansone and Judith Harackiewicz and their collaborators. They argue that intrinsic motivation is there whenever people do something because they find it interesting. This is totally consistent with Deci and Ryan's intrinsic side of the continuum. Things we find interesting are usually going to be those where we find the task valuable and often they are going to be things that we feel autonomous about doing.

The difference from the self-determination theory perspective is that from this Sansone and Harackiewicz's view, a task could actually flip around on that autonomy-heteronomy continuum; that is, sometimes we might feel intrinsically motivated by a task, and sometimes that same task might leave us feeling a little bit more extrinsically motivated.

More importantly, Sansone and Harackiewicz argue that we can actively move ourselves around on that continuum. We can turn play into work and we can also more happily turn work into play via employing good strategies.

As a first step in understanding their approach, you can think about two kinds of goals that often operate simultaneously in learning, a "what" goal, and a "why" goal. Listening to this lecture is part of the goal of learning about motivational factors in learning that is the "what." The "why" goal is your purpose in doing so, and this could vary across different people listening to this lecture. You might be listening because you are interested in understanding how learning works and this is part of that. You might be specifically interested in understanding motivational factors. Or, you might be listening just because you and a friend decided to listen to the course together and this is a way to enjoy time together.

From this beginning point, you then may engage in the activity, listening to the lecture. At that point, you are going to determine if you find it interesting or not. If you do, you probably feel like listening further and hearing more. If not, now you have to problem You have to figure out how to engage with this lecture in a way that is going to work for you, or you have to decide to skip it in which case you are not going to learn about motivation, and you are not going to be hearing what I am saying.

One of the major findings from this work is that a match between the experience itself and your "why" goals produce a stronger interest and more motivation to sustain your engagement in some activity. In several studies, Sansone and colleagues have looked at people whose "why" goals include making social connections. These are people that are called high in interpersonal orientation and they are compared to people whose "why" goals seldom involve relationships or connections to others.

They ask these two different kinds of people to engage in an activity in the laboratory. They are often quite interested in learning activities and learning situations, so often the task in the laboratory is an online learning task.

They then vary the conditions under which people get to do this learning task. They either get to work by themselves or they get to work with others. Then, as with many motivational studies, what they do is they look at behaviors that suggest the person is going to keep pursuing learning in that area in the future. They look at whether people request information about related coursework at the University.

What do they typically find? Well first of all, if the learning context, whether you are with others or by yourself, matches your interpersonal orientation— as if you're socially oriented and you are learning in a social context or if you are not socially oriented and you are by yourself; those are matching situations—and that turns out to benefit motivation. Social people like to learn with others, and relatively less social people prefer to learn by themselves. Further, if you are a non-social person, when you learn with others, your motivation takes a hit when the others engage in off-task social activity. The opposite is true for social people who learn with others. In that case the more off-topic socializing they do, the more they are motivated to pursue the learning activity in the future.

At the end of this tour of motivation in learning, what can we do about our own learning experiences? One of the first things that we can do is to try to create the circumstances that foster intrinsic, autonomous engagement with learning. That includes trying to structure learning so that we experience meaningful choice. Maybe about topics, but also meaningful choices can be made about where and when we learn and we also want to try to find ways to get meaningful feedback that is informative about our progress. This could include self-testing, but it can also include just trying to tell others what we are learning, because in the process of talking with others, we often acquire a clearer sense of what we do and do not understand.

Another thing we can do is to cultivate a belief in incremental theories of intelligence and ability. As we already noted, this belief is consistent with a great deal of data, so I am not telling you to delude yourself, rather I am telling you to try to see that people really can improve capabilities with practice and time. This is about believing this is not only true of other people, but it is also true of ourselves.

In the last several lectures we have been discussing principles about learning that apply to everyone or at least most people. We have been acting as though who is doing the learning largely does not matter. In the next section, we will actually begin to ask whether the specific and unique characteristics of the person learning make a difference, and if so, how. We will look at intelligence, learning styles, individual differences in interests, and finally the role of age in learning.

Intelligence and Learning
Lecture 20

In the last several lectures, we have been discussing principles about learning that apply to everyone. In the next section of the course, we will move from a consideration of general factors that relate to learning to a consideration of how different people might learn differently—with different capacities and preferences or with different motivations. To begin this segment, we're going to ask whether there are individual differences in the capacity for learning, and then we'll consider a controversial topic within and outside psychology—namely, intelligence.

Implicit Learning

- One general learning mechanism or set of mechanisms is an implicit, nonconscious capacity to monitor probabilities of events in our environment—what we have called system one. This learning mechanism has long been touted as one that doesn't differ much between people.

- This type of learning can be examined with artificial grammar learning and sequential reaction time tasks, and there are reliable individual differences in implicit learning as assessed by these tasks.

- In addition, performance on these types of tasks is unrelated to measures of general intelligence and to measures of working memory capacity or executive function. That is, implicit learning is a distinct individual difference.

- Furthermore, people whose processing speed is faster show higher implicit learning scores, and people perform better on foreign-language learning and mathematics when they are better at implicit learning.

- If people's performance on one occasion is not similar to their performance on another occasion, it is unclear how much individual differences in implicit learning can help us understand broader differences between people in learning. Furthermore, we don't know yet if we have one set of mental processes for implicit learning or multiple such processes—in which case, the sequential reaction time task assesses only one.

- However, individual differences in this type of learning are related to academic achievement—which is usually viewed in terms of explicit, deliberate attempts to learn material—and to the long-established approach to individual differences in learning capacity: intelligence.

- Intelligence may not be a great explanation of differences in learning, at least in the ways we measure it; implicit learning offers a potentially useful alternative idea for researchers to explore.

The History of IQ Tests

- We think of intelligence as the capacity for adaptive, successful problem solving. In its earliest history, French scientist Alfred Binet argued that human intelligence involved such abilities as memory, judgment, reasoning, and social understanding.

- An intelligence quotient, or IQ, is a measure of someone's intelligence that is based on a relatively limited examination of their ability to do certain types of problems, often under conditions of limited time—these are called IQ tests.

- Binet developed some of the earliest IQ tests in France to determine whether children were ready to start school or whether they should wait. Around the onset of World War I, IQ testing became a way to sort out the strengths and weaknesses of army recruits for various positions.

- Today's IQ tests generally measure two distinct but related capacities that are often termed fluid and crystallized intelligence. Fluid intelligence consists of tests of speed of information processing, and crystallized intelligence consists of measures of vocabulary and knowledge.

- After these initial military applications, IQ tests were more fully developed for widespread use. This included adapting them for groups that weren't literate or couldn't speak English, which led to using IQ tests to evaluate immigrants and a number of other dubious contexts.

- The use of IQ tests shifted from an evaluation of a person's readiness to learn to the idea that IQ is a static element of a person's capacities and not something that changes or can be improved.

- In fact, when we speak of IQ, many people now presume that we are born with IQ and that it is what makes learning easier or harder for some people than others. In other words, IQ is an aptitude or talent that makes it easier to learn. However, IQ is the innate potential and is distinct from learning.

- This is why the data showing that one or another group, on average, scores lower on IQ tests is so troubling. If we instead assumed that IQ was some temporary state related to readiness to learn, we might view that same type of finding as indicating the need for remedial programs or other solutions—rather than as a claim of a group's fundamental inferiority.

IQ, Learning, and Genetics
- Evidence for IQ as an ability that facilitates learning needs to show two things: that IQ predicts learning and that it is a stable aptitude of a person.

- IQ scores tend to predict learning pretty well. In many cases, people with higher IQ scores appear to learn and then perform at a higher level than those with lower IQ scores. This is consistent with the notion that IQ is the ability to learn and perform a variety of tasks.

- Additionally, IQ needs to be a stable aptitude of a person; otherwise, it could be argued that IQ doesn't reflect ability to learn but perhaps the person's current state of learning. In fact, IQ test scores are quite stable over time.

- Furthermore, IQ seems to be highly heritable, which means that identical twins show more similar IQ test scores than other siblings, and this is true even when they are reared in different homes. In a given environment, there may be genetically linked differences in IQ, but these differences are not independent of the environment.

IQ test scores tend to predict learning and are stable over time. In addition, IQ seems to be highly heritable.

- Under the assumption that intelligence is the capacity to learn and that it is genetic, researchers selectively bred rats who were either good or bad at maze learning. Rats from each strain were then reared under three different conditions: the usual laboratory conditions, impoverished conditions, and enriched conditions.

- Then, rats were tested under standard conditions. Researchers only recorded differences in the environment that the rats were typically bred and reared in. Under enriched conditions, both strains performed better, and they did equally well; under impoverished conditions, both strains performed worse, and they did equally poorly.

- Therefore, the effects of any gene—including any gene involved with intelligence—are intertwined with the environment so much that you can't separate them. In the case of IQ, this finding means that IQ may have to do with genetic effects but only in the way that specific genes are operating within a person's specific environment over time.

- The stability of IQ may not mean that IQ comes first and is genetically based and that learning relies on IQ; rather, the stability of IQ may mean that people who start out having learned more in their environment continue to have advantages over time because most people who start out having learned more maintain their environmental advantages or disadvantages—the circumstances that led them to learn more or less than their peers.

IQ Tests as Measurements of Achievement

- A psychologist named Steve Ceci argued that IQ tests are actually measuring achievement. In other words, IQ tests don't measure your ability to learn; instead, IQ tests measure what you have previously learned, which gives you an advantage on subsequent learning.

- In making his argument, Ceci found that the more school people attend (measured by the highest grade completed), the higher their IQ; this relationship remains strong even when controlling for potential confounding variables.

- In addition, during summer vacation, children's IQ scores drop, and over the school year, children's IQ scores rise. The summer drop is particularly bad for low-income children. This means that over the school year, as children learn more, their IQ scores increase. Over the summer, as they forget some of their newly learned material, IQ scores drop. This drop is worse in children whose summers are likely to involve less intellectual activity because their families are less able to afford stimulating summer camps and other academic experiences.

- Work on children who attend school only intermittently suggests that as they get older, their IQ declines steadily. Some of this work comes from historical studies of migrant workers and similar families in which younger children attend school regularly, but older children increasingly work rather than regularly attend school.

- Across a wide array of historical periods, people who delay beginning school because of war, lack of an available teacher, or segregation and racism lose a significant number of IQ points per year of delayed schooling.

- Similarly, people who drop out of school early, without finishing high school, also show IQ deficits. Furthermore, in the studies Ceci reviews, the relationship between IQ and dropping out is not nearly enough to explain the lower adult IQ of those who left school before the end of high school.

- If you look at effects of age on IQ independently of effects of schooling, which can be done by examining differently aged children within the same school grade, you find that a year of schooling has a larger effect on IQ scores than one year of development.

- Many historical shifts in IQ scores, such as large increases in IQ scores of World War II recruits compared to World War I recruits, can be attributed to historical expansions in the typical person's education.

- Finally, achievement tests, which purport to measure learning, are so identical to IQ tests that it is folly to think they are distinct. Not only are these two types of tests highly correlated, but they are also related to other variables—demographic variables such as socioeconomic status and factors such as years of schooling—in identical ways. In every way that has been examined, achievement tests and IQ tests seem to be measuring the same thing.

IQ and Schooling

- In his review, Ceci showed that schooling may affect basic cognitive capacities such as attention, perceptual abilities, memory, executive function—and IQ.

- Schools provide direct instruction on many elements tested in standard IQ tests. Schooling also provides children with instructions on strategies for thinking, such as ways of classifying items. Furthermore, school experiences give children skills at sitting still, decoding instructions, following adult directions, and other capacities that foster better IQ test performance.

- Ceci doesn't argue that IQ is meaningless or that schooling can make all children equally bright; rather, he suggests that IQ is better conceived of as a complex measure of achievement that indexes past learning, and past learning is a function of experiences provided to people over their lifetime—as well as whatever innate differences there might be in people's learning abilities.

- IQ is a fraught concept in our society in part because, historically, a test designed to help assess children's readiness for schooling became linked to ideas about ingrained and unchangeable mental superiority and inferiority, the inequality of individuals and groups, and the justification of social inequities.

- From Ceci's point of view, increasing intelligence involves the goal of promoting and supporting learning as the route to promote intelligence, and this means supporting the basic biologically healthy state that gives children a foundation for learning as well as supporting access to education for everyone.

Suggested Reading

Ceci, "How Much Does Schooling Influence General Intelligence?"

Kaufman, DeYoun, Gray, Jimenez, Brown, and Mackintosh, "Implicit Learning as an Ability."

1. Implicit learning ability seems to be related to intuition. How might the capacity to learn patterns without awareness relate to intuition?

2. Traditional IQ tests focus heavily on information processing and knowledge of vocabulary. What are other aspects of intelligence that might be poorly captured by such tests but that might be relevant to learning?

Intelligence and Learning
Lecture 20—Transcript

In this next part of the course, we will move from a consideration of general factors that relate to learning for all of us, to a consideration of how different people might learn differently with different capacities and preferences, or different motivations. We are now on to the "who" is doing the learning.

To begin this segment, we are going to ask whether there are individual differences in the capacity for learning. I am going to work historically backwards, today. I am going to beginning with a more recent effort to look at individual differences in learning capacity. Then, we will take up what is a controversial topic within and outside of psychology, one with a much longer history, namely, intelligence.

As we noted earlier, one general learning mechanism or set of mechanisms is an implicit, non-conscious capacity to monitor probabilities of events in our environment. This is what we have called system one. This learning mechanism has long been touted as one that does not differ much between people. This is the type of learning that is examined with artificial grammar learning and also with tasks like what is called a "sequential reaction time task."

In a sequential reaction time task, people are asked to watch objects on a screen and to press keys that indicate the location of the objects. Although the participants are not told this and they usually do not know it, there is a complicated, probabilistic pattern in the way the objects are appearing in the different locations. Over time, based on system one learning, people start to respond faster when the pattern is an expected one compared to when a less likely pattern occurs. Importantly, people do not realize they have learned a pattern, and they could not explicitly tell you what the pattern is, but their reaction time is telling us that they have learned something.

In fact, this faster responding to expected versus less expected patterns is what we call implicit learning. I want you to keep in mind implicit learning isn't the same as the speed of reacting. It is the difference in speed that indicates, on some level, that one pattern is likely versus how slow you are when a pattern is less likely.

First of all, it turns out based on very recent research. There are reliable individual differences in implicit learning assessed by these tasks. What reliable means is that people's performance on one set of trials in the task is similar to the way they performance on a different set of trials. Some people are doing better at such learning. Some people are faster to show evidence of implicit learning, and others are slower to show that evidence.

Another important and very interesting fact here is that this kind of performance on tasks that measures implicit learning turns out to be unrelated to measures of general intelligence, and it also turns out to be unrelated to measures of working memory capacity or executive function. In other words, implicit learning of slow reaction time tasks is the distinct individual difference. Just because you have a superb working memory doesn't mean you will have a strong capacity to learn in the implicit and non-conscious way.

Implicit learning is related to processing speed, and people whose processing speed is faster—and we know that because they are quicker to push a button in a reaction time task—they show higher implicit learning scores. Finally, and maybe most importantly implicit learning abilities measured in this way are related to academic achievement. For example, people do better at foreign language learning and at mathematics when they are better at implicit learning.

What does this mean? First of all, I want you to know this is very recent research. It was done in the last few years and published in 2011. Many aspects of individual differences in implicit learning remain to be established. We don't for example know how reliable these differences between people are over time. If someone's performance on one occasion is not like their performance on another occasion, it becomes unclear how much individual differences in implicit learning can help us understand broader or more long-term differences between people in learning.

We also don't yet know if we have one set of mental processes for implicit learning, or whether there are multiple sets of implicit learning processes, and in that case, serial reaction time tasks might assess only one kind of implicit learning and there might be lots of others.

What is interesting is that individual differences in this kind of learning are related to academic achievement. Usually academic achievement is viewed in terms of system two explicit and deliberate efforts to learn material and individual differences in this kind of implicit learning are also unrelated to the more long-established approach to individual differences in learning ability, and that is intelligence.

As we will see next, intelligence may not be a great explanation of differences in learning, at least as we currently measure intelligence. Implicit learning offers a potentially useful alternative idea that researchers can explore.

In addition to the work that I just described on individual differences in implicit learning, the more long-standing area of focus on individual differences in learning is that of intelligence. Are differences in people's learning related to differences in their intelligence? The answers we arrive at today may, in fact, surprise you. They certainly surprised me. To begin with, we have to consider what intelligence is, and the history it has both within the field of psychology and also beyond.

We think of intelligence as the capacity for adaptive, successful problem solving. What might that capacity entail, and how could we go about to measure it? In its earliest history, Alfred Binet, the French scientist who was responsible for developing one of the earliest intelligence tests, Binet argued that human intelligence involved our abilities for memory, judgment, reasoning, and social understanding.

An intelligence quotient, or IQ, is a measure of someone's intelligence that is based on a fairly limited examination of their ability to do certain kinds of problems, often under time pressure conditions, and those are what we call IQ tests. Typical problems on IQ tests include reasoning from a set of given premises, substituting symbols for digits, answering general knowledge questions, completing patterns of numbers, words, or visual images, recognizing the meanings of words, and so on.

Binet developed some of the earliest tests in France and he had a very specific goal. He wanted to figure out whether kids were ready to start school or whether they should wait a little bit longer before beginning school.

The timing of his work and the timing of these developments was right around the onset of World War I. That meant that IQ testing took off pretty quickly as a way to sort out the strengths and weaknesses of army recruits for various positions within the army. In the context of making IQ tests more useful for that military application, IQ tests developed into their current form.

Today's IQ tests generally measure two distinct, but fairly related capabilities and they are often termed fluid and crystallized intelligence. Fluid intelligence consists of tests of speed of information processing, the capacity to detect patterns and predict what comes next in sequences, the ability to mentally rotate figures, the ability to remember new information that you are given, and so on. Crystallized intelligence consists of measures of vocabulary and general knowledge. Fluid intelligence is what you can do with new information on the fly, and crystallized intelligence is what you have accumulated already.

As an aside, non-verbal tests of IQ that have been developed and applied to humans and chimpanzees actually suggest many of the visual and spatial aspects of IQ tests are actually pretty similar across species. Humans have additional abilities that seem to be less relevant for chimpanzees, and those include some of our abilities with respect to social understanding that we talked about earlier.

After these initial military applications, IQ tests were more fully developed for widespread use. This included adapting them for groups that were not literate, or could not speak English. As all these developments occurred, IQ tests played a role in evaluating immigrants and in a number of other what we might think of as dubious contexts. As this happened, the use of IQ tests shifted from evaluating someone's current readiness to learn, to a more problematic, and essentialist idea that people differing in some fundamental capability for learning. Essentialist means an entity idea of intelligence. That is, it is the idea that IQ is a static element of someone's capacities. It is not something that changes. It is not something that can be improved. Binet's original idea for IQ was not this way. It was not the idea that there was some immutable quality of children that determined whether they could go to school, but IQ quickly became viewed in this way.

In fact, when we speak of IQ, many people now presume that IQ is what we are born with. They assume that it is IQ that makes learning easier or harder for some people than others. Another way to think about this is to say that IQ is viewed as an aptitude or a talent that makes it easier to learn. Those who have a higher IQ will perform better in school. They will get better grades and they will get better test scores. IQ is the innate potential and it is distinct from learning.

This is why the data that show that one or another group, on average, scores lower on IQ tests, this is why that data is so troubling. If we assumed that IQ was some temporary state of a person, that basically told us how ready they were to learn, we might view that same set of finding as indicating the need for remedial programs or different instructional methods rather than as a claim about a group being fundamentally inferiority or superior.

What would count as good evidence for IQ as an ability that facilitates learning? What would help us feel like this essentialist count is right? You need to show two things. One thing you need to show is that IQ scores predict learning. Here IQ scores look pretty good. IQ scores predict learning quite well.

For example, let me just give you a list of some of the things that can be predicted pretty well based on knowing someone's IQ. These things include school grades, scores on achievement tests, which measure how much students have learned in school settings (and we are going to come back to that fact later today), military recruits' ability to steer a tank, mechanics' ability to repair engines, postal workers' speed and accuracy at mail sorting, and so on.

In all these cases, people with higher IQ scores appear to learn and then to perform at a higher level than those with lower IQ scores. All of this is totally consistent with the idea that IQ is the ability to learn and perform a wide variety of tasks.

A second thing you need to show is that IQ is some kind of stable aptitude the person has, otherwise, it could be argued that IQ does not reflect ability to learn, but may reflect the person's current state of learning. Then, all those predictions that I listed above, they cannot be understood as findings about differences between people in the ability to learn. Instead, they involve differences between people in starting knowledge that lets some people better learn new skills or new material than others.

Well, over time, IQ test scores are quite stable. What that means is that for most of us, if we are above average we stay above average in our IQ tests scores, and if we are below average, we stay below average in our IQ test scores. Further, IQ actually turns out to be highly heritable. What that means is that identical twins have more IQ test scores than fraternal twins and the normal siblings, and this is true even when identical twins are reared apart in different homes.

This could be because our environments actually also tend to be fairly pretty stable over time. Even when identical twins are reared apart in different families, there are many reasons why their environments tend to end up pretty similar. These include the nature of the adoption process, because that adoption process targets particular kinds of families. It also includes the fact that we as in other people respond quite similarly to people who look and act in similar ways. That is, we all go around creating or eliciting our environments and twins may elicit similar experiences from their surroundings even when they are reared apart.

Am I saying that people are not different in intelligence? Not quite, but I am trying to suggest to you that there is no environment-free ability difference. In a given environment the typical environment we have in our country now, for example, there may be genetically linked differences in IQ, but these differences are far from independent of the environment.

This brings me to a really wonderful study of genetics and learning in rats. Under the assumption that intelligence is the capacity to learn, and that it can be selectively bred for, that is, it is genetic, some researchers took rats who were good or bad at maze learning, and bred them selectively to create strains actually are labeled "maze-bright" and "maze-dull" rats.

The researchers then took rat pups from each strain maze-bright rats and maze-dull rats, and they reared them under three different kinds of environmental conditions. In one case they reared them under the usual laboratory conditions, and these were the conditions that were in effect, as they bred these different strains of rats. In another condition, the rats were given impoverished conditions. They were given poor nutrition, and they were not given toys. Another group of the rats got enriched conditions. They got better food than the typical laboratory situation, and they got a lot of space and a lot of toys.

The researchers then went on to test the rat's ability to learn mazes under the usual maze learning conditions. What they expected, based on the assumption that genes will out, was that the good environment would enhance learning for both kinds of rat, but the differences between the two rat strains would remain. That is, maze-bright and maze-dull rats would always differed even though they would both do better in good conditions, and they would both do more poorly at maze learning under poor conditions; that's not what they saw.

Instead, the researchers only saw differences in the environment that the rats were typically bred and reared in. Under enriched conditions, both strains of rats did better and they did equally well. Under impoverished conditions, both strains did worse, and they did equally badly.

What this tells you is that the effects of any gene, including any gene involved in intelligence and for a complex quality like intelligence as we have defined it, there are going to be a lot of genes involved. The effects of any gene are intertwined with the environment so much that you actually cannot pull them apart. In the case of IQ, this means that IQ may have to do with genetic effects, but IQ has to do with genetic effects only in the way that the genes are operating within that person's environment, over time.

What this means is that the stability of IQ test scores may not mean that IQ comes first and it is genetically based, and learning relies on IQ. Rather, the stability of IQ may mean that people who start out having learned more in their environment continue to have advantages over time, because most people who start out having learned more maintain their environmental advantages over time, the circumstances that initially led them to learn more than their peers.

Where am I going with this? Some years ago, a psychologist named Steve Ceci began to take a good, careful look at the evidence that IQ was stable, and that it predicted learning. What he discovered was quite surprising, and it may radically change your perspective on IQ, as it did mine. What Ceci did was to argue that what IQ tests are really measuring is achievement. IQ doesn't measure your ability to learn, IQ measures what you have previously learned, and what you have previously learned can give you a leg up on subsequent learning as we have discussed before in this course.

In making his argument, Ceci brought in eight different pieces of evidence, and we will consider them in turn. Before we go there, however, I have to make a very brief statistical digression. In many fields, to quantify the relationship between two variables, like IQ and learning, researchers compute something called a correlation coefficient, or correlation, for short.

A correlation coefficient ranges from -1 to $+1$. A correlation of 0 or somewhere around there means that two different variables, again let us think of IQ and learning, have no relationship at all. What that means is knowing someone's IQ tells me nothing about how well they are going to learn.

A correlation of $+1$ would mean that IQ and learning are perfectly positively correlated. That would mean that knowing someone's IQ allows me to perfectly predict their learning, and because it is a positive correlation it would also mean that the higher their IQ, the better their learning.

A correlation of -1 means again that IQ and learning have a perfectly correlation, but this time it is a negative one. Knowing someone's IQ would allows me to perfectly predict his or her learning, but in this case, that negative sign means that the higher their IQ, the worse they are learning.

In practice, correlations of about 0.3 or somewhere in that arena, whether they are positive or negative are the norm for variables that we think of as being related to one another, but not the same. When two variables correlate at 0.7 or 0.8 or higher, you have to wonder if they are not essentially the same variable being measured in two different ways with the small differences that make the correlation a little less than 1 being due to differences in measurement and a little bit of error in our measurements.

This is important, because some of the evidence Ceci compiles on IQ as achievement versus IQ as ability, relies on the magnitude of correlations between IQ and other variables.

First off, the more school people attend, measured by the highest grade they complete, the higher their IQ. This relationship remains very strong even when you control for other variables that might explain that effect. In fact, the relationship involves correlations of between 0.6 and 0.8. These are relationships that are getting close to the "measuring the same thing" idea.

Second, and this one is really kind of interesting, during summer vacation, children's IQ scores drop. Over the school year, children's IQ scores rise. The summer drop is particularly bad for low-income kids. What does this mean? What it means is that over the school year as kids learn more, their IQ scores go up. Over the summer, as they forget some of their newly learned material, IQ scores drop. The drop is worse in kids whose summers are likely to involve less intellectual activity, because their families are less able to afford academically stimulating summer camps and other sorts of summer experiences.

Work on kids who attend school only intermittently also suggests that as they get older, their IQ declines steadily. Some of this work comes from interesting historical studies of migrant workers and other families where the younger kids go to school pretty regularly, but older kids increasingly begin to work to contribute to family income. They do not regularly attend school. In these families, kid's initial IQ scores are within the normal range for their age group, but the IQ scores of older children are significantly lower than those of their peers.

People who delay beginning school because of war or the lack of an available teacher, or segregation and racism, across a wide range of historical periods, lose an average of five to seven IQ points per year of delayed schooling.

Similarly, people who drop out of school early without finishing high school also show IQ deficits relative to their same age peers. You might be thinking, "Well, the people with lower IQ drop out of school because it is too hard." This is not the case in the studies Ceci reviewed. The relationship between IQ and dropping out is not nearly big enough to explain the lower adult IQ of people who left formal schooling before the end of high school.

Three additional pieces of evidence were marshaled by Ceci. One is that if you look at the effects of age on IQ, and primarily in childhood independently of the effects of schooling, and you can do this by looking at kids who are in the same school of grade but are different in age. What you find is that one year of schooling has a bigger effect on IQ scores than one full year of development. In my son's third grade class, then, the difference in IQ between the barely eight-year-olds like my son, and the already-nine-year-olds is going to be smaller than the IQ difference in the barely eight-year-olds from the beginning of the school year to the end of the school year.

It is also the case that many historical shifts in IQ scores, such as the large increases in IQ scores of WWII recruits compared to WWI recruits, can be attributed to historical expansions in what a typical person's education entailed.

Finally, last, but by no means least, achievement tests, which purport to measure learning, are so identical to IQ tests, that it is almost foolish to think they are distinct. Not only are these two types of tests highly correlated in the range of 0.8 correlations, they are also related to other variables, demographic variables like socioeconomic status, factors like years of schooling as I have outlined above. They are related to those factors in identical ways. In every way that has been examined, achievement tests and IQ tests look like they are measuring the same thing. Perhaps, Ceci concludes, this is because they are.

Ceci went on, in his review, to also show that schooling may affect basic cognitive capacities like attention, perceptual abilities, memory, and what we would call executive function as well. The question is how does school do this? How does school affect IQ? There are at least three ways that school works to affect people's IQ scores.

One is that schools provide direct instruction for many of the things that are tested in standard IQ tests. My son has spent two years learning Latin roots for words, and this was all before he turned nine. The Latin roots are very helpful, in direct ways, for deciphering difficult and unusual vocabulary words on an IQ test.

Schooling also provides kids with instructions about strategies for thinking, ways of classifying items. For example, it is in school that we learn to put apples and oranges together because of their botanical status as fruits, rather than because they are both round or can be eaten, or have seeds. These latter categorizations are viable. They are even useful, but they are just not consistent with IQ test rules.

Finally, school experiences give kids some skills at sitting still, at figuring out written instructions and verbal instructions, at following adult directions, and other capacities that are also likely to promote better IQ test performance.

IQ is a fraught concept in our society in part because historically, a test designed to help assess children's readiness for schooling was linked to ideas about engrained and unchangeable mental superiority or inferiority, ideas about the inequality of individuals in groups, and ways of justifying existing social inequities. It is not surprising that a lot of researchers and scholars also find the idea of IQ problematic and troubling. One real issue to think about is what we are trying to do with the idea of IQ. What is this concept being used to accomplish? If we are just trying to assess where someone is in order to tailor education or training or other opportunities specifically for that person, IQ tests probably do a pretty decent job. If we are trying to sort people into groups or to treat IQ as an immutable aspect of people, then we are likely to actually fail to capitalize on at least some of our human potential.

Also, remember that we talked about confirmation biases and the self, and we talked about how people who think badly of themselves work kind of hard to maintain those negative views and to get others around them to share those negative views. Well this also certainly applies to self-perceptions about IQ and to teacher perceptions about IQ.

When teachers developed the idea that a child is stupid, or that child him or herself develops the idea that he or she is stupid, you can imagine very similar ways in which both teacher and child might work to maintain that belief. That happens at the child's expense, but it also happens at the expense of all of us.

Note that Ceci does not argue that IQ is meaningless, and he does not argue that schooling is going to fix everything and make all kids equally bright and equally smart. Rather Ceci suggests that IQ is better thought of as a complex measure of achievement, as something that indexes past learning. Past learning is a function of experiences that a person has over their lifetime as well as whatever innate differences there might be in the ability to learn.

The idea of tacit learning that I started with suggests that there will be real differences between people in learning capacities too. IQ just may not be the best route to getting at those differences. A more promising route may involve looking at individual differences in more basic aspects of cognition like speed of information processing, the ability of working memory to deal with more or less information, the ability to inhibit distractions and this kind of implicit learning capacity.

This work is at its very beginning because researchers in those traditions, researchers interested in attention and working memory, have not been historically as interested in differences between people as researchers in other fields. Another answer to the problems raised by work on IQ and one we will address in the next lecture is ideas about learning styles and multiple kinds of intelligence.

As a historical note, Binet lived to see his test and its later iterations are linked up with all kinds of ideas about inferior groups and people. He was horrified. He referred to the way that IQ tests were developed and were being used as involving what he called "brutal pessimism." He set about toward the very end of his career and life trying to develop exercises that would increase intelligence and that would demonstrate, forcibly and convincingly, that intelligence was not an unchangeable aspect of people.

Unfortunately, Binet died before completing the project to increase intelligence. From Ceci's point of view, we know a great deal about how to increase intelligence, and most of what we know points to the goal of promoting and supporting learning as the route to promote intelligence. This means supporting the basic biologically healthy state that gives kids a good foundation for learning through good prenatal care, good nutrition, and early childhood interventions for poverty. It also points to supporting access to education for everyone.

Are Learning Styles Real?
Lecture 21

Intelligence has been viewed as a capacity for learning, but it increasingly seems like it might reflect people's learning history rather than their ability to learn in the future. Additionally, individual differences in implicit learning remain consistent with the idea that some people are simply better than others at learning in general. In this lecture, we'll consider two overlapping ideas that are more optimistic: We're all good at some things but not others, and we may all differ in the way we like to learn. These ideas are, respectively, the notions of multiple intelligences and learning styles.

Multiple Intelligences

- The idea of multiple intelligences was initially proposed by Howard Gardner several decades ago. From Gardner's view, the nature of an intelligence depends in part on the type of information that it is being used to process.

- In contrast to the types of abilities measured on IQ tests, Gardner argued that people actually demonstrate intelligence in what is called a domain-specific way. Because of this, in our focus on IQ, we ignore many ways in which people could demonstrate intelligence.

- Initially, Gardner proposed seven types of intelligence.

  - Logical-mathematical intelligence is one of the types of intelligence assessed by IQ tests. This intelligence is what contributes to various types of reasoning and mathematical computation.

  - Spatial intelligence is another type of intelligence that is partially captured by IQ tests, and it has to do with people's understanding of space.

- Verbal intelligence allows people to play with words, make elegant and persuasive arguments, understand and make inferences from what they read, and is also measured on IQ tests.

- Interpersonal intelligences involve the ability to navigate relationships and social interactions with skill.

- Musical intelligence involves great abilities in melody and rhythm.

- Kinesthetic intelligence involves capacities for movement.

- Intrapersonal intelligence refers to the ability to be aware of one's own feelings, motivations, and thoughts.

- More recently, Gardner proposed that there might be additional intelligences—having to do with spirituality and with nature and natural systems—but he cautions about the relatively little evidence on these new types of intelligence as of yet.

- To demonstrate the intelligences, we need evidence that the different intelligences are, in fact, separate from one another. However, for many of Gardner's proposed intelligences, there are no easily administered tests.

- For standard IQ tests, we can measure logical-mathematical, spatial, and verbal. In many cases where it has been possible to measure, the relationships among two intelligences fall in a gray area; these tests suggest that the intelligences are related but are not quite the same.

- In the rare cases where more intensive assessments of ability have been made, such as observing actual job performance, these measurements are often highly correlated with IQ tests.

- Therefore, researchers in favor of the idea of a single intelligence view the evidence as indicating Gardner is wrong and that all intelligences are related whereas Gardner and his supporters view the evidence in precisely the opposite way. This is an example of confirmation bias.

Multiple Intelligences and Learning

- Across a large number of studies, Tim Hoeffler found that higher spatial intelligence is associated with better learning from visualizations. Therefore, people who score higher on spatial IQ tests who are then presented with pictures learn more from the pictures than those whose spatial IQ scores were lower. However, it matters what types of visual images you are trying to learn from.

- Hoeffler also found that this was most evident when the visual images were static and learners had to use their own minds to rotate the diagram or imagine how a process unfolded from the starting point that was depicted. When the images were made dynamic, people with lower visual ability were able to benefit from visualization also.

© Brand X Pictures/Thinkstock.

Experts, including chess players, process new expertise-related information differently than novices.

- For spatial intelligence, it looks like learning from visualization is easier for those with higher spatial ability, but does this mean that there are different intelligences—or does it really mean that people who are more experienced in visualization, as indicated by higher visual ability tests, do better at learning from visualization?

- As with standard IQ, is it possible that these intelligences reflect not some type of pure ability but really expertise? It is very difficult to disentangle these two issues—a priori ability versus more experience.

- In both cases, experience and prior learning give someone an advantage in learning something new. Therefore, the findings regarding spatial intelligence and learning from visualizations hold, but we are interpreting them differently—as differences in existing knowledge that influence the ease of future learning.

- While there are relatively few studies looking at multiple intelligences and learning, there are many studies that show that experts process new expertise-relevant information quite differently than novices.

Multiple Intelligences versus Learning Styles
- While Gardner himself focused primarily on the concept of intelligences, many educators seized on his ideas as relevant to differences in learning styles, and the idea that we have different learning styles is enormously prevalent in today's world.

- Learning styles are distinct from the idea of multiple intelligences because they are presumed to reflect differences in the way people learn rather than in abilities.

- As of 2004, there were 170 different models and measures of learning styles. One example of learning styles includes the V.A.K. category system, in which people may be either visual, auditory, or kinesthetic learners.

- To begin with, learning styles are real: There are reliable, measureable differences in people's preferences for learning, and these can be measured and described with most of those 170 different systems.

- Some people think better when moving while others need to be still. Many people need to build things to see how they work while others would rather look at diagrams or listen to a lecture about a structure.

- These preferences are stable over time—that is, you won't change your mind about being an auditory learner over a period of a few months, but over decades, things can shift. Furthermore, these preferences will tell you something about how you might choose to learn.

- Does this mean learning styles or learning preferences matter for actual learning? In terms of learning, we know that elaborative encoding is a very useful and helpful aid in learning, and we know that most things we learn involve integrating across many areas of the brain. Moreover, we know that prior knowledge and expertise matter enormously in learning.

- All of this suggests that adapting material to a preference for visual stimuli by excluding auditory information, for example, doesn't make sense. It would result in less elaborative encoding because you have reduced one arena for the development of connections— an arena where there could be prior knowledge and experience that would facilitate learning, for example.

- We also know that what people choose to do—their preferences for strategies, in that case—doesn't always correlate with what they should do to maximize learning.

- The core issue is that these preferences for different ways of learning do not seem to matter, in the sense that adapting teaching or learning contexts to the preferences of the individual results in better learning—faster-acquired or better-retained learning.

- The learning styles hypothesis has three components.

    - People will learn better with one approach than with another.

    - The approach that is best will differ for different people because, otherwise, we aren't talking about styles and individual differences but about metacognition and learning strategies that work for everyone, such as repeated testing.

    - Most importantly, people will learn best when they are taught in a way that matches their learning style.

- To fully test this hypothesis, researchers need to conduct studies in which learning styles are identified, and within each learning style, people get randomly assigned to an instruction that either matches or doesn't match their preferred style. After instruction, all participants are evaluated for their learning with the same test.

- A comprehensive literature review by several prominent psychologists found a small number of studies that actually tested the learning styles hypothesis in this way.

- One study looked at learning of computer-presented information about electronics and visual or verbal learning styles assessed in several different ways. Across variations of the study and many different ways of classifying people as visual or verbal learners, the researchers found no evidence that people should receive information matched to their learning style in order to optimize learning.

- Only one study supported the idea of learning styles, and that particular study had some strange features—such as the use of unusual methods for assessing learning outcomes—that make it less than ideal evidence.

- Overall, multimodal presentation works better than matching learning styles for most people. Additionally, visual presentations can be very strong for learning in general, but our expertise, or prior learning, about how to use visualizations matters in this regard.

Implications of Learning Styles

- For those that have more prior knowledge, more knowledge is acquired and with greater ease. One way to think about this phenomenon is that this is the core of specialization in a complex society—that is, it's acceptable for people to differ in their experiences, expertise, and subsequent learning.

- The same psychologists who reviewed research on learning styles and suggested that there wasn't much evidence for attending to them admitted that there are enormous implications for learning of differences in prior knowledge.

- Instead of looking at multiple intelligences or learning styles as an opportunity to fix the way we educate people, researchers interested in enhancing learning might focus on how we can assess individual differences in prior knowledge and how we can make use of that information to tailor education to what people do know and where they need to learn more.

- More advanced and knowledgeable people may be better able to benefit from discovery-based learning than truly novice learners. This is consistent with the fact that discovery-based learning, in its moderate forms, works better in adulthood than earlier in the lifespan.

- This possibility is also consistent with findings that more advanced learners benefit from having less structure—that is, less teacher-directed, explicit guidance—while less advanced learners, or those with less prior knowledge, benefit from having more teacher direction and explicit guidance.

- In addition, understanding what assumptions learners bring into their learning can be helpful for shaping the way that instruction unfolds. When we discussed work on scientific understandings by Michelene Chi, we talked about the process of learning as a change in models, and that change is easiest to support for learners if we know what their starting models are.

- Furthermore, all people may benefit from knowing more about metacognition—the things that can distort our understanding of our own learning and the strategies that are effective but unused by learners.

- Where learning styles may need to be retained as an idea is in the area of motivation because while learning in one's preferred style may not have anything to do with learning outcomes, if it affects people's interests and motivations, it may still be a useful concept.

Suggested Reading

Geake, "Neuromythologies in Education."

Pashler, McDaniel, Rohrer, and Bjork, "Learning Styles."

Schaler, ed., *Howard Gardner under Fire*.

Questions to Consider

1. A different way to take the idea of multiple intelligences seriously is to view them as indicating acquired expertise. If we view them this way, what would the implications for teaching and learning be?

2. Given the absolute paucity of evidence on learning styles, what do you think accounts for their enormous popularity? Given the evidence, can you give up on a belief in learning styles? Why or why not?

Are Learning Styles Real?

Lecture 21—Transcript

As we discussed last lecture, intelligence has been viewed as a capacity for learning, but increasingly looks like it might reflect people's learning history rather than necessarily their ability to learn in the future. As we also considered, the history of IQ research has been very tarnished by its use for maintaining stereotypes about groups and justifying inequality.

We also noted the search for individual differences that are related to learning ability is far from over. Last time, we touched on the idea that there may be individual differences in implicit learning. Such differences although, remain totally consistent with the idea that some people are simply better than others at learning in general, an idea which many people find distasteful or troubling. It is certainly not egalitarian.

Today, we will consider two overlapping ideas about individual differences in learning that share a distinctly more optimistic message, namely that we are all good at some things but not others, and that we may all differ in the way we like to learn. These ideas are, respectively, the notion of multiple intelligences, and the notion of learning styles.

The idea of multiple intelligences was initially proposed by Howard Gardner several decades ago. From Gardner's view, an intelligence was a biopsychological information processing capacity, and the nature of an intelligence depended in part on the type of information that it was being used to process.

In contrast to the kinds of abilities measured by IQ tests, Gardner argued that people actually demonstrate intelligence in what he called a "domain specific" way. Because of this, if we focus too heavily on intelligence tests and IQ, we ignore many other ways in which people could demonstrate high levels of intelligence.

Initially Gardner proposed seven kinds of intelligence. Logical-mathematical intelligence, which is one of the kinds of intelligence assessed by IQ tests, was one. This is the kind of intelligence that contributes to reasoning, mathematical computation, and other kinds of math and logic tasks. A second kind of intelligence Gardener proposed was spatial intelligence. This is different kind of intelligence and it is also partially captured by IQ tests. It has to do with people's understandings of space.

A third kind of intelligence is verbal intelligence. This is the kind of intelligence that lets people play with words, make elegant and persuasive arguments, understand and make inferences from what they read, and even make a really good pun now and then, and this is a kind of intelligence that is also measured on IQ tests.

As an aside, some research suggests that this type of intelligence is the most evident to others actually. That verbal intelligence is one of the ways we come to decide that someone in our everyday lives is more or less intelligent.

In addition to those three though, Gardner also proposed that there were interpersonal intelligences; these are the abilities to navigate relationships and social interactions with skill. Some people might actually call this political acumen.

There is also musical intelligence, which involved great abilities with melody and rhythm. There is kinesthetic intelligence; this involves capacities for movement. Michael Jordan is a shining example of this kind of intelligence.

Finally, Gardener proposed that there is a kind of intra-personal intelligence, intelligence about the within the person, and this is the ability to be aware of your own feelings, motivations, and thoughts and to be accurate in perceiving those feelings and motivations and thoughts.

More recently, Gardner has proposed that there might be additional kinds of intelligence having to do with spirituality, and having to do with intelligence about nature and natural systems. He cautions us that, currently, there is relatively little evidence to demonstrate that these new types of intelligence exist.

That brings me to the issue of what would we need to demonstrate that there is a kind of intelligences? One thing that we need is we need evidence that these different kinds of intelligence, these seven kinds that Gardener proposed a well as any other are actually separate from one another, that they are distinct abilities.

Recall that last lecture we talked about this idea of a correlation—that is, a number that indexes how closely related two different variables are to one another. Remember, correlations can range anywhere between negative one and positive one, and a correlation of zero means there is no relationship between two variables, and a correlation of negative one or positive one means the two variables are perfectly related if I know the value of one variable, I can tell you the variable of the other. Positive correlations mean variables follow a pattern where more of one variable goes with more of another. We talked about more IQ being related to, say, more education. Negative correlations go in that other direction, the fewer stressful events in a person's childhood the more life satisfaction the person experiences as an adult.

Of course in the real world of real data we do not see correlations around one very often, we usually get numbers in between and you may recall that correlations around 0.3 suggest that two variables are meaningfully related but they are still distinct. Correlations around 0.8 and up, 0.7 and up suggest two variables are more or less capturing the same thing.

To collect this kind of evidence about distinct forms of intelligence we face some problems. For many of Gardner's proposed intelligences, there are not any easily administered tests. For standard IQ tests, of course, we have those three. We can look at logical and mathematical intelligence, spatial intelligence, and verbal intelligence, and we can measure all three of those.

It turns out in many cases where it has been possible to do so, the relationships among spatial intelligence and verbal intelligence for example they fall in a gray zone. They certainly are not zero. They are actually quite a bit larger than 0.3, which would suggest separate but related abilities. They are not so large that you can definitely say, "These are one thing." That is, they fall a bit short of that 0.8 mark.

In the rare cases where people have done more intensive assessments of abilities, like observing actual job performance, those measurements also turn out to be highly correlated with IQ tests. Given what you know about confirmation biases, what this means is everyone can draw his or her own conclusion about those abilities. Researchers in favor of the idea of one intelligence view this evidence as indicating Gardner is wrong, all intelligences are related, and in fact, one quote is, "There are no multiple intelligences, but rather, it is argued, multiple applications of the same multifaceted intelligence."

Not surprisingly, Gardner and his supporters view the evidence in precisely the opposite way. This, after our lecture on learning as theory testing, should surprise none of us. It is confirmation bias in action.

Let us suppose we throw Gardner a bone, and we say, okay, let us treat these as distinct performances on tests that are related to distinct forms of intelligence. Let us assume they are not just multiple indicators of one underlying intelligence.

If we do that, there are two additional issues we have to resolve because for our purposes, we are not really interested in multiple intelligences per se. Rather, we are interested in whether different intelligences are related to differences in how different people learn.

A first and obvious question is whether the intelligences relate meaningfully, to learning. Are people better at learning in areas where they have higher intelligences? Possibly.

Let us look at just one focused piece of evidence in this regard. In math and science, we often encounter material that is presented visually. If we have higher spatial abilities, or spatial intelligence, are we better able to learn from visualizations? Remember spatial intelligence includes things like navigation and way finding, and constructing cognitive maps. It also includes some other visual abilities, like being able to mentally rotate an object we are looking at.

Tim Hoeffler pooled a large number of studies to look at this. In general, across the studies that he looked at, higher spatial intelligence measured on standard IQ type tests is associated with better learning from visualizations.

If I take someone who scored high on a spatial IQ tests, and then I then give them some pictures, they learn more from those pictures or figures than someone whose score on the spatial IQ test was lower.

It matters what types of visual images you are trying to learn from. Hoeffler also found, by comparing across different studies, that the effect was most evident when the visual images were static, because that means learners had to use their own mind to rotate the diagram or they had to imagine how a process unfolded from the starting point that the diagram or figure depicted.

When the images were made dynamic, people with lower visual ability were able to benefit from visualization also. We will revisit this finding later in this lecture, because it is pertinent to the topic of learning styles.

At least for spatial intelligence, it looks like learning from visualization is easier for those with higher spatial ability. Does this mean there are different intelligences? Or does it really mean that people who are more experienced in visualization, as indicated by higher performance on a visual ability tests, do better at learning from visualization?

This is a second issue, and it is a trickier one in a way. As with standard IQ, is it possible that these intelligences reflect not some kind of pure ability in, say, spatial mental rotation, but instead they reflect an established expertise?

In other words, if you have high verbal IQ, say, is it because you have a special aptitude or talent for learning verbal material? Or, is it because you started reading early (that's something many kids can do given the right context), and therefore, by IQ-testing time in second grade or so, you had learned a very large vocabulary, and you had a big repertoire of knowledge about sentence structure because you just had more years of reading behind you?

It is very difficult to disentangle these two issues, *a priori* ability versus the accumulation of more experience and expertise. If I have, in relative terms, a lousy kinesthetic IQ, and I am going to assure you that I do, is it because during my childhood, I spent a lot of time on my bum reading rather than being out moving around?

In both of these cases, as we have learned in this course, experience and prior learning give a person a leg up, and a lack of experience and prior learning can give someone a serious disadvantage when it comes to learning something that is related, although new.

The findings I just described about spatial intelligence and learning from visualizations hold. Those findings are real, but we might interpret them somewhat differently. We might interpret them as differences in existing knowledge that influence the ease of future learning.

Some researchers actually think that our visuo-spatial IQ is actually increasing across the population because we are currently exposed to more images and more visual stimuli than we have ever been exposed to before historically.

While there are relatively few studies that really look directly at multiple intelligences and learning, there are many studies that show experts process new, expertise-relevant information quite differently than novices. Here is an example. Where I, a novice player, see randomly distributed pieces on a chess board, experts chess players see meaningful configurations that tell them how play has proceeded and also give them a really good sense of how play is likely to proceed in that game.

Where my daughter, a non-pianist, hears melody, I both hear the melody and on a more tacit level, there is some part of me that also has a feel for the motor movements that are required to produce that melody. You can also recall the early example in this course of golfers and non-golfers who were asked to learn a series of actions. Golfers were better at learning the actions as long as they were related to golf.

While Gardner himself focused primarily on the concept of intelligences, many educators seized on his ideas as being relevant to differences in learning styles, and the idea that we have different learning styles is also enormously prevalent in today's world. Private schools promise, at some expense, to match instruction to your child's unique learning style. You can hear people sometimes say things like, "I'm not a very visual person."

Learning styles are distinct from the idea of multiple intelligences, because they are presumed to reflect differences in the way people learn, rather than in their abilities, per se.

One prominent example of learning styles is the V.A.K. category system, and in this system people are either visual, V, auditory, A, or kinesthetic K learners. There are other ideas out there. In fact, there are actually so many ideas out there. I could spend several years teaching you the details of all of the available models. As of 2004, many years ago, there were 170 different models or measures of learning styles.

Are learning styles real, and are they meaningful for thinking about the learning process? These are two different questions, and we are going to look at them in sequence.

Are learning styles real? Yes. First, there are reliable, measureable differences in people's preferences about how they learn. These can be measured and they can be described with most of those 170 different systems, although every system has its own idiosyncratic way of describing differences.

To give you a concrete example, maybe you like listening to lectures as a way of learning. Or you might be a person who prefers to read about an issue you are interested in. You might not really like to talk directly to an expert, and your friends may feel just the opposite.

Some people think better when they are moving, running, or walking, and others need to be very still. Many of you may need to touch something or build something to see how they work, and others might prefer to read about it and look at diagrams rather than get their hands dirty.

These preferences exist and they are stable over time. That is, you do not change your mind about being an auditory learner over a period of a few months, although over decades, people's preferences can move around a little bit.

Left here on your own devices, these preferences will tell you something about how you might choose to learn when you are making all of the choices. Does this mean learning styles or learning preferences matter for actual learning?

To think this through a bit, let us first step back and consider something about what we know of learning so far. We know that elaborative encoding is a very useful and helpful aid in learning. We know that most things we learn involve integrating across many areas of the brain. The brain actually works not in separated chunks, but in the interconnections across perception, sensation, memory and association, motor skills, and planning and decision-making areas.

Moreover, we know that prior knowledge and expertise matter enormously in learning. All of that knowledge suggests that if we adapt material to, say, a preference for visual stimuli by keeping auditory information out of the picture it does not make sense. It is not likely to help people learn better.

It would result in less elaborative encoding because you have reduced one arena for the development of connections, an arena where there could be prior knowledge and experience that would facilitate learning.

Going a bit further, we also know from the lecture on judgments of learning and choices about learning strategies, that what people choose to do, their preferences for strategies, in that particular case, does not always map onto what they ought to do to maximize learning.

The fact that I might choose a certain modes for learning, when I have the freedom to do so, does not always mean that choice is what will serve me best.

This is the core issue. Do these preferences for different ways of learning have meaning, in the sense that adapting teaching and learning contexts to the preferences of the individual results in better learning? By that, we might mean faster learning or we might mean learning that is better retained. The answer to this question is. So far, no.

The learning styles hypothesis has three components, and often, we lump them together when we are thinking quickly, but it is important to elaborate them when we look for evidence in favor of learning styles.

The first component of the hypothesis is this, people will learn better with one approach than with another. The second component is, the approach that is best will differ for different people, because otherwise, we are not talking about styles and individual differences, but about meta-cognition and learning strategies that work really well for everyone like repeated testing. The third, last, and most important component of the hypothesis is the idea that people will learn best when they are taught in a way that matches their learning style.

To fully test this hypothesis, researchers need to conduct studies where learning styles are identified, and within each group of people that shares a particular learning style, people are randomly assigned either to get instruction that matches their preferred style, or to get instruction that does not match their preferred style. Then everyone is evaluated for how much they have learned or how quickly they have learned after instruction using the same test.

The learning styles hypothesis would get support if the results were something like the following. For each learning style group, people who got their matching instruction like visual learners who got a visualization heavy instruction do better than participants who have that style but get, say, auditory instruction.

A comprehensive review of this literature by several prominent psychologists found a very tiny number of studies that actually tested the learning styles hypothesis in this way.

One of their favorite studies looked at learning of computer-presented information about electronics, and visual or verbal learning styles assessed in a number of different ways. Across three experiments, people were assigned to receive a help screen that were either verbal or visual in nature.

For some people, the help screens matched their preferences, but for other people the help screen was at odds with their preferences, so a visual learner got a verbal help screen

Across all three of the studies, and many different ways of classifying people as visual or verbal learners, the researchers found no evidence at all that people should receive information matched to their learning style in order to optimize learning.

Another example study assessed people's preferences for visual or verbal learning using a questionnaire. People were then randomly assigned to be presented with a list of concepts visually in the form of line drawings or verbally as a spoken list, or both visually and verbally. You saw the pictures and you heard the list spoken out loud.

Then, recall was used to assess the extent to which participants had learned the lists. In this case, visual presentation, with or without verbal stimuli, yielded superior learning regardless of what participants preferred in terms of learning styles.

Only one study of all of the studies that the researchers looked at actually supported the idea of learning styles, and that particular study had some odd features. Somewhat unusual methods were used to assess learning outcomes, and the authors of this particular article felt like those features of the study made it somewhat suspect. It wasn't ideal evidence.

Is the take home message that everyone benefits from certain ways of learning, and we should drop our search for individual differences that might require different approaches to learning? To some extent, yes. Given what we have covered thus far, multi-model presentation works better for most people regardless of whether they are right/left brained or v, a, or k. Visual presentations can be very strong for learning in general. We are very visual creatures, but our expertise or our prior learning about how to use visualizations is also going to matter in this regard.

Let's focus on one area where there is good reason to keep investigating possibilities, and to do so actively. Recall in the Bible, the book of Matthew the phrase, "To them that hath, more shall be given." We learn over and over again that there is a kind of Matthew effect in learning. To those that have more prior knowledge, more knowledge is acquired, and with greater ease.

One good way to think about this phenomenon is that this is the core of specialization in a complex society. That is, I do not need to be kinesthetically gifted because most of what I do does not involve motor skill. I am no surgeon and my family can put up with my less than perfect skills at harvesting vegetables from our summer garden. It is okay, people differ in their experiences, in their expertise, and they differ in their subsequent learning.

This is the idea of playing to one's strengths, and that is a very appealing idea. Often the goal of an educator is to improve areas of weakness. You do not pay an expensive tennis coach to improve your perfect forehand. Rather you pay him or her to help you shape a more effective serve out of your presently weak one. Therein lies a very different way of thinking about the findings we have reviewed today.

The same psychologists who reviewed learning styles work and suggested there was not much to rely on there, had the following take on this issue. We know there are enormous implications for learning of differences in prior knowledge.

Instead of looking at multiple intelligences or learning styles as the place to "fix" the way we educate people. Researchers interested in enhancing learning might spend more time and effort on other things. Specifically, they could focus on how we can assess individual differences in prior knowledge, and how we can make use of that information to tailor education to what people do know, and to where they need to learn more.

Experienced teachers face this problem every single day in their classrooms, and at every level, and many do a fabulous job of navigating what their students already know and getting those students to where they need to be for the next level. I routinely have students who know scientific methodology inside and out, sitting side by side with students who do not have a clue what would make for an experiment, versus some other kind of study. My charge is to help the ones who know a lot already think about the tougher material and grow, while also ensuring that the complete newcomers leave my course understanding the basics.

Research in this area is in many ways not integrated into a single understanding, but we know enough to already outline some important possibilities just from previous lectures in this class, and those possibilities are supported by some findings in the available research literature.

First, we discussed how the more advanced and knowledgeable people might be better able to benefit from discovery-based learning as compared with truly novice learners. That's consistent with the findings that discovery based learning in its moderate forms, actually works better in adulthood than earlier in the lifespan.

It is also consistent with other research findings. For example, that more advanced learners, people who come in with more prior knowledge, they benefit from having less structure. That is, they do better when the teacher is less directive and when they get less explicit guidance. Less advanced learners, the people with less prior knowledge actually benefit quite a bit from having the teacher do more explicit and directive things in the classroom, give them more structure.

Second, understanding what assumptions learners bring to their learning can be really helpful for shaping the way that instruction unfolds. For introductory psychology majors, for example, they often don't conceive of psychology as a scientific field. This needs to be introduced to them before we begin to lecture about this or that research experiment.

For more advanced students within the major, the idea of psychological science is an old hat idea. Similar to this, when we discussed work on scientific understandings by Michelin Chi, we talked about the process of learning as a change in models. That change is easiest to support for learners if we know what their starting model is about.

A third implication from our past work is that all people may benefit from knowing more about metacognition—the things that distort our understanding of our own learning, and the strategies that are effective, but strangely un-used by learners.

Where learning styles may need to be retained as an idea is in the area of motivation. While learning in one's preferred style may not have anything to do with learning outcomes, if it affects people's interests and motivations, it may still be a very useful concept for us to think about. As we mentioned preferences about how to learn are real, and they are somewhat stable.

It is really true that I prefer to read in order to learn, while my mother prefers to watch videos. When we find a chef who can teach us how to prepare a south Indian style foods, my mother watches the chef's public television show, and I buy the chef's cookbook. To some extent, learning styles may be a useful starting point for thinking about how to motivate people, and in the next lecture, we will actually consider individual differences in interests and in motivation, as they affect people's learning.

Different People, Different Interests
Lecture 22

Thus far, we have focused on whether individual differences in abilities or learning preferences are related to individual differences in learning, and we have continued to encounter the importance of individual differences in prior learning. In this lecture, we'll analyze the issue of motivation—but from the perspective of individual differences—from the standpoint of interest. That is, are there individual differences in what people find interesting? If so, do those differences affect learning? Then, we'll consider a personality trait that might be interpreted in terms of general interest in learning—openness to experience—and how it affects learning.

Interests and Learning

- In fact, there are differences among people in what they find interesting, and these differences are evident very early in our lives. Furthermore, it seems very likely that these differences influence learning.

- We all make choices about the activities we do and the topics we seek information about, and when it comes to leisure, what drives our choices is interest. Because interest is shaping our attention and actions, and over time, our knowledge, it should influence learning.

- It would be important to know whether interest shapes learning because from an educational standpoint, it means that you need to devote time to making your topic interesting—as well as clear and understandable.

- To test the effect of interests on learning requires creating similar learning materials that reflect or relate to different interests and exposing each person to materials that are consonant with his or her interests—and materials that are not. In addition, if you don't make the materials similar and you find learning differences, you can't tell whether it was the materials or the people. Furthermore, researchers have to ensure that these comparisons involve items that are in general of similar interest.

- In a project conducted by K. Ann Renninger and her colleagues, preschool children were shown pictures of their interest objects and other objects. The other objects reflected the interests of other children, which implies that the object is not fundamentally boring. The researchers examined the direction of children's gaze to evaluate their attentional focus and were able to show that children were more likely to look at their interest objects than at the other objects.

- Children also showed biases in recognition and recall of images they were shown in other parts of this study toward their individual, idiosyncratic interests. Shifting attention and differences in memory suggest that interests will also influence learning—at least in three- to four-year-old children.

- This type of research becomes more interesting and more important when we start looking at required learning in older children or adults, such as reading comprehension or math, and whether tailoring that learning to individual interests is helpful.

- More recently, Renninger and her colleagues conducted this type of work with 11-year-old children and looked more explicitly at learning from texts and at solving word problems in math.

- As in the preschooler study, they initially sought to identify children's idiosyncratic interests. Then, the researchers developed reading and math materials that incorporated children's interests and examined whether children learned better when the text concerned material in which they were interested.

- They found that when students are allowed to work on tasks related to their individual interests, their learning is sometimes enhanced. This is more true for reading than for math problems. However, interests sometimes masked students' comprehension difficulties, so they were less aware of gaps in their understanding.

- This research suggests that tailoring educational materials to individual interests is something worth examining with caution because it's pretty difficult to do it well, and it may not pay off all that well for how much children learn—though it may help keep children motivated.

Differences in Interests

- Theorists have developed a model that linearly describes the process of how people develop interests: First, people may experience what is called a triggered situational interest, which is a momentary experience of the emotion of interest that is triggered by some ongoing event. Then, people cither maintain that situational interest or lose it.

- Maintained situational interests are not yet part of a person's identity, but they result in repeated experiences of interest. Researchers refer to a third stage that involves actively seeking out engagement as an emerging individual interest, which is an interest that is sufficiently part of a person's sense of self that it motivates his or her choices of situations and behaviors.

- Over time, individual interests can become sustained—perhaps over a lifetime. By the time you have a developed or sustained individual interest, you also have substantial competence in that area.

- From self-determination theory, we learned of our need to be autonomous—to control and direct our own lives—and how learning experiences that undermine autonomy have serious costs. Self-determination theory proposes that there are three fundamental needs humans have: Autonomy is one, but two others are to connect with others and to feel competent.

- In terms of what types of things trigger situational interests and maintain situational interests—an important precursor for interests getting to be part of our sense of ourselves—it may not be surprising that self-initiation, perceiving oneself as talented or potentially talented, and feeling connected to other people are part of the triggering of initial interest.

- In other words, an activity or topic seems interesting to us initially when engaging with that topic, or activity fuels autonomy, competence, or relatedness.

- When we take a long-term perspective and look at how those situationally triggered interests might be sustained and turned into individually owned interests, social support, which refers to the role other people play in fostering our interests, turns out to matter.

- In many of the studies on social support, the other people are parents and teachers. Parents support interests financially in the way of time and resources for a pursuit and by showing interest and enthusiasm. These actions show people that their emerging interests is valued and allows them to increase their competence within the interest area.

- Teachers who provide clear structure and monitoring also help students develop interests; structure and monitoring are ways to help students acquire competence, and monitoring in particular communicates the value of competence.

- Longitudinal studies of students' interests in academic contexts point to self-perceived competence as a major foundation for the development, maintenance, and enhancement of individual interests over time. In other words, interests were relevant to students' course selections, but over time, achievement was a far stronger predictor of future interest than was initial interest.

- Therefore, interests matter, but they tend to matter more in terms of how they catalyze expertise. That is, the way individual interests appear to play out long term is via fostering initial learning, which in turn catalyzes greater interest and greater subsequent learning. Furthermore, competence itself is fundamental to interest; we like what we feel good at.

- Thus far, we've emphasized prior knowledge as making learning easier because encoding things is easier when you can more easily make connections between new knowledge and what you already know. However, prior knowledge can also make it feel more interesting to learn something, perhaps because the learning experience is more likely to feed your needs for competence.

Differences in Openness to Experience

- Researchers in personality have arrived at a consensus that personality is best described in five or six broad dimensions. One of these is central to the idea of individual differences in interest, and that is the dimension of openness to experience.

- People vary in the extent to which they are high or low in openness to experience. Those who are high on this trait welcome novelty, find aesthetic experiences like looking at art and architecture to be interesting, enjoy reading and learning about new things, and enjoy thinking about the meanings of what they experience.

- This is a trait that captures a general orientation toward intellectual, learning, creative, and aesthetic pursuits, and people do vary on this dimension—with some people wanting to do more exploring, thinking, and learning and others wanting less. Broadly, this can be thought of as a difference in the interest in learning.

- Like other personality traits, openness to experience is largely stable after early adulthood—by about age 30. Being high on openness to experience appears to have important advantages in people's ability to experience an array of feelings without trying to suppress them or distance from them and in the way people deal with stressful experiences.

- Openness to experience could be linked to better learning in at least two distinct ways. First, openness could work indirectly, by simply being related to people pursuing more learning—after all, it is an individual difference in interest in learning.

- Small differences in interests lead to larger differences in acquired knowledge, which in turn lead to larger and larger differences in subsequent learning. Likewise, openness could motivate people to seek further education, which in turn increases learning.

- In addition, openness might work directly, by changing the way people engage with the same learning experience.

- Some studies examine relationships between openness to experience and various types of cognitive performance tests, including tests of general knowledge. Basically, these tests are indirect evidence for the idea that openness to experience fosters seeking out more learning opportunities because such cognitive performance tests suggest a history of learning in various areas.

Personality and Learning

- Across many studies, openness to experience is consistently linked to knowledge-based aspects of IQ test performance. However, these are somewhat unsatisfying as tests of whether openness differences influence learning because a much more controlled approach would be needed in which people who differ in openness to experience all try to learn the same material under the same circumstances.

- In one project, researchers looked at a pilot training program, which was interesting for several reasons. First, it had two stages—computer simulation and actual cockpit training—so it permitted the researchers to look at how traits like openness predict the transfer of initial learning to a new phase of learning, with different demands. In addition, it standardized what people had to learn. Furthermore, the training is a kind of learning that isn't stereotypically intellectual, so it makes for a harder test.

Research on pilot training programs shows that being more open to experience fosters general learning and is linked to a better ability to transfer learning.

- While both phases of training involve similar actions, they involve them under quite different circumstances with different levels of seriousness and risk.

- Before people began the program, they reported on their personality—specifically on openness to experience, emotional stability, and conscientiousness. For phase one learning, none of these traits were relevant to how well people performed and how quickly they mastered that phase.

- For phase two learning, one major predictor of how people did was phase one learning. However, personality also mattered: The higher someone's openness to experience, the more quickly they learned in phase two.

- Therefore, there is some evidence that being more open to experience fosters general learning and is linked to better ability to transfer learning from one context—a computer simulator—to another.

Suggested Reading

Herold, Davis, Fedor, and Parsons, "Dispositional Influences on Transfer of Learning."

Hofer, "Adolescents' Development of Individual Interests."

Questions to Consider

1. If competence plays a role in interest, how can people develop interests in areas where they are initially not so competent? What strategies could be useful in mitigating the role of early inability in a learning process?

2. Could you cultivate greater openness in personality?

Different People, Different Interests
Lecture 22—Transcript

So far we have focused on whether individual differences in abilities, or in learning preferences are related to individual differences in learning, and largely, we keep coming back to the importance of individual differences in prior learning. In this lecture, we are going to go back to the issue of motivation, but this time from an individual differences perspective from the standpoint of interest. That is, we are going to ask, "Are there individual differences in the things people find interesting? If so, could those affect learning? Do they affect learning?" Then, we will consider a personality trait that might be interpreted as general interest in learning and how that trait actually affects learning.

I know this may come as a shock to some of you, but in fact, there are differences among people in what they find interesting. I hope you were sitting down when I said that. In fact, these differences, in one form or another, are evident very early. For example, one study of preschool children—three and four-year-old children—showed that children had clear, well-developed interests already with respect to the play materials in their preschool. The interests were really obvious and really evident and that means you could figure it out really fast by just hanging around in the classroom which kid was interested in what. Different kids had different interests. Kids' interests stayed the same over three weeks so it wasn't just a matter of kids randomly choosing different activities on a single day when they were observed. Rather, kids consistently went after particular activities that seemed to really interest them. Could these differences influence learning? It seems very, very likely that they do if you just think about your own experiences of interest.

Let us consider an example or two. I am really interested in nutrition and fitness in my non-work life. What does that mean? Well, in part, it means that some of my discretionary and leisure time is spent involved in activities related to nutrition and fitness. I like to run. I like to lift weights. I really enjoy hiking. I enjoy biking. I swim. When the weather lets me, I cross-country ski. I also do a lot of cooking and I focus on healthy cooking in the cooking that I do.

In all of those activities, there are aspects of learning. I am probably continuing to learn things relevant to fitness and nutrition as I do those activities. For example, with running I am probably fine-tuning my running skills, my posture, my balance, and my stride rate. When I am cooking I am honing my understanding of cooking to techniques, my ability to do those techniques, and I am shaping my knowledge about food combinations all the time.

The activities alone are not the only way that my interest is contributing to further learning. I also read a lot about nutrition and fitness. I read books, I read blogs, and I read newspapers. Given limited time, say, to read the paper, I will almost certainly check for the latest news on fitness before I check for the latest news on the Middle East peace-and/or-fight-of-the-day news. Over a few years, even, what I have actually done to myself is to develop my knowledge about fitness and nutrition quite extensively and possibly at the expense of being an informed world citizen.

We are all this way. You may not be a nutrition research buff, but we all make choices about the activities we do, and the topics we seek information about. When it comes to leisure, what drives our choices is interest. Interest, because it's shaping our attention and our behavior and over time, our knowledge, ought to influence learning. There is also a fair amount of learning that we have to do rather than want to do, right? And so in somewhat more controlled studies, we can also ask whether it is true that interest shapes learning. It would be important to know this, because from an educational standpoint, it means that you need to devote time to making your topic interesting for people, as well as clear and understandable.

We did talk earlier about Sansone and Harackiewicz's research about people who differ and how interested and motivated they are by social interaction. You may remember that in that work, people who were highly motivated by social relationships and social exchanges were more motivated to learn a task when they could do it together with someone else. Here is the catch, we do not know if their actual learning was better, we only know that they were more interested in the topic and they asked for more information about related course work. Those motivational factors might lead them to go on and to learn more, but the studies just don't tell us that.

However, doing the right kind of research that would really answer the question turns out to be extremely labor intensive and difficult, so there are surprisingly few studies available in this area to really directly look at the relationship between individual interests and learning. A good deal of the work that does directly test this relationship was done by Renninger and her colleagues.

"Why is it so difficult?" you might be thinking. First, to test the effects of individual interests on learning requires that researchers make similar learning materials that reflect or that relate to quite different interests, and then they have to expose each person to materials that are consonant with or congruent with his or her interests, and materials that are not congruent with his or her interests. If you do not make the materials similar, which is a big part of the work, and you find learning differences, you cannot tell whether it was because people learned a different "what," or because the people had different interests.

Even more complicated, researchers have to ensure that when they are comparing different topics or items of interest, they have to compare items that are in general possibly interesting, right? It is not a matter of differences between toys and socks, but of differences between one kind of toy and another kind of toy, so to speak.

In one relatively early project, the preschool children in the study above were shown pictures of their interest objects and other objects. The other objects actually reflected the interests of other children in the classroom. This is a really nice strategy because that way, it is not just that the object is fundamentally stupid or boring it could be of interest to a kid, it just doesn't interest this kid.

The researchers then went on to look at children's eye-gaze direction and that helped evaluate where the children were focusing their attention, and they were able to show that kids were more likely to look at their interest objects than at the other objects.

Then, the children also showed biases in recognizing and recalling the images they were shown in other parts of the study. Again, these biases were oriented toward their individual, idiosyncratic interests. The fact that interests shift attention and result in differences in memory means that interests influence learning, at least in these three- to four-year-old kids.

The nice thing about studying preschoolers is that the scope of interests they might have is kind of small. The downside is we are not really that interested in kids learning lists of toys. Worse still, three- to four-year-olds are less able to avoid learning than other age groups. They are just not in a position to not go to class, or to tune out during a lecture. They also have a lot of learning that happens just as they try to go about doing every day things. They are pretty motivated learners.

Where this all gets more interesting and more important is when we start to look at older kids or adults learning stuff that they have to learn, like reading comprehension or math, when we start to ask whether tailoring the learning of those topics to individual interests could be helpful.

Renninger and colleagues more recently conducted some work of this sort with 11-year-olds and it looked more explicitly at learning from texts and at solving word problems in math. This is a really important way to examine these issues because reading to learn and being able to use math to solve problems that aren't always given to you in the form of a math problem, these are really important skills kids need to acquire and adults use all the time. You can somewhat equate the "what" that is being learned across kids who differ in interests in that everybody is learning reading comprehension and math skills.

As in the preschooler study, they initially sought to identify kids' idiosyncratic interests. Then, the researchers went on to develop reading and math materials that incorporated an individual child's interests, and then they were able to test whether kids learned better from a text that concerned material in which they were already interested.

What they found was that when students are allowed to work on tasks related to their individual interests, their learning is sometimes enhanced. This is more the case for reading than for math problems. That said, interests also sometimes masked or hide a student's difficulties in understanding. Students were sometimes less aware that they had a gap in their understanding when the material was something in their area of interest.

One way to think about this problem is that when we read about an area we have strong interests in, we also tend to have strong prior knowledge in that area. I will say a little more about this later. As a consequence, we may actually gloss over gaps in our understanding of a passage, or we might fill those gaps in with knowledge from our already acquired learning. Sometimes this is good when we have the right knowledge, but when we lack the right knowledge, it sometimes does not work out so well.

Another way to think about this comes from a related body of work on what are called seductive details in learning from texts. Seductive details are interesting facts and trivia, funny cartoons and illustrations that are not really important for understanding a given body of work, but they are used because they are thought to help engage a reader's attention and keep them reading.

Careful studies have shown that seductive details do draw the reader's attention, but in fact, they draw the reader's attention to the wrong material. They actually divert attention from the central things that students need to be learning to the trivial details that are making the text more entertaining.

All of this suggests that tailoring educational materials to individual interests is something worth examining with caution because it is pretty hard and pretty labor intensive to do it well, and it may not pay off all that well for how much kids learn, although it may help keep kids motivated and interested. Some researchers would say it helps emotional interests but at some cost to kids learning.

So far we have not given much attention to how differences in interest develop. This is also important because if we could figure out how an interest begins, maybe we could figure out how to get people interested in the stuff they actually have to learn. We could sort of circumvent this whole issue of idiosyncratic already developed interests.

Theorists have developed a model that lays out the process of interest development in a kind of linear fashion, and it goes something like this.

First, people may experience what is called a triggered situational interest. A triggered situational interest is a momentary experience of the emotion of interest, and it is triggered by some ongoing event. One common experience might be to catch a news phrase on public radio and it triggers more focused attention to the story being told.

Afterwards, people can maintain that situational interest or they can lose it. I once heard a snatch of a story on the bacteria in our intestinal tracts on NPR, and I was really captivated by this idea. It was easy to sustain my interest even when the material became more technical.

To give you a different example, I also got temporarily interested in a form of exercise class called Zumba when I heard the music playing while I was running at my gym. A maintained situational interest is not necessarily part of my identity yet, but it can result in repeated experiences of interest. I have a maintained situational interest in gut bacteria. It means I read news stories on it when they show up in the Sunday *Times*, but I do not really pursue further information on it beyond that. After a few Zumba classes, I actually lost my interest in pursuing the activity. It felt more repetitive and it was just less interesting than I thought it would be.

For something where people begin to seek out actively engagement in that activity or involvement in that topic, researchers call that an emerging individual interest. It is kind of a third stage. An emerging individual difference means an interest that is sufficiently part of my ideas of myself, my identity but it actually motivates my choices about of situations and behaviors.

Over time, individual interests can become sustained. From my own perspective, part of someone's identity in a way that will sustain them over many years, maybe even a lifetime. One of the important points here is that by the time you have a developed or a sustained individual interest, what that means is you also have some competence in that area. You have some foundational knowledge in the area. Keep that in mind as I go on to the next issue today, which is this.

This descriptive notion of moving from point A, which is sort of the triggered situational interest, "Hey, that is kind of cool," to point D, "I am really interested in and devoted to this topic or activity." It is not that satisfying or useful. That is because it leaves out the why and the how. How do you get from point A to point D? What affects that process?

To answer this, one way to think about this is to actually go back to self-determination theory, and we discussed that earlier in the first lecture on motivation. In that lecture, we primarily focused on the issue of our need to be autonomous, to control and direct our own lives, and how learning experiences that undermine autonomy have some serious costs.

Self-determination theory actually proposes that there are three fundamental needs for human beings. Autonomy is one, but two others are connecting with other people, and feeling competent.

In terms of what kinds of things trigger situational interests and maintain them over time, an important precursor for an interest becoming part of our identity, it is probably not going to surprise you that self-initiation, choosing the activity yourself, perceiving yourself as talented or potentially talented at the activity, and feeling connected to other people through that activity are all part of how initial interests get triggered. In other words, activities and topic seem interesting to us initially when engaging with the topic because the activity fuels autonomy, competence, or relatedness.

When we take a long-term perspective, and we look at how those situationally triggered interests might be sustained and turned into individually identified interests, social support turns out to matter. Social support means the role other people, and in many of these studies, the other people of interest are parents and teachers, play in fostering our interests.

Social support plays out in many ways. Parents support their children's interests financially by giving time and resources for their kid's interests, and by showing interest and enthusiasm in a child's interest. All of these show someone that their emerging interest is valued, and they allow them to increase their competence within the interest area.

Teachers who provide clear structure and monitoring also help students develop interests. If you think about it, structure and monitoring are ways to help students acquire competence, and monitoring in particular communicates the value of competence.

In fact, one nice project followed preschoolers over time to see which preschoolers maintained their individual interests and which preschoolers did not. It turned out that the kids who maintained their interest had parents who believed in supporting kid's curiosity, provided more materials related to their kid's interest in the home, and more frequently read their child non-fiction books about the interest area.

Here is the big story in this area. Longitudinal studies of students' interests in academic settings point to self-perceived competence as a major foundation for the development, maintenance, and enhancement of individual interests over time.

What this means concretely is that interests are relevant to students' course selections in the beginning of an academic period, but over time, it is their achievement. It is their actual competence or actual learning in the courses that really predicts future interest. Their achievement, their competence predicts future interests better than their initial interest in a topic.

Interests matter, but they matter more in terms of how they catalyze expertise. The way individual interests play out long-term is by fostering initial learning. It is initial learning that catalyzes greater interest and greater subsequent learning. Competence itself is fundamental to interest. We like and we are interested in the things that we feel good at.

This really brings home another valuable aspect of prior knowledge. Thus far, we have emphasized prior knowledge as making learning easier because it changes encoding. Encoding things is easier when one can more easily make connections between new stuff, and what you already know. Prior knowledge can also make it feel more interesting to learn something, perhaps because the learning experience is better at feeding your need for competence.

Before we leave the topic of interests and individual differences, there is also a general, broader individual difference in personality that we need to consider. Researchers in personality have arrived at a consensus that

444

personality is best described in five or six broad dimensions. Many of these dimensions are not important for us to think about today, but one of them, in my view, is central to the idea of individual differences in interest—that is the dimension of openness to experience.

People vary in the extent to which they are high or low in openness to experience. What does it mean to be high or low on this trait? Those who are high on this trait like novelty. They find aesthetic experiences like looking at art and architecture to be interesting. They enjoy reading and learning new things. They enjoy thinking about the meanings of their experiences.

This is a trait that captures a general orientation toward intellectual, learning, creative, and aesthetic pursuits. People do vary on this dimension. Some people want to do more exploring, thinking, and learning, and other people are somewhat less interested in doing so. You can think of this as a difference in interest in learning, broadly.

Like other personality traits, openness to experience is largely stable after early adulthood, by about age 30 or so. It is also something that we, our friends, and our family generally agree on. By that, I mean if I describe myself as high in openness to experience, my husband will likely agree, and my friends will likely agree. In point of fact, the audience for this lecture is likely to score higher in openness than a general population sample, because buying great courses is the kind of thing people high on openness do.

Being high on openness to experience appears to have some important advantages for people in terms of being able to experience lots of feelings without suppressing them or distancing from them, and it seems to have some real advantages for how people deal with stressful experiences.

What about learning? Is openness to experience linked to better learning? This could be the case in at least two different ways. One way is that openness could work indirectly. It could work because it motivates people to pursue more learning because it is an individual difference in interest in learning.

As with interests as I mentioned earlier, small differences in interests can lead to larger differences in acquired knowledge, which in turn lead to larger and larger differences in subsequent learning. Likewise, openness could motivate seeking further education, which in turn, increases learning.

Openness might also work directly. It might work by changing the way people engage with a learning experience.

There are a few studies that can be looked at to evaluate these ideas. Some studies actually examine relationships between openness to experience and various kinds of cognitive performance tests. These include tests of general knowledge. We can think of these as being indirect evidence for the idea that openness to experience fosters seeking out more learning opportunities, which in turn fosters the acquisition of more knowledge. As we discussed in the lecture on IQ, these kinds of tests suggest a history of learning in various areas.

In a very large longitudinal study of Swedish people, those higher on openness to experience scored higher on an entire array of cognitive tests including many tests indicating acquired knowledge, like verbal ability tests. It was true for men and women, and importantly, this was true even when researchers statistically controlled for people's level of education. That's important because openness to experience might just be linked to the pursuit of more education. And remember, we discussed the strong possibility that differences in IQ type performances might simply reflect more education.

In a second study, researchers looked at university students, and they assessed their openness to experience, as well as their general knowledge. To measure general knowledge, they looked at a questionnaire that assesses knowledge of literature, general science, games, fashion, and finance, so a pretty broad assessment. Openness to experience was linked to higher general knowledge. Across many studies, openness to experience is consistently connected to knowledge-based aspects of IQ test performance.

This is all somewhat unsatisfying as a test of whether openness differences influence learning, because for that, we would like to see a more controlled approach, where people who differ in openness to experience all try to learn the same material under the same circumstances. For that kind of study, I would like to tell you about a different project.

In this project, researchers looked at a pilot training program. The pilot training program was interesting for several reasons. First, it had two stages, and that lets researchers look at how a trait like openness predicts the transfer of initial learning in phase one to phase two part of learning that has different demands. The second thing this does is it standardizes what people have to learn. They would have to learn how to pilot an aircraft. The last thing that is really great about this is that this is a kind of learning that is not stereotypically intellectual. Rather it involves visual spatial and motor skills. It makes for a little bit of a more demanding test.

Eighty-five participants, and almost all of them were men, came to the flight academy and they wanted to earn a private pilot's license. They began as true novices. They had little to no flight experience prior to beginning the program.

The training program's first phase is a computer-based flight simulation program that has a series of lessons. In these lessons, trainees have to execute simple maneuvers. They have to climbing, descending, and turn their aircraft, and they have to do so within some constraints; that is, they have to hit good enough performance before they are allowed to go on to the next lesson. They have to complete all of the computer-based lessons successfully before they get to go on to phase two of training. For this computer-based phase, the researchers looked at how many tries people needed to pass each lesson and they used that as a measure of how effectively they were learning.

The second phase of training involves actual cockpit training with a flight instructor and it culminates in a test flight that if you do it successfully, certifies you to get a private pilot's license. As you can see, both phases of training involve similar actions. They involve those actions under very different circumstances and they are different levels of seriousness or risk. In phase two, things are higher stakes. For the second phase, researchers looked at how many hours it took before people got their private pilot's license as an indicator of successful learning.

Before people began the program, they reported on their personality. They specifically reported on openness to experience, and a couple of other traits, emotional stability, and conscientiousness. These latter traits have not been widely linked to learning, but they do reflect the extent to which people are likely to experience negative emotion, and the extent to which people are reliable and follow through on promises, and so on. They might be related to how well people do in the training.

First off, there were no personality traits that predicted performance in phase one learning. For phase one learning, that computer based learning, openness, emotional stability, and conscientiousness were all irrelevant to how well people performed and how quickly they mastered that phase.

The real action was in phase two learning. For phase two learning, one major predictor of how people did, how many hours they needed to get their private pilot's license, was not surprisingly phase one learning. Personality also mattered. The higher someone's openness to experience, the more quickly they learned in phase two. There is some evidence that being more open to experience fosters general learning and is linked to better ability to transfer learning from one context, the computer simulator, to another.

Openness to experience is a personality trait, and that often means we think of it as not changeable. And, openness to experience is pretty stable in adulthood. If anything, it tends to decline as people get older. But researchers have been looking at how and when personality does change, and drawing from their work, we might speculate that there could be ways to cultivate greater openness to experience. In particular, people's personality changes over adulthood are related to their social and occupational roles. Usually, this is a good thing; those roles tend to encourage us to become kinder, more agreeable, less neurotic, and more reliable and trustworthy. But those same roles may not do as good a job encouraging us to stay curious and interested in learning new things because we get expert at what we're supposed to do in those roles. One way to think about this is that you could attempt to build in the demands for new learning in your life in other ways, by trying to make learning new things a regular part of your leisure life.

More broadly, today we have considered how individual interests foster learning, and how this process is in part fueled by the fact that interests focus attention and learning activities which allows the development of initially higher knowledge, and that then facilitates further learning and further interest.

This section of our course has been focused on individual differences relevant to learning, and we have emphasized abilities and interests. Next lecture, we will consider the role of age as an individual difference which affects learning over the entire life span, in part through its impact on cognitive abilities and motivation.

Learning across the Lifespan
Lecture 23

This section of the course has been focused on individual differences relevant to learning, and we've emphasized abilities and interests. In the last lecture, we learned that people differ in their interests and that it does influence learning. People also differ by age, and we've hinted at the role of age differences in learning throughout the course. In this lecture, we're going to centrally focus on the role of age as an individual difference that affects learning—in part through its impact on cognitive abilities and on motivation.

Age-Related Differences in Information-Processing Abilities

- Across the entire course, there are a few principles that will serve as an introduction for thinking about how learning might differ at different ages.

- The first principle is that development is not learning because development happens in similar ways for all healthy individuals with relatively little dependence on experience beyond the minimal typical environment.

- The second principle is that learning relies on information processing and associated abilities. Those abilities mature, and they can take a while to do so. At ages when those abilities are not mature, they actually limit some of what children can learn.

- Furthermore, those abilities also decline in adulthood. That is, as people age, they become less able to juggle information in working memory and less able to engage executive functions to inhibit distractions.

- In the case of childhood and old age, there is increasing evidence that the rise and fall of basic information-processing abilities is biological based—rooted in changes in the brain.

- Together, the first and second principles point to a very important issue about age differences in learning: Developmental differences in information-processing abilities constrain or enable more effective learning at different points in the lifespan.

- Young children's learning is constrained by their relatively immature cognitive abilities. Elderly adults' learning is constrained, even among healthy older adults, by age-related deficits in those same cognitive skills.

- There is a wealth of research on older adults' verbal learning and other kinds of explicit, deliberate learning tasks, such as learning lists of words. Virtually all of this work shows that older adults perform more poorly, on average, than young adults.

Older adults have somewhat reduced information-processing abilities, making a broad search for new information a more difficult task than for younger adults.

- In an important study of this phenomenon, Paul Baltes and his colleagues attempted to look at verbal learning in a way that tested the limits of older adults' performance. The first conclusion from this study was that older adults were capable of learning a new strategy for learning word lists and employing that strategy.

- Another conclusion is that older adults benefitted enormously from the new strategy as compared to their initial ability to learn the words. However, the best of the older adults were well below the worst of the younger adults.

451

- In this study, age-related, biologically based changes in basic information-processing capacities limited learning performance—even when strategies and expertise were matched.

- Older adults' more implicit learning processes appear relatively preserved from any changes relative to capacities like those for working memory and executive function.

- It is not clear whether implicit learning processes are a single mechanism or many different nonconscious mechanisms; in the latter case, many of these mechanisms could be adversely affected by aging.

- For reading, for typically developing children, children of the same age with higher working memory capacity show higher reading performance because reading draws heavily on the ability to hold items in mind and put them together to understand texts.

- Therefore, even though children may be equally good at recognizing phonemes and decoding individual words, if they are developmentally behind or ahead in working memory capacity, it will affect the speed with which they can learn to read.

- Additionally, we think of children as excellent learners despite their cognitive limitations, so the fact that there are cognitive limitations associated with aging, too, doesn't mean we should be pessimistic about the possibilities of truly lifelong learning.

Age-Related Differences in Prior Knowledge

- The third principle we will examine is that prior knowledge matters. Different age groups have different levels of prior knowledge on which to draw when learning new things. Mostly, it is helpful to have more prior knowledge, but it can sometimes be a problem for people because if prior knowledge is incorrect or leads us astray, we sometimes fail to incorporate information into our existing beliefs and ideas.

- If we take aspects of IQ like vocabulary and general knowledge as reflecting acquired learning over time, studies tend to show that the older the research participant, the higher, on average, their scores on these types of IQ measures.

- Longitudinal studies also show growth in these types of assessments into old age. In fact, we don't really begin to decline in any meaningful fashion until after age 70. As we get older, we know more, and that means we could have more prior knowledge on which to draw in learning; we are particularly likely to know ourselves better.

- One interesting place where this age advantage in prior knowledge might play a role is in allowing older adults, as compared with younger adults, to make more efficient decisions—decisions that require less information but that are equally good

- This is especially important given that older adults have somewhat reduced information-processing abilities, making a broad search for new information a more difficult task.

- Decision-making studies often look at occasions in which people have to choose between two or more alternatives and are able to search available information to help them choose. The decisions examined range from relatively controlled, artificial choices presented to people in a laboratory to real-world, significant choices, such as breast cancer treatment choices by patients.

- A recent examination looked at studies of older adults' decision making across different studies of consumer choice, which falls somewhere in between those extremes because it includes real-world decisions with consequences but ranges from trivial choices among everyday products to medical choices about treatments.

- Overall, this review suggested that older adults consider less information than do young adults on average. These authors also detected that the differences in the information search of age groups weren't the same in all studies.

- When they examined why this might be, they found that older adults' information search was most similar to younger adults' information search in the context of health decisions and was most different in nonhealth domains. This may have to do with motivational issues.

- Less information could be good or bad: If the result is that older adults make poorer decisions, then less information is bad, but if the decisions reached by older and younger adults are similar in quality, then less information is good—it's about efficiency. The idea is that prior knowledge might reduce the need for information searching, resulting in equivalent decision quality.

Age-Related Differences in Motivation and Interest

- The fourth principle is that motivation and interest matters, and motivation also varies over the lifespan in ways that are importantly connected to learning.

- Generally, openness to experience declines in later life, and this decline is found longitudinally, when we compare individuals to themselves earlier in their lives. It is also found cross sectionally, when we compare people of one age to others of different ages. This pattern has also been found in virtually every country that has been studied.

- That general age-based change suggests that as we age, we may be less interested in learning new things in general, and that is consistent with decision-making research.

- A well-established perspective on adulthood and aging, selectivity theory, suggests that we are going to be motivated by different aspects of our worlds as we approach the end of life.

- Laura Carstensen and her collaborators argue that we have at least two major motives as we go about our daily lives: One is an information-seeking motive, or curiosity drive, and the other is an emotion-regulation motive. Respectively, these can be encapsulated as finding out and feeling good.

- Carstensen points out, however, that the availability of information and its general utility to us may diminish over adulthood as we become older because we tend to know more as we get older, meaning that there is less to learn.

- Additionally, the available new information in the world is of less utility and relevance to us as we get older for two reasons. First, when we have established our lives, we often know the information and skills we need for living our lives, so remaining things to learn are less necessary. In addition, information often has more long-term payoffs. As people approach the end of life, they may be less interested in pursuing things that don't have immediate rewards.

- Emotion in terms of feeling good has immediate rewards. Carstensen has shown in several studies that as people get older, their relative emphasis on new information versus feeling good shifts, and emotion becomes more important and more salient.

- Socioemotional selectivity theory has spawned a wide range of investigations, including explorations of social activity, personality change, preferences for products, and everyday emotional experience. However, the more pertinent issue is the effect of shifting motives on learning.

- A relative shift in concerns for emotion regulation over adulthood appears to change people's ways of paying attention to new information, learning that information—as reflected in memory— and even the way their brain responds to that information.

- Age-related differences in attention, learning, and memory have been labeled the positivity effect, which is an effect in which older adults, relative to younger adults, pay more attention to emotionally relevant stimuli—especially positive ones. They learn them more effectively and recall them better.

- The positivity effect has been shown with pictures, words, texts, and autobiographical memories and with measures of attention, retention, and even brain-based responding.

- The fact that positive and emotionally relevant information draws more attention from older adults can actually make up for some age-related losses.

- Adolescents, by contrast to older adults, are highly motivated by information. This is in part reflected by a phenomenon known as the reminiscence bump, in which our learning of songs, news events, TV shows, movies, and the events of our own lives is enhanced during adolescence.

Preserving Information-Processing Abilities

- Pursuing the following actions can preserve our ability to learn, although there are never guarantees that research findings about people on average will work for all individuals.

- The same actions that preserve information-processing abilities also contribute to other aspects of living a long and healthy—not to mention happy—life.

- Get some exercise. Both cardiovascular and strength training exercises appear to help preserve information-processing abilities, probably by enhancing blood flow in and outside the brain.

- Keep mentally active in meaningful ways. Examples of this include continuing education, traveling, volunteering efforts, and community involvement.

- It may be useful to try to learn something truly new every so often—something that is radically different from the usual things you do but that is still meaningful and enjoyable. Try a new dance class or sculpture course, or learn a new language.

Suggested Reading

Hertzog, Kramer, Wilson, and Lindenberger, "Enrichment Effects on Adult Cognitive Development."

Questions to Consider

1. What do you think makes individuals who are higher in openness to experience and still seek new information even in later life different from the averages reported in this lecture?

2. Given greater prior knowledge in older adulthood, decision making might become more efficient—at least under some circumstances—but could prior knowledge also distort or make decision making problematic?

Learning across the Lifespan
Lecture 23—Transcript

Last lecture, we talked about different interests. People differ in their interests and that does influence learning. People also differ by age, and we have hinted at the role of age differences in learning here and there, throughout the course. We have mentioned to name just a few examples, age differences in executive function, age differences in the ability to learn source information, age differences in who benefits from discovery based learning, and age differences in openness to experience. Age has not been our primary focus in those cases.

In this lecture, we are going to centrally focus on the role of age in learning. Let us start by recapping a few principles from across the entire course, because these few principles are going to be our starting off point for thinking about how learning might differ at different ages. They are going to let us frame our thinking about age differences so that we come away with more than just a kind of hodgepodge list.

Principle one is that learning is not the same as development. Sometimes both learning and being able to use learned information although depend on development. Principle two is that learning is related to information processing and abilities associated with information processing, and by that, we mean attention, working memory, and executive function, those abilities to plan, to flexibly change strategies and to inhibit distractions.

The third principle is that learning is related to prior learning. Learning new things relies on and it builds on what we already know. Finally, a fourth principle is that learning is related to what motivates us and interests us. That includes our general interest in learning new things, our openness to experience. It is easier and it is more enjoyable to learn things that we want to learn and when we find learning to feel easy, our sense of competence motivates us to learn more.

If we think about these four principles, it gives us a framework for thinking about the role of age in learning. Let us start with principle one, which goes all the way back to the first lecture of the course. Development is not learning remember, because in this course we are thinking of development as what happens in similar ways for all healthy people with relatively little dependence on specific experiences beyond what you would expect as typical for us.

Examples of developmental phenomena include the growth and development of the frontal lobes, which enable executive function. That growth and development happens from infancy through early adulthood, ending in the early- to mid-20s. The decline of executive functions is also linked to changes in the brain that happen with aging, particularly in the frontal lobes. These are developmental phenomena. The role of the frontal lobes in enabling executive function means that these developmental changes are going to be important for what people can and cannot or at least cannot easily learn at a given age.

That brings me to that second principle. Principle two is this idea that learning relies on information processing and associated abilities. As I just noted, those abilities mature and they can take a while to do so. At ages when those abilities are not mature, they actually limit some of what kids can learn.

It is also the case that those abilities decline across adulthood. That is, as people age, they become less able to juggle information in working memory, they are less able to engage executive functions to do things like inhibit distractions.

In fact, studies looking across childhood and adulthood, beginning as young as age 6, show that people are at the maximum ability in their mid-20s for most of these basic cognitive capacities that are important to learning. That is especially true for speed of information processing. We are never as fast at taking in new things was we are in our late adolescence and early adulthood. Speed and these other basic cognitive abilities actually often begin to decline after early adulthood.

Principles one and two together point to a very important issue about age differences in learning. Developmental differences in information processing abilities constrain or enable more effective learning at different points in the life span. Young children's learning is constrained by their relatively immature cognitive abilities. Elderly adults learning is constrained even among healthy older adults by age related deficits in those same cognitive skills.

There is an absolute wealth of research on older adult's verbal learning and other kinds of explicit, deliberate learning tasks like learning lists of words. Virtually all of this work shows that older adults perform more poorly on average than young adults. As with other age differences, it is actually important that we ask whether an age difference is really do to ageing or development, or whether some other factor like the different everyday and environments of older versus younger adults is actually what is explaining the difference.

If older adults and younger children are worse than young adults at learning lists of words, is it because of developmental changes in the brain, or is it something about the amount of practice that young adults and perhaps especially college students, get at memorizing lists.

One very important landmark study of this phenomenon was done by Paul Baltes and his colleagues. What they decided to do was to look at verbal learning in a way that tested the limits of older adults' performance. The results are actually very instructive for those of us interested in learning.

What they did was to first recruit a group of older and younger adults and then they trained these individuals to use a specific really effective mnemonic strategy for learning lists of words. It is called the method of loci. In this method, participants associate words on the to-be-learned list with specific locations, using vivid visual imagery.

Everyone was trained. Everyone got practice using the method until they did not get any better. At this point, we can already draw one conclusion from the study and that is this: Older adults were quite capable of learning that new strategy for word list learning and they were very capable of employing that strategy. When they used the strategy, they learned the words much better than at their initial baseline test of word learning.

However, now Baltes and colleagues could look at people engaged in learning lists of words who were all using exactly the same optimal learning strategy, and who all had an equivalent degree of training in using that strategy. What they found was that although older adults benefitted enormously from the new strategy, compared to their initial ability to learn the words, the best of the older adults were well below the worst of the younger adults.

It is not often that when we compare groups of people on some cognitive task, it is not often that we do not have a lot of overlap in the two groups. This is a very unusual finding. In other words, when Baltes and his colleagues matched older adults with younger adults, gave them the same strategies and the same level of expertise, they still performed more poorly at a verbal learning task. This is very strong evidence that it is age-related, biologically based changes in basic information processing capacities and the underlying brain structures that are limiting learning performance among older adults because we have matched some of those other experience differences.

A further twist on older adult cognitive abilities also warrants mention here. Older adults' more implicit learning processes, what we have been calling system one in earlier lectures, those appear relatively preserved from changes, relative to capacities like those for working memory and executive function.

As an example, let us think about motor learning of dynamic balance. In one study, older adults were asked to stand on a platform that was oscillating. Unknown to the participants, the oscillation was following a pattern. Remember, we are actually pretty good at picking up these kinds of patterns and making use of them to help us perform actions even when we are not really aware that a pattern exists. Later, participants came back and they were tested on their ability to balance using that same oscillation pattern, and they were also given a test of whether the skills would transfer.

Participants got better at balancing in spite of the oscillation, and they did so at the same rate that younger adults got better. There is a lot of work to be done. As we noted in the lecture on learning commonalities, it is not clear whether implicit learning processes are one mechanism, or many different non-conscious mechanisms. In the latter case, it could be that some implicit learning is adversely affected by aging while other implicit learning is spared.

Aging is not the only place we can pick on in the lifespan, so let us briefly think about how age-related differences also constrain children's learning as well. The findings we reviewed earlier indicate that working memory and executive function abilities show significant growth over early childhood. Do age differences in working memory help explain differences in kids learning? For reading, for typically-developing kids, yes. Kids of the same age with higher working memory capacity show higher reading performance because reading draws heavily on the ability to hold items in mind and put them together to understand texts.

Even though children may be equally good at recognizing phonemes and decoding individual words, if they are developmentally behind or ahead in working memory capacity, it will affect how well they can learn to read at a given age.

Also note that we think of kids as excellent learners and we have this idea despite their cognitive limitations. The fact that there are cognitive limitations associated with aging too, does not mean that we should be pessimistic about the possibilities of truly lifelong learning.

Principle three is that prior knowledge matters. When we think about age, different age groups have different levels of prior knowledge on which to draw when they are learning new things. Mostly, it is helpful to have more prior knowledge. As we also noted, it can sometimes be a problem for people because if prior knowledge is incorrect or if it leads us astray, as in the case of language we sometimes fail to incorporate information into our existing beliefs and ideas or to acquire new features of a language.

If we take aspects of IQ like vocabulary and general knowledge as reflecting acquired learning over time, as reflecting prior knowledge, study after study after study shows that the older the research participant, the higher, on average, their scores on these kinds of IQ measures. Longitudinal studies, which follow the same people over many years, also show growth in these assessments into old age. In fact, some studies suggest we do not really begin to decline in a significant or meaningful way in these abilities until after age 70. As we get older, we know more, and that means we could have more prior knowledge on which to draw in learning. We are particularly likely to know ourselves more.

One interesting place where this age advantage in prior knowledge might play a role is in allowing older adults, as compared with younger adults, to make more efficient decisions. By that, I mean a decision that requires less information, but is equally good. You can think of this as being like getting more bang out of a little less learning, in some sense.

This is especially important because older adults have somewhat reduced information processing abilities, and that makes a broad search for new information a more difficult and demanding task in later life.

Decision-making studies often look at occasions where people have to choose between two or more alternatives, and they are able to search a variety of available information in order to help make their choice. The decisions that get examined in these studies range from relatively controlled and artificial choices that are presented to people in a laboratory all the way to real-world significant choices, such as the kinds of breast cancer treatment choices that patients make.

A recent study looked at a wealth of studies. This was a meta-analysis of older adults' decision-making across studies of consumer choice. Consumer choice falls somewhere in between the extremes I outlined above, in that it is a real-world decision that has with consequences for people, but it ranges from trivial choices like choosing what toothpaste to buy to more significant choices like choosing a medical treatment to purchase.

In this review the findings suggested that overall older adults consider less information than do young adults. The difference looks something like this. Generally older adults look at about 56 percent of the available information and younger adults consider about 65 percent. This is not as you can already see a really big difference, but it is a consistent difference and it is consistently there across different studies.

The authors also found that the differences in age groups' information search were not the same in all studies. When they looked at why this might be, what they found was that older adults and younger adults look most similar when they are making health decisions. They look the most different when it is non-health domains. This might have to do with motivational issues, which we will consider in more detail below.

Less information could be good or bad. If the result is that older adults make poorer decisions, then less information is bad. If the decisions reached by older and younger adults are similar in quality, then less information is good. This is about efficiency.

Remember, the idea is that prior knowledge might reduce the need for information searching, resulting in equivalent decision quality for older adults despite looking at less information. One way to test this is to use computer-based simulations of decisions, and these are based on the way that older and younger adults search information. When you do this, what you are really doing is you are asking a computer to act like an old decision-maker or act like a young decision-maker in terms of information search. Then you ask the computer to follow various models for making its decision.

Those models can rely on lots of information, or on relatively little information. What you learn when you use this approach is that the decisions reached by the computer under "be old" or "be young" conditions are virtually identical. There are tiny differences that favor young adults, but the greater information search identified in studies of actual decision-making really does not result in a big payoff in terms of decision quality.

One of my favorite, although somewhat poignant examples of this is in a study of decision-making about breast cancer. In that study, 75 women who were recently diagnosed with breast cancer were surveyed about their treatment decisions. It turned out in the study, that older women sought less information, as with many of the studies above on decision-making. Older women made equivalent decisions to the younger adults, and they made them actually more quickly.

What these findings suggest is that prior knowledge may help older adults make good decisions on less information than younger adults in many circumstances.

In this case, we can really think about the importance of prior knowledge because the women with breast cancer really need to draw on prior knowledge about themselves and their preferences and their lives and how the different treatment options would impact those things.

Principle four is that motivation and interests matters, and as we shall also see today, motivation varies over the lifespan in ways that are importantly connected to learning. Most generally, we talked about the fact that openness to experience declines in later life, and this decline is found longitudinally, when we compare individuals to themselves earlier in their lives. It is also found cross-sectionally, when we compare people of one age to different people of another age.

It is also a pattern that has been found in virtually every country that has been studied, and there are many countries that have been studied in this way. That general age-based change is consistent with the idea that as we age, we may be less interested in learning new things. That is also consistent with the decision-making work that I just talked about.

One well-established perspective on adulthood and aging, socio-emotional selectivity theory, suggests that we are also going to be motivated by different aspects of our worlds as we approach the end of life. Laura Carstensen and her collaborators argue that we have at least two major motives as we go about our daily lives. One is an information-seeking motive. This is that curiosity drive that we discussed early on in this course. The other is an emotion regulation motive. We might encapsulate these as "finding stuff out and feeling good."

Carstensen points out, although, that the availability of new information and its utility to us may diminish over adulthood, as we become older. Why? For one thing, as noted earlier, we tend to know more as we get older, and that means there may be less out there left to learn. For another, the available new information in the world is of less utility and relevance to us, as we get older, for at least two reasons.

First, when we have established our lives, we often know the information and skills we need for living those lives, and so remaining things to learn are somewhat less needed, and information also has more long-term payoffs. The pursuit of a college degree, for example, is a rather lengthy process. It involves a fair amount of work and significant economic cost. The payoff is a more long-term thing. It involves lifetime earnings potential and in the short term, actually people go into debt for college degrees.

As people approach the end of life, Carstensen argues, they may be less interested in pursuing something that doesn't have an immediate reward. What has immediate rewards? Emotion. Feeling good is a payoff right here and right now. Carstensen has argued, and she has shown in several studies, that as people get older, their relative emphasis on new information versus feeling good shifts. Emotion becomes more important and more salient.

The perspective of socio-emotional selectivity theory has spawned a wide range of investigations, and these include explorations of social activity, personality changes, preferences for products, and everyday emotional experience. Some of this work has shown that older adults as compared with younger adults make different choices about possible people to spend time with. They prefer close friends or family over interesting strangers.

When asked to imagine themselves with a great deal of healthy lifetime left they go back to being interested in meeting someone like the author of the book they enjoyed or a new and interesting person. Young adults in situations that limit their time (an impending move or a serious illness) shift their social preferences toward familiar and close relationships.

Even this shift has to do with learning. As Carstensen notes, the author of a book or an interesting new stranger offer a greater opportunity for learning new stuff. They are more likely to know things that we do not already know. By contrast, someone we have known for our entire adult lives is likely to be a lot better at helping us to feel good, to feel safe, to feel secure, to feel loved and to feel connected. They may not offer us nearly as much in the way of new information or new perspectives, at least not as much as that more unknown and unfamiliar person might.

The relationships between making choices about who we spend time with, the warm and familiar or the new with the potential for learning as I just expressed it is a theoretical one. That is, that the studies that test social partner preferences, who I want to spend time with, do not really test actual learning of new information. Other work although does so more directly.

In that work the kind of increased focus on emotion, on managing feelings that characterizes aging also appears to change people's ways of paying attention to new information, of learning that information as reflected in memory and ultimately even the way their brain is responding to information depending on how emotional that information is.

Age-related differences in attention, learning, and memory have been labeled the positivity effect. Briefly put, the positivity effect is one in which older adults as compared to younger adults pay more attention to emotionally relevant stimuli, and especially positive ones. They learn positive stimuli more effectively than negative stimuli, and they recall them better.

The positivity effect has been shown with pictures, words, texts, autobiographical memories, and with measures of attention, memory, and even brain-based responding.

The fact that positive and emotionally relevant information draws more attention from older adults can actually compensate for some age-related losses. For example, there are some very clear deficits in source learning in later adulthood. Some types of source recollection do not show any differences between young and old adults. Not surprisingly, perhaps, it tends to be those that involve more emotionally relevant queues to source.

Adolescents in contrast to older adults are highly motivated by information. You can see this when you look at a phenomenon known as the reminiscence bump. This phenomenon is one in which our learning of songs, news events, television shows, movies, and even the experiences of our own lives is actually enhanced in this period of life. The way we know this is that if you ask people over the age of 50 to recall various kinds of memories (songs, famous faces, personal experiences) they are disproportionately likely to remember things from the years between 10 and 30.

In fact, adolescent and young adult's exploration and risk taking is something of a cliché. Adolescents explore even to the point of taking serious risks and of experiencing hurt and pain in order to learn and find out about themselves and their worlds. This is not only true for humans, in our stereotypical understanding of different age groups. It is also actually true of rats.

One of my favorite recent studies actually looked at the exploratory behavior of teenage rats, compared to adult rats. The goal of the study was for the rats to learn to poke into a hole to get food pellets. They could only poke the hole every so often to get the food pellets. Other times it did not really work. Adolescent rats in this context they make what are called task irrelevant pokes more than adults. They are more than likely, especially when they are hungry, to run around an open enclosure and explore all the options available to them in that enclosure.

To summarize, when we consider what learning is about for people of different age groups, we can look at age differences in information processing abilities, in prior knowledge, and age differences in motivations and interests.

When we do this, we get a distinctly different picture for different periods in the life span, distinctly different for childhood, adolescence and early adulthood, and for midlife and beyond.

Childhood is about the simultaneous processes of development and learning and in childhood those processes are hard to separate. Development constrains what kids can learn, but it is also probably fair to say that kids are like sponges. They are highly motivated to learn, and they are constantly learning, because so little is prior knowledge for little kids.

Adolescence and young adulthood by contrast is about maximum information gain. Information processing abilities are at their lifetime peak during this age period. The motivation to learn new things is also still very high and in contrast to kids, prior knowledge is also probably at a good basic foundational level that can facilitate learning.

Midlife and beyond is a time that is dominated by the issue of maintaining what we have learned and maintaining the capabilities that we have acquired in earlier parts of our lives. This is the time when we can capitalize on what we already know, we can shift our goals a bit, and we are vulnerable to cognitive declines that are going to affect basic information processing abilities. These declines can constrain our learning, or they can make it take us a bit longer to pull off the same level of learning as a young adult.

Before we leave middle and older adulthood, I want to focus on some factors that actually appear like they are going to help us preserve information-processing abilities to the extent that this is possible into late life.

There is an important caveat here. Pursuing these actions can preserve our ability to learn, but there are never guarantees that research findings about people on average will work for you as an individual specifically. I have to underscore that point: You can try these things. They have many benefits. They do not guarantee that you are going to preserve your cognitive abilities without decline.

The good news is that the same things that preserve information-processing abilities also contribute to other aspects of living a long and healthy and happy life. There are a lot of reasons why doing these things is a good idea.

The first one is really simple, get some exercise. Both cardiovascular and strength training exercises appear to help preserve information processing abilities. People thing this is probably because they really enhance blood flow in and outside the brain. Even mild exercise like walking is a great thing, and there are studies of weight training interventions with even frail, nursing home–dwelling elderly adults.

Another thing is to keep mentally active in meaningful ways. Examples of this include all kinds of continuing education efforts, Great Courses DVDs and CDs, Elderhostel, volunteering efforts, and community involvement.

Finally, It may be useful to try to learn something truly new every so often, something radically different from the usual things that you do, try a new dance class, try a sculpture course, try to learn a new language.

Again, this should be something that is meaningful to you and enjoyable, not a punishment, but more of an effort at staying open and curious and at maintaining cognitive flexibility.

Finally, researchers interested in ways of maintaining learning into late life do caution against current commercial products, because while some of these computer games could turn out to be useful at maintaining information processing abilities, most are untested, and it is an unregulated industry. Meaningful, and established activities are available without buying expensive software unless, like my husband, you are an avid gamer and if you would simply enjoy those computer games, knock yourself out.

Next time, we will bring all the lectures together to think about the big picture of how we learn that I have tried to paint for you in this course. We will consider some new directions in learning research, how what we have learned in this course can be applied to optimize our learning, and what implications we can draw for the teaching side of learning.

Making the Most of How We Learn
Lecture 24

In this final lecture, we will begin by reviewing what we have learned with a special focus on how to optimize learning in everyday life. Additionally, we will expand our consideration of learning in two ways. First, we will consider the role of teachers, coaches, and other people in learning. Then, we will consider the frontiers of learning research—the questions that seem still unanswered and some of the exciting developments that are on the horizon for learning.

Optimizing Learning

- In this final lecture, we're going to revisit ways of optimizing learning with a special focus on two different second-language learning situations: In the first, you are learning a second language for fun, and in the second, you are a refugee—a stranger in a strange land—with a vital need to learn to communicate.

- Elaborative encoding involves linking what you learn to other things, making connections across different aspects of your experiences.

- If you are learning a language, you will do better if you both hear and see the words when learning them. Repeating them after hearing and seeing them helps, and so does visualizing objects or actions for nouns and verbs.

- The refugee, in the new country, is surrounded by the new language—both hearing and seeing words and having many chances to visualize. Second-language courses offer these opportunities in more formal ways.

- Space your learning: Take breaks between learning episodes and use sleep to enhance learning.

- Don't try to learn vocabulary two days before a trip; start early and work in chunks with breaks.

- For the refugee, this part is complicated. Because so much is new, it is difficult to have breaks between learning, and one of the only breaks available from language learning can be spending time with family and others from one's home country and speaking in one's native language.

- Making your learning variable involves learning in different situations so that your ability to use what you have learned is enhanced.

- Looking at vocabulary words in books, news articles, and menus will help make your practice of those words variable.

- This is an area where refugees and immigrants have an advantage in language learning; they will necessarily encounter the new language in many different settings and in many different ways. They have to use the language to accomplish basic tasks.

- In the latter part of the course, we have also learned that metacognition expands what we think of as effective rehearsals, which involve both what we know and what we are still working on learning.

- For those learning a second language in our home country, don't stop practicing vocabulary words you think you've learned—you still want to rehearse now and then.

- Refugees don't have trouble with this; the vocabulary they acquire will get used as they go about the business of their new lives.

- However, there is a dilemma for any newcomer to a strange country: Once you acquire a basic, functional ability in the language, you need to work to keep adding new vocabulary and new capacities rather than letting yourself make do with what you know well.

- Finally, we have discussed that a good rehearsal sometimes means giving yourself a test.

- As a second-language learner yourself, don't just read over the materials; you need to test yourself. Produce your vocabulary words without any cues, and then see how you did. Trying to talk is even more effective.

- In this case, the refugee has the advantage again because the situation requires talk tests all the time, which is exhausting but will end up producing better learning.

- We discussed the fact that prior knowledge matters a lot for future learning. Know what your prior knowledge is and how it might be used for and against effective learning.

- To learn a new language requires temporarily inhibiting the old one, so prior knowledge of the native language can get in the way, and the native language—for both you and the refugee—has probably made it more difficult to speak the new one.

- Additionally, if the refugee is illiterate, then he or she lacks the prior knowledge that literacy provides, and literacy helps with learning a new language. As we learn new languages, in fact, we learn them both by looking at words in print and hearing them spoken. We use our literacy to more quickly acquire parts of a new language.

- The refugee, however, has advantages when it comes to inhibiting the native language. If you are in your home country, you will have a difficult time doing that. If, as refugees, you are in a place where most people don't speak your language, that inhibition task is easier.

- Let system one work on your behalf when possible. Especially as adults, we overemphasize that rational, deliberate, conscious set of processes in learning and often fail to capitalize on system one's potential to help us.

- Simply playing books in the language you are trying to learn in the background, without focusing attention on them may help you learn rhythms and grammar rules in that language—and that may be another reason why immersion is so helpful for second-language learning.

- Hone, enhance, and maintain basic cognitive abilities for attention, working memory, and executive function. Executive function is going to be key to overcoming confirmation biases and using scientific reasoning to learn well.

- Learning a new language is helped by good executive function, and learning a language in turn may help executive function improve; given that this is true for learning of all different types of languages, both you and the refugee can benefit from second-language learning efforts.

- Capitalize on your metacognitive knowledge. Remember that there is an increase in variability of performance before acquiring a new level of skill. When learning, a bad practice day with a lot of mistakes sometimes is followed by better performance.

- For language learning, this translates directly into grammatical mistakes and accent horrors perhaps before acquiring a new level of proficiency. Knowing this can help people through the more difficult moments in language acquisition.

- Capitalize on what you know about motivation and interest development. One of the major conclusions from the latter half of this course is that we are generally motivated to attain competence, and competence motivates interest.

- In other words, if we can struggle through the initial phases of learning something, we may be in a better position to find it interesting. This is especially important when we have to learn something rather than choosing it freely because feeling that you have to learn something violates the need for autonomy.

- Finally, find a way to return some autonomy to the experience by making choices and engaging your creative juices in figuring out how you'll learn the language.

- For the refugee, this is another area where there are serious disadvantages; learning the new language is not a choice, and it is often a source of experiencing no sense of competence. However, many refugees do describe having chosen the country to which they're relocated, and thinking of their situation this way may be very helpful to preserve autonomy about learning that specific language.

The Role of Others in Learning

- Teachers include coaches, parents, and even friends. Teaching needs to be attentive to the way learning is affected by prior knowledge. Effective teachers have a clear sense of what students usually think at the beginning of a class and know how they can change that model toward one more consistent with the available knowledge in a field.

- Teaching needs to be attentive to the constructive nature of learning. For example, inquiry-based learning isn't always a great option for learners. However, lectures, although they are widely criticized, turn out to be efficient ways of helping people learn.

- Finally, good teaching also needs to be sensitive to motivational and metacognitive aspects of learning, and there are many reasons to believe that teaching situations vary in their capacity to do this effectively.

- Teachers often create external rewards for children, but research suggests that such rewards are risky and might further undermine motivation, making learning in those contexts feel coerced and externally controlled.

- For younger children, the work of Deanna Kuhn and others suggests that maturation of executive function, which develops into early adulthood, constrains how well people can think about or reflect on the process of learning. Adults don't do this very well, and children are even less capable of it and need more help. Therefore, we may need to think about how teaching, in various settings, can incorporate some metacognition.

Emerging Areas in Learning Research

- Neuroscience deals with the way our brains enable us to learn, remember, and do anything we do. Neuroscience shows that the brain is highly integrated and highly plastic, or changeable.

- What that means is that we use all our brains all the time, and that is important for thinking about learning because it gives an optimistic picture about the possibility of linking system one and system two processes. The plasticity of the brain also can be interpreted as support for lifelong learning.

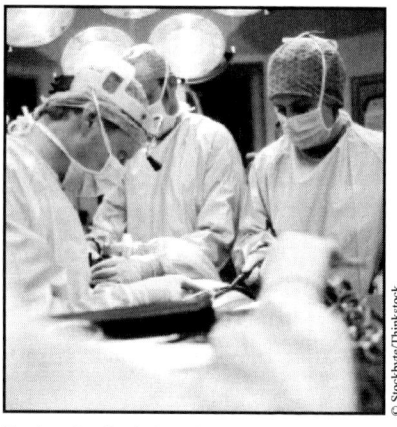

© Stockbyte/Thinkstock.

- The rise of virtual reality and high-fidelity simulators is another emerging area in learning

Technological developments in brain imaging and related research methods have led to an explosion in our ability to assess how the brain learns.

research. Some of the most interesting examples are in medicine, in which book training and videos can only take people so far. However, virtual reality gives us a way to train doctors and nurses on virtual patients in ways that come very close to real experience.

- Virtual reality and high-fidelity simulators are also important tools for studying learning; they are allowing cutting-edge investigations such as how visual perspective changes our models of a space.

- Finally, computers are playing an increasing role in helping researchers test ideas about how we learn. In this work, researchers study human learning, develop an idea about how we learn, program a computer to follow that idea, and then see if the computer responds like a person.

- In other words, we don't learn like computers, but we might be able to program computers to learn like us—and use that ability to test ideas about how we learn.

Suggested Reading

Moreno and Mayer, "Personalized Messages That Promote Science Learning."

Questions to Consider

1. Imagine how you can employ the principles from this course in some learning you want to do—or even in some learning you have to do.

2. How—and at what age—might teachers better incorporate metacognitive strategies into the classroom context?

Making the Most of How We Learn
Lecture 24—Transcript

We have had an amazing tour of learning over the past 23 lectures. How do we learn? We actively create meaning from our experiences, then we alter the information we are learning to connect it to what we already know. Our learning depends on how we do it, where we do it, when we do it, with whom, and from what sources, and of course definitely on why we do it and who we are.

I think that the definition we started with—learning as a change in a person's understanding, knowledge, or abilities arising from the person's experience—holds up pretty well.

Let us take just a few minutes to consider a couple of frontiers of learning research, both the questions that seem unanswered in our past lectures, and some of the exciting developments that did not quite make it into our overview. Then, we will try to pull together what we have learned, with a special focus first on revisiting the myths we began with, and second, on using our new and more accurate understanding to optimize learning in everyday life.

Finally, we will end by considering what teachers and other educators can do to make best use of this understanding of how people learn. There are at least three frontiers of learning research that are very exciting for me, and as with many innovations in any area of science, they are all connected to emerging technologies that have opened new possibilities for researchers.

One of those frontiers is neuroscience, which deals with the way our brains enable us to learn and remember, and pretty much do anything we do. Neuroscience as a field has a long and distinguished history, but technological developments in brain imaging and related research methods have led to an explosion in our ability to look at how the brain does its thing, including learn.

So how are neuroscientists changing our understanding of learning? Well neuroscience is showing us more and more that the brain is both highly integrated and highly plastic. This radically changes what we know about learning.

What integrated means is that we use all our brains all the time, and this is important for thinking about learning. For one, it tells us there is not unused potential in the brain. There are not these dusty corridors of neurons that never get used. For another, it makes it less surprising that system one learning like when we track the statistical properties of a speech stream, can help system two actions like when we have to decide whether something sounds like a word or not. It is helping us to understand how the brain enables system one and system two processes, which areas of the brain are involved in those two processes, and how the brain enables the two systems to interact.

The plasticity of the brain refers to the fact that the brain is extremely malleable and extremely flexible. When there is damage to one part of the brain, other parts of the brain can be recruited to fill in, and that is different than what people once thought, which was that functioning was really tied to one region and damage to that region of the brain would forever destroy the function that was identified with that region.

The brain is always changing in response to new experiences. It's always adapting. That plasticity is a source of major optimism about what is possible for us as lifelong learners. Recall the myth that old dogs don't learn new tricks. Well, not only do old dogs learn new tricks, their brain enables them to do that. In fact, they may be doing it with brand new neurons. Learning is not the sole province of the young, even for something like a second language.

Another frontier area involves the rise of virtual reality and high fidelity simulators. For many of us, including all the video-gamers in my life, virtual reality is really a new frontier for entertainment because these kinds of simulators take playing to a new level of reality. If you have ever played with a Wii or a Kinect or any of their emerging market rivals, you know how vivid that simulated experience can be. You can be sparring in a simulated boxing ring, and find yourself ducking a punch or you can be serving in tennis and in virtual reality, I really can serve a tennis ball.

Entertainment uses aside though, virtual reality also offers us the possibility for new ways of approaching learning. Some of the most interesting examples of this from my view are in medicine. In medicine, book training and videos can only take people so far, and eventually doctors have to learn on, us. That is really scary because we know that learning something like a surgical procedure takes a lot of repetition and probably will involve mistakes. Virtual reality gives us a way to train doctors and nurses on virtual patients in ways that come very close to real experience, and this is something many medical schools are already actively doing.

The way it works is that doctors and nurses operate on a patient simulator. This consists of a kind of doll that looks and responds much like a real person. A sophisticated computer program generates that simulated doll's responses. That computer can be programmed to mimic various operating room scenarios like adverse drug reactions, shock, and so on. This lets doctors and nurses practice a procedure without putting a real person in harm's way.

Virtual reality allows us to train doctors on more than just how to do a procedure, it also opens up possibilities for looking at how doctors cope with and could learn from mistakes.

Virtual reality is also used to train pilots in aviation and drivers for commercial transportation, just as in the medical school situation, simulators allow people to practice tasks like take off and landing or navigation under difficult driving conditions, in ways that don't place other people at risk.

Virtual reality and high fidelity simulators are also important tools for studying learning in the laboratory. They are allowing cutting edge investigations into things like how visual perspective changes our models of space and how our perceptual and motor systems adapt to changing environmental conditions.

I've actually always wondered what it would feel like to walk if I were actually tall, and my colleagues in this area actually tell me that they might be able to let me try it out soon (again, using virtual reality).

You could say if architects made use of virtual reality in design, they might stop making buildings that none of us can navigate, but it might be that aesthetics always trump utility for some domains.

The last frontier is also one that like virtual reality, involves using computers, but in this case, rather than have computers simulate the learning situation, be the patient or be a traffic situation, computers are used to simulate the learner in ways that can help researchers test ideas about how people learn.

If I think we learn categories by memorizing examples and associating them to a category, I can program a computer to learn in this way, and I can see if its behavior, how long it takes to learn, how well it can classify new examples, and the kinds of mistakes that it makes. I can see if those look a lot like human behaviors when human beings are learning categories. If the computers behaviors do not match what humans do, it suggests that the theory of category learning I have programmed that computer with is probably not accurate in accounting for how humans learn categories.

These are really going to be interesting areas to watch. In this course, we have also covered some fundamentals, which I think are not going to change, and I want to take a few minutes now to think about those and as we do so, let us reconsider some of the myths that we started with in this course.

Remember the myth that we always know when we are learning and that we learn intentionally. Well as you now know, this myth comes from the fact that we often overemphasize that rational, deliberate, conscious set of processes and learning. The processes where we sit down and we actively look at the material we are trying to learn.

In overemphasizing those system two processes, we often fail to capitalize on system one's potential to help us learn. Note that those relatively nonconscious systems, those system one processes, they do not even always need feedback about whether they are getting it right.

It never occurred to me until I prepared this course that just playing books in the language you are trying to learn in the background without listening to them might help you learn rhythms and grammar rules in that language without expending as much effort and without getting feedback on whether we are right or wrong. Doing that probably will help us, and that may be another reason why emersion is so helpful for second language learning.

Recall that in the beginning of the course, I asked you to imagine that you were a refugee from sub-Saharan Africa, a former subsistence farmer. I asked you to imagine arriving in the United States to start a new life and to learn a new language. Although it is overwhelming, the emersion in an English language world is likely to help you more quickly acquire a basic functional sense of words and rhythms in English. In a kind of funny way, your task is easier than if you were a middle class American trying to learn Italian for an upcoming vacation tour of Venice because in that case, you are probably learning from tapes in a setting where nothing but English is being spoken.

Another myth with which we began was the idea that prior knowledge does not matter for how we learn, and I am going to repeat myself. There is no tabula rasa in learning, so how do we make use of this knowledge that prior knowledge, prior learning plays an important role in learning.

It can be particularly useful to enter new learning situations, with an eye to what you already know and how it can be used to help you. It is also worth knowing when prior knowledge may make your life more difficult. For example, learning to type if you already play the piano is made easier, because some of the finger movements involved is going to draw on similar already automated motor patterns. Learning to play on racket sport can capitalize on another that you have already acquired.

One clever undergraduate that I once had in a class pointed out that websites which are organized like a print newspaper are easier to navigate, because they let people draw on long practice knowledge, although this may be changing as our culture shifts away from print media.

On the other hand, prior knowledge can also hurt us. This is true in some ways for switching between, say, racket ball and tennis because although they have similar motor patterns, they are also some distinct elements of those sports, but it is perhaps most clear in learning a second language.

Whether you are a refuge or a tourist, your native language is a kind of prior knowledge that may get in your way.

Remember we discussed that often you have to suppress words from your first language in order to get to the words you need in a second language, and when it comes to inhibiting our native language, if we are in our home country while we are learning, we are going to have a hard time doing that. If as refugees we are in a place where most people do not speak our language at all, that inhibition task actually just got a little easier.

It is important to know, prior knowledge in the form of literacy in one language is a different matter. If you were literate prior to migrating to a new country, you can also make use of print materials to enhance your learning of that new language.

We also talked about the idea that you have to be interested in order to learn, that interest comes first and learning second. You now know that actually having a little competence can enhance interest. In other words, if we can struggle through the initial phases of learning something, we may be in a better position to find it interesting. This is especially important when we have to learn something rather than chose it freely, because as you also know, feeling that you have to learn something is going to violate your need for autonomy, and it is a little bit unmotivating.

If you have to learn a language because, say, your spouse wants to learn the language and travel or because you are a refuge and there are no other options, here are some ways to use what you know about motivation. Well first, you can just be reassured that if you will like learning the language more after a basic foundation of ability within it.

You can also try to craft learning situations that help you learn the language while feeding your other interests. My own learning of German skyrocketed when I found class where we discussed academic topics like the book *Guns, Germs and Steel* with absolutely atrocious beginner level German. I so desperately wanted to be able to express my thoughts about that book I was willing to work at it with my minimal skills.

Doing this crafting learning situations that do feed your interests, helps to return some autonomy to the experience and ought to improve your motivation that way as well.

Another myth related to motivation and learning is the notion that we always feel clear and confident when we are learning well. Now you know better. You know that sometimes before we get to the next level, our performance is full of variability. We looked at that issue briefly when we talked about mass strategies and how kids acquire those.

Here is another illustration of it in a very different domain. My five-year-old daughter is learning to play the violin. Some days she plays very well and other days, no matter how long practice drags on, she sounds awful. In the absence of invoking knowledge about variability, you might conclude that the bad practice days are no good. In fact, maybe you might think they are even harmful, because clearly she is not practicing the correct ways to play the pieces on those days.

Here is the thing, knowing how math-learning proceeds means that what might be happening with my daughter is an increase in the variability of her playing before she acquires a new level of skill or becomes able to play a new piece.

The same applies to all of us when we are learning. A bad practice day or a lot of mistakes are sometimes a kind of storm before the calm, of a new level of skill. For language learning, this translates directly into mistakes and grammar awfulness or accent horrors, perhaps right before you get to a new level of proficiency.

Knowing this can really help people through the more difficult moments in language acquisition. You can know that when things seem awful and are not going well, you may need to just stick with it a little bit longer to get through his hurdle and onto that next level.

Another set of myths we discussed was the idea that smart people know how to learn, and we know when we are learning well versus when learning is not going well. You now know about the elements of effective rehearsal. Some of those are probably not surprising. You need to use elaborative encoding, and linking what you are learning to things you already know.

We also discussed the need to space your rehearsals including taking breaks. You know that sleep is a very effective kind of break to take because it is so fundamental to helping us consolidate and hold onto what we have learned. You know that you need to make your rehearsals variable in many cases, because that way, you can use what you are learning in a wider variety of circumstances.

You also now know some of the mistakes people make when they choose strategies for rehearsal. For example, you know that effective rehearsal involves both what we know and also what we are still working on learning. What you stop practicing you are going to risk forgetting. If you are learning a second language, you have to practice both the words you already know and the words you are trying to acquire.

Perhaps most importantly, and perhaps most difficult to do, you now know that good rehearsals sometimes mean testing yourself. For motor learning and spatial learning, we naturally test ourselves as we practice in most cases. You cannot learn to play the piano without well playing the piano. Our refuge cannot learn to drive a car without actually driving the car. You will not learn to get from the house to the office without actually doing it because even studying it on a map is not sufficient and it definitely will not help you avoid new construction kinds of delays.

In other cases, we sometimes don't test ourselves as much as would be ideal. If you are a refugee, you have to use your new language, which is a kind of test because you can't communicate without it. If you were working on Italian with your spouse in your living room, well you can quite easily read through vocabulary words without forcing yourself to try to talk. In that second case, you are actually going to have to work pretty hard to force yourself into testing your knowledge, and it is not easy.

My husband is a native speaker of German, but his English was so much better than my German when we met, that we have never spoken German to one another. That is because when we converse, we humans want to communicate as fully as possible, maybe particularly with our mates, and that means we go with the language that is going to maximize communication at the expense of the language we might be trying to learn.

My secretary, when he was learning Italian, had what I still think is a really clever way to get around this problem. He and another person in our department decided to translate the book *Charlotte's Web* from English into Italian. It let them work together. They are both very social people. That was a lot of fun for them. It forced them to fully use their fledgling Italian, and because it is a children's book, the Italian was not too complicated to do.

It also got them around the awkwardness of trying to have a difficult effortful and unsatisfying conversation with someone where if you would just switch to English, you would enjoy it so much more. We are all social creatures as a matter of fact, and that bring me to my next point.

Through all of this course, we have not focused on the role of other people— teachers and coaches and parents and friends—in helping learning in any direct way. I would like to end by thinking about the roles that other people play in our learning, and how those roles relate to the things we have discussed in this course. Knowing what we now know about learning, we can think a bit more about how teaching can support or undermine learning.

One thing we know now is teaching needs to be attentive to the way learning is affected by prior knowledge. Some of the most effective teachers I know are effective because they have a very clear sense of what students usually think at the beginning of a class, and they know how they can change that model toward one that is more consistent with the available knowledge in a field.

Teaching also needs to be attentive to the constructive nature of learning, to the way that we create learning out of the information we encounter, but there are debates about what that would mean. For example, one way of thinking about that is to point toward discovery based learning, or inquiry based learning, and as we saw earlier in this course, that is not always the best option for learners. Lectures actually, while they are widely bashed as bad and unengaging, turn out to really be pretty efficient ways of helping people learn.

Guided discovery learning looked really great for adolescents and particularly adults in several studies, and here, I want to go back to this idea of scaffolding. Scaffolding is what happens whenever a more experienced person guides a novice person through some activity or through a field of knowledge.

We saw scaffolding in this course in the context of learning to tell stories. It is very evident in that context. What you see in parents' scaffolding of kids' stories is that parents build in a structure for the story that tacitly communicates what should go in a story and where.

Parents do this structuring in a way that leaves openings for the child to participate actively. They might structure the child's narrative in time and content, but they get the child to produce the content in response to their questions. Good scaffolding, then, is a kind of teaching that takes into account the person's existing skills and existing knowledge, and it creates opportunities for them to be active in their learning.

Teaching also needs to take into account meta-cognitive, which is what learners know about learning. It is clear to me as a college educator that we seldom teach meta-cognition in our schools. Often, meta-cognition is not an explicit part of any teaching. To think about this further, let us think about just strategic information like the sort we outlined earlier about how to rehearse when we are trying to learn and what kinds of practice and rehearsals are most effective.

You know now that self-testing is very important in acquiring new information and retaining it. College students as it happens don't know this. In fact, a recent survey of students showed that they do not report using self-testing as a study strategy, and they don't even really always endorse it as effective. This is in huge contrast to the findings that show just how effective self-testing is as a learning strategy.

I am going to make a confession here, I admit with some embarrassment it is very seldom that I explicitly tell my students how they can improve their learning. Rather, I conduct review sessions in my courses where I model the behavior of self-testing. Let me give you an example. In my research methods course, I hold regular review sessions in class just prior to the exam. These usually take place about two to four days prior to the test.

When students come into the review session, I say to them, "Please pull out a sheet of blank paper. In the next five minutes I want you to write down everything you have learned over the past several weeks." They look at me with horror. They are hoping that I am going to say, "Just joking," but I am not. I wait for five and sometimes even seven extraordinarily painful seconds. After a minute or so, they realize I am serious, and they start writing. I give them about five minutes, and then I ask them to start telling me what they have written down.

I put the items up on a white board and draw lines and organize things and when we finish, we have usually managed to place on the board all the material that was covered and in the process, to review how the material is related.

Until this year, I had sort of assumed that students would get that this was modeling how they might study at home or more precisely, I had not really thought that much about it at all. Here is why I was wrong. For students to get the modeling of how to review, for them to get that I was showing them how to study, would require them to engage that system two deliberate reflective processing, but to engage it not about the content of what we were reviewing. Remember, that is what they are interested in. Their goal is to pass the test. Rather, they would have to engage system two processing about the process by which I was talking them through the review. Of course, they were not thinking about the process. They were worried about the content.

The upshot of this is that teachers could help more. This year, I will be pointing their attentions specifically not just to what we are reviewing, but also to the process by which we are reviewing it, and I will also be making them read a few articles on study strategies including self-testing.

Self-testing is just one example of one part of meta-cognition, strategy knowledge. It seems to me more broadly that we may need to think harder about how teaching in various settings can incorporate information about meta-cognition to help students learn more effectively.

Finally, good teaching also needs to be sensitive to motivational aspects of learning, and there are many reasons to believe that teaching situations vary in their capacity to do this effectively.

Consider motivation. In many cases, we initiate learning. I decided to take a German course while working in Germany, and you have all decided to take this class from the Great Courses. We know that that element of choice and autonomy is highly motivating for people.

In other cases, however, we are taught because we are required to learn something. We are doing training for our jobs, or we are attending school. In the school case, teachers often create external rewards for kids, which might range from things like praise and being the student of the week, to—at least in my son's school—candy and soda rewards for good behavior and good academic work. Everything we know about motivation from this course suggests that those kinds of rewards are risky, and they might further undermine motivation. They might make learning in those contexts, in those school contexts feel coerced and externally controlled.

Learning is best when it is its own reward. Achieving a level of competence is a really great thing, and we ought to recognize that as such and not confuse the issue with things like soda and candy.

We do need to ask why we have so many schools that function in this way, that undermine kids' motivation to learn. We need to ask what the alternatives might look like. Montessori schools for example, provide children with no incentives to learn other than their own and their teacher's pleasure in their developing competence. There are likely to be other ways teachers can motivate kids intelligently and effectively, and many teachers work really hard to do that, and we should recognize and support them in those efforts.

I am an optimist. I think our motivation to learn is so basic to whom we are as a species, that I think it is resilient to or at least we can recovered it from setbacks like a coercive school setting. In fact, one of the bigger messages from this course is that we can all learn at any age. Learning is a kind of human birthright. It is one of the most amazing things about us. Everything about human beings is built for lifelong learning from our extended, unusually long childhood and our large prefrontal cortices to our interest in novelty and challenge as long as we feel safe enough to explore.

I think this capacity for learning is also a reason for being optimistic about the future of humanity as well. There is an awful lot we need to learn at this point in our history in order to avert the kinds of difficulties that we are facing as a species.

In closing, I hope you have enjoyed this tour of how we learn. It is something of a cliché, but in the process of developing the course, I have also learned a great deal. From learning some areas of research that I did not previously know very well, to some basic gross motor skills like how to walk around in a TV studio without looking like a rat in a maze full of shocking devices.

I would like to thank you for your attention, your engagement, and maybe your elaborative encoding. And as a certain Vulcan might have once said, "Learn well and prosper."

Bibliography

Adams, J. A. "Historical Review and Appraisal of Research on the Learning, Retention, and Transfer of Human Motor Skills." *Psychological Bulletin* 101 (1987): 41–74. This is an overview of motor learning, which, while somewhat dated, is still accurate and provides a good background.

Alfieri, L., and P. J. Brooks, N. J. Aldrich, and H. R. Tenenbaum. "Does Discovery-Based Instruction Enhance Learning?" *Journal of Educational Psychology*, November 15, 2010. Advance online publication. doi: 10.1037/a0021017. This article reports on the state of the art about discovery-based instruction and learning outcomes, which suggests that enthusiasm about discovery-based learning needs to be tempered with serious thinking about how, and with whom, it is best implemented.

Allen, G., ed. *Human Spatial Memory: Remembering Where*. Mahwah, NJ: Lawrence Erlbaum Associates, Inc., 2004. Spatial learning is often quite technical in the primary literature; this textbook provides a more accessible overview for those interested in deepening their understanding of spatial learning and memory.

Ashby, F. G., and W. T. Maddox. "Human Category Learning." *Annual Review of Psychology* 56 (2005): 149–178. This is a somewhat technical overview of category learning but provides a good review of what we know about how people learn categories.

Baars, B. J. *The Cognitive Revolution in Psychology.* New York: Guilford Press, 1986. An overview of the major conceptual shifts in the cognitive revolution in psychology, along with interviews from major players within and outside the field.

Baillargeon, R. "How Do Infants Learn about the Physical World?" *Current Directions in Psychological Science* 3 (1994): 133–140. A concisely written account of how infants are not a tabula rasa and about the built-in mechanisms that help them acquire further understanding about their physical environments.

Bartlett, F. C. *Remembering: A Study in Experimental and Social Psychology.* New York: Cambridge University Press, 1932. This is a classic in memory research but also provides many illustrations about the ways that our learning draws upon prior knowledge and understanding—sometimes in ways that distort our learning.

Beck, H. P., S. Levinson, and G. Irons. "Finding Little Albert: A Journey to John B. Watson's Infant Laboratory." *American Psychologist* 64, no. 7 (2009): 605–614. This article reports on efforts to identify Little Albert, the participant in Watson's behaviorist work on phobias, and to find out what happened to him after his participation in Watson's study.

Boroditsky, L. "How Language Shapes Thought." *Scientific American*, February 2011. This is an elegant and accessibly written examination of how the languages we learn have potentially much broader implications for what we can and cannot perceive and learn about other nonlinguistic subjects.

Brice-Heath, S. *Ways with Words.* Cambridge, UK: Cambridge University Press, 1983. A vivid ethnography that examines how children in different communities learn to tell stories and use language in other ways and how this learning may influence their success in other arenas, such as school.

Carlson, L., C. Hoelscher, T. Shipley, and R. Conroy Dalton. "Getting Lost in Buildings." *Current Directions in Psychological Science* 19 (2010): 284–289. A concise account of factors that influence whether buildings are difficult or easy to learn to navigate.

Ceci, S. J. "How Much Does Schooling Influence General Intelligence and Its Cognitive Components? A Reassessment of the Evidence." *Developmental Psychology* 27 (1991): 703–722. A seminal look at the relationship between intelligence and schooling that may change your perspective on the role of IQ in people's capacity to learn.

Dent, C. H., and P. G. Zukow, eds. *Developmental Psychobiology* 23, no. 7 (1990). Special Issue: "The Idea of Innateness: Effects on Language and Communication Research." A variety of contributions to this special issue look at the debate over whether aspects of human language and communication are innate versus whether they can be learned from input via sophisticated statistical tracking capacities, which we share with other species.

Diamond, A., W. S. Barnett, J. Thomas, and S. Munro. "Preschool Program Improves Cognitive Control." *Science* 318, no. 5855 (2007):1387–1388. A concise account of how dramatic play leads to gains in executive function in preschool children.

Doidge, N. *The Brain That Changes Itself.* London: Penguin Press, 2007. A look at how learning changes the brain and at the endless potential of the brain for learning. A neuroscience addendum to much of what is discussed in this course.

Doughty, C. J., and M. H. Long, eds. *The Handbook of Second Language Acquisition.* Oxford, UK: Blackwell Publishing, 2003. This book addresses a range of topics in the acquisition of second languages, including the critical period hypothesis and other ways of understanding the difficulty of learning second languages after early childhood.

Evans, J. St. B. T. "Intuition and Reasoning: A Dual-Process Perspective." *Psychological Inquiry* 21 (2010): 313–326. This article helps to introduce two different ways in which we learn: a more intuition-based, nonconscious way and a more explicit, deliberate way. It provides a nice overview of how these two systems differ and why scientists think there are, in fact, two systems.

Fredrickson, B. L., and C. Branigan. "Positive Emotions Broaden the Scope of Attention and Thought-Action Repertoires." *Cognition and Emotion* 19 (2005): 313–332. A good example of an experimental article showing effects of positive emotion on learning.

Geake, J. "Neuromythologies in Education." *Educational Research* 50 (2008): 123–133. This is a pointed critique of some persistent and pernicious ideas in education about how we learn.

Hansen, M., and E. Markman. "Children's Use of Mutual Exclusivity to Learn Labels for Parts of Objects." *Developmental Psychology* 45 (2009): 592–596. A great empirical example of a study showing how a presumably inborn mutual exclusivity constraint can help children rapidly learn new words.

Herold, D. M., W. Davis, D. B. Fedor, and C. K. Parsons. "Dispositional Influences on Transfer of Learning in Multistage Training Programs." *Personnel Psychology* 55 (2002): 851–869. This study examines the effects of being open to experience on pilot's learning, as well as the influence of other traits.

Hertzog, C., A. F. Kramer, R. S. Wilson, and U. Lindenberger. "Enrichment Effects on Adult Cognitive Development." *Psychological Science in the Public Interest* 9 (2009): 1–65. An authoritative and accessibly written review of what adults can do to maintain or even enhance cognitive abilities.

Hofer, M. "Adolescents' Development of Individual Interests: A Product of Multiple Goal Regulation." *Educational Psychologist* 45 (2010): 149–166. A somewhat technical account of how individual interests develop with an emphasis on adolescence, but it is applicable to other age periods as well.

Hyltenstam, K., and N. Abrahamsson. "Maturational Constraints in SLA." In *The Handbook of Second Language Acquisition*, edited by C. J. Doughty and M. H. Long, 539–588. Oxford, UK: Blackwell Press, 2003. A fairly clearly written explanation of the idea that second-language acquisition is difficult in adulthood and a review of the evidence for that claim.

Kaufman, S. B., C. G. DeYoun, J. R. Gray, L. Jimenez, J. Brown, and N. Mackintosh. "Implicit Learning as an Ability." *Cognition* 116 (2010): 321–340. One of the first articles examining whether implicit learning differs across people in ways that are consistent over time.

Kuhn, D. "Children and Adults as Intuitive Scientists." *Psychological Review* 96 (1989): 674–689. An examination of how children and adults learn about science and a gentle but pointed criticism of the idea that we operate as intuitive scientists.

Kumkale, G. T., and D. Abarracin. "The Sleeper Effect in Persuasion: A Meta-Analytic Review." *Psychological Bulletin* 130 (2004): 143–172. A somewhat technically presented but powerful review of how messages we initially dismiss can come to influence us more than we'd like as time passes.

McAdams, D. *The Redemptive Self: Stories Americans Live By*. New York City: Oxford University Press, 2006. A look at some particular features of the stories Americans tell about their lives and an argument that these features are deeply part of our culture.

Moreno, R., and R. E. Mayer. "Personalized Messages That Promote Science Learning in Virtual Environments." *Journal of Educational Psychology* 96 (2004): 165–173. This is a look at two features of virtual reality that suggests that feeling personally engaged promotes learning while more immersive visuals do not. It is an interesting illustration of where research on learning is headed in relation to current technological advances.

Nadler, R., R. Rabi, and J. P. Minda. "Better Mood and Better Performance: Learning Rule-Described Categories Is Enhanced by Positive Mood." *Psychological Science* 21 (2010): 1770–1776. An example of the usefulness of positive emotion for some types of learning.

Nelson, K. *Language in Cognitive Development*. Cambridge, UK: Cambridge University Press, 1996. This book offers a look at how language, learning, and development are inextricably intertwined in early childhood. It also contains some of the most readable, clear explanations available of how and why infants are not a tabula rasa in the earlier half of the book.

Nelson, K., ed. *Narratives from the Crib.* Cambridge, MA: Harvard University Press, 1989. A classic within child development, this book compiles transcripts of a child's nighttime self-directed talk along with analyses from experts on child development. It provides many illustrations relevant to this course—from the way that Emily learns to tell coherent stories to the way that she uses the process of telling stories as a tool to learn about important scripts and schemas.

Pashler, H., M. McDaniel, D. Rohrer, and R. Bjork. "Learning Styles: Concepts and Evidence." *Psychological Science in the Public Interest* 9 (2008): 106–119. An authoritative compendium of the gap between claims and evidence when it comes to learning styles; an essential read before investing in any learning style–based products or services.

Perry, L. K., L. K. Samuelson, L. M. Malloy, and R. N. Schiffer. "Learn Locally, Think Globally: Exemplar Variability Supports Higher-Order Generalization and Word Learning." *Psychological Science* 21 (2010): 1894–1902. A somewhat technical but good account of how variability is important for learning—how pure repetition is inferior to somewhat varying repetition.

Pinker, S. J. *The Blank Slate: The Modern Denial about Human Nature.* New York: Viking Press, 2002. A well-written book for the general public that presents accounts of evolutionary thinking within psychology.

Powell, R. A., D. G. Symbaluk, and S. E. MacDonald. *Introduction to Learning and Behavior.* 2nd ed. Belmont, CA: Thomson-Wadsworth, 2005. A fairly up-to-date overview of classical conditioning, operant conditioning, and other behaviorist approaches to learning.

Rankin, C. H., et al. "Habituation Revisited: An Updated and Revised Description of the Behavioral Characteristics of Habituation." *Neurobiology of Learning and Memory* 92 (2009): 135–138. A somewhat technical overview of the concept of habituation as it is currently understood. Useful for those who want a very in-depth grasp of this most basic of learning processes.

Ryan, R. M., and E. L. Deci. "Self-Regulation and the Problem of Human Autonomy: Does Psychology Need Choice, Self-Determination, and Will?" *Journal of Personality* 74 (2006): 1557–1585. A treatment of autonomy and its role in both individual lives and within the field of psychology by authors who have been doing research on autonomy for decades.

Sansone, C., and J. L. Smith. "Interest and Self-Regulation: The Relation Between Having To and Wanting To." In *Intrinsic and Extrinsic Motivation: The Search for Optimal Motivation and Performance*, edited by C. Sansone and J. M. Harackiewicz. 341–372. San Diego: Academic Press, 2000. Autonomy and intrinsic motivation are great, but sometimes we have to learn things for extrinsic reasons. Sansone and Smith present a very important perspective on how people can turn having to do something into wanting to do something.

Savage-Rumbaugh, S., P. Segerdahl, and W. M. Fields. "Individual Differences in Language Competencies in Apes Resulting from Unique Rearing Conditions Imposed by Different First Epistemologies." In *Symbol Use and Symbolic Representation: Developmental and Comparative Perspectives*, edited by L. Namy. Mahwah, NJ: Lawrence Erlbaum Associates, Inc., 2005. A treatment of the learning of human languages by apes with an emphasis on how learning processes for the apes varied depending on the assumptions researchers had about human language learning. This article is not only interesting with respect to learning but also with respect to the history of one part of comparative psychology.

Schaler, J. A., ed. *Howard Gardner under Fire: The Rebel Psychologist Faces His Critics.* Peru, IL: Open Court Publishing, 2006. This book takes a look at Gardner's theory of multiple intelligences and some of the major criticisms of his theory along with some of his other less-known research and critiques of that work. It is a fairly readable overview for the nonexpert.

Schmidt, R. A., and C. A. Wrisberg. *Motor Learning and Performance.* Champaign, IL: Human Kinetics, 2008. A comprehensive, basic textbook that provides a good overview of motor learning for those who want to know more but are not interested in the more technical reviews intended for researchers.

Siegler, R. and M. Svetina. "What Leads Children to Adopt New Strategies? A Microgenetic/Cross-Sectional Study of Class Inclusion." *Child Development* 77 (2006): 997–1015. A terrific example of the way that looking at a few children intensively can reveal the process by which learning takes place.

Stark, L., and T. J. Perfect. "Whose Idea Was That? Source Monitoring for Idea Ownership Following Elaboration." *Memory* 15 (2007): 776–783. An illustration of the difficulty of learning sources of information as well as the information itself. In contrast to the more academic examples, this article applies to a context of more widespread interest.

Swann, W. B. *Self Traps: The Elusive Quest for Higher Self-Esteem.* New York: W. H. Freeman, 1996. This book is written for the general public, and it serves to illustrate the way that what we know can distort what we learn as applied specifically to our beliefs about ourselves.

Swingley, D. "The Roots of the Early Vocabulary in Infants' Learning from Speech." *Psychological Science* 17 (2008): 308–312. A readable explanation of how very young infants learn words from the speech around them, and an illustration of the clever and very precise experiments that allow us to figure out how infants do this learning.

Taylor, H. A., S. J. Naylor, and N. A. Chechile. "Goal-Specific Influences on the Representation of Spatial Perspective." *Memory and Cognition* 27 (1999): 309–319. A clearly presented study outlining experiments on how our goals for learning an environment change what we learn about that environment.

Weinstein, Y., K. B. McDermott, and H. L. Roediger III. "A Comparison of Study Strategies for Passages: Rereading, Answering Questions, and Generating Questions." *Journal of Experimental Psychology: Applied* 16 (2010): 308–316. This article discusses research on optimizing students' study strategies and offers insights into our decisions about what to study and how.

Bibliography

Zaromb, F. M., J. D. Karpicke, and H. L. Roediger III. "Comprehension as a Basis for Metacognitive Judgments: Effects of Effort After Meaning on Recall and Metacognition." *Journal of Experimental Psychology: Learning, Memory, and Cognition* 36 (2010): 552–557. This article presents research that shows how much we can be misled in our judgments about how much we have learned.

Notes

Notes

Notes

Notes

Notes